AFRICA SINCE 1800

This history of modern Africa takes as its starting point the year 1800, because, although by that time the greater part of the interior of Africa had become known to the outside world, most of the initiatives for political and economic change still remained in the hands of African rulers and their peoples.

The book falls into three parts. The first describes the precolonial history of Africa, while the middle section deals thematically with partition and colonial rule. The third part details the emergence of the modern nation states of Africa and their history. Throughout the 200 years covered by the book, Africa, and not its invaders, is at the centre of the story. The authors are as concerned with the continuity of African history as with the changes that have taken place during this period.

The new edition covers events up to the middle of 2003, and takes account of the fresh perspectives brought about by the end of the Cold War and the new global situation following the events of 11 September 2001. It is also concerned with the demographic trends that are at the heart of so many African problems today, with the ravages of diseases such as HIV/AIDS and malaria and with the conflicts waged by warlords fighting for control of scarce resources.

Africa Since 1800

ROLAND OLIVER
ANTHONY ATMORE

Fifth Edition

PUBLISHED BY THE PRESS SYNDICATE OF THE UNIVERSITY OF CAMBRIDGE
The Pitt Building, Trumpington Street, Cambridge, United Kingdom

CAMBRIDGE UNIVERSITY PRESS
The Edinburgh Building, Cambridge CB2 2RU, UK
40 West 20th Street, New York, NY 10011-4211, USA
10 Stamford Road, Oakleigh, VIC 3166, Australia
Ruiz de Alarcón 13, 28014 Madrid, Spain
Dock House, The Waterfront, Cape Town 8001, South Africa

http://www.cambridge.org

First published 1967
Reprinted 1969
Second edition 1972
Reprinted with corrections 1974
First paperback edition 1977
Third edition 1981
Reprinted 1981, 1982, 1983, 1985, 1986, 1988, 1989, 1992
Fourth edition 1994
Reprinted 1995, 1999, 2000, 2001
Fifth edition 2005

Printed in the United States of America

Typeface New Aster 10/13.5 pt.   *System* LaTeX 2_ε [TB]

A catalog record for this book is available from the British Library.

Library of Congress Cataloging in Publication Data
Oliver, Roland Anthony
Africa since 1800 / Roland Anthony Oliver, Anthony Ernest Atmore. – 5th ed.
p. cm.
Includes bibliographical references (p.   ) and index.
ISBN 0-521-83615-8 – ISBN 0-521-54474-2 (pbk.)
1. Africa – History – 19th century.   2. Africa – History – 1884–1960.
3. Africa – History – 1960– I. Atmore, Anthony.   II. Title.
DT28.O4   2004
960′.23 – dc22   2003063544

ISBN 0 521 83615 8 hardback
ISBN 0 521 54474 2 paperback

Contents

Maps

ONE. Africa North of the Equator

The Sahara and Islam: The Bonds Unifying Northern Africa

The geography of the northern half of Africa is dominated by the Sahara desert. Throughout its vast area, 2,800 km (1,700 miles) from north to south and nearly 8,000 km (5,000 miles) from east to west, rainfall is less than 13 cm (5 inches) a year. Except around a few oases where underground supplies of water reach the surface, agriculture is impossible, and the desert's only inhabitants have been nomadic herdsmen, breeding camels and moving their animals seasonally from one light grazing ground to another. To the north of the desert lies the temperate Mediterranean coastland – its rainfall concentrated between January and March, with wheat and barley as its main cereal crops and sheep, the main stock of its highland pastures. Southward are the tropics, the land of the summer rains, favouring a different set of food crops from those grown around the Mediterranean. In the desert and northward live Berbers and Arabs, fair-skinned peoples speaking languages of the Afroasiatic family. South of the desert begins the 'land of the blacks' – to the Greeks; 'Ethiopia', to the Berbers, 'Akal n'Iguinawen' (Guinea); and to the Arabs, 'Bilad as-Sudan'.

The desert has always been a formidable obstacle to human communication, but for two thousand years at least – since the introduction of the horse and the camel made travel easier – people have persevered in overcoming its difficulties. Before the days of the motorcar and the aeroplane, it took two months or more to cross. Nevertheless,

1

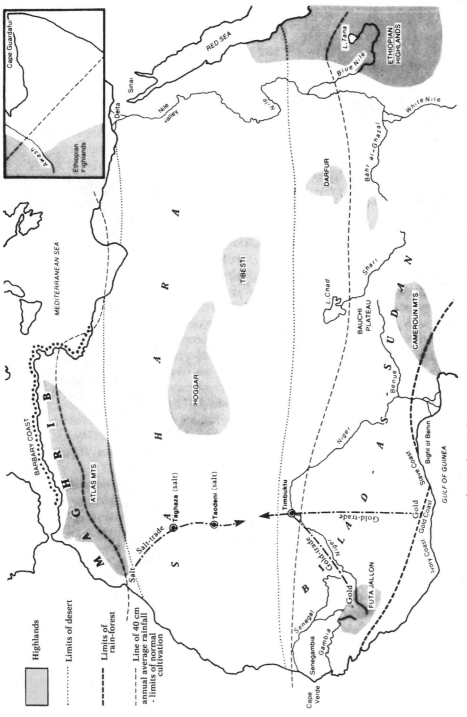

1. Northern Africa: geographical features and vegetation.

Highlands
········· Limits of desert
━ ━ ━ Limits of rain-forest
─ ─ ─ Line of 40 cm annual average rainfall - limits of normal cultivation

people did cross it, not merely in isolated journeys of exploration, but, regularly, year after year, in the course of trade, education, and pilgrimage. The essential intermediaries in this traffic were the pastoral nomads of the desert itself. They bred the camels, trained them for carrying, and accompanied and protected the caravans on their journeys. They also controlled what was, until the twentieth-century discoveries of oil and natural gas, the one great natural resource of the Sahara, which was the salt deposited in almost inexhaustible quantities by the evaporation of ancient lake basins situated in the very middle of the desert, dating from prehistoric periods of much greater rainfall. The salt was in high demand to the north, and more especially to the south of the desert. The nomads brought in slaves to mine it and supplied the all-important camels to transport it in bulk. Given the salt caravans, which by the nineteenth century were employing hundreds of thousands of camels to carry tens of thousands of tons of salt, the exchange of many other commodities from north and south of the desert becomes much easier to understand. The gold from the tributary valleys of the upper Niger, the upper Volta, and the Akan forest was an early and important element in the trans-Saharan trade. Slaves, captured all along the southern edges of the Sudanic belt, accompanied nearly every northward-moving caravan. And, as time went on, leather goods and cotton textiles manufactured in the Sudan were carried northwards in considerable quantity. The staples of the southward traffic were the woollen textiles of North Africa; the cottons and muslins of the Middle East; and the weapons, armour, and other hardware of southern Europe.

Therefore, long before any sailing ship from Europe reached the Atlantic coast of West Africa, the Sudanic lands to the south of the Sahara were in touch with those of the Mediterranean not only by exchanging produce but also by the sharing of skills and ideas. Whereas the Latin Christianity of the Roman provinces never crossed the Sahara, Greek-speaking missionaries, both Orthodox and Monophysite, converted the Nubian kingdoms on the upper Nile and the kingdom of Aksum in northern Ethiopia. In the west, Islam first spread through the conquest of Egypt and North Africa in the seventh century, and then moved on across the desert with little delay. By the ninth century, the nomads of the central and western Sahara were converting to Islam. By the eleventh century, at least, the new faith was beginning to penetrate the Negro kingdoms to the south of the desert, where it appealed first and foremost to those who travelled beyond their own communities and language areas as participants in an already active system of regional and interregional trade. To them, Islam offered wider intellectual and spiritual horizons and membership in a universal brotherhood which looked after its members in very practical ways. Between the eleventh and eighteenth centuries, at least, the townsfolk of the Sudanic countries learned to be Muslims like the Arabs and the Berbers to the north. Their learned and pious men studied Arabic, the language of the Holy Koran, and a few made the pilgrimage to the holy cities of Mecca and Medina, passing through the great cities of Egypt and North Africa on the way. The rulers and the rich men on both sides of the desert worshipped the One God, read the same books, and discussed the same things.

It would, of course, be a great mistake to imagine that all the civilisations of the Sudanic belt of Africa were due to contact with the world of Islam. We now know that a pattern of urban life in walled towns existed in widely scattered parts of West Africa long before the spread of Islam, and that the characteristic political formation of small 'city states' grouped in clusters – each cluster speaking a common language and observing common customs – must have been a development indigenous to the region. The periodic and sporadic incorporation of city–states into larger political hierarchies, described by outsiders as kingdoms or empires, is likewise to be seen as a response to various local factors, including differences of economic opportunity and military power and the ambitions of individual rulers, and not as the transfer of political ideas from the north of the desert to the south. Nevertheless, the growing presence of Islam and the proximity of the Islamic heartlands as the most obvious point of reference in the outside world did help to provide a certain element of unity to the northern half of Africa, extending from the Mediterranean almost to the Atlantic coast of West Africa. Within all this vast area, despite multitudinous differences of language and culture, interregional trade and travel were practised by a small number of people and, by the beginning of the nineteenth century, nearly all of these were Muslims, so that there was a certain pool of common ideas in circulation from one end of it to the other.

It is debatable just where the southern frontier of northern Africa lay at different times in history. Until the twelfth and thirteenth centuries, it probably included little more than the open grasslands, forming a belt 500 or 600 km (300 or 400 miles) wide to the south of the desert margin, from the Senegal to Lake Chad and eastwards through Darfur and Kordofan to the Ethiopian highlands. Throughout this region, beasts of burden, especially donkeys, could circulate, and troops of armed horsemen could control and levy tribute upon the populations of quite large states. To the south again lay the woodland belt, thickening progressively into dense equatorial rain forest. Here, because of tsetse fly in the woodlands and lack of forage in the forest, all goods had to be carried by canoes or porters, and soldiers fought on foot. Markets and states were smaller, and there were few towns large enough for Islamic religion and learning to gain a foothold. Nevertheless, by the fourteenth and fifteenth centuries, some interregional trade was beginning to penetrate even these southern lands. Gold was found in the Akan forest, and kola, the one luxury stimulant permitted by Islam, was grown exclusively within the forest belt. When the Portuguese discovered the West African coast, they found that the trading frontier of the Mande traders from the Niger bend had already reached the coastline of modern Ghana. During the three centuries that followed, the European traders operating from the Atlantic beaches pushed the frontiers of interregional trade northwards again, but only by a matter of 300 to 500 km (200 to 300 miles). By 1800, there was still far more of West Africa which looked northwards for its contacts with the outside world than southwards to the seaborne trade with Europe. And, of course, throughout the whole vast region to the east of Lake Chad, there remained no other source of outside contacts but the northern one.

Countries of the Mediterranean Coast

By the end of the eighteenth century, people in the Muslim world as a whole had lost much of the energy and sense of purpose that had driven them to produce such a brilliant culture in the early centuries of Islam. They failed to keep abreast of the new inventions and techniques being discovered in western Europe, particularly in military affairs and transport – such as the improvements made to sailing ships. This failure to make progress affected all parts of Africa considered in this chapter in one way or another. It applied especially to the lands north of the Sahara, from Egypt in the east to Mauritania in the west. Since the sixteenth century, all these countries, except Morocco, had formed a part of the Turkish Ottoman empire, with its capital at Istanbul. By the eighteenth century, Ottoman power had declined considerably from the peak reached two centuries earlier. Provincial rulers now acted almost independently of the Ottoman sultan, and even tribute payments had become fairly nominal. While the situation varied in detail from one country to another, the ruling elite in all of them was composed of the descendants of the original Turkish garrisons, who augmented their numbers in each generation and their sense of separateness from the local people by recruiting slave soldiers from the northern confines of the Ottoman empire in southern Russia and the Caucasus. It was in supplying these recruits that the Ottoman sultans came nearest to ruling their North African possessions.

It was in Egypt that the system of military rule had its deepest roots. When they conquered the sultanate in 1517, the Ottomans took over an institution which had been operating since the thirteenth century; the elite cavalry soldiers, imported as slaves but then educated and trained to occupy a highly privileged status, were known as *mamluks*. At the end of their professional service, they were freed and generously pensioned. Their children, however, were forbidden to enter the army. The commanders of the mamluks, the *amirs*, directed the military and civil services of the state, and each amir on his appointment imported a fresh supply of mamluks to be his bodyguard or 'household'. Much of the cultivable land of the country was divided into fiefs for the support of the military elite, and for the peasant millions of Egypt who toiled and were taxed Mamluk rule was a harsh one. But it supported a leisured and educated class which made Cairo, at least, a centre of luxury and learning as outstanding as any in the Muslim world.

To the west of Egypt, the countries of Tripoli, Tunis, Algeria, and Morocco were known collectively to the Arabs as *al-Maghrib* (the West). Here, in contrast with Egypt, the authority of governments rarely extended far beyond the main cities. In the hinterlands lived fiercely independent nomadic tribes – both Berbers and bedouin Arabs. They could only be rather loosely controlled by playing off one against the other. In Tripoli, the Ottoman government had been represented since 1711 by the local Karamanli family, which had concentrated its efforts mainly on developing the trans-Saharan trade from Bornu and the Hausa states. By this route came a steady supply of Sudanese slaves, who were distributed by the merchants of Tripoli to Istanbul, Damascus, Cairo, and all over the western part of the Muslim world. Tripoli was likewise a distributing centre for the splendid leatherwork of the Hausa cities, already well known in western Europe as 'Morocco leather'. Tripoli's exports southwards consisted mainly of arms, armour, and Arab horses. They also included mercenary soldiers trained in the use of firearms, who joined the bodyguards of the Sudanese rulers.

Tripoli, however, had no monopoly of the trans-Saharan trade. Probably, the largest hub of the desert traffic was at the oasis of Ghadames, where the borders of Tunisia, Algeria, and Libya now meet. Here, caravan routes from the central and western Sudan converged, and Ghadames merchants were well known in Hausa-land and Timbuktu alike. From Ghadames, some of the Sudan trade was carried to Tunis and Algiers. These were busy ports from which merchants could more easily reach the markets of western Europe than from Tripoli. The rulers (*beys*) of Tunis had been drawn since 1705 from the local Hussainid family, whose armed forces protected a large settled population from the attacks of the nomad Berbers of the eastern Atlas. These peasant farmers of the Tunisian plain were some of the greatest wheat producers of the whole Mediterranean basin. In the coastal towns, a sophisticated middle class of merchants and officials, enjoying a long tradition of Islamic civilisation and learning, ran a more orderly system of government than was possible in any other Maghrib country.

The Ottoman rulers of Algiers were known as *deys*. Unlike the rulership of Tunis, this office had not fallen into the hands of a single family, to be passed down from father to son. It was filled on the death of the reigning dey by election from among a group of merchants and soldiers who were the most influential men in the city. The merchants, called *corsairs* by Europeans (from an Italian word meaning 'to chase'), traded by sea with the European countries, using galleys rowed by Christian slaves. Legitimate trade was sometimes combined with acts of piracy against European shipping and coastlines, for which they became infamous. During the seventeenth century, Algiers had been one of the most attractive cities of the Mediterranean. Dr Shaw, an English traveller in the early eighteenth century, commented favourably on its surroundings:

The hills and vallies round about Algiers are all over beautiful with gardens and country seats, whither the inhabitants of better fashion retire during the heats of the summer season. They are little white houses, shaded with a variety of fruit trees and ever-greens, which, besides the shade and retirement, afford a gay and delightful prospect towards the sea. The gardens are all of them well stocked with melons, fruit and pot-herbs of all kinds. The natives of Algiers live extremely happy, for though the government is despotic, it is not so in reality.[1]

Even at the time of its surrender to the French in 1830, Algiers was described as 'perhaps the best regulated city in the world'. The French conquerors found that the majority of the Algerines were better educated than the majority of the local Frenchmen. And this was after half a century of grave political disorders, due to revolts among the Arab and Berber tribes who roamed over the high plateaux of the interior behind the coastal plains. These tribes were led by *marabouts*, the Muslim holy men, who carried their attacks to the very outskirts of the cities on the Mediterranean shore.

Morocco had never been a part of the Ottoman dominions, and its armies were composed mostly of black slaves from the Sudan, of whom by the mid-eighteenth century there were said to be some 150,000 – half of them housed in a specially constructed military town, and the rest dispersed in forts guarding the central lowlands of the country from the incursions of the Berber nomads of the Atlas. The extent of territory paying tribute into the sultan's treasury had greatly diminished since the late sixteenth and early seventeenth centuries, when for a few years the kingdom had stretched right across the desert to Timbuktu. Now, as in Algeria, tribal groups from the High Atlas and the desert fringes were apt to raid the settled areas and extort their own tribute from the peasants of the plains, and the

---

[1] T. Shaw, *Travels and Observations Relating to the Several Parts of Barbary and the Levant* (Oxford, 1738), p. 71.

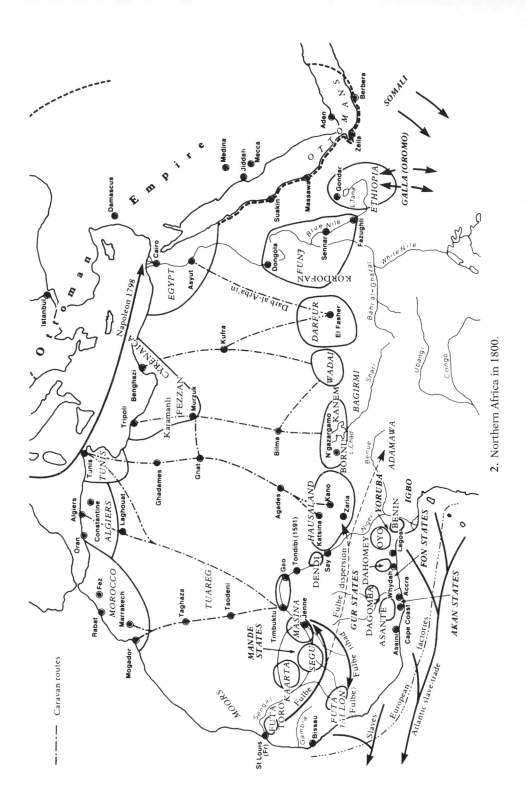

2. Northern Africa in 1800.

armies of the sultan were powerless to prevent them. Nevertheless, Morocco was still the terminus of a considerable trade with the south. The salt trade conducted by the desert Berbers from near its southern borders still attracted much of the gold of the upper Senegal–Niger region, despite the attempts of the French at St Louis to obtain it. Slaves from the Niger bend still went northwards to Morocco in considerable numbers. Despite the opening of the sea routes, a great many European manufactures, especially English cotton goods, were distributed over West Africa by Moroccan merchants who bought them at Mogador on the Atlantic coast of southern Morocco. Arabic-speaking Moors lived all over the western fringes of the Sahara as far south as the banks of the Senegal. Their holy men practised the characteristic Maghribi forms of devotion, becoming followers of such religious orders as the Ramaniyya, which was founded in 1770 in Kabylia (Algeria), and the Tijaniyya, established in 1781 by Sidi Ahmad Tijani at Ain Mahdi, near Laghouat, on the desert fringe of Algeria. Tijani's teaching was accepted at the great Moroccan university at Fez, and his order prospered in Mauritania and among the Tuareg tribesmen of the central Sahara.

States of the Sudan Region

Most of the larger states existing to the south of the Sahara were affected in some degree by the stagnation of the Islamic world as a whole. Generally, there was less security for traders and pilgrims than there had been and, in consequence, less wealth, less learning, and less religion. Among the states most affected was Ethiopia, which, though Christian in religion, lay close to the Arabian heartlands of Islam and suffered severely from the decline in the trade of the Red Sea. More seriously still, Ethiopia had been suffering since the sixteenth century from the progressive infiltration and settlement of its southern and eastern provinces by its Oromo neighbours. The Christian monarchy had responded to the situation by moving its headquarters away from its traditional medieval bases in Shoa (the region around modern Addis Ababa) to the region north of Lake Tana, where it finally established a fixed capital at Gondar. But this attempt at regroupment had not been successful. The Oromo pressure continued, and the new frontiers could only be defended by attracting Oromo contingents into the royal service by granting them the right to raise tribute from the Christian peasantry. Jesus II (1730–55) was the last of the eighteenth-century emperors to exercise any real authority outside the Gondar region. After his death, the feudal rulers of the other provinces became virtually independent, and rival emperors were recognised by different factions. By the early nineteenth century, one of them had fallen into such abject poverty that, when he died, there was not enough money in the treasury to pay for a coffin.

Bordering Ethiopia to the west lay the territory of the Funj sultanate, which in the sixteenth century had replaced the southernmost of the Christian kingdoms of Nubia. The Funj made their capital at Sennar on the Blue Nile, which became the centre of a rich trade in Ethiopian gold and Sudanese ivory, which were exported to Jiddah in exchange for Indian textiles. By the mid-eighteenth century, however, the dynasty was becoming increasingly dependent on its black slave troops. When the Scotsman James Bruce, who wrote a marvellous description of his dangerous travels in Ethiopia, passed through the country on his way down the Blue Nile in 1770, there was still a standing army of 1,800 horses and 14,000 infantry, but control of the western province of Kordofan had been lost, and trade had shrunk to a trickle. Bruce was not impressed by what he saw. 'War and treason', he wrote, 'appear to be the only occupations of this horrid people, whom Heaven has separated by almost impassable deserts from the rest of mankind.'[2]

More vigorous than the Funj sultanate were now those of Darfur and Wadai, one on each side of the modern frontier between the Sudan Republic and Chad. Though nominally Muslim, it is clear from the early nineteenth-century accounts of Muhammad al-Tunisi, a distinguished Arab scholar who made voyages of exploration to both countries, that here, as in many states of the western Sudan, ancient pre-Muslim ideas of divine kingship still persisted. Al-Tunisi described an annual ceremony of re-covering the royal drums, when a boy and a girl were sacrificed; he also described the sultans taking part in almost Pharaonic rituals of seedtime and harvest:

---

[2] James Bruce, *Travels to Discover the Source of the Blue Nile 1768–1773* (London, 1790), vol. 4, p. 437.

At the beginning of the planting season the Sultan rides out in great pomp, escorted by more than a hundred young women, by his slave boys and by a troop of flute-players. When he reaches the open fields, he dismounts from his horse, takes different kinds of seeds and sows them, while a slave hoes the ground.[3]

The wealth of these two states were derived from the slaves raided by the armies of horsemen from among the animist peoples living to the south of them, who lacked any kind of state organisation. Both sultanates traded in copper from the rich deposits at Hofrat en-Nahas near the headwaters of the Bahr al-Ghazal, and both sent their trading caravans northwards by the *Darb al-Arba 'in* (the Forty Days' Road), which reached the Nile valley at Asyut.

At the end of the eighteenth century, the ancient empire of Kanem–Bornu, with its wide territories to the east and west of Lake Chad, was still the most stable and civilised of the Sudanic states. To be sure, it had lost some of the imperial outreach achieved in earlier periods when it had pushed its military garrisons northwards to occupy the salt mines at Bilma and to touch the southern marches of Tripoli in the Fezzan. But its rulers were still pious and literate Muslims and, throughout their kingdom, justice was administered according to Islamic law. The interregional trade of Kanem–Bornu was indeed based upon the horrific slave raids annually conducted by the armies of the ruler (*mai*) upon the stateless peoples of the Mandara mountains and other peripheral regions to the south; but, within the state's boundaries, there was peace and prosperity of a kind, which impressed all foreign travellers. The capital at that time was the brick-built town of N'gazargamo, some 95 km (60 miles) west of Lake Chad – the ruins of which can still be seen and which cover an area about 3 km (2 miles) in diameter. Here, the mais lived a dignified and secluded existence, supported by the tribute collected for them by their provincial governors from the peasantry of a kingdom measuring perhaps 1,000 by 500 km (600 by 300 miles), much of it light grazing land, but including also the densely populated alluvial farmlands west of Lake Chad.

In terms of interregional trade, the most active part of the central Sudan was not Kanem–Bornu but the city–states of Hausaland lying

[3] Muhammad bin 'Umar al-Tunisi, *Voyage au Ouddây*, tr. Dr Perron (Paris, 1851), p. 159.

along its western flank. Though never united, these Hausa cities were unique in the Sudan in that they possessed manufacturing industries on a really important scale. Weaving, dyeing, leatherwork, glassmaking, smithing, and metalwork of every description were carried out, mostly by slave artisans living in the towns and fed by agricultural slaves living in special villages in the surrounding countryside. At the end of the eighteenth century, Katsina was still the leading city; soon it was to be Kano, with Zaria a close third. It was from these cities rather than from N'gazargamo that the great caravan routes radiated outwards across the Sahara to Tripoli and Ghadames, and from there to Tunis and Algiers. Bornu, with its cavalry armies, supplied most of the slaves that were exported northwards. The manufactures came from Hausaland, and their distribution covered the whole of northern Africa.

South of the Sahara from the Maghrib, the powerful empires of the medieval western Sudan had broken up by the end of the eighteenth century into many weak kingdoms. The great empire of the Songhay Askias, which had stretched in the sixteenth century from the upper Senegal to the frontiers of modern Nigeria, had come to an end with the Moroccan invasion of 1591. At the battle of Tondibi, the Moroccans used firearms for the first time against Sudanese cavalry and foot soldiers armed only with bows and spears. The conquerors settled down, and their descendants formed a new ruling class, the *arma* (shooters, gunmen), which soon became independent of the Moroccan sultan, the soldiers electing their own *pashas* (rulers) at Timbuktu and their *kaids* (governors) in the garrison towns around the loop of the Niger bend from Jenne to Gao.

After the Moroccan conquest, what remained of the ruling class of Songhay retreated down the Niger and set up an independent government in the southern province of Dendi. Upstream from Jenne, on the western side of the Niger bend, the Mande subjects of the Songhay empire reverted to their pre-imperial pattern of government as a cluster of small states, each centred around a little walled town called a *kafu*. Here and there, as at Segu and Kaarta, successful warlords, getting firearms in exchange for war captives, managed to establish some larger states – each incorporating several kafus. However, the most vital region of the western Sudan during the seventeenth and eighteenth centuries was the far west. Here, in Futa Toro to the south

of the middle Senegal, there had sprung up during the medieval period a people of mixed Berber and Negro descent known as the Fulbe
(French: Peul; Hausa: Fulani). Unlike the states of the Mande, those
of the Fulbe included many groups of nomadic pastoralists, who
herded their cattle in the parts of the country which were too arid for
agriculture even during the wet season and brought them southwards into the farmlands to manure the fields after the cereal
harvest had been gathered. Unlike their farming relatives, the pastoralists migrated far and wide in search of new grazing grounds
and established similar relationships with the farmers of other language groups. As early as the fifteenth century, they were spread out
in small communities all over the savanna belt of West Africa to as
far east as Lake Chad. Until the eighteenth century, these scattered
Fulbe were mostly animist in religious belief. However, those Fulbe
who remained in their Futa Toro homeland were converted to Islam
by marabouts from Mauritania in the sixteenth and seventeenth centuries and joined Muslim brotherhoods – full of zeal for their new
faith. One Fulbe clan, the Torodbe, became the missionary and clerical leaders of the whole of the Fulbe people. Wherever Fulbe were
dispersed, Torodbe preachers would be found teaching the necessity
for conversion and Islamic reform and advocating *jihad*, the holy
war, as the means of obtaining it. The twin bases of the Fulbe movement were Futa Toro and Masina, a Fulbe-led state to the south-west
of Timbuktu, once tributary to Songhay, which became independent
after the Moorish conquest. From Masina in the eighteenth century,
Torodbe missionaries carried the jihad to Futa Jallon, the mountain
country on the borders of Guinea and Sierra Leone, and eastwards
across the Niger bend to Say. From this background of missionary
zeal and holy war, the great Fulbe jihad of the early nineteenth century arose.

It is often said that the seventeenth and eighteenth centuries were
a period of decline in the western Sudan, and certainly it was a time
of great political disorder. But, thanks to the Torodbe and other religious leadership groups, much of the learning of the medieval Sudan
was kept alive. It is possible that by the end of the eighteenth century, both Islam and Arabic education were more widely spread than
they had been during the great days of the medieval empires. Despite the political disorders, trade continued to flow. There seems to
have been a breakdown in communications between the western and

the central Sudan. This was because, after the defeat of Songhay, no other power was able to control the fierce Tuareg nomads living to the north and east of the Niger bend. The routes running north-west from Timbuktu and north from the Senegal remained open and active well into the nineteenth century – more active by far than the routes from Timbuktu westwards to the Atlantic coast.

States of the Woodland and the Forest

By the eighteenth century, the opening of the Atlantic trade by the Europeans had made a crucial change only among the states of the woodland and forest zones to the south of the savanna belt. From their earliest days, these states had all in their external relations faced towards the north. The Akan states of modern Ghana and the Ivory Coast had looked towards Mali, Songhay, and the successor states of the Mande, while the states of the Yoruba- and Edo-speakers in southern Nigeria looked towards Hausaland. As Samuel Johnson, the historian of the Yorubas, pointed out,

It should be remembered that light and civilisation with the Yorubas came from the north... The centre of light and activity, of large populations and industry, was therefore in the interior, whilst the coast tribes were scanty in number, ignorant and degraded, not only from their distance from the centre, but also (later) through their demoralising intercourse with Europeans and the slave trade.[4]

It was the same in Ghana and the Ivory Coast as it was in Nigeria. The most important of the woodland and forest states had at first been those on the northern side. The smallest and the most backward, populated only by fishermen and salt-boilers, had been the little states on the coast.

The Atlantic slave trade, which was begun by the Portuguese in the late fifteenth century when a trickle of Africans were shipped across the ocean – first to Europe and later to the Spanish and Portuguese colonies in the New World – had developed by the end of the seventeenth century into a steady flood. Most of the European maritime countries then took part in it, especially Britain and France. The brisk competition for slaves among the rival Europeans meant that

[4] Samuel Johnson, *History of the Yorubas* (Lagos, 1921), p. 40.

the states at or near the coast had easy access to firearms, which they used at first in wars of conquest against their neighbours and eventually against the formerly more important inland states. Within the woodland and forest states, there had been considerable change in the balance of power by the end of the eighteenth century. The rising states were those based near the coast, especially Asante and Dahomey, which had grown as a result of the use of firearms acquired through the Atlantic trade. The most dramatic demonstration of this shift in power occurred in 1745, when the musketmen of Asante defeated the armoured cavalry of Dagomba who, in any earlier period, would have chased them mercilessly out of any open country they had dared to enter. This process, begun in the seventeenth and eighteenth centuries, was carried much further in the nineteenth.

The Encircling Power of Europe

The only significant imperial power in the northern half of Africa at the end of the eighteenth century was Ottoman Turkey. Its dependencies in Egypt, Tripoli, Tunis, and Algiers were admittedly almost 'self-governing', but they did at least contribute some revenue to the sultans in Istanbul. The European powers trading with North and West Africa had, in contrast, nothing but a few footholds, in the shape of fortified trading factories scattered along the West African coast, from St Louis on the Senegal to Whydah in Bénin. These forts, whether British, Danish, Dutch, French, or Portuguese, were designed mainly to protect the operations of one group of European traders from the competition of others. Few of the castles could have withstood a determined attack by local Africans, and their governors had to be circumspect in exercising any jurisdiction outside the walls. They carried on their trade with the help of African middlemen living in the adjacent towns. Although by the end of the eighteenth century, they were exporting around 100,000 slaves a year from West Africa alone, the Europeans seldom captured a slave by themselves and, save for the French on the Senegal, it was the rarest thing for any European to venture 20 km (12 miles) inland. Nor did there seem at any time in the eighteenth century the slightest likelihood of a change in the pattern of these relationships, which were satisfactory to both the European and the African traders. It is true that by the end of the eighteenth century, the slave trade was under attack in one or two European countries. A judge in an English court declared in 1772 that there was no such thing as slavery on English soil. And, fifteen years later, a group of philanthropists in England bought a few square miles of the Sierra Leone peninsula for the purpose of settling Negro slaves freed in England and across the Atlantic in Canada. From this tiny beginning, the result of the stirring of consciences among a few well-to-do men, truly 'a cloud no bigger than a man's hand', sprang the ever-growing flood of European interference in tropical Africa during the century to come. But nobody at the time could have foreseen it.

To contemporaries, the change in the balance of power in the Mediterranean must have seemed much more impressive than any growth of European power in tropical Africa. To Britain and, therefore, to France, India and the routes to India were already a matter of the most serious strategic importance. When these two powers were locked in combat at the end of the century, it seemed a natural move that Britain should forestall the French by seizing the Cape of Good Hope from the Dutch. That Napoleon should reply by occupying Egypt was surprising only in that it finally showed the weakness of the Ottoman empire in relation to European military might. The mamluk soldiers surrendered to the French in a single battle fought near the Pyramids in 1798. The French were removed three years later only through the powerful assistance of the British. It was all very well for al-Jabarti, a citizen of Cairo and an eyewitness to these events and the last of the traditional Muslim chroniclers of Egypt, to write:

The presence of the French in Cairo was intolerable... Muslims died of shame when they saw their wives and daughters walking the streets unveiled, and appearing to be the property of the French... It was bad enough for them to see the taverns that had been established in all the bazaars and even in several mosques... The scum of the population was doing well, because it benefited from the new freedom. But the elite and the middle class experienced all sorts of vexation.[5]

What had happened once could happen again. It was only surprising that it did not happen for another eighty years.

---

[5] *Chronique d'Egypte 1798–1804*, ed. and tr. Gaston Wiet (Cairo, 1950), p. 45.

TWO. Africa South of the Equator

The Lands of the Bantu

The geography and climate of Africa south of the equator is much less simple than that of the northern half of the continent. Very briefly, however, high and rather dry steppe country runs south from the Ethiopian highlands through the middle of East Africa. It then crosses over towards the western side of the subcontinent, ending up in the Kalahari desert, with the dry lands of Botswana and the Orange Free State on one side and those of Namibia on the other. On the other hand, low-lying and distinctly humid country extends from southern Cameroun right across the northern half of the Congo basin to Lakes Tanganyika and Malawi, and from there it continues down the Zambezi valley to the Indian Ocean coast and round through southern Mozambique into Natal. In general, the steppe country is more suited to pastoralism than to agriculture and, therefore, tends to be only lightly populated. Equally, in the dense equatorial forest, agriculture is only practicable in clearings and beside riverbanks where sunlight can penetrate, and so here again population is very thin and until quite recently was virtually confined to the rivers and the seacoast, where a little agriculture could be combined with fishing. The best conditions for food production are found in the borderlands between the two zones, mostly therefore in the middle of the subcontinent. This is where population is densest and where, by the end of the eighteenth century, the most complex and centralised political institutions were found.

18

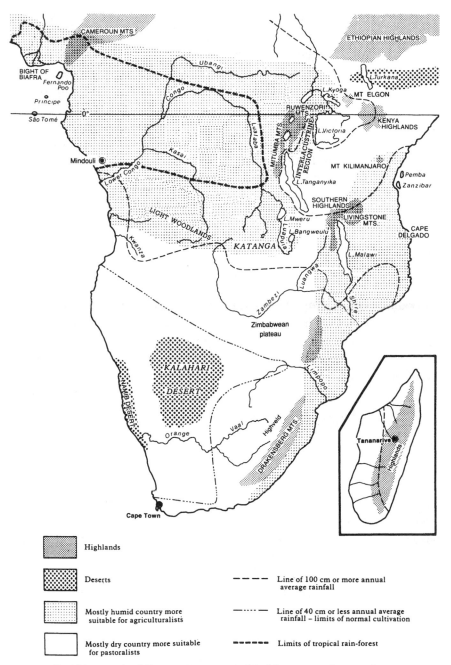

Highlands

Deserts

Mostly humid country more
suitable for agriculturalists

Mostly dry country more suitable
for pastoralists

– – – – Line of 100 cm or more annual
average rainfall

– · – · – Line of 40 cm or less annual average
rainfall – limits of normal cultivation

▬ ▬ ▬ Limits of tropical rain-forest

3. Africa south of the equator: geographical features and vegetation.

One particularly striking fact about the peoples who live in Africa south of the equator is that nearly all of them speak closely related languages of a single subfamily called Bantu (from the common word *muntu*, a man; plural *bantu*, people), of which the nearest relations outside the area are with the languages of southern West Africa. The exceptions to this rule – the people who do not speak Bantu languages – are all found in the dry zones of the north-east (parts of Kenya and Tanzania) and the south-west, where the practice of agriculture is difficult. It looks, therefore, as though the Bantu-speakers were the first agriculturalists in this part of Africa, and as though the 'cradleland' from which they dispersed was the woodland region to the north-west of the equatorial forest in what is today central and southern Cameroun. Starting perhaps around 3,500 years ago, the early Bantu spread southwards from this area, some groups expanding across the Congo basin by the rivers until they reached the savannas to the south of the forest, while others kept to the lighter woodlands bordering the forest to the north, the east, and the south. From these rather distinct lines of dispersion there developed, first, a Western Bantu tradition, in which political leadership tended to be associated with skill in metal-working – above all, in the forging of tools and weapons – and (later) an Eastern Bantu tradition in which rulers tended to be recognised by their possession and political manipulation of large herds of cattle.

The Western Bantu

For the Western Bantu, the region of light woodland extending for 800 to 1,000 km (500 to 700 miles) to the south of the forest offered almost ideal conditions for Iron Age food production. Rainfall was adequate, but not excessive. There was excellent fishing in the northward-flowing tributaries of the Congo River system and hunting in the strips of forest which lined the riverbanks, with plenty of open country for agriculture between the streams. The whole region was rich in iron ore, and there were large copper deposits both north of the lower Congo at Mindouli and southwards in Katanga. In the part of the region to the north and south of the lower Congo were peoples speaking the Kongo and Mbundu languages, who early formed small states based around dynasties which specialised in working iron and copper into tools and weapons. At some time around the fourteenth century, a local migration of well-armed Kongo-speakers moved southwards across the lower Congo and conquered the northern Mbundu. This resulted in the formation of a large state, covering most of northern Angola. When it was discovered by the Portuguese at the end of the fifteenth century, the Kongo kingdom was at the height of its power. A sixteenth-century document preserved in the Vatican archives describes the authority of the Kongo kings in the following terms:

At the head of the Kongo kingdom is a king of kings who is the absolute lord of all his realm, and none may intervene in any of his affairs. He commands as he pleases. He is not subject to any law. The village chiefs have above all to take care to collect from their subjects the taxes which are due to the king, and which they each of them carry to the governor of their province. The governor presents himself twice in each year at the royal capital in order to pay in the tribute, and if the king is satisfied, he replies with the one word, *wote*, which means 'you have done well'. In this case the governor esteems himself highly favoured and makes many clappings of his two hands. As a sign of his joy he throws himself on the ground, covering his body with dust. His servants do the same, and then take him on their shoulders, and go through all the city crying his praises. But if the king does not say this word *wote*, he retreats greatly discomfited, and another time he takes care to bring a larger tribute. The tribute is not fixed as to quantity: each brings as much as he can. But if the governor does not do better, the king addresses to him a strong reprimand, and takes away his post. Such a man then becomes as poor as the most miserable of all the blacks.[1]

By the end of the eighteenth century, the Kongo kingdom was little more than a memory. During the first century of its contact with the Portuguese, it had overextended its frontiers through wars of conquest, and thereafter the Portuguese found better slaving partners in the independent Mbundu kingdoms to the south of Kongo, near which in 1575 they established a permanent colony on the island of Luanda, the nucleus of the future Angola. Other Europeans traded with the Vili kingdoms north of the Congo estuary, where local merchants organised successful long-distance trade routes into the interior, using the rivers wherever possible. Kongo meanwhile disintegrated, first into its constituent provinces and later into smaller divisions still. As the Portuguese colony slowly expanded its footholds

---

[1] Vatican document cited in J. Cuvelier and L. Jadin, *L'Ancien Congo d'après les archives romaines* (Brussels, 1954), pp. 33–4.

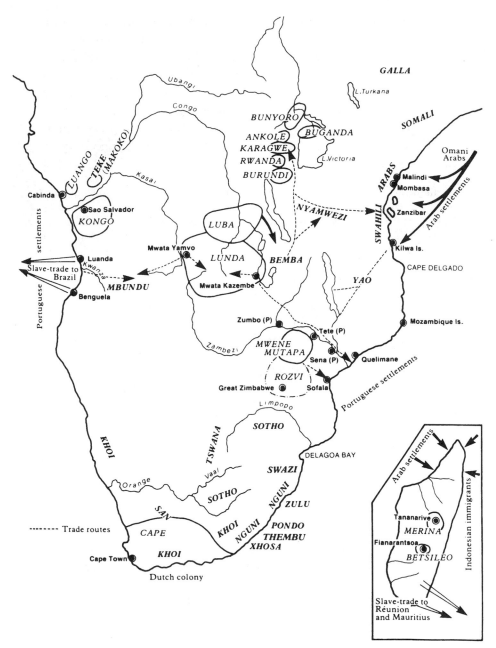

4. Africa south of the equator in 1800.

northwards up the coast, the successor states of the Kongo kingdom became its commercial hinterland, in which merchant families
wielded most of the influence.

Eastwards from the sphere of the Kongo and Mbundu, right across
to Lake Tanganyika, the savanna country to the south of the equatorial forest was occupied by another set of Western Bantu peoples,
of whom the most significant were the Luba and the Lunda. The
Luba lived astride the headwaters of the Congo River, known in
these latitudes as the Lualaba, which along with its many tributary
streams flows northwards from the copper-rich Katanga plateau,
which forms the watershed between the Congo and the Zambezi.
A little to the north of the watershed, the Lualaba flows through a
sequence of lake basins known as the Upemba depression, where
a happy mixture of fishing and farming, combined with advanced
metal-working in iron and copper, gave rise early in the present millennium to a very dense population, organised in a series of small
kingdoms reminiscent of the Kongo model. The earliest states would
appear to have been formed by the Luba.

By the end of the eighteenth century, however, the two most important kingdoms were those of the Lunda, farther to the west and south.
These were the kingdom of Mwata Yamvo, which occupied the whole
south-western corner of modern Democratic Republic of Congo, and
the kingdom of the Mwata Kazembe, astride the Luapula River in
southern Katanga. These great states, however, were but the centre
of a whole cluster of smaller ones, which filled up most of southern
Congo, eastern Angola, and northern Zambia. The rulers of the two
big Lunda kingdoms, and of several of the outlying states, were 'divine kings', in the style of those of Darfur and Wadai (see Chapter 1)
and of many other states in sub-Saharan Africa. They ate and drank
in secret, practised 'royal incest' with their queen sisters, shared ritual authority with their queen mothers, and used spirit mediums
to communicate with their royal ancestors. As the symbol of their
authority, they used fire from the royal forge, from which burning
brands were carried annually to the headquarters of all tributary
chiefs.

The capitals of the Lunda kings, though not as permanent as
the towns of West Africa, were considerable centres of government
and trade. The palace population was large because the kings took

hundreds of wives drawn from all the main families in the country. The court officials were numerous, and so were the skilled
craftsmen – potters, smiths, weavers, basketmakers, brewers, wood-
carvers, huntsmen, and traders – who congregated around the capital
and lived off the foodstuffs sent in as tribute from the surrounding
countryside. Describing such towns, which he visited in 1906, the
German explorer Leo Frobenius wrote:

> When I penetrated into the region of the Kasai and the Sankuru I found villages
> still existing whose principal streets were lined on both sides, and for miles on
> end, with four rows of palm-trees, and whose charmingly decorated houses were
> each of them a work of art. There was not a man who did not carry sumptuous
> weapons of iron or copper, with inlaid hilts and damascened blades. Everywhere
> there were velvets and silken stuffs. Every cup, every pipe, every spoon was a
> piece of artistry, fully worthy of comparison with the creations of Europe.[2]

The Eastern Bantu

Although Western Bantu peoples settled as far south as Namibia,
in most of the region to the south of the Katanga copperbelt they
were interspersed with Eastern Bantu peoples whose ancestors had
expanded around the north-eastern fringes of the equatorial forest,
bringing their cattle, sheep, and goats and establishing a very different pattern of settlement in dispersed homesteads rather than
concentrated villages. Their earliest settlements in eastern Africa
were in the 'interlacustrine' region around Lakes Albert, Victoria,
and Tanganyika. From here, during the early first millennium A.D.,
they spread eastwards to the Indian Ocean coast and southwards
into central and southern Africa. Where their populations grew dense
enough, the Eastern Bantu, like their Western counterparts, formed
states on a monarchical pattern, and the process of competition and
conquest among the initial small states led gradually to the emergence of some larger ones. In the interlacustrine region, by the end of
the eighteenth century six large states had grown up – Buganda, Bunyoro, Ankole, Karagwe, Rwanda, and Burundi – which are shown
on Map 4. Though not as big as the states of the Sudanic belt, all of
them probably had populations of half a million or more. As with

---

[2] L. Frobenius, *Histoire de la civilisation africaine* (Paris, 1952), p. 15.

the pre-Islamic states of the Sudan, they were ruled by divine kings who governed through elaborate hierarchies of court officials and provincial chiefs. As with the kingdoms of the Mwata Yamvo and the Mwata Kazembe, many smaller states clustered around these bigger ones, some of them paying tribute to one or other of the large kingdoms, but most in practice independent of all of them.

The first European travellers who came upon this region in the mid-nineteenth century felt that they were entering a new world. They had walked 1,250 to 1,400 km (800 to 900 miles) from the east coast along tortuous footpaths never more than a few inches wide, through sparsely inhabited country where provisions were hard to come by and even drinking water was often a problem. Along most of their route, every day's march brought them into the territory of some petty potentate with whom they had had to negotiate permission to pass. And then, suddenly, they found themselves in a world of plenty and of order. Here a ruler's writ or authority could run for a hundred miles from his capital. His messengers sped along wide, well-beaten roads to the provincial or district headquarters they were trying to reach. In 1862, Speke and Grant stayed with the 'ever-smiling' King Rumanika of Karagwe while runners were sent to announce their arrival to Kabaka Mutesa of Buganda. Their passports granted, they were accompanied for the rest of their journey by royal guides, and food and lodging were arranged at the end of each day's march.

Another region where large centralised states were developed by Eastern Bantu peoples was that between the Zambezi and Limpopo Rivers, in Zimbabwe and southern Mozambique. This was a region rich in gold, copper, and ivory; where Indian Ocean traders had been present from at least the tenth century; and where by about the same date some concentrated settlements were being built with stone walling and platforms indicating their function as capital towns. The earliest examples were in or near the Limpopo valley, but the world-famous site of Great Zimbabwe was built some 240 km (150 miles) to the north of it in predominantly pastoral country on the southern slopes of the Zimbabwe plateau, and was occupied and gradually improved from the mid-eleventh until the mid-fifteenth century, when it was suddenly abandoned. A new centre of power then emerged on the northern edge of the plateau, overlooking the Zambezi valley, where there reigned a king of kings called the Mwene Mutapa, who owned great herds of cattle which grazed over the plateau country, and took tribute from the elephant hunters and ivory traders of the Zambezi valley. When the Portuguese colonised the lower part of the valley in the sixteenth century, they began to intervene in the succession struggles of the Mwene Mutapa's kingdom by extending support to their own favoured candidates. By the late seventeenth century, the main ruling house had come so much under their influence that a rival dynasty, that of the Rozvi, claimed the paramountcy for their state of Butwa, which controlled most of the region during the eighteenth century. Although the medieval capital site at Great Zimbabwe lay within this state, it was no longer a place of any importance. The Rozvi capitals were built farther to the west, between Gweru and Bulawayo, where ruins like those at Naletale and Dhlo–Dhlo have yielded finds dating to this period.

The Trade of Bantu Africa

The most striking fact about these Bantu states was that, unlike their counterparts in the Sudanic belt of Africa, they were almost completely cut off from contact with the outside world. The larger Bantu states were situated in the interior of the continent and, until after the eighteenth century, they virtually lacked any of the Islamic influence which was so important a feature of the Sudan. The infestation by tsetse fly was so widespread that beasts of burden were unknown, although herds could be pastured in limited areas. Everything had to be carried except on the rivers and, so far as we know at present, the only water routes running deep into the continent during medieval times were those which ascended the Zambezi and the Limpopo from the coast of southern Mozambique. Here, the Swahili Arabs from Kilwa and points farther north were trading cloth and beads for gold and ivory at least by the tenth century. In the sixteenth century, the Portuguese replaced the Swahili Arabs on the Zambezi and, henceforward, this line of communication ran through their hands.

The more important part of the Portuguese contribution, however, was their opening of the Atlantic coast of Bantu Africa to seaborne trade with Europe and South America. Their first venture in this direction was with the Kongo kingdom, where they made the Kongo kings their allies. They also supplied them with Christian missionaries and technical and military aid. In the course of a hundred years, however, their interests shifted southwards to Luanda and Benguela, where they found it easier than in Kongo to obtain slaves, which were needed in ever-increasing numbers to work the sugar plantations of their colony of Brazil. The demand of the Portuguese for slaves was supplied on the one hand by the little wars fought by their Mbundu allies against other Mbundu living a little farther away from their forts in the Kwanza valley, and on the other hand by the purchases made by their African trading agents (*pombeiros*, from Pumbe, a market on the Malebo Pool) in the interior markets. The slave-trader James Barbot observed in 1700 that

These slaves have other slaves under them, sometimes a hundred, or a hundred and fifty, who carry the commodities on their heads up into the country. Sometimes these pombeiros stay out a whole year, and then bring back with them four, five or six hundred slaves.[3]

In this way, the Portuguese made indirect contact with the Lunda kingdom of Mwata Yamvo and its many satellites. By the end of the eighteenth century, the main Lunda kingdoms had acquired guns, cloth, and other European luxuries, and their own industries had developed greatly by learning from European examples. Splendid axes and cutlasses were made by the Lunda smiths in the period following the European contact. Manioc (or cassava) – the South American root crop – was introduced by the Portuguese to feed the slaves awaiting shipment to the New World, and soon became the staple food for the whole of the southern Congo region.

The important region which remained right out of touch with the outside world until late in the eighteenth century was the interlacustrine one. To the west of it lay the equatorial forest, to the north the Nile swamps, and to the east the Kenya highlands, inhabited by warlike pastoralists such as the Nandi and the Masai. The easiest line of approach was from the south-east, but it was a long time before even this was developed. Apparently, the early Swahili Arab communities of the east coast had no contact with any but the coastal peoples anywhere to the north of the Zambezi. Certainly, the Portuguese, when they occupied this part of the coast during the sixteenth and

---

[3] A. and J. Churchill, *Collection of Voyages and Travels* (London, 1732), vol. 5, p. 522.

seventeenth centuries, had no knowledge, even by hearsay, of the interior that lay behind. It was, in fact, only when the Arabs of Oman
(in the Persian Gulf) seized the northern part of the east coast from
the Portuguese at the beginning of the eighteenth century that contact with the interior began to develop; even then, the main agents
of it appear to have been the Nyamwezi people of western Tanzania,
who found their way down to the coast with ivory for sale. Throughout the eighteenth and early nineteenth centuries, it was still the
Nyamwezi who organised and operated most of the carrying trade in
East Africa. Their caravans covered the whole region from Katanga
to the Indian Ocean. They marched great distances with heavy loads,
eating little and sleeping in the bush. The early European travellers
reported how the Nyamwezi boys used to prepare themselves for this
way of life by carrying small tusks on their shoulders as they went
about their home villages. Traditional history relates that it was in the
late eighteenth century that the first consignments of plates, cups,
saucers, knives, and cotton goods reached the kingdom of Buganda
at the heart of the interlacustrine region. From this time onwards,
the traditions tell of a steadily growing trade passing to the south of
Lake Victoria and through the Nyamwezi country to the Zanzibar
coast.

South Africa: Bantu and Boer

Another part of Bantu Africa which had almost no contact with
the outside world until late in the eighteenth century was the region south of the Limpopo in what is now the Republic of South
Africa. Two main groups of Eastern Bantu peoples lived here – the
Sotho–Tswana on the plateau to the west of the Drakensberg mountains, in what was to become the Transvaal and the Orange Free
State, and the Nguni peoples (Zulu, Swazi, Pondo, Thembu, Xhosa)
in the fertile and well-watered coastal lowlands of Natal and the
Transkei. So long as they still had room for expansion by clearing
the bush and occupying the more marginal lands, these peoples created no centralised states. The Sotho lived in large, almost urban
concentrations of 10,000 to 15,000 people, their settlements often en-
closed within stone walls. When one settlement grew inconveniently
large, colonists were dispatched to found another. The Nguni lived in

dispersed homesteads, grouped in chiefdoms, each with around 10,000 subjects; and once again, when political units grew too populous, they divided. Only toward the end of the eighteenth century did two Nguni groups living at the northern extremity of Nguni country begin to face the problem of overpopulation by recruiting their young men into military regiments with a view to conquering and subjugating their neighbours.

These groups were to emerge during the early nineteenth century as the Zulu and Swazi nations. Until then, despite the fissiparous political systems, the South African Bantu appear to have lived fairly prosperously – especially after the introduction of maize, another New World food crop, which spread outwards from the Portuguese trading stations in southern Mozambique. Such European visitors as passed through the land in the sixteenth and seventeenth centuries – mostly survivors of shipwrecks off the notoriously stormy coast – commented on the large herds of sleek cattle. They noticed, however, that iron tools were scarce except in the neighbourhood of Delagoa Bay. The governor of the Cape, Simon van der Stel, wrote a dispatch to his superiors in Holland in 1689, telling them of the journey of the crew of a wrecked vessel, the *Stavenisse*. The country of the 'Magossebe' (AmaXhosa) is described as follows:

Their riches consist in cattle and assegais, also copper and iron. The country is exceedingly fertile and incredibly populous, and full of cattle, whence it is that lions and other ravenous animals are not very apt to attack men, as they find enough tame cattle to devour. They preserve their corn in cavities under ground, where it keeps good and free from weavils for years. In their intercourse with each other they are very civil, polite and talkative, saluting each other, whether young or old, male or female, whenever they meet; asking whence they come, and whither they are going, what is their news, and whether they have learned any new songs or dances. The kings are much respected and beloved by their subjects; they wear the skins of buck and leopard. One need not be under any apprehension about meat and drink, as they have in every village a house of entertainment for travellers, where they are not only lodged, but fed also.[4]

It was more than a century before the Dutch colony planted at Cape Town in 1652 made any contact with these south-eastern Bantu peoples. Most of the western Cape province was still the country of the

---

[4] D. Moodie, *The Record, or a Series of Official Papers Relative to the Condition and Treatment of the Native Tribes of South Africa 1838–1842* (Amsterdam, 1960), vol. 1, p. 431.

Khoi (Hottentots) and San (Bushmen) – the pastoral and hunting predecessors of the Bantu, now reduced to the south-western corner of a subcontinent of which they had once been the principal inhabitants. The Dutch settlers at the Cape expanded only slowly into the interior, driving out the Bushmen, and making servants and herdsmen of the Khoi, whose tribal organisation was broken by the double impact of colonists and smallpox. This labour force was supplemented by slaves brought from both the western and eastern coasts of Africa and the Dutch possessions in the East Indies. The Dutch settlers and their slaves increased at an almost equal pace – there were some 17,000 of each by the end of the eighteenth century. Intermarriage between all of the racial groups at the Cape – Europeans, Negroes, Khoisan, and Malays – was beginning to produce the mixed Cape Coloured population. Not until about 1770 did Afrikaner (Cape Dutch) and Bantu face each other across the Fish River, thieving each other's cattle by night and arguing about its return by day. Soon there were frequent armed conflicts. In 1795, when the British first seized the Cape from the Dutch at the time of the Napoleonic wars, the problems on the eastern frontier were threatening and dangerous, but might still have been satisfactorily solved, given goodwill on both sides and a firm determination to maintain a permanent frontier between the Cape Colony and its Bantu neighbours. But, by the time the British returned permanently in 1806, the situation on the frontier had passed beyond the hope of peaceful negotiation and control.

The East Coast: Arabs and Swahili

At the end of the eighteenth century, therefore, Bantu Africa was still a very secluded region in comparison with most of Africa north of the equator. The only part of it which had been for any long period in contact with a literate civilisation and a universal faith was the coastal belt of East Africa. Here, trading settlements were known to Greek geographers in the first century A.D., while early mosques built of mud and thatch have been found which show the presence of Islam as early as the eighth or ninth century. Commercial settlements were established by Arab merchants from the Red Sea and the Persian Gulf; from the tenth century on, some of these were prosperous enough to have their public buildings made of the coral blocks abounding on the coast. The Swahili people, in origin perhaps the indigenous Bantu inhabitants of the Lamu archipelago, who would have been among the northernmost of the Eastern Bantu, early learned to make and handle seagoing canoes and small sailing vessels, and so managed the coasting trade, of which the Arabs supplied the long-distance, oceanic element. It was the indigenous Swahili, as much as or more than the Arabs, who built and populated the thirty or forty coastal towns spread out along the coast of Kenya, Tanzania, and northern Mozambique. Kiswahili is unequivocally an Eastern Bantu language, though using some hundreds of Arabic loan-words, many of them recently introduced. By the seventeenth and eighteenth centuries, however, if not much earlier, most inhabitants of the Swahili towns were Muslims, and it was this factor more than any ethnic or linguistic one which made them feel different from, and superior to, the other Bantu peoples who were their neighbours. Beyond the coastal belt, however, the influence of this Swahili Arab civilisation was very restricted indeed. Swahili Arab traders had preceded the Portuguese on the Zambezi, where they had built the riverside ports of Sena and Tete. Here also, Swahili Arabs resident at the Mwene Mutapa's court had in 1569 instigated the murder of the Roman Catholic missionary, Gonçalo de Silveira, following which the Portuguese began a policy of extermination against them. Elsewhere, however, until late in the eighteenth century, there is scarcely a reference to Swahili Arab activities more than a few miles from the Indian Ocean coast.

The Portuguese in Africa South of the Equator

After the Swahili Arabs came the Portuguese, whose direct influence was confined to the Kongo kingdom, the Kwanza and Zambezi valleys, and to a few offshore islands, including Luanda, Mozambique, Kilwa, and Mombasa. In Kongo, some thousands of people, including the royal family, became Christians. The Portuguese king corresponded with the king of Kongo as an equal, addressing him as 'Most high and powerful prince and king, my brother'. Many of the Kongo people remained Christian for eight or nine generations, until the last links with Europe were cut by the quarrelling and fighting which broke out inside the country from the end of the seventeenth century onwards. On the Kwanza, and again on the Zambezi, some tens of thousands of Africans came to regard themselves as the subjects or allies of the Portuguese rather than of any indigenous African state. Of these, perhaps the majority became in some sense Christians, but only a tiny handful acquired any literary education or became assimilated to the Portuguese way of life and culture. In any case, the example of Portuguese manners in such isolated settlements in Angola and Mozambique was not very inspiring. In one way or another, by conquest or by taking people under their protection, the Portuguese destroyed most of the African states with which they came into direct contact. Much more important were the indirect effects of their presence upon those living a little farther away from them. Undoubtedly, the opening of the Atlantic trade encouraged the expansion of African states in the hinterland of Angola and Mozambique, as it had done also in West Africa. While Portuguese interference diminished the Mwene Mutapas, it created the conditions for the Rozvi dynasty of Butwa to take their place and to establish the first effective customs control upon the gold production of the Zimbabwe plateau. Again, the Portuguese destroyed the kingdom of Kongo, but their presence in Angola certainly assisted the rise of the Mwata Yamvo dynasty farther inland. Whoever had guns had power. Whoever had cloth had the prestige goods with which to reward loyal subjects. These things were obtained in exchange for slaves and ivory, which could best be supplied and transported to the Portuguese frontier markets by a state with well-armed hunters and protected caravan routes. Such states could be, and usually were, established and run on completely African lines. The Mwata Yamvo, the Mwata Kazembe, and the Rozvi Mambo were all 'divine kings' and their political institutions were of a fully African kind. But it is unlikely they would have developed as far as they did without the Portuguese presence in Luanda and on the Zambezi.

Madagascar

The large island of Madagascar, lying some 500 km (300 miles) off the coast of Mozambique, furnishes yet another example of how, in the early stages of trade with Europe, it was better to be living just beyond the range of direct contact than within it. Until the early Christian era, Madagascar had remained uninhabited, and it was first colonised by immigrants from maritime South-East Asia in much the same way as the islands of the Pacific. The newcomers travelled in outrigger canoes, bringing with them seedlings of their native food plants, notably bananas, rice, and taro. Their Malagasy language, the nearest relatives of which are found on the island of Borneo, established itself so firmly that all subsequent immigrants came in time to adopt it. Although Madagascar had neither ivory nor precious metals, it supplied foodstuffs for the coastal trade of the Swahili Arabs, who had established settlements on the island by the eleventh century. Perhaps as a result of this contact, the western coast of the island came to be settled by Africans from the Mozambique coastlands, who brought their own food crops and cattle. The Portuguese and the Dutch called there for supplies on their voyages to the Far East, but it was not until the eighteenth century, with the introduction of coffee-planting on the neighbouring islands of Mauritius and Réunion, that Madagascar began to play a significant part as a supplier of slaves. The response of the Malagasy to this trade was similar to that of the African peoples on the mainland. The best-armed among scores of small states grew at the expense of their weaker neighbours and sold their war captives to the Europeans, a motley collection of pirates drawn from all the maritime nations of the West. With the aid of European firearms, some powerful states emerged, in particular that of the Hova people, whose homeland was a small, intensively irrigated area around the capital of Tananarive, high on the central plateau. Between 1787 and 1810, a great warrior-king, Nampoina, embarked on a career of systematic conquest and political expansion. By the time of his death, the Hova-ruled state of Imerina controlled most of the centre of the island. From his inland fastness, and using the advantage of interior lines, Nampoina laid the foundations of a powerful, centrally administered kingdom.

At the end of the eighteenth century, therefore, the southern half of Africa, no less than its northern half, was still standing very much on its own feet. If European influence was somewhat more noticeable in the south than in the north, the influence of the Islamic world was much less so. With one exception, the foreign-ruled enclaves on African soil were of negligible size and small significance; on the whole, African political systems had proved capable of adapting

and regrouping in response to the new economic opportunities offered by the outsiders. Thus far, at least, most of the modern weapons
which had entered Africa through trade with the outside world had
found their way into the hands of Africa's traditional rulers and had
been used to strengthen existing institutions. The exception to the
general rule was, of course, the Dutch colony at the Cape, where
the absence of any African occupation denser than that of hunters
and pastoralists had left a local power vacuum that was unique in
the continent. It was not that any European government yet wanted
anything more than a refreshment station at the Cape for its oceanic
shipping, which could be defended and denied to competitors. It was
rather that the few hundreds, and later the few thousands, of company servants-turned-settlers were able to establish a bridgehead for
local population growth of the same kind that Europeans had established in the coastlands of North America. The enclave of Mediterranean climate around the Cape peninsula, which made it unsuitable
for African cereal farmers, was to make it also the Achilles' heel of
Africa, but no one in 1800 had foreseen it.

THREE. The Opening up of Africa: (1) From the North-East

H istorians have often written of the nineteenth century in Africa
mainly as a period when Europeans were increasing their influence and power in preparation for later conquest. It should rather
be seen as a period when, with the aid of a greatly increased supply of firearms from the new coal-fired furnaces and of cheap textile
manufactures from the steam-driven factories of the industrialis-
ing countries, world trade was pressing remorselessly into Africa in
search of whatever might be exportable with the limited means of
transport available. For most of the nineteenth century, the agents
of this pressure were the rulers and traders of the coastal regions,
including, first and foremost, those of the predominantly Muslim
countries bordering on the Mediterranean and the Red Sea.

Muhammad Ali (1805–1849): The Revival of Red Sea Trade

In all this part of the world, the French conquest and occupation of Egypt between 1798 and 1800 had marked a turning point.
Napoleon's decisive victory at the battle of the Pyramids had revealed
the weakness and technical military inferiority of the whole of the
Ottoman empire, and, like many other such victories in history, it
provoked a compelling desire in the conquered to learn the skills of
the victors. Soon after the end of the Napoleonic wars, French military instructors were to be found throughout the Ottoman lands, and
in addition to their military manuals, the intelligent and ambitious
among the Turkish officer class were reading widely in European

35

history and political philosophy. Above all, in Egypt the Napoleonic episode threw up an outstanding leader, able to understand the significance of events and to apply the lessons he had learned. The history, not only of Egypt, but of the whole of North-East Africa and the Red Sea area, was dominated during the first half of the nineteenth century by the figure of Muhammad Ali Pasha. This remarkable man combined the talents of an oriental despot with a shrewd understanding of the very different world of Europe. Muhammad Ali was a man of great charm and utter ruthlessness, an able administrator, and a cunning diplomat. Although he himself was not an outstanding military leader, several of his many sons were extremely efficient commanders. He was concerned, above all, to secure his position as Ottoman viceroy in Egypt and to make the office hereditary within his own family. In addition, however, he restored the beginnings of order and prosperity to the Red Sea area and provided Egypt with the framework of a modern state.

Born in 1769 in Macedonia, one of the Ottoman territories in the Balkans, Muhammad Ali first entered Egypt as an officer in the Ottoman forces sent there to deal with the French invasion. With the support of a body of Albanian soldiers loyal to him personally rather than to the far-off Ottoman sultan, he made himself by 1805 the most powerful military boss in Cairo. The following year he was appointed *vali* (Turkish: viceroy, governor) by the sultan. His power was at first tenuous, there being many other military groups opposed to his own. In 1811, he dealt with this opposition with characteristic ruthlessness by inviting the principal Mamluk amirs to a banquet in Cairo and then having some 300 of them massacred in a narrow alley leading out of the citadel on their way home. His power in Egypt now secure, for the next eight years Muhammad Ali devoted his main efforts to the pacification of the Red Sea area. First and foremost, this involved the suppression of the Wahhabis, the followers of a puritanical Muslim sect which had arisen among the bedouin tribesmen of the Arabian desert. The Wahhabi leaders denied the authority of the Ottoman government and disrupted the annual pilgrimage caravans travelling to the holy cities of Mecca and Medina. Muhammad Ali's armies cleared the Hijaz of the Wahhabis and, in 1818, finally overcame the dissident tribesmen in the heart of Arabia. The holy places were restored by Muhammad Ali to the authority of his overlord.

The Ottoman garrison ports of Suakin and Massawa, on the African side of the Red Sea, remained under Ottoman control until the end of the viceroy's reign when, in 1846, they were leased by the sultan to Egypt. Only in 1865 were the towns permanently annexed to the Egyptian Sudan.

Nevertheless, Muhammad Ali's early operations in the Red Sea area brought about a complete revival of the pilgrimage and an even more striking revival of trade. The Red Sea route began to be used by the British for rapid communications with India; Jidda, the Ottoman port in the Hijaz, became temporarily the most important commercial town between Bombay and Cairo. This, in turn, revived all the local trade routes running inland on the African side of the Red Sea, especially those to the Ethiopian highlands. From this region, the most highly valued female slaves were sent to the Hijaz, where they were bought as concubines by the more prosperous class of pilgrims. Also in great demand in the Hijaz and elsewhere in the Muslim world was the musk obtained from the glands of the civet-cat, which was the speciality of the Sidama kingdoms. There was a similar revival in the gold trade from Innarya in the south-western highlands, and also in the splendid coffee grown all over the highlands region. The political recovery of the Ethiopian state (in the northern provinces of Tigre and Amhara) and of its powerful daughter state of Shoa – which began in earnest in the 1830s and 1840s – was made possible largely through the revenue from this commercial revival. The increased trade enabled the rulers of these states to start re-equipping their soldiers with firearms in place of spears.

The Egyptian Conquest of the Sudan

From the Red Sea, Muhammad Ali turned his eyes in 1820 towards the Sudan. The Arabian campaigns had been costly in troops, and he hoped to secure an inexhaustible supply of Negro slave recruits for his armies in the southern Sudan. The Funj sultanate was incapable of offering any resistance. It had already lost control of all the northern part of the Sudan; Dongola was in the hands of a group of Mamluk refugees who had escaped from Muhammad Ali's clutches in Egypt. With only 4,000 well-armed men, Muhammad Ali's son Ismail was able to make steady progress up the Nile, overcoming the

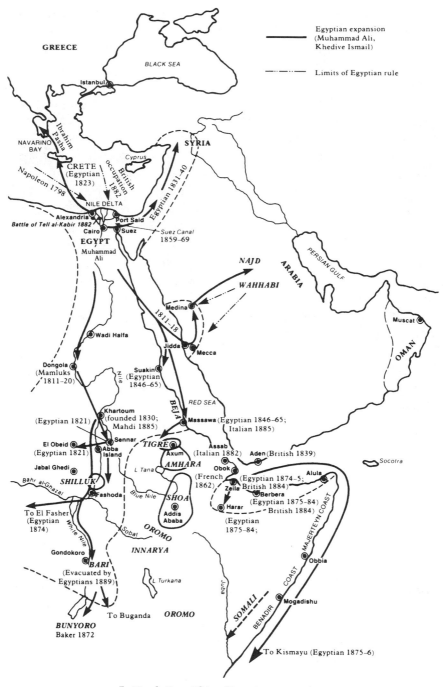

5. North-East Africa: Egyptian expansion.

Mamluks at Dongola and entering the Funj capital at Sennar unopposed in June 1821. The Funj sultan was deposed, and he and his family received an Egyptian pension. There was one brief uprising in 1822, in which Ismail lost his life. After this had been suppressed, the Egyptian colonial capital was founded in 1824 at Khartoum, at the junction of the White and Blue Niles, and the Sudan remained under Egyptian rule until the Mahdi's rebellion of 1881–4.

The economic benefits which Muhammad Ali's reign conferred upon Egypt and the Red Sea coasts did not generally extend to the Sudan. Attempts made by the Egyptian administration to widen the range of agricultural production, such as the settlement of Egyptian peasants in the Gezira around Sennar, were not very successful. The Arabic-speaking groups living in the Nile valley in the north were regularly taxed by the government, and some of them became quite prosperous through their involvement in the considerable shipping traffic that developed on the river; others became even more wealthy by partaking in the slave and ivory trades in the southern Sudan. The nomadic tribes in the deserts to the east and west of the river supplied the large numbers of camels and other domestic animals which, after slaves and ivory, formed the main exports of the Sudan. All the serious efforts of the Egyptian government were concentrated, however, on the region to the south of Khartoum. 'You are aware', Muhammad Ali wrote to his treasurer in 1825, 'that the end of all our effort and of this expense is to procure negroes. Please show zeal in carrying out our wishes in this capital matter.' Every year, the Khartoum government dispatched military expeditions southwards to Dar Fung and westwards to Kordofan and the Nuba mountains on official slave raids, which returned with as many as 5,000 captives each. For a time, the Shilluk with their centralised kingdom on the White Nile above Fashoda made an effective limit to the Egyptians' southward penetration. But Muhammad Ali, hoping for the discovery of gold, was always urging his governors to press farther south. In 1838, he even visited the Sudan himself to encourage these efforts. From 1839 to 1841, one of his Turkish sea captains, called Salim, broke through the opposition of the Shilluk in a series of expeditions up the White Nile. He proved the river to be navigable for 1,600 km (900 miles) south of Khartoum, as far as Gondokoro in the land of the Bari near the modern Sudan–Uganda frontier. The dream of gold did not come true. In its place appeared the reality of nearly a million square miles of elephant country, the human inhabitants of which were still ignorant of the value of ivory. From then on, the penetration of the traders developed quickly, with European firms based on Khartoum in the forefront. Through their consuls, these firms resisted the attempt by the Egyptian government to set up a monopoly over the ivory trade.

At first, the forces at the disposal of the traders and of the local inhabitants were fairly evenly balanced. The traders with their armed sailing-boats were superior so long as they kept to the river, but on land the local people had the advantage. While these conditions lasted, the exchange of goods, though unequal in value, was peaceful enough. There came a time, however, when few elephants could be shot near the riverbanks and when the local demand for beads and cheap trinkets was satisfied. To obtain ivory, it now became necessary to leave the riverbanks and to try to find trade goods which would arouse the interest of the peoples of the backcountry, who were even less sophisticated than the groups alongside the rivers. The traders responded to the new conditions by bringing up bands of armed Arab followers, recruited mainly from the Nile valley north of Khartoum. They placed these men in fortified encampments called *zeribas* spread over the whole backcountry of the White Nile and the Bahr al-Ghazal. There was little surplus food available for them, and they were often forced to raid the villages in order to feed themselves. The local people – mostly Nilotic pastoralists with the simplest material needs – wanted only cattle and more cattle. Armed raiding parties as a result scoured the countryside for cattle, and exchanged them (often with the people from whom they had been captured) for ivory and slaves. Petherick, the British Consul in Khartoum, described the situation in 1863:

Instead of the introduction of more valuable and civilising merchandise, such as cutlery, or cloth for wearing apparel, as articles for barter – when the value of glass and copper ornaments began to decline and lose their charm – the traders disgraced themselves by descending to enrich themselves by the plunder and destruction of tribe after tribe.[1]

[1] J. Petherick, *Travels in Central Africa, and Explorations of the White Nile Tributaries, 1869* (London, 1869), vol. I, p. 229.

By the late 1860s, the zeriba system had spread all over the vast territory of the Nile–Congo watershed, embracing not only the south-west of the modern Sudan Republic, but also the southern half of Chad and most of the Central African Republic. One single warlord trader, al-Zubeir Rahman Mansur, who set out from Khartoum in 1856, was by a decade later employing 1,000 armed men, and exporting some 1,800 slaves each year as well as an unmeasured quantity of ivory, using a route through Kordofan which bypassed all the control points in the upper Nile valley. In 1873, the Egyptian government recognised his position by appointing him governor of the Bahr-el-Ghazal province, and supplying him with a small garrison of regular troops in return for a tribute in ivory worth about £15,000 a year. In 1874, Zubeir invaded the kingdom of Darfur, killing the sultan and gaining control of the caravan routes across the desert to both Egypt and Tripoli.

Muhammad Ali and the European Powers

By the 1820s, Muhammad Ali had made himself far stronger than his overlord, the Ottoman sultan. He realised the importance of sea power in the military forces of the European states and, at great expense built an Egyptian navy in the Mediterranean. In 1821, the first major revolt broke out in the Ottoman empire, when the Greeks rose to claim their independence. The sultan was not strong enough to suppress the revolt, and called upon Muhammad Ali to help him. Egyptian forces rapidly overwhelmed the rebels on the island of Crete and, in 1824, a great military expedition under the viceroy's eldest son, Ibrahim Pasha, set out for Greece from Alexandria. So successful was Ibrahim in the Morea (the southern part of Greece) that it seemed that the Greek revolt was doomed. At this point, Russia threatened to intervene on the side of the Greek Christians. To prevent this, a joint French and British naval force was sent to Greece in an attempt to enforce an armistice between the rebels and the Egyptian army. Almost by accident, hostilities broke out and, at the battle of Navarino Bay in 1827, the Egyptian fleet was destroyed. The following year, Ibrahim Pasha had to evacuate his troops from the Morea, and Greece became independent.

This was the first serious reverse suffered by Muhammad Ali, and he naturally wanted recompense from the sultan for the costly Greek campaigns. The sultan went back on a promise to make him pasha (governor) of Palestine and Syria; so, in 1831, Ibrahim's army took over these provinces from direct Ottoman control. By now, the sultan was thoroughly alarmed at the power of his overmighty subject but could do nothing to curb it. In 1833, Muhammad Ali was officially recognised as governor of Syria and Palestine. A further attempt by the Ottomans in 1839 to drive him out of these provinces ended in the defeat of the sultan's forces by Ibrahim Pasha; the Egyptian forces seemed ready to march to Istanbul and dictate terms to a new sultan, who was only a young boy. Again, the European powers intervened. Britain was committed to uphold the ramshackle Ottoman empire and, in 1840, in concert with other European countries and in spite of French support for Muhammad Ali, forced him to withdraw from Syria. Yet, he obtained one solid gain – the viceroyalty of Egypt was made hereditary in his family and, with this his authority over the Sudan was tacitly recognised by the sultan.

To meet the shortage of recruits for the army after his Arabian and Sudanese campaigns, and because of the failure of his plan to obtain Negro slave soldiers, Muhammad Ali took in 1822 the new step of forcing into his army as conscripts the Egyptian *fellahin* (Arabic: peasants). Since the Arab conquests of the seventh century, all soldiers in Egypt had been foreigners. Now, native Egyptians began to be recruited into the ranks and, later in the century, they were even trained as officers. This was to have a potent effect on the growth of nationalism in Egypt. Muhammad Ali also imported European – mostly French – military advisers and instructors to establish army medical, artillery, and engineering schools. One result of this was that European textbooks were translated into Turkish and Arabic, and some of the cleverest young Egyptian officers learned French and became familiar with western political as well as military ideas. In this period, when European countries had a near monopoly of the manufacture of modern weapons, Muhammad Ali was dependent on Europe for arms and military equipment. These were very expensive, and one factor in the tremendous drive toward economic and administrative reforms in Egypt, which characterised much of his reign and for which he is above all remembered, was the need to obtain money to pay for armaments. Muhammad Ali and his ministers were seriously concerned to modernise Egypt for the benefit of its people, who had long been living under oppressive conditions. The amount of land under irrigation was greatly increased. Cotton and sugar were introduced as economic crops, and grain cultivation was expanded. The old Mamluk land-owning aristocracy was largely replaced by the family and favourites of the viceroy. This did not put an end to corruption and exploitation, but it helped to spread new ideas. Muhammad Ali is justly considered by Egyptians and many other historians to be the founder of modern Egypt. The main failing of Muhammad Ali's government was that all power remained so closely concentrated in his own hands. Weaker and less capable successors were unable to control the machine he had created.

The Khedive Ismail (1863–1879)

Muhammad Ali died in 1849 and was followed as viceroy by undistinguished successors – the brilliant Ibrahim Pasha had died the year before. Abbas I (1849–54), Muhammad Ali's conservative grandson, was hostile to European ideas, and his son Muhammad Said (1854–63), the uncle of Abbas, a rather weak man, was by contrast too much under the influence of European favourites. During his reign, in 1859, the construction of the Suez Canal was begun. A new chapter, however, opened both for Egypt and for North-East Africa as a whole with the accession of another of Muhammad Ali's grandsons, Ismail. Ismail had grand ideas that were enlightened, but were not backed by good judgement or by any sense of financial prudence. At home, Ismail lived the luxurious life of a mighty sovereign, and he was given the old Persian title of *khedive* by the Ottoman sultan. His public policies were undertaken in the same spirit, and were no doubt modelled upon the reforming drive of his grandfather. Egypt should be projected at one bound into the world of railways, telegraphs, factories, schools, and town-planning. The Suez Canal, which Muhammad Ali had consistently refused to sanction – rightly foreseeing that it would place Egypt at the mercy of the much more powerful navies of the nations of Europe – was completed by Ismail (in 1869). A fleet of steamships was ordered, which were to ply between the Mediterranean and the Red Sea ports. In the year of Ismail's accession, the

British explorers Speke and Grant passed through Cairo with the tale of the rich interlacustrine kingdoms at the head of the White Nile, and at once Ismail's imagination responded. He would pass round the Nile cataracts with a railway, and he would place steamers on the White Nile and the equatorial lakes. All the ivory flowing eastwards to Zanzibar would be diverted northwards to Cairo. In 1869, he commissioned Baker, the explorer of Lake Albert, at the huge salary of £10,000 a year, to put this immense scheme into effect. In four years, Baker achieved little in a practical way other than the assembling of some steamers on the White Nile, but the record of his travels in the southern Sudan and northern Uganda showed that the penetration of this whole region by the traders from Khartoum was proving as destructive as the activities of Zubeir and his colleagues in the Bahr el-Ghazal. By the 1870s, the 'Khartoumers' had reached as far south as Bunyoro and Buganda, becoming deeply involved in the succession struggles of Bunyoro, where rival traders supported rival candidates in exchange for handsome gifts of ivory. In 1873, Baker was succeeded by Charles Gordon, who insisted that the grand design could only work if Ismail occupied a base on the east coast of Africa. He noted in his diary on 21 January 1875:

I have proposed to the Khedive to send 150 men in a steamer to Mombaz Bay, 250 miles north of Zanzibar, and there to establish a station, and then to push towards M'tesa. If I can do that, I shall make my base at Mombaz, and give up Khartum and the bother of steamers, etc. The centre of Africa would be much more effectually opened out, as the only valuable parts of the country are the highlands near M'tesa, while south of Khartum is wretched marsh. I hope the Khedive will do it.[2]

Ismail agreed, and later the same year sent another expensive expedition, this time to Kismayu at the mouth of the Juba River. This expedition, however, was recalled as the result of British pressure exercised on behalf of the sultan of Zanzibar. At the same time, Ismail's forces occupied Zeila in the Gulf of Aden and Harar inland, but attacks on Tigre from Massawa resulted in heavy defeats at the hands of the Ethiopian emperor, John.

Although Ismail's scheme for making Egypt the head of a great African empire collapsed, in many respects Egypt greatly benefited

---

[2] *General Gordon in Central Africa, 1874–79*, ed. G. B. Hill (London, 1881), pp. 65–6.

from the reign of the magnificent khedive. A considerable network of communications – railways, telegraphs, urban amenities – was built up, including of course the Suez Canal. Muhammad Ali had done much to modernise Egypt, but it was only in Ismail's time that the urban centres at least – Cairo, Alexandria, and the Canal towns – achieved a distinctively modern aspect. But because Egypt was so dependent on European capital for the implementation of these development policies, the khedive was forced to borrow money at exorbitant rates of interest. Already in 1875, he was forced to sell his own shares in the Suez Canal in order to meet his most pressing debts. By 1879, the Egyptian treasury was bankrupt, and later the same year Ismail himself was deposed by the sultan at the suggestion of the European powers. A committee representing the European countries to whom Egypt owed money took over the direction of the Egyptian finances. European financial experts took seats in the cabinet of Ismail's son and successor, Tawfiq.

The economy measures introduced by Tawfiq's European advisers hit the army officers hard, amongst other classes of Egyptians. Many were put on half-pay, and a group of them, led by Colonel Urabi Pasha, rebelled in 1881 and set up military control over the khedive's government. They threatened to repudiate the national debt. This military revolution led at last to the direct intervention of the European powers. Britain and France planned to act together to restore the weak authority of Tawfiq and to protect European financial interests. In the end, France was prevented from taking part by an internal political crisis and by events in Tunisia and Indo–China. Thus, Britain invaded Egypt alone in 1882, and defeated the forces of Urabi Pasha at the battle of Tell al-Kabir. Britain's occupation of Egypt was to be a major factor in the partition of Africa that followed.

The Sudan and the Mahdiyya (1881–1898)

Only a year before the British occupation of Egypt, the Sudan revolted against its Egyptian government. This was not a movement originating in the Negro south of the Sudan, where Egyptian rule had been most oppressive. The core of the rebels came rather from the nomadic groups to the west of the Nile, especially the Baqqara – Arabic-speaking cattle-owning people of Kordofan and the Nuba mountains. The nomads were the first to rally to the standard of revolt. They resented the Egyptian government's attempts to tax and to control them more than did the settled agriculturists of the Nile valley north and south of Khartoum. These riverain Arabs, descendants of the old population of the Funj kingdom, tended to sit on the fence, waiting until it was clear that the Mahdi was successful before joining him. Economically, their grievance was that the Egyptian government in the early days had conscripted many of their slaves on whose labour they had depended for their livelihood. More recently, since the reign of Ismail, the government had prevented the importation of more slaves from the south, and had kept even the ivory trade in its own hands. Religious grievances were also important. The Egyptians had increasingly brought into the Sudan their own Muslim teachers and religious dignitaries, whereas Sudanese Islam had its own strongly established *shaikhs* (holy men) and religious brotherhoods, who resented the newcomers and their different ways. Ismail's appointment of Gordon, a Christian deeply committed to the antislavery campaign, as governor–general of the whole Sudan, upset the local Muslims still further. The nomads, at least, were ready to follow a religious leader who promised to overthrow Egyptian rule, which in their eyes was impious and heretical as well as being at times harsh.

Such a religious leader appeared in the person of Muhammad Ahmad, who was born in 1844, the son of a boat-builder near Khartoum. After an intensely religious upbringing, he became a teacher and was granted the title of shaikh. In 1881, he proclaimed himself the *mahdi*, the Saviour of the Muslims, who would reestablish Islam in its primitive purity. At first, the British authorities in Egypt took little notice of what seemed to be a local religious movement. When, after the capture of El Obeid by the Mahdi's Baqqara horsemen in 1883, they realised its seriousness, it was already too late to restrain it except by a major military expedition far beyond the means of the bankrupt Egyptian state. The British government had at this time no wish to extend its responsibilities in Egypt and, therefore, decided that the reconquest must wait until Egypt's own finances were sufficiently restored to undertake it. Meanwhile, it was clear that the Mahdi had the enthusiastic support of most sections of the Muslim Sudanese. Khartoum fell to him in 1885, and Gordon, who had been sent to evacuate the garrison, was killed in the fighting. The Mahdi himself died shortly after the capture of Khartoum and was succeeded by his general, Abdallahi, who was known as the *khalifa* (Arabic: successor). Abdallahi established a strong secular administration in place of the Mahdi's dream of a society that would be organised on a religious basis similar to the Muslim state in the earliest days of Islam.

The Khalifa's rule lasted for thirteen years. It might have lasted longer if the European powers had not by then been partitioning Africa among themselves. As it was, the government of the Mahdiyya in the Sudan continued until almost the end of the nineteenth century. The reconquest of the Sudan by Anglo–Egyptian forces was almost the closing episode of the partition. It was one of the few cases in which a government that was still carrying out most of its functions had to be defeated and overthrown by an invading army in order to make way for colonial rule.

The Reunification of Ethiopia (1855–1889)

Perhaps the most remarkable development in the whole of Africa during the later nineteenth century was the reunification and development of Ethiopia into a state which could not merely survive the partition of Africa but even in a sense take part in it. As we have seen, the opportunity for this revival had been created by the reopening of the Ethiopian region to external trade during the second quarter of the century. This enabled the more enterprising local rulers to build up their power by buying firearms. So far, there was nothing essentially different from what was happening in all the more powerful native states of tropical Africa. In Ethiopia, however, there was, in addition, the memory of a great state which had existed in the past. The ancient Christian Church still existed as a single national organisation in Tigre, Amhara, and Shoa and the other almost completely independent provinces of the old empire. It acted as a unifying influence. It marked off the Christian core of the country in the highlands from the Muslim states to the north and east and from the Oromo homelands and Oromo-ruled states to the south and south-west, which were rapidly becoming Islamised during the early nineteenth century. Because of the education provided by the

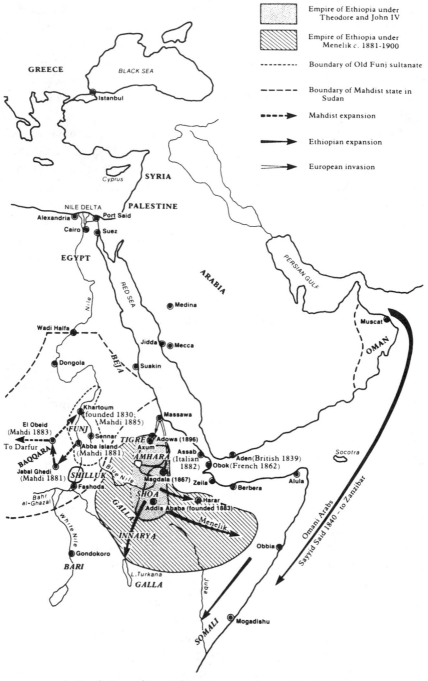

6. North-East Africa: Ethiopian expansion and the Mahdiyya.

Church, there was still a small class of literate and sophisticated people. This educated class had some idea of how to enter into diplomatic relations with the outside world and how to give foreigners the impression of a civilised power. All these factors were waiting to be used by a national leader as soon as one arose. The first to do so was Ras Kassa, a successful robber chief from the north-western frontier, who in 1855 managed to have himself crowned as emperor by the leaders of the Church at the ancient capital of Axum in Tigre. Ras Kassa took the name of Theodore. Two consuls from the British Foreign Office visited Theodore soon after his coronation and captured their impressions of him in their official report:

King Theodorus is of a striking countenance, peculiarly polite and engaging when pleased, and mostly displaying great tact and delicacy. He is persuaded that he is destined to restore the glories of the Ethiopian Empire, and to achieve great conquests. Indefatigable in business, he takes little repose night or day; his ideas and language are clear and precise; hesitation is not known to him, and he has neither counsellors nor go-betweens. He is fond of splendour and receives in state even on a campaign. He regards nothing with pleasure and desires but munitions of war for his soldiers.[3]

Though fanatically pious and utterly ruthless, Theodore undoubtedly believed that it was his mission to revive the Ethiopian nation, and in the twelve years after 1855, he did much to achieve this ambition. He was, however, already subject to fits of madness when his career was cut short by a British military expedition, sent in 1867 to protest against the maltreatment by him of two British envoys. Surrounded by the British forces in his fortress at Magdala, he eventually shot himself.

His successor as emperor, John IV, fought his way to the throne with arms obtained from the British, who had encouraged him as a rival to Theodore. In the 1870s, the main external enemy of the empire of Ethiopia, which was still more a collection of semi-independent provinces than a unified kingdom, was Egypt. The expansionist policies of the Khedive Ismail, directed towards the Red Sea and Somali coasts, threatened to revive the previous long isolation of the Christian lands in the interior mountains. As we have seen, Egypt took over control of Suakin and Massawa in 1865 from

[3] Walter C. Plowden, *Travels in Abyssinia and the Galla Country* (London, 1868), pp. 455–6.

the Ottoman sultan, and occupied much of Eritrea. In 1875, Ismail extended an Egyptian protection over the Muslim rulers of Zeila and Harar and launched an Egyptian attack upon Ethiopia from both the north and the east. The Emperor John was successful in halting the Egyptian invasion, but the continued Egyptian occupation of the more important Red Sea and Somali ports severely curtailed the supply of arms and other goods to Ethiopia. This weakened John in his conflicts with Menelik, the powerful young ruler of Shoa, with whom he had to contend for the title of emperor. Shoa, which lies to the south of Tigre and Amhara, had suffered greatly from the Oromo encroachments of the sixteenth to eighteenth centuries. The two rulers of Shoa before Menelik had been engaged during the previous fifty years on a course of rearmament and expansion similar to that undertaken by Theodore. In 1878, John had to make terms by which Menelik married his daughter and was recognised as his successor. Even so, concealed hostility and competition continued between the two until John's death in battle against the Khalifa Abdallahi in 1889, when Menelik at last became emperor. In the early years of his rule over the state established by the Mahdi, Abdallahi had attempted to extend his control over all the Sudanese lands formerly occupied by the Egyptians. This inevitably brought him into conflict with Ethiopia, which resulted in the fulfilment of Menelik's ambitions.

In a long reign which lasted until 1913, Menelik completed the process begun by Theodore. He united the provinces of Tigre and Amhara with Shoa, and extended Ethiopian rule over the Muslim and animist states to the south. He fully understood the importance of modern weapons; long before he became emperor, he bought arms and ammunition from every available source, especially from the Italians. They were replaced by the French (who operated from their Somali coast possession of Obok) in the 1880s as the principal external influence in Ethiopia. Italian consuls from Aden had made arrangements with Menelik in 1878–9 and, after the establishment of a colony at the port of Assab in 1882, Italian envoys were in regular attendance at Menelik's court. As we shall see (Chapter 10), this Italian presence in Ethiopia led to the Wichale Treaty of 1889. Yet, it was the Italians whom Menelik defeated in their attempted invasion of Ethiopia from their possessions in Eritrea, at the decisive battle of Adowa in 1896. To obtain money for his weapons, Menelik, like all his contemporary rulers in North-East Africa and in the inter-lacustrine lands, relied mainly on the profits of ivory, for which he raided deep into the lands of the animist peoples to the south-west and south-east of Shoa. He extended his political control behind the raiding armies. Ethiopian expansion at the expense of the Somali of Harar and the Ogaden was a factor in the last great southward mi-gration of the Somali peoples. By the turn of the century, they were spilling over into the dry northern province of Kenya.

Long before direct European intervention in East and North-East Africa, the Muslim and Christian rulers of the more powerful and wealthy states in Africa itself were using firearms obtained from Europe to extend their trade with the peoples of the interior. They followed up these commercial activities with an extension of their political control. Egyptian expansion in the Sudan and Shoan expan-sion in the lands to the south and east of the Ethiopian highlands are examples of this process in North-East Africa. The Swahili Arab penetration of East Africa, based on the sultanate of Zanzibar, offers another example (see Chapter 8). Only the Ethiopian rulers, how-ever, were skillful enough to use the advantages of contact with the outside world while avoiding the financial and diplomatic entangle-ments which could lead to European intervention.

FOUR. The Opening up of Africa: (2) From the Maghrib

North-West Africa and the European Powers (1800–1830)

We have seen that at the beginning of the nineteenth century, North Africa west of Egypt consisted of four Muslim states. Three of them – Tripoli, Tunis, and Algiers – were nominally dependencies of the Ottoman empire. The fourth – Morocco – was an independent kingdom. Although all of them traded extensively with western Europe, their religious and cultural connections – as well as a great part of their trade – lay with the eastern Mediterranean on the one hand and with the Muslim states of the western Sudan on the other. All four Maghrib countries regularly imported Sudanese slaves for their own use as soldiers and servants, wives and concubines. In addition, all of them, but especially Tripoli, acted as entrepôts for the re-export of slaves to Egypt and Syria, Turkey and the Balkans. During the first third of the nineteenth century, this basic pattern changed very little. Thereafter, the growing power of western Europe made itself felt in a variety of ways which, in the long term, introduced important changes in the lives of the people of North-West Africa. First, there was the British campaign against the slave trade, waged both in the Mediterranean and in the Atlantic. Next, there was the Greek war of independence (1820–9), fought with the support of the Christian powers. The success of the Greeks drove Muslim rule, and with it the institution of slavery, from a Christian country and provided an example later to be followed by the other Balkan states. Finally, with the invention of the steamship and the consequent growth in the power

and mobility of European navies, there came the concentration of
the nations of western Europe on the Mediterranean Sea. For Britain
and France, the Mediterranean was a route to the rich lands of India
and the East Indies. It was also the outlet (through the narrow strait
of Istanbul) for the Russian fleet in the Black Sea. It was to prevent
the establishment of Russia as a Mediterranean power that Britain
intervened against Muhammad Ali, in Greece in 1827 and in Syria in
1840. As was to be expected from its geographical position, France's
interest in the Mediterranean was more regional and less global than
that of Britain. France was concerned with its commercial activities
in the Levant and North Africa and, indeed, welcomed the growth of
a strong, friendly North African power based upon Egypt. In 1829,
not long before the French attack on Algiers, the French government
encouraged Muhammad Ali to think of including the Maghrib in his
sphere of influence. Thus, governments in France, in Spain, and later
in Italy were interested in North Africa both for its value as a counter
in the Great Power game played by the European states and for its
economic and commercial possibilities.

At the beginning of the nineteenth century, however, there was little awareness in the Maghrib countries that Christian Europe would
prove the main threat to their continued independent existence. Certainly, there was no idea among them of presenting a united front
to European advances. In Tripoli, for example, the hereditary pasha,
Yusuf Karamanli, who ruled the country from 1795 until 1830, had
begun his reign by aiding the British against the French in Egypt, and
thereafter enjoyed British support in maintaining his freedom from
Ottoman control. This freedom he used to extend his authority over
the Fezzan, the semi-desert country to the south of Tripoli, through
which ran the caravan routes to the central Sudan. By 1811, Yusuf
was master of the Fezzan and, by 1818, he had established treaty relations with the rulers of Bornu and Sokoto, the two most important
states of northern Nigeria. Tripoli supplied Bornu with arms and ammunition for its annual campaigns against the peoples of Mandara
and Bagirmi on its southern borders, and received a greatly increased
supply of slaves in exchange. Despite friendly relations with Britain,
the city of Tripoli became at this time the largest slave-market of the
Mediterranean. Of the 10,000 slaves brought annually across the
Sahara, more than half passed through Tripoli or else through

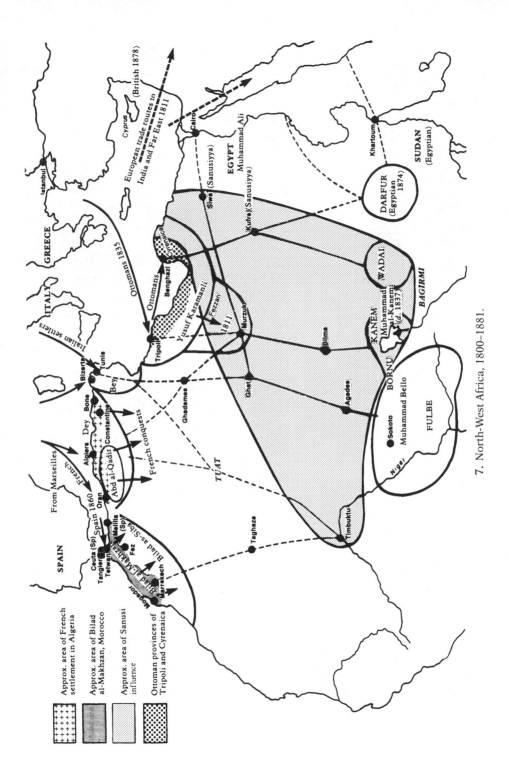

7. North-West Africa, 1800–1881.

Approx. area of French settlement in Algeria

Approx. area of Bilad al-Makhzan, Morocco

Approx. area of Sanusi influence

Ottoman provinces of Tripoli and Cyrenaica

European trade routes to India and Far East 1811   (British 1878)

Cyprus

Cairo

Khartoum

SUDAN
(Egyptian)

DARFUR
(Egyptian)
1874)

EGYPT
Muhammad Ali

Siwa (Sanusiyya)

Kufra (Sanusiyya)

WADAI

BAGIRMI

KANEM
Muhammad
al-Kanemi
(d. 1837)

Benghazi

Cyrenaica

Ottomans

Yusuf Karamanli

Fezzan

1811

Murzuk

Bilma

BORNU

FULBE

Muhammad Bello

Sokoto

GREECE

ITALY

Ottomans 1835

Italian settlers

Tripoli

Tunis

Bizerta

Bey

Ghadames

Ghat

Agades

Istanbul

From Marseilles

French

Algiers   Dey   Bone

Oran   Spain 1860

Abd al-Qadir   Constantine

French conquests

TUAT

Niger

Timbuktu

Taghaza

SPAIN

Ceuta (Sp)

Tangier   Melilla (Sp)

Tetwan

Fez

Rabat al-Makhzan   Bilad as-Siba

Marrakech

Mogador

54

Bengazi, the port of Cyrenaica. Naturally enough, all the main journeys of exploration to the central Sudan by European travellers, including those of Clapperton, Barth, and Nachtigal, used this line of approach, and owed most of their security to the pashas of Tripoli, who provided them with escorts and introductions to the rulers of lands to the south.

The rulers of Tunis, like those of Tripoli, based their country's almost complete independence from the Ottoman sultan on their friendship with Britain. Algiers, in contrast, was linked more closely with France. During the wars which the Revolutionary government of France and the French emperor Napoleon fought with most of the other European powers between 1792 and 1815, Algiers had supplied grain to the French forces, including those which had attacked Egypt. A large war-debt to the government of the dey of Algiers had been incurred by France during these years. After the defeat of Napoleon in 1815, the new French government refused to pay this debt. This poisoned relations between the two countries and led to the French invasion of Algeria in 1830.

Alone among the North African countries, Morocco did not have the Ottoman sultan as a nominal master against whom it was necessary to seek an ally. Morocco, therefore, reacted to the increased European activity in the Mediterranean and the Atlantic by seeking to cut itself off from the outside world. Sultan Mawlai Sulaiman (1792–1832) forbade his subjects to leave the country and restricted their dealings with Christians to a minimum. The European consuls and merchants were confined to the ports of Tangier and Mogador. The efforts of the British consuls to interest the sultans in antislavery measures met with blank refusals even to consider the matter. In 1841, Sulaiman's successor, Abd ar-Rahman, declared firmly that he would not forbid a practice which had been sanctioned by the laws of every sect and nation 'from the times of the sons of Adam up to this day'.

The vital element in the lives of the great majority of the people of the Maghrib, however, was not that of their relations with distant European powers, but rather the vibrant social and religious community provided by Islam. It was Islam, in its many forms, which linked the Maghrib to sub-Saharan Africa, as well as to the Arab lands to the east. The Tijaniyya brotherhood, which had been founded on the northern edge of the Sahara (see Chapter 1), was highly successful in propagating its ideas and institutions throughout the Sudanic region of West Africa, and this was only the largest of several orders. The saintly marabouts were often key figures in the social structures of the Maghrib, and the fame of the most saintly extended over vast areas. Moroccan marabouts, for example, were venerated as far afield as the Nilotic Sudan. Muslim education was a further bond between Mediterranean and sub-Saharan Africa, with the celebrated and ancient universities of Cairo, Kairouan, and Fez drawing students from African lands to the south of the desert as well as from the Middle East. Although marabouts, brotherhoods, and university mosques transcended the vague frontiers of states, they played a key role in political affairs, both local and national. Drawing all these strands together was the pilgrimage to Mecca, which gathered people from all over the Muslim lands of northern Africa to share the arduous journey and the religious experience. It was into one corner of this in many ways self-contained world that the French rudely thrust when they invaded Algeria.

The French in Algeria (1830–1879)

The French invasion of Algeria was one of the most unprincipled and ill-considered acts of policy in the whole of the nineteenth century. It was undertaken for no positive reason at all, but for the purely negative one of diverting the attention of the French people, by a spectacular military success abroad, from their resentment of the misgovernment of the kings Louis XVIII and Charles X. It did not even succeed in this objective, for within a few months of the attack on Algiers, Charles X had been overthrown by a popular revolution. But the French stayed in Algiers.

The excuse for the attack was a fit of anger by the dey of Algiers, Husain, who in 1827, in the course of one of the endless discussions about the war-debt, struck the French consul in the face with his fly-whisk. Three years later, the French government, announcing that it would put an end to the piracy of the Algerian corsairs, landed troops and defeated Husain's forces. Algiers and Oran fell almost at once, and Bône, the port of eastern Algeria, fell in 1832. There remained for the French the far more difficult task of ruling what they had conquered.

Like all previous conquerors of Algeria, the French imagined that they would be able to confine their occupation to the coastal plain. Indeed, the inhabitants of the coastal towns and those social groupings which had traditionally made up the *makhzan* (Arabic: allies) of the dey proved friendly to the French and anxious to accept their protection. The reason was simply that the French were able to exploit the age-old rivalry between the townsfolk and the peasants of the coastal region on the one hand and the men of the hills and mountains on the other. The leader of the hill-folk was Abd al-Qadir, the son of a famous marabout of the Atlas region, who in 1832 declared a great jihad against the French (and against the makhzan), saying:

We have assumed this important charge [the office of *amir*, commander] hoping that it may be the means of uniting the great body of Muslims and preventing dissensions among them, of affording general security to all dwellers in the land and of driving back the enemy who had invaded our country with a view to placing his yoke upon our necks.[1]

With great skill and tact, Abd al-Qadir held together the quarrelsome tribes of western and central Algeria, organised an administration similar to that of the old Ottoman government, and built up a standing army with which he inflicted a number of defeats upon the French. His jihad made it impossible for the French to limit their occupation to the coastal plain: like all other conquerors of North Africa, they were drawn, whether they liked it or not, into the interior.

In 1841, General Bugeaud began the systematic conquest of Abd al-Qadir's territory. District after district was occupied by French military posts and patrolled by flying columns of mounted soldiers. This was no longer a war of armies which, while fighting one another, could spare the civilian population. These small campaigns were brutal. One of the sons of the French king, serving with the French army, wrote, 'Our soldiers returning from the expedition were themselves ashamed. About 18,000 trees had been cut down; houses had

---

[1] Cited in Col. Churchill, *The Life of Abd el Kader* (London, 1867), p. 28.

been burnt; women, children and old men had been killed.' Similar
ferocity was shown by the Arabs toward French soldiers and civilians
whenever the chance occurred. Resistance continued long after the
capture of Abd al-Qadir himself in 1847, and great bitterness seeped
into the relations between conquerors and conquered.

In these circumstances, the settlement of French colonists, of
whom there were by 1847 about 100,000, could not be a peaceful
process. Bugeaud saw that the newcomers would have to be settled in concentrated areas, where they could be protected by the
army. This meant the clearance (French: *refoulement*) of the more
fertile regions in the coastal plains and movement of the former inhabitants into remoter, less fertile, and already inhabited districts.
This policy was carried out by force, and the fighting in Algeria
continued until the 1870s. Once conquered, the Muslim areas were
administered by a form of indirect rule. French officials governed
the people through their territorial chiefs and councils. The system had much in common with the old Ottoman administration.
While the deys had maintained their government with a force of
15,000 men, the French required 100,000, and in the interior regions military government gave way to civil administration only in
1879. Even then, Kabylia and other mountain districts remained un-
pacified.

The colonists, who in 1880 numbered some 350,000, did little to
bring prosperity to Algeria. Nearly all of them were poor people. Most
of those who settled on the land were small wine-growers from the
south of France whose vineyards had been attacked by disease. In
the towns, most of the settlers were not even French, but Spaniards,
Italians, and Maltese from overcrowded homelands, who came to
seek paid employment and to engage in petty trade. As time went on,
even the French agricultural settlers tended to drift into the towns,
leaving the land which had been so expensively cleared for them to
fall into the hands of a few wealthy individuals and companies who
built up great estates. Unlike colonists in other parts of the world,
the French settlers in Algeria, especially the wealthy ones, were able
to keep close touch with their homeland across the Mediterranean.
They came to have an influence on French politics out of all proportion to their numbers or real importance.

Morocco (1830–1894)

Morocco was much affected by the French occupation of Algeria. Abd al-Qadir's resistance was conducted mainly from western Algeria, and Sultan Abd ar-Rahman (1822–59) supported him with arms and, on occasion, provided him with refuge in Morocco. This brought French action against him in 1845, when Moroccan forces, fighting a European enemy for the first time since the sixteenth century, were badly defeated at the battle on the river Isly. Fortunately for Morocco, the French were too busy with Algerian affairs to follow up their victory. In 1859, Morocco also became involved with Spain, which claimed that the ports of Ceuta and Melilla on the northern coast, which it had held since the sixteenth century, were being constantly raided by the sultan's subjects. A Spanish army invaded Morocco and inflicted a series of defeats on the sultan's forces. The war was ended in 1860 by the Treaty of Tetuan, under which Morocco promised to pay Spain a huge indemnity. This indemnity opened Morocco to further European interference. To pay it, the sultan had to raise a loan in London on the security of the Moroccan customs and to accept control over them by foreign commissioners.

Within Morocco, the government had the difficult task of upholding the sultan's authority against the religious movements of the marabouts and the hostility of the nomadic groups. Traditionally, the country was divided into the *bilad al-makhzan* (the friendly country), which paid taxes into the sultan's treasury, and the *bilad as-siba* (the unfriendly country), where the government could exert its influence only by threats and bribes. The relative size of these two areas depended very much on the personality of each particular sultan. Mawlai al-Hasan (1873–94), the last great sultan before the French occupation, was continually on campaign reducing the area of the unfriendly country. For the first time since the seventeenth century, the sultan's authority was carried into the High Atlas region and also deep into the Sahara in northern Mauritania. Mawlai al-Hasan was thus trying to make certain that no ungoverned groups existed which could cause frontier incidents of the kind which had led to the Spanish war. The fact that Morocco was able to keep its independence until 1912 is a tribute to Mawlai al-Hasan's enterprise and skill.

Tripoli under Ottoman Rule (1835–1911): The Sanusiyya

After the death of Yusuf Karamanli in 1830, two parties contended for the office of pasha, one supported by the British, the other by the French. After several years of confusion, during which the bedouin of the Fezzan broke away from the control of any authority in Tripoli, the Ottoman government decided to reassert its authority over Tripoli, to counter Muhammad Ali's power in Egypt and the French presence in Algeria. In 1835, an Ottoman governor arrived in Tripoli and declared the Karamanli dynasty deposed. By 1842, this government had subdued most of the coastal tribes, but it could not control the Fezzan. The trans-Saharan trade suffered gravely, both from these events and from the wars which broke out around the frontiers of Bornu after the death of the ruler in 1837. During the 1830s and 1840s, the central Sahara was so disturbed that traffic on the routes from Bornu and Wadai was restricted to a single annual caravan on each main route.

Peace returned to the central Sahara with the rise of another Muslim brotherhood, that of the Sanusi. The founder of the order, Muhammad al-Sanusi, was born in Algeria about 1790 and studied in religious schools in Morocco before making the pilgrimage to Mecca. He established his first *zawiya* (Arabic: religious centre) among the bedouin of Cyrenaica in 1843. His simple teaching of a return to the original practices of Islam, and his considerable tact and diplomacy, appealed to the feuding tribesmen and held them together in a way in which neither the Karamanlis nor the Ottomans had been able to do. The order spread rapidly into the Sahara and the western Sudan, and its popularity was still increasing when Muhammad al-Mahdi (not to be confused with the Mahdi of the Egyptian Sudan) succeeded his father as shaikh in 1859. Zawiyas of the Sanusi order were set up all over Cyrenaica, the Fezzan, Wadai, Kanem-Bornu, and as far west as Timbuktu. The followers of al-Sanusi were closely connected with trade, and paid regular dues out of their trading profits which went to enrich the zawiyas. These became the centres not only of religious propaganda, but also of agricultural and commercial development. At the beginning of the nineteenth century, the route from Benghazi to Wadai had been the least busy of the trans-Saharan routes. After the establishment of the Sanusi movement in Cyrenaica and in Wadai, at both ends of it, it became the most important. The Ottoman governors of Tripoli were forced to acknowledge the authority of the leaders *(ikhwan)* of the order over the desert peoples and to keep on good terms with them, since they controlled the trade on which the prosperity of Tripoli and Benghazi depended. As a result of British pressure at Istanbul, the Ottoman government abolished the trade in slaves throughout the empire (except the Hijaz) in 1857. In Tripoli and Cyrenaica, this law could not be enforced against the determination of the Sanusi traders to continue their operations. In this region, the trans-Saharan slave trade survived until the French occupation of Niger and Chad and the Italian occupation of Cyrenaica, at the beginning of the twentieth century.

The Regency of Tunis (1830–1881)

All through the nineteenth century, the *beylikat* (regency) of Tunis was the most progressive and westernised of the Maghrib states. As early as 1819, the bey outlawed piracy. The beys were also the first Muslim rulers to abolish slavery and the first to adopt a constitutional form of government. The economy of Tunisia was varied enough to withstand the effects of the abolition of privateering and slavery. The plains of northern Tunisia provided rich harvests of grain and fruit, while Tunis and the other coastal cities produced many manufactured goods, such as cloth, leather goods, and metalware. The political situation, however, was by no means so secure, especially after the French invasion of Algeria and the restoration of Ottoman authority in Tripoli. The Tunisian government felt itself in a trap between two sources of likely attack and turned to Britain for protection. In 1837, after the French occupation of Constantine, the Algerian fortress city near the Tunisian border, the British government promised to support the beys not only against France but also against the Ottoman sultan. It was this reliance on Britain that led Ahmad Bey to abolish slavery in a series of decrees issued between 1841 and 1846. The bey's government had sufficient authority to enforce these laws throughout the country.

The constitutional decrees of 1857 and 1861 were passed, at the suggestion of the French and British consuls, in order to satisfy the ambitions of the wealthy, well-educated Tunisian middle class and of the influential French and Italian trading communities. The constitution granted equality of all men before the law and guaranteed freedom of trade. It also set up nominated councils to advise the bey. In practice, the common people were not much helped by this constitution, which gave political power to the wealthy few. The government largely ignored the constitution, and it soon fell into disuse. However, the memory of it survived, and when nationalist political parties emerged in Tunisia during the twentieth century, they took the name Destour (Arabic: constitution).

During the 1860s and 1870s, British influence in Tunisia declined in relation to that of France, which was determined that no other European country should occupy a position of strength on the borders of Algeria. After a prolonged diplomatic and commercial struggle with Italy, which was by the 1870s united and was beginning to show interest in North Africa, France decided to take strong action. A dispute between the bey's government and a French trading company, and the incursions of Tunisian hill-tribes across the Algerian frontier, provided the necessary excuse. In 1881, French forces captured Bizerta and Tunis. The bey was forced to sign a treaty allowing France to occupy Tunisia and to take charge of its finances and foreign affairs. Unlike the dey of Algiers fifty years earlier, the bey and his government continued to function under French supervision.

The French occupation of Tunis, as much as the British occupation of Egypt which occurred in the following year, was one of the opening moves in the partition of Africa among the European powers. It was in fact the result of an informal agreement made in 1877 among Britain, France, and Russia, by which each of these powers was to 'take one bite at the Ottoman cherry' with the tacit support of the others. Britain's bite was Cyprus, which was ceded to it under pressure by the Ottoman government in 1878. Russia's bite consisted of three formerly Ottoman provinces in the Caucasus mountains. Though viewed by Britain and Russia as a Mediterranean and Middle Eastern agreement, the French were conscious of its African implications. In occupying Tunis, they were not merely protecting the borders of Algeria, but were extending a French North Africa which was ultimately to connect with the area of French conquests on the Senegal and the Niger.

FIVE. West Africa before the Colonial Period, 1800–1875

The Fulbe Jihads

Although the nineteenth century was to see great changes in sub-Saharan West Africa resulting from the gradual abolition of the Atlantic slave trade and its replacement by other forms of commerce, such changes came about only very slowly and, for a long time, affected only a small part of the region. In general, the first half of the nineteenth century witnessed mainly a continuation of the eighteenth-century pattern, with the slave trade actually increasing in volume, and with events in the interior being moulded more by influences emanating from the Islamic world to the north than by seaborne contacts with Europe and America. At the beginning of the century, the most significant events in the region were the holy wars or jihads of the Fulbe people scattered across the savanna belt from the Senegal River to the Cameroun highlands. These events had nothing to do with direct European intervention in the region, yet they affected the whole of the western and central Sudan.

As we mentioned in Chapter 1, these jihads had their origin in the revival of Islam in the western Sudan, which was brought about by the Arabic-speaking Moors who came into Mauritania from across the Sahara in the fifteenth and sixteenth centuries. This was not a once-for-all impact, but rather a continuing impulse toward religious reform, which renewed itself in every generation. The leaders of such revivals retired from the hustle and bustle of politics and trade, and went to live in remote places. They trained small bands of devoted disciples in the study of both the Islamic scriptures and legal traditions and in their own methods of prayer and devotion. The disciples were formed into brotherhoods (*tariqa*) called after the name of the founding teacher (for example, the Tijaniyya brotherhood named after Ahmad Tijani, who lived in southern Algeria at the end of the eighteenth century). The eighteenth-century jihads waged in Futa Toro and Futa Jallon were organised by Fulbe teachers, most of whom belonged to the ancient brotherhood called the Qadiriyya. Usuman dan Fodio, the leader of the nineteenth-century jihad in northern Nigeria and Niger, was a member of this brotherhood.

Usuman dan Fodio was born into the Torodbe clan in 1754, in Gobir, the northernmost of the Hausa states. He studied under a famous teacher at Agades, the capital of the Tuareg state of Aïr in the Sahara north of his home. Here, he came in touch with the reformist ideas then stirring throughout the Muslim world. These were a part of the reaction of Islam as a whole to the advance of the Christian West. It had begun in Arabia with the Wahhabi movement in the eighteenth century, and led to the reform of old brotherhoods like the Qadiriyya and to the foundation of new ones. Typical of these new brotherhoods were the Tijaniyya, which became particularly powerful in the western Sudan, and the Sanusiyya in Cyrenaica and the eastern Sahara. There was, of course, no European menace on the spot to react to in West Africa at this time. However, it does seem that, along with the desire to reform the practice of Islam in the Sudan, the religious leaders did have the sense of a threat to the Islamic world in general from expanding European Christendom. Early European explorers of the Sahara region, for example, encountered Muslim teachers who asked them why the British had conquered India (which had a large number of Muslims amongst its population).

This, then, was dan Fodio's background when he returned from Agades to become tutor to the son and heir of the Hausa *sarki* (ruler) of Gobir. In this position, he gained a considerable influence in the councils of the state, which he used to spread his zeal for religious reform. In 1802, dan Fodio's pupil Yunfa became sarki on the death of his father. Yunfa proved a bitter disappointment to his former tutor, who now retreated from the court to his native village, where he was soon joined by members of the reforming party. These became so numerous that Yunfa threatened him with military action. Dan Fodio, pointing to the historical parallel of the Prophet Muhammad's flight (*hijra*) from Mecca, then retired to the remote district of Gudu (21 February 1804). At Gudu, his supporters rallied round him in such numbers that he found himself at the head of a formidable army of warriors (Arabic: *mujahidun*, from 'jihad'), all burning with religious fervour and intent on jihad. Dan Fodio was unanimously proclaimed *Amir al-Mu'minin* (in Hausa *Sarkin Musulmi*, Commander of the Faithful), which was the traditional title of the caliphs, or successors, of the Prophet. (The caliphs were the rulers of the Arab empire in the early, glorious days of the Muslim era.) After being proclaimed Commander of the Faithful, dan Fodio swore to the disinterestedness of his intentions, saying, 'If I fight this battle that I may become greater than my fellow, or that my son may become greater than his son, or that my slave may lord it over his slave, may the Kaffir [infidel] wipe us from the land'.

After the declaration of jihad, dissatisfied men came from all the Hausa states to swear allegiance to the Amir al-Mu'minin and to receive in exchange the green banner of the True Believers. The puritanical motives of the leaders of the jihad are well described by Muhammad al-Tunisi (see Chapter 1), who was in Wadai in 1810 and heard news of its success:

The Falata [Fulbe] accuse all other Sudanese of impiety and of heresy, maintaining that only by force of arms can they be brought to repentance. They assert that the other Sudanese have altered and adulterated the principles of Islam, that they have broken the criminal code by allowing compensations of money for criminals, which is illegal and proscribed by the Holy Book. They claim that they have undermined the foundations of religion by proclaiming illegal and criminal innovations to be legitimate, by shameful customs such as adultery, the use of fermented drinks, passion for amusement, song and dance, neglect of the daily prayers, and refusal to offer alms for the poor. Each of these crimes and shameful deeds deserves vengeance and calls for a *jihad*. These ideas kindled the minds of the Fula for years, until suddenly there arose amongst them one renowned for his piety and godliness; the *Zaki* [Hausa: lion] who became a reformer and proclaimed the holy war.[1]

Not all the mujahidun were animated by such purely religious enthusiasm. The leaders were drawn for the most part from the educated

[1] *Voyage au Ouddây*, tr. Dr Perron (Paris, 1851), p. 163.

Muslim Fulbe of the towns (Hausa: *Fulanin gidda*), who had come to despise, as al-Tunisi shows, the corrupt, half-pagan conduct of the old Hausa ruling families, known collectively as Habe. They were supported by many of the town Hausa, who treated the movement as an opportunity to free themselves from the Habe rulers and to fight among themselves. The jihad was also supported by virtually all of the pastoral Fulbe (Hausa: *boroje*) of the countryside. These were mostly still pagan, but they felt a racial affinity with the town Fulbe and even belonged to the same clans. The main motive of most *boroje* was doubtless the hope of being able to loot the wealth of the Hausa towns.

The revolt swept all over Hausaland, the leading towns of Katsina and Kano yielding to dan Fodio's mujahidun in 1807 and 1809, respectively. The Habe dynasties were replaced by Fulbe amirs, most of whom had been appointed by dan Fodio in 1804 and 1805. Beyond Hausaland to the east, Adamawa, which had long been penetrated by pastoral Fulbe, became part of the new empire after a struggle lasting nearly thirty years. The political intrigues of the Fulbe religious teachers paved the way for the penetration of the mujahidun into Nupe and Yorubaland. They occupied the northern provinces of the old Oyo empire (see p. 73) which, as the emirate of Ilorin, became a base for the spread of Islam among the Yoruba. To the north-east, the jihad was halted only in Bornu, where Muhammed al-Kanemi, a warrior and cleric from east of Lake Chad, successfully drove out the invaders. Al-Kanemi took over control of the affairs of Bornu, but the mai of the ancient dynasty was allowed to retain his court ceremonial although deprived of all real power. The Scottish traveller Clapperton, who visited Bornu in 1821, remarked on the position of the mai:

The Sultanship of Bornu is but a name; the court still keeps up considerable state, and adheres strictly to its ancient customs, and this is the only privilege left them. When the sultan gives audience to strangers, he sits in a kind of cage, made of bamboo, through the bars of which he looks on his visitors who are not allowed to approach within seventy or eighty yards of his person.[2]

---

[2] D. Denham, H. Clapperton, and W. Oudney, *Narrative of Travels and Discoveries in Northern and Central Africa, in the Years 1822, 1823, and 1824* (London, 1826), cited in Thomas Hodgkin, *Nigerian Perspectives: An Historical Anthology* (London, 1973), p. 205.

The conquest period over, Usuman dan Fodio, always more of a scholar than a ruler, returned to his books. His empire was divided into two: his son Muhammad Bello ruling the eastern part from the newly founded city of Sokoto, and his brother Abdallah the western part from Gwandu. After Usuman's death in 1817, Bello was recognised by Abdallah as sultan of Sokoto, and he ruled there until his death in 1837. By this time, the religious fervour of the movement was largely spent. The Fulbe had turned from religious reformers into a ruling class. Moreover, although an enormous area now paid theoretical allegiance to a central dynasty, in practice the Sokoto 'empire' was nothing more than a loose association of like-minded ruling groups, which had sprung into existence by responding to Usuman's invitation to join the jihad. There was no central bureaucracy and no imperial army. The Fulbe emirates were no better able to organise collective defence against outside aggression than the Habe states which they succeeded. Nevertheless, it was under Fulbe rule that Islam first spread outside the towns into the country districts. Their rule was, in general, more progressive and more effective than that of their Habe predecessors, and their importance was by no means ended when Britain and France began to impose their power.

The Jihad in the Western Sudan

The successes of the Fulbe in Hausaland had important effects farther to the west. In 1810, Hamadu Bari (also known as Ahmadu Lobo), one of Usuman's early followers, led an army westwards across the Niger bend and drove out the Bambara overlords from his homeland, the Fulbe state of Masina. Here, as in Futa Toro and in Futa Jallon, the ground for reform had been prepared by the jihads of the previous century. The whole of this area was now undergoing a further period of revival as a result of the spread of the new and powerful brotherhood of the Tijaniyya. In 1826, a young cleric called Umar from Futa Toro made the pilgrimage to Mecca. He was initiated into the Tijaniyya in the holy city and then returned slowly homewards through the Bornu of al-Kanemi, the Sokoto of Muhammad Bello (whose sister he married), and the Masina of Hamadu Bari. Known now as al-Hajj Umar (the pilgrim), he settled in Futa Jallon and began to prepare the fiercest of the West African jihads.

He equipped his force with firearms obtained from the Europeans at the coast, and at last in 1850 he launched them on the Bambara kingdoms of Segu and Kaarta and then on Masina. Had he not been checked by the French (see pp. 76–7), he would have made for Futa Toro as well. As it was, when he captured Timbuktu in 1863, his empire, based now at Hamdillahi near the old Bambara capital of Segu, stretched over the whole of the country from the Niger bend to the upper Senegal.

The empire of al-Hajj Umar did not last as long as that of Usuman dan Fodio. Umar himself was killed in 1864, and it took his son Ahmadu Sefu nearly ten years to establish his right to rule throughout his father's dominions. Even then, his rule lasted only until 1884. Nevertheless, the active survival of Islam under French colonisation throughout most of the region occupied by the Mande-speaking peoples was largely due to the revivalist movements carried forcefully into the whole of this region by al-Hajj Umar.

The Forest States and the Outside World

Unlike the situation in the Sudanic region, the changes in the woodland and forest belt of West Africa came about only slowly and sporadically during the first sixty years or so of the nineteenth century. It is true that the whole attitude of the main trading nations toward West Africa underwent a sea change during the last years of the eighteenth century and the earliest years of the nineteenth. Denmark made the slave trade illegal for its own nationals in 1805, Britain in 1807, Holland in 1814, and France in 1818. In 1815 and 1817, Spain and Portugal restricted their slave traders to the seas south of the equator (as far as Portugal was concerned, this meant the trade between Angola and Brazil). Britain even carried this new anti-slavery policy so far as to establish a naval patrol in West African waters and to declare the freed-slave settlements on the Sierra Leone peninsula a Crown Colony (1808).

If they intended to continue trading in West Africa, all these nations had to seek a new basis for their commerce. This search for trade was one of the main reasons why so many European explorers undertook dangerous and arduous expeditions in West Africa during the first half of the nineteenth century. The first were the journeys of Mungo Park to the upper Niger in 1795 and 1805. The greatest was the journey of the German, Heinrich Barth, made between 1850 and 1856, as a result of which he wrote a magnificent description of the central and western Sudanic region. Here, as an example of his penetrating eye for detail, is a little of his description of the Tasawa region of northern Hausaland (not far from Usuman dan Fodio's Gobir), which he entered by the desert route from Agades:

Tasawa was the first large place of Negroland proper which I had seen, and it made the most cheerful impression upon me, as manifesting everywhere the unmistakable marks of the comfortable, pleasant sort of life led by the natives: the courtyard fenced with a 'derne' of tall reeds, excluding to a certain degree the eyes of the passer-by; then near the entrance the cool shady place of the 'runfa' for ordinary business and for the reception of strangers . . . the whole dwelling shaded with spreading trees, and enlivened with groups of children, goats, fowls, pigeons and a horse or a pack-ox. With this character of the dwellings, that of the inhabitants themselves is in entire harmony, its most constant element being a cheerful temperament, bent upon enjoying life, rather given to women, dance, and song, but without any disgusting excess. Drinking fermented liquor cannot be strictly reckoned a sin in a place where a great many of the inhabitants are pagans; but a drunken person, nevertheless, is scarcely ever seen; those who are not Mohammedans only indulge in their 'giya', made of sorghum, just enough to make them merry and enjoy life with more light-heartedness.[3]

This was a state of affairs very similar to that about which the Fulbe reformers had complained some fifty years previously, apparently to little effect.

Side by side with the search by Europeans for trade routes and for objects of a new and legitimate commerce, there was the beginning of the first genuinely unselfish Christian activity in Africa. Some Christians in Europe were deeply concerned for Africans as people with a right to share in the benefits of Christianity as well as the useful skills and knowledge built up by Christian civilisation in western Europe. Earlier Roman Catholic missionary efforts had only touched West Africa briefly and at one or two scattered points. The beginning of the nineteenth century, however, saw the establishment of flourishing Church of England (Anglican) and Methodist missions in Sierra Leone. Their converts were to play a most important part

[3] *Travels in Africa* (Centenary edn., London, 1965), vol. I, pp. 439–40.

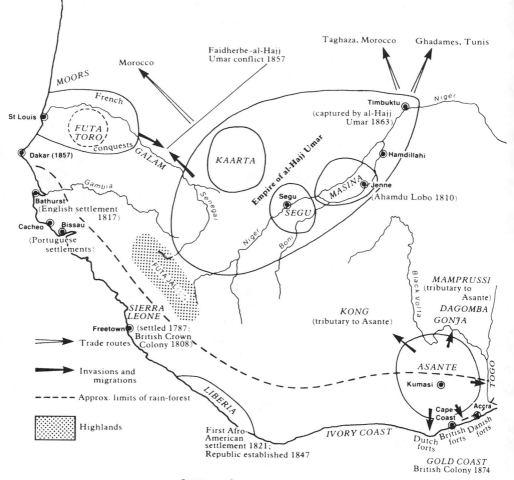

8. West Africa, 1800–1875.

in the later history of the whole of the southern part of West Africa. The 1820s saw the coming of the Presbyterian Basel missionaries to the Gold Coast and, by the 1840s, all the main Protestant denominations were represented in the Gold Coast, Dahomey, and in western and eastern Nigeria. Roman Catholic missions followed between the 1840s and 1880s.

Still, all these exploring and missionary activities were only the first stages in the development of European influence. The first half of the nineteenth century, from the point of view of African history

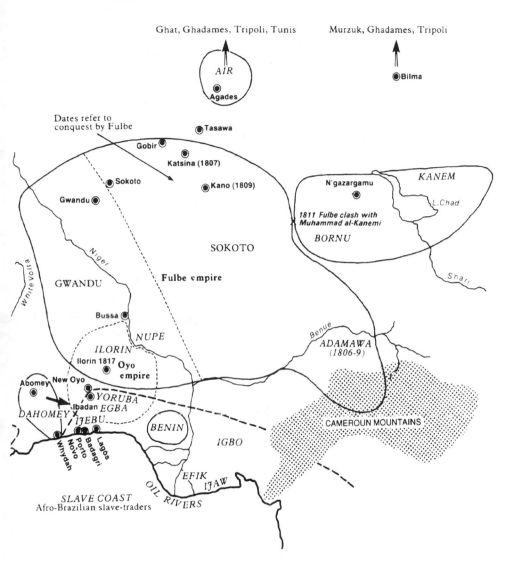

as opposed to colonial, saw little more than a continuation – and even a strengthening – of the eighteenth-century pattern amongst the woodland and forest peoples of West Africa. Despite the anti-slavery legislation in European countries, and despite the constant patrolling of the British navy, the slave trade not only continued, but actually increased in scale. Whereas most authorities have estimated the export of slaves from the whole of West Africa at about 100,000 a year at the end of the eighteenth century, by the 1830s it had risen to about 135,000. Slavery, as distinct from the slave trade, continued to be legal in the southern states of America until 1863 and, throughout this period, the illicit trade yielded great profits. The trade to Brazil and Cuba continued, though on a decreasing scale, until the 1880s, and as European and American merchants dropped out of the trade for fear of the punishments involved, their places were taken by Brazilian Negroes (Afro–Brazilians), whose operations were much more difficult to detect and prevent.

It would be misleading, however, to draw from these figures the simple conclusion that all the states of the Guinea forest were irretrievably committed to a continuation of the slave trade. Asante, at least, had long outgrown its period of active expansion, during which the disposal of war captives had temporarily eclipsed the export of gold dust and ivory. By the nineteenth century it was concerned mainly to hold its wide dominions. It was the sheer military power of Asante, fed by regular exchange of gold dust for firearms with the Dutch at Elmina, which kept the British and their Fante allies along the central stretch of the Gold Coast in a state of constant alarm. The forts were expensive to maintain. They could pay their way only by the levying of customs duties on legitimate trade. Yet, the trade routes were constantly subject to closure through the military operations of the Asante against their tributary states in the interior. Even the Fante were discouraged from agricultural production for export by threats of Asante invasion. Officially, British jurisdiction, whether vested in an unofficial Council of Merchants, as it was for most of the time until 1842, or in a Colonial Office governor, as it was thereafter, was limited until 1874 to the coastal forts. Such informal influence as was exercised upon the coastal states was largely concerned with resistance to Asante pressure.

If a militaristic and still partially slave-trading Asante continued to dominate the affairs of the Gold Coast, the situation on the Slave Coast to the east of it was even more similar to what it had been in the eighteenth century. Here, as the modern air traveller so clearly sees, the coast is nothing but a narrow surf-hammered beach, behind which a vast system of interconnected lagoons provides secure access for canoes to all the rivers of Togo, Dahomey (Bénin), and western

Nigeria. The methods of the slave traders of the 1830s along this stretch of coast were described by Richard Lander:

As soon as a vessel arrives at her place of destination, the crew discharge her light cargoe, with the manacles intended for the slaves, and land the captain at the same time. The vessel then cruises along the coast to take in country cloth, ivory, a little gold dust, etc., and if a British man-of-war be near, the crew having nothing on board to excite suspicion, in most cases contrive to get their vessel searched whilst trading with the natives. They return to the place where the cargoe had been loaded, and communicate with the captain on shore who then takes the opportunity of acquainting his crew with the exact time in which he will be in readiness to embark. The vessel then cruises a second time up and down the coast, till the appointed day approaches, when she proceeds to take in her living cargoe.[4]

Dahomey, like Asante, had by the nineteenth century reached its full territorial extent. Unlike Asante, however, it had no export with which to procure the guns which it needed to maintain its military power. So long as the demand for slaves continued, therefore, the kings of Dahomey continued, however unwillingly, to supply it.

The bulk of Slave Coast slaves did not, however, in the nineteenth century at least, come from Dahomey. They came from Yorubaland and were exported through Porto Novo, Badagry, and Lagos. All these ports were to the east of Whydah on the same lagoon system. Although there was a thriving Afro–Brazilian stronghold at Lagos, the main reason for this was the decline and disintegration of the ancient Oyo empire. This was the result of tensions from both north and south. On the one hand, the southern Yoruba states – Egba, Ijebu, and Ondo – had been growing steadily in power through access to the coastal trade. On the other hand, Ilorin and other northern districts of the empire had been penetrated, as had the Hausa states, by the Fulbe and were, therefore, involved in the jihad. The beginning of the end came in 1817, when the great chiefs of Oyo, led by Afonja of Ilorin, sent an empty calabash to the *alafin* (king), Aole, thus signifying that they no longer acknowledged his authority. Aole accepted the hint in the traditional fashion by committing suicide, but not before he had uttered his famous curse. From the palace forecourt

---

[4] *Records of Captain Clapperton's Last Expedition to Africa* (London, 1830), vol. 2, p. 238.

he shot three arrows, one to the north, one to the south, and one to
the west, saying,

'My curse be on you for your disloyalty and disobedience, so let your children
disobey you. If you send them on an errand, let them never return to bring you
word again. To all the points I shot my arrows will you be carried as slaves. My
curse will carry you to the sea and beyond the seas, slaves will rule over you, and
you, their masters, will become slaves'. Then, smashing an earthenware dish,
he shouted, 'Broken calabash can be mended, but not a broken dish; so let my
words be irrevocable'.[5]

The curse seemed to take immediate effect, for shortly afterwards
Oyo was abandoned by its inhabitants, and those who stayed in that
area became subjects of the Muslim emirate of Ilorin. The majority
of the people moved away, however, some founding a new town of
Oyo about 150 km (90 miles) to the south on the edge of the forest,
while others settled at Ibadan, which grew to be the greatest Yoruba
city within the forest belt. The states and provinces of the Oyo empire
became independent of central control and started to fight each other
both for extended frontiers and for control of the trade routes. The
principal gainers from these wars were the Egba, who founded a new
capital city at Abeokuta in 1830, controlling the routes to Porto Novo
and Badagry, and the Ijebu, whose territory controlled the main route
from Ibadan to Lagos. One result of these destructive, internecine
struggles among the Yoruba was that vast numbers of captives
were taken as slaves, so that by the 1840s Lagos and Badagry had
become the biggest slaving ports in West Africa.

The Yoruba wars were a tragedy, for much of southern Yorubaland
lies within that part of the forest belt where the oil-palm grows wild
and, where, therefore, there was an easily marketable alternative
to the slave-trade. Because of these wars, the oil-palm in southern
Yorubaland was not commercially exploited. It is, indeed, one of
the curious facts of West African history that the one region where
a peaceful changeover to legitimate commerce took place was the
region where in the past the slave trade had been most active. This
was the region roughly corresponding to the east of the Niger delta,
which at the end of the eighteenth century had supplied 20,000 slaves
a year. Here, the Efik and Ijaw villagers of the lagoon area used to

[5] Samuel Johnson, *History of the Yorubas* (Lagos, 1921), p. 192.

take their great war canoes up the rivers to the Igbo slave markets, and now they showed an equal enterprise in converting the Igbo to the collection of palm-nuts which were taken down the rivers to be sold to the Europeans. By the 1820s, the region was beginning to be known as the Oil Rivers.

The European traders realised that if they could take steam-driven ships (which were starting to be available in the 1820s, though it was not until much later that they replaced sailing ships on the open seas) up the larger rivers into the forest region where the oil-palms grew, they could buy the produce more cheaply and eliminate the coastal middlemen. This was the real significance of the discovery of the Niger mouth by John and Richard Lander in 1830, as the result of a journey down the river by canoe from Bussa to the delta. Eleven years later, the British government was persuaded by philanthropists and traders alike to send an ambitious expedition to penetrate the interior using the new water route. But the west coast was extremely unhealthy for Europeans – it was known as 'the white man's grave'. The reign of the malarial mosquito had still another fifteen years to run before the use of quinine helped Europeans to overcome the fever that was so deadly for them. The Niger expedition of 1841–2 was a failure, more than one-sixth of its European members dying in the space of two months. The commercial navigation of the Niger was delayed until the 1860s.

The Beginnings of European Intervention

Halfway through the century, therefore, the main characteristics of the societies of the southern, forested part of West Africa had changed very little except in the Oil Rivers district. This was in spite of the legal abolition of the slave trade by the European powers, in spite of the British navy, and in spite of the small and scattered possessions of the French and the British, the Danes, and the Dutch. In general, the slave trade was still flourishing, and the strength of the main military states, Asante and Dahomey, was still increasing. The only significant increase in European power, even during the third quarter of the century, was along the coast itself. Here, on the eastern sector of the Gold Coast, Britain in 1850 bought the Danish forts in order to be able to impose customs duties along a sufficient stretch of coast to pay the expenses of its occupation. In 1872, the Dutch, finding their forts along the western sector of the coast no longer profitable, ceded them freely to the British. Another factor was Britain's intervention in the affairs of Lagos. The British supported the claims of Akitoye to the title of *Ologun* (the ruler of Lagos, at one time appointed by the Oba of Benin), and in 1851 helped him drive out his nephew and rival Kosoko. In return for British help, Akitoye promised to end the slave trade from Lagos, but he could not keep his hold over the island city without further British support. When, in 1861, Dahomey again threatened to attack Abeokuta, Britain rid itself of the Akitoye–Kosoko dispute by annexing Lagos as a colony. From this point, an almost inevitable path led forward to further intervention – on the one hand, the punitive expedition against Asante in 1873 and the incorporation of the coastal states into the Gold Coast colony in 1874; on the other hand, the gradual expansion of Lagos along the coast to the east and the west and the increasing interference of the British consuls in the affairs of the Oil Rivers states.

In the French colony on the Senegal, a new phase of active intervention began with the appointment as governor of Louis Faidherbe in 1854. Since its reoccupation by the French in 1817 (it had been in British hands during the Napoleonic wars), the colony had consisted of little more than a circle of agricultural villages around the port of St Louis. The only active trade was that in gum arabic with the Moorish tribes living in the desert to the north of the river. Trade with the interior, which the French so much wanted to develop, was prevented by the powerful Fulbe state of Futa Toro higher up the river on the southern side. Convinced that the Senegal would prove the commercial highway for the trade of the whole of the western Sudan, the French had a clearer motive for interior conquests than the British at any of their coastal bases. Conquest of the lower Senegal valley was, therefore, Faidherbe's declared policy, and in ten years he had carried it out, encouraging economic crops – especially ground-nuts – in the conquered lands, and establishing schools as well as administrative centres in each newly acquired district.

Any kind of European intervention on African soil was likely to lead to more. Britain's creeping protectorates along the Lagos and Gold Coast stretches of the West African shore were one example.

Faidherbe's policy of military conquest inland was another. It was, however, more difficult to call a halt to this inland conquest than to the growth of Britain's coastal possessions. The farther the French advance went inland, the more sharply it came into conflict with the Muslim states of the interior of the western Sudan. Already by 1857, Faidherbe was involved with the forces of al-Hajj Umar. The Muslim leader of the jihad temporarily checked the French advance southeast up the Senegal, but was unable to prevent their attacking Futa Toro to the south of the river. The French conquest of Futa Toro was a blow to the prestige of al-Hajj Umar. Most of his mujahidun were emigrants from Futa Toro, which had been the original Fulbe jihad state. Clearly, this was a situation which could end only in the defeat of the French and their retreat to St Louis, or else in the defeat of the Muslims and the French advance to Timbuktu and beyond.

In West Africa, therefore, events were tending by the third quarter of the nineteenth century to increasing intervention by both France and Britain. There was still in 1875 nothing that could suggest the speed of events that were to follow in the next twenty-five years, however. Had France and Britain not been pushed by other European powers into a scramble for outright partition, their intervention would undoubtedly have proceeded much more slowly than in fact it did. Still, military forces armed and trained by professional soldiers from Europe had already been in action against the indigenous soldiery of African states before 1875 and had proved their superiority in weapons, discipline, and tactics over the numerically very much larger forces brought against them. In West Africa, at least, the broad pattern that the partition was to follow had been laid down and could lead only to an ever-growing area of colonial occupation.

SIX. Western Central Africa, 1800–1880

The region we call 'Western Central Africa' encompasses the region of the Congo forest and the light woodland country to the south of it. Today this area is occupied by Angola and the states of Congo (DR), Gabon, the People's Republic of Congo, and the Central African Republic. In terms of the older African states, it includes the area of the Luba–Lunda and the lower Congo kingdoms. The Portuguese were the most active external influence in this region, but not the only one. During the first three-quarters of the nineteenth century, the northernmost frontier of Angola was at the Loge River, and from here northwards to Mount Cameroun and up both sides of the Congo estuary, there was a kind of commercial no-man's land, the shore dotted with the trading factories of English, Dutch, American, French, and Spanish as well as Portuguese firms. During the second half of the nineteenth century, an even more important source of external influence was that of the Swahili Arabs and Nyamwezi from East Africa. Only during the colonial period was the region as a whole reconnected with its natural ports of exit on the Atlantic coast.

The Pombeiros and the Mwata Kazembe

During the early part of the century, Portuguese influence reached the interior by two main routes, one of which started in Luanda, the other in Benguela. The Luanda route was the older and, by the beginning of the nineteenth century, it led in a sense right across the continent. Portuguese merchants themselves seldom left Luanda: indeed,

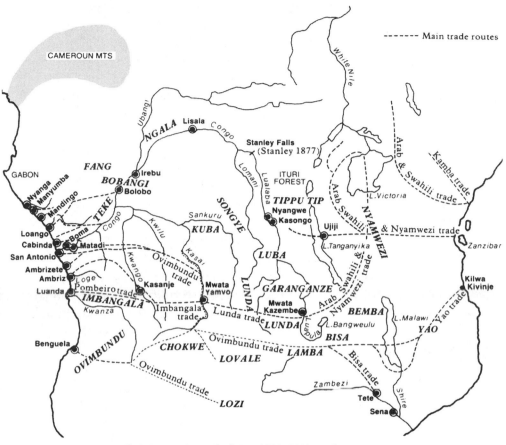

9. Western Central Africa, 1800–1880: trade routes.

the Portuguese government always did its best to prevent them from doing so. It knew that relations with the peoples of the interior went much more smoothly if trade was handled by the pombeiros. These, as we noted in Chapter 2, were African, or sometimes Mulatto, agents from the colony. They were employed by the Portuguese government or by private traders to lead caravans into the interior and to reside at the *feiras*, or garrisoned marketplaces. Peoples living beyond the Portuguese borders would bring their produce for sale to these markets. The most distant feira on the Luanda route was about 500 km (275 miles) up-country at Kasanje. It had been founded in the seventeenth century as the capital of a tributary state, the inhabitants of which

were a people called the Imbangala, who had originally formed a part
of the Luba–Lunda dispersion. The pombeiros did not normally go
beyond Kasanje. From there to the Mwata Yamvo's kingdom, trade
was organised by the Imbangala. The Mwata Yamvo sent his own
caravans still farther inland to the Mwata Kazembe's capital on the
Luapula River. And, by the end of the eighteenth century, the Mwata
Kazembe in his turn was in commercial contact with the Portuguese
station at Tete on the Zambezi – the usual carriers on the last stretch
of the route being the Bisa people of the north-eastern part of modern Zambia. At the end of the eighteenth century and several times
during the early nineteenth century, the Portuguese tried to survey
this route. They hoped by this means to extend their own power and
influence from coast to coast. In 1798, an expedition commanded by
Lacerda reached the Kazembe's capital from Tete, but had to turn
back. In 1806, however, two pombeiros called Pedro João Baptista
and Amaro José were sent out from Luanda and accomplished the
double journey to Tete and back on foot, with no greater hardship
than that of being detained for nearly four years on the outward journey at the court of the Mwata Kazembe. Baptista wrote of the king
in his journal:

The Kazembe is powerful in his capital, and rules over a great many people. His
place is rather smaller than the Mwata Yamvo's. His orders are harsh, and he
is feared by all the great chiefs, who are also lords in their own lands... When
there are no travellers trading at his capital, he will order slaves and ivory to
be collected, and will go with his ambassadors to chastise such chiefs as stop
the way to traders coming from Tete to his country. The territory of Kazembe is
supplied with provisions all the year round – manioc flour, millet, maize, beans,
bananas, sugar-canes, potatoes, yams, gourds, ground-nuts, and much fish from
the rivers Luapula and Mouva which are near. He owns three salt districts... He
possesses victuals and oxen... which he sends and buys from the Huizas [Bisa]
in exchange for slaves... King Kazembe has tea-pots, cups, silver spoons and
forks... and gold money. He has a Christian courtesy: he doffs his hat and gives
good day.[1]

The pombeiros noticed that the Kazembe, whose capital was almost
in the middle of the continent, would normally export his slaves
westwards via the Mwata Yamvo's kingdom to Luanda, whereas he

[1] *Lands of the Cazembe: Lacerda's Journey to Cazembe ... Also the Journey of the Pombeiros*, tr. R. F.
Burton (London, 1873), p. 231.

sent his ivory eastwards to Tete. This was probably a just reflection of the market for slaves and ivory in the trade of the Atlantic and Indian Oceans at that time.

The Ovimbundu and the Chokwe

By the middle of the nineteenth century, great changes had taken place along the old transcontinental route. On the one hand, as we shall see, the trade eastwards from Kazembe had changed its direction from the Portuguese on the Zambezi to the Swahili Arabs of the Zanzibar coast. On the other hand, the old Luanda route to the Mwata Yamvo, using the Imbangala as intermediaries, had been superseded by a more southerly route from Benguela. Trade on this route was in the hands of the Ovimbundu of the Bihe plateau. The Ovimbundu, like the Imbangala, were people who had been organised into small states by conquering migrants from the Lunda area. From the eighteenth century on, they had been joined by considerable numbers of European refugees – some escaped convicts, some deserters from the Portuguese army. These people had passed on to their hosts their own skill with firearms and had helped to make them the greatest traders of the whole of the dry, upland region of the Congo–Zambezi watershed to the south of the Mwata Yamvo's kingdom. By 1850, their caravans, usually numbering two or three hundred porters, had penetrated south-eastwards into the Lovale and Lozi countries of the upper Zambezi valley, eastwards as far as the Lamba of the Zambian Copperbelt, and northwards right across the Mwata Yamvo's country and down the Kasai as far as the southern fringes of the Congo forest. In part, the decline of the Luanda route and the rise of the Benguela one reflected a change in the commodities exported. The Luanda route had been, above all, a slaving route, and the Imbangala had for two-and-a-half centuries been specialists in the supply of slaves. Luanda continued to export slaves openly and actively until 1838, when slavery was officially abolished in all the Portuguese possessions. Illegal shipments continued for another two decades, but from lesser ports and not from the capital of the colony. Hence, the downfall of the Imbangala. And, simultaneously with the abolition of the slave trade, the Portuguese lifted the government monopoly of the ivory trade. This opened up new trading opportunities, which the Ovimbundu were better placed to exploit than the Imbangala. The Ovimbundu were traders rather than hunters. But their eastern neighbours, the Chokwe, were the great ivory-hunting specialists of the mid-nineteenth century. Their methods were ferocious in the extreme. They were well supplied with firearms and were continuously on the warpath. They lived by pillage, taking slave-prisoners and incorporating them in their own war-bands, seizing stocks of dead ivory, and hunting out the elephants systematically in one region after another. The Ovimbundu traders, in fact, advanced behind a screen of Chokwe hunters and warriors, buying their ivory and supplying them with firearms in exchange. Thus, the Chokwe, a small and almost unheard-of people in 1800, had by the end of the century conquered large areas between the upper Zambezi, the Kwango, and the middle Kasai Rivers and western Katanga, and it was they who in 1885 at last made an end to the great kingdom of the Mwata Yamvo.

The Nyamwezi and the Arabs

While the Ovimbundu and the Chokwe were displacing the Lunda and the Imbangala at the western end of the transcontinental route, the Mwata Kazembe, in the centre of it, was likewise being displaced by newcomers from East Africa. The story of the Nyamwezi and Swahili Arab penetration of East Africa during the nineteenth century is told in Chapter 7: here, we are concerned only with that part of the movement which affected Western Central Africa. As early as 1832, the Kazembe rebuffed a Portuguese trade mission which visited him, saying that he was already getting all the foreign goods that he needed from the Zanzibar coast and that he no longer wished to trade with the Portuguese on the Zambezi. If he had foreseen the consequences of these new East African trading contacts, he might have been more cautious in rejecting the Portuguese proposals. For, about 1856, a Nyamwezi merchant, Msiri (the 'Mosquito'), who had already made several trading expeditions to Katanga, settled down with an armed following at Bunkeya, on the northern edge of the Kazembe's kingdom. There, he steadily built up his power and influence until he was strong enough to defy the Kazembe and to make himself the effective overlord of a large region, which included the whole of the north and west of the Kazembe's kingdom. He also spread into the Luba kingdoms to the north of it. Msiri, with his Nyamwezi warriors, known in Katanga as the Bayeke, now added to his trading profits with regular tribute in ivory, salt, and copper levied from the chiefs who had formerly paid it to the Kazembe or to the Luba kings. Like the Kazembes before him, he traded these products in many directions. The salt and copper (cast in small bars or crosses) went down the Kasai and the Lulua Rivers to the peoples of the forest margin like the Kuba and the Songye, who traded it for ivory. The ivory Msiri exchanged for guns, obtained from both the Ovimbundu and the Portuguese in the west and from the Swahili Arabs in the east. Msiri's empire, known to the early European explorers as Garanganze, lasted until the coming of the Belgians in 1891, when Msiri himself was shot in a scuffle with a Belgian officer. His Bayeke followers continued – even after independence – to form an important element in the politics of Shaba. Godfrey Munongo, for example, who was minister for the interior in Tshombe's Congolese government, was a Yeke – and a grandson of Msiri himself.

What Msiri was doing in southern Katanga was occurring simultaneously in northern Katanga and the Kivu region by other groups of East Africans, led in this case mostly by Swahili Arabs from the Zanzibar coast. They had first crossed Lake Tanganyika about 1840 from their lakeside ferry-port of Ujiji. By about 1860, there was a regular Arab settlement at Nyangwe on the Lualaba (the upper Congo). Soon they were trading and raiding over the whole area between Lake Tanganyika and the Lomami River, where they came within the sphere of the Chokwe raiders coming from the west. Like the Chokwe, they could penetrate where they wished, as the possession of firearms made them all-powerful, and the ancient Luba and Songye kingdoms were even more defenceless than the Lunda kingdoms to the south. Like the Yeke invaders to the south of them and the Chokwe to the south-west, they were ruthless and rapid in their exploitation of the ivory resources of the country. They hunted elephants in armies, and the armies lived off the local populations and savaged them, levying tribute in foodstuffs and ivory, and burning and looting the villages at the slightest signs of resistance.

Nevertheless, behind the first line of advance of the elephant-hunters, the invaders of eastern Zaire settled down to an organised

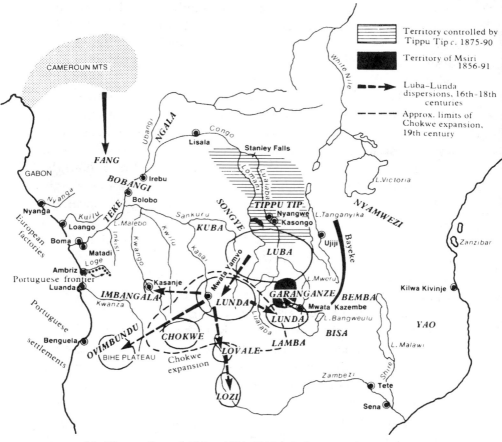

10. Western Central Africa, 1800–1880: tribal areas and migrations.

way of life. Their townships, many of which still exist, were equipped
with mosques, and the principal houses had all the little luxuries
of urban life on the East African coast – beds, furniture, coffee ta-
bles, even the beautifully carved doorways of Zanzibar. Around their
settlements, the Arabs developed thriving agricultural plantations.
Europeans were much impressed by these Arab achievements, as
can be seen from the following description of Kasongo, written by
Sidney Hinde, the English medical officer of the Congo Free State
forces that conquered the Arab lands of eastern Congo in 1893:

Kasongo was a much finer town than even the grand old slave capital Nyangwe.
During the siege of Nyangwe, the taking of which was more or less expected,

the inhabitants had time to carry off all valuables, and even furniture, to places of safety. At Kasongo, however, it was different. We rushed into the town so suddenly that everything was left in its place. Our whole force found new outfits, and even the common soldiers slept on silk and satin mattresses, in carved beds with silk mosquito curtains. The room I took possession of was eighty feet long and fifteen feet wide, with a door leading into an orange garden, beyond which was a view extending over five miles. We found many European luxuries, the use of which we had almost forgotten; candles, sugar, matches, silver and glass goblets and decanters were in profusion. The granaries throughout the town were stocked with enormous quantities of rice, coffee, maize and other food; the gardens were luxurious and well-planted; and oranges, both sweet and bitter, guavas, pomegranates, pineapples, mangoes and bananas abounded at every turn. The herd of cattle we found in Kasongo was composed of three distinct breeds...

I was constantly astonished by the splendid work which had been done in the neighbourhood by the Arabs. Kasongo was built in the corner of a virgin forest, and for miles round all the brushwood and the great majority of trees had been cleared away. In the forest-clearing fine crops of sugar-cane, rice, maize and fruits grew. I have ridden through a single rice-field for an hour and a half.[2]

Tippu Tip

In the early days, each of these Arab settlements was ruled by its founder and followers, who exercised a kind of loose political authority over the local African chiefs. The man who brought the Arabs of this region together, to recognise his own supremacy and, ultimately, that of the sultan of Zanzibar, was Muhammed bin Hamed, more generally known by his nickname of Tippu Tip. He was born in 1830 in Zanzibar, and his mother was a Muscat Arab of the ruling class. His father and his paternal grandfather were coastal Swahili who had taken part in the earliest trading expeditions to the interior. His paternal grandmother had been the daughter of a Nyamwezi chief, and Tippu's own earliest journeys were with Nyamwezi caravans travelling round the south end of Lake Tanganyika to Katanga. He was for a time associated with Msiri, but later left him and set up his own headquarters at Kasongo on the Lualaba, where he described himself as sultan of Utetera. This was in the late 1860s and the early 1870s. From then on, for twenty more years, Tippu Tip was the most powerful man in the eastern part of what later became the Democratic

[2] S. L. Hinde, *The Fall of the Congo Arabs* (London, 1897), pp. 184, 187.

Republic of Congo (DRC). He was loyal to the sultan of Zanzibar, yet – unlike most of the Arabs – he maintained excellent relations with the Nyamwezi. The Nyamwezi territory lay between him and the east coast, controlling his line of communications with Zanzibar. In 1877, he met the explorer Stanley – at Nyangwe and accompanied him down the Lualaba to Stanley Falls (later Stanleyville), thus extending his ivory-hunting and other trading activities into the Ituri forest region.

By the 1880s, Tippu Tip was said to have 50,000 guns at his command. His territory touched that of the Chokwe in the south-west, while his station at Stanley Falls was only a fortnight's journey for the river-steamers which Stanley – by then in the employment of King Leopold of the Belgians – had launched at Lake Malebo. Tippu Tip realised that the European powers were closing in on tropical Africa. From 1883 to 1886, therefore, he made a great effort to rally the Arabs of eastern Zaire to acknowledge the political authority of the sultan of Zanzibar, in the hope that the sultan's dominion over East Africa would be recognised by the Europeans. In this way, Tippu Tip hoped that his rule in eastern Congo would become more permanent. But his efforts were in vain: the European powers at the Berlin Conference (see Chapter 9) did not uphold the sultan's claims over the interior of East Africa. Tippu Tip's last years in the Congo (1877–92) were spent in the improbable role of King Leopold's 'governor' at Stanley Falls. After his eventual retirement to Zanzibar, his former lands were conquered, as we have seen, by European forces. However, as with Msiri's Katanga, the Belgians took over many of the institutions of Arab rule in eastern Zaire and employed many Swahili in positions of subordinate authority. In fact, the Swahili language, known locally as Kingwana, remains the common language of this part of the DRC to this day.

The Lower Congo Region and the Congo River Route

The part of Western Central Africa least known to Europeans at the beginning of the nineteenth century was the region north and south of the lower Congo, which at the end of the century was to be the main centre of interest and of the struggle for political control. The most important factor in this region was the geographical one. The Congo

River and its tributaries that converge upon Lake Malebo provide some 6,500 km (4,000 miles) of waterways which are navigable without interruption. But the 400 km (225 miles) of river between Lake Malebo and the Atlantic Ocean passes through a district of steep and broken hill country in a series of cataracts and waterfalls. This country is as hard to travel through as any in the world. Only with immense difficulty did Stanley and other officials of the Congo Free State have a road cut across the stony hills and forested valleys to transport parts of steamships up to Lake Malebo to be reassembled for use on the navigable waterways. But prior to this, so long as water transport on the upper river was by canoe and so long as head porterage was the only means of transport over the cataract region, the economic possibilities of the Congo River system were limited. At the beginning of the century, when the Portuguese government maintained its monopoly of the ivory trade, a certain amount of ivory and other traffic used the northward-flowing tributaries of the Congo in order to bypass Portuguese territory. This trade did not come together at Lake Malebo, which was not yet – as it later became – a commercial bottleneck. Instead, it passed from the rivers to the scores of European trading factories scattered along the coast to the north of the Portuguese possessions in Angola, along numerous side routes through the forest and down the streams that flowed directly into the Atlantic. The staple product of this trade was ivory, but, as the nineteenth century went on, it came to include also palm-oil and palm-kernels, beeswax, coffee, raw cotton, and rubber. By the 1870s, the volume of British trade alone from the Western Central African coast rivalled that from the Oil Rivers district of southern Nigeria.

It was ivory, however, which formed the backbone of the trade. It was ivory which had the highest value and which did not deteriorate in transport. It was ivory, therefore, which came from farthest afield – from the Lunda-dominated countries of the Kwango and the Kasai, and from the forest peoples of the main river. Among these, the Teke from the northern shores of Lake Malebo acted as the main traders and carriers for the whole region below Bolobo. Above Bolobo, the Bobangi took their place as far as Irebu and, beyond that, the Ngala, who traded as far as Lisala, 1,600 km (1,000 miles) from the sea. This was the farthest point from the west coast where Stanley found

European merchandise during his journey down the Congo in 1877. The European guns and cloth which he saw here had taken five years to reach their destination.

North of the main river, in the region between the Ubangi and the coast, the part taken by the Chokwe farther south was played by the Fang (French: Pahuin) people. They were immigrants into Western Central Africa from the interior of Cameroun. They had moved southwards from the savanna into the rain forest and had become the preeminent ivory-hunters, exchanging their ivory, generally through African middlemen, for European goods, especially guns, at the factories on the Gabon coast. The Fang at this time were very fierce and were widely reputed to be cannibals. Mary Kingsley, a courageous Englishwoman who travelled through their country in 1894, described how the inhabitants of a Fang village tried to sell her their store of elephant tusks and india rubber:

> I did not want these things then, but still felt too nervous of the Fangs to point this out firmly, and so had to buy...I found myself the owner of balls of rubber and some tusks, and alas, my little stock of cloth and tobacco all going fast...To be short of money in a Fang village is extremely bad, because these Fangs, when a trader has no more goods to sell them, are liable to start trade all over again by killing him and taking back their ivory and rubber and keeping it until another trader comes along.[3]

The whole of this pattern of trade which found its way by lateral or side routes to European trading factories scattered along the coast from Mount Cameroun to Angola was, however, placed in danger by Stanley's journey down the Congo in 1877 and by his demonstration that above the lower Congo cataracts, there were thousands of miles of smoothly flowing waterways, easily navigable by steamers. The British government was satisfied with the old pattern of trade and took no action when Stanley returned to England and told of his discoveries. However, King Leopold of the Belgians, who had by this time spent nearly twenty years studying the colonial activities of other nations and looking for an opportunity to establish an empire of his own, listened with interest to Stanley's stories. Already Leopold's eyes were fixed upon the Congo basin, though he was

---

[3] 'Some Unpublished Travels', cited in Stephen Gwynn, *The Life of Mary Kingsley* (London, 1933), pp. 109–10.

planning to approach it from the east, using the Swahili Arab routes. With Stanley's report before him, he completely changed his plans: he would bypass the cataracts on the lower river with a railway and launch steamers on the upper river. At once the Congo would become a bottleneck, funnelling the trade of the whole vast river basin into his net. The Arab and Nyamwezi empires would be rolled back. The Chokwe would cease to be of any commercial importance. Under a European reorganisation of its trade, the region as a whole would resume its natural unity.

King Leopold's design, as we shall see, did more than anything else to spark the European scramble for Africa. It brought to an end an old chapter of African history. When the Portuguese first came to Western Central Africa in the fifteenth century, they had opened its trade westwards – to the coast and to the lands across the Atlantic Ocean. Through their subsequent concentration on the slave trade, however, and through their unenlightened attempt to hold down the price of ivory by a royal monopoly, they allowed the East Africans during the first three-quarters of the nineteenth century to divert most of the ivory trade away from its natural Atlantic outlets into the trading system of the Indian Ocean. From the point of view of geography, this was all wrong. Stanley Falls and Bunkeya (Msiri's capital) were both much nearer to the west coast than to the east. But it took Stanley's journey and King Leopold's commercial vision to reverse the swing of the pendulum, which otherwise would have left Western Central Africa a dependency of Eastern Central Africa and a part of the Muslim world.

SEVEN. Eastern Central Africa, 1800–1884

Eastern Africa, for the purposes of this chapter, includes not only the modern states of Kenya, Uganda, and Tanzania, but also northern Mozambique, Malawi, Burundi, and Rwanda. All these lands were to fall under some kind of European rule before the end of the century, but, from 1800 until 1884, the predominant outside influences were not European, but Swahili Arab or Turco–Egyptian. Before 1884, only a handful of Europeans attempted trading ventures of their own in the interior. In general, European and American enterprise was limited – like that of the Indians from the British empire in India – to supplying Arab and Egyptian merchants with manufactured goods, especially cloth and firearms, in exchange for ivory and a few less important products such as hides, beeswax, and gum arabic. It was the Muslim merchants who traded directly with the African peoples. The work of Christian missionaries was the main European activity in East Africa before the partition took place. The missionaries, however, arrived in this region much later than the Muslim traders, and their work was still in the pioneer stage when the colonial period began. They were not responsible for the establishment of European political control, which came, when it did, mainly as the result of happenings outside East Africa.

The Penetration of the Interior by the Swahili Arabs

The evolution of the Swahili Arab population in the coastal belt of East Africa and on Zanzibar and the other offshore islands is described in Chapter 2, as are the origins of trade between the interior and the coast. This trade from the interlacustrine kingdoms and from Katanga, most of which was carried originally by the Nyamwezi, seems to have been mainly a peaceful activity. Early European travellers were much impressed by the prosperity and sufficiency of many of the inland districts they visited. For example, Sir Richard Burton, who was by no means prejudiced in favour of African achievements, wrote after his journey to Lake Tanganyika in 1858: 'The African is in these regions superior in comforts, better dressed, fed and lodged than the unhappy Ryot [peasant] of British India. His condition, where the slave-trade is slack, may indeed be compared advantageously with that of the peasantry in some of the richest of European countries.' Traditions among peoples who were to suffer from the violence that was to come recall, in the exaggerated way that people often do, the good old days:

In the old times, long long ago, in their old homes, the Yao were in accord and united. If a quarrel arose they used to fight without rancour, avoiding bloodshed. If strangers came to a village, would they have to pay for their food? No, it was bestowed on them free; directly a man heard that a stranger was at his door, he would rejoice and say 'I have the plant of hospitality at my door, bringing guests.'[1]

As the nineteenth century approached, however, two factors combined to hasten changes in the old way of life. The first was the rapidly growing demand at the coast for ivory and slaves. The second was the great desire of the peoples in the interior for more and more firearms. There was still, as there had always been, a ready market for domestic and plantation slaves in and around all the coastal towns, as well as in Oman and the other states of Arabia and the Persian Gulf. From the mid-eighteenth century until the mid-nineteenth, the French added greatly to the demand with their labour requirements for the sugar and coffee plantations in Réunion (and, until the Napoleonic wars, in Mauritius). In the early nineteenth century, the Portuguese, because of the restrictions imposed on the West African slave trade north of the equator, shipped an increasing number of slaves round the Cape from Mozambique to Brazil and Cuba. And, above all, the nineteenth century saw a vast development of the plantation agriculture of the

---

[1] Yohannah B. Abdullah, *The Yaos*, ed. and tr. M. Sanderson (Zomba, 1919), p. 11.

Swahili Arabs, and with it a growing demand for slaves from the interior. But, as the nineteenth century went on, the demand for ivory – and, therefore, the prices paid for it – became even greater than that for slaves. The age-old market for East African ivory was the Asian one. By the middle of the nineteenth century, however, demand in Europe and America had very greatly increased. Wealth derived from the industrial and commercial changes taking place in European countries and in North America had developed an almost insatiable appetite for the luxury objects made from ivory, such as knife-handles, piano keys, billiard balls, and ornaments of every kind.

A few of the Swahili Arabs who had been settled on the coast for centuries began to respond to these opportunities at the end of the eighteenth century, soon after the Nyamwezi traders had pioneered the routes. The great advance of the coastal people, however, developed only during the long and brilliant reign (1806–56) of Seyyid Said, imam of Muscat and hereditary overlord of the Arab settlements along the Zanzibar coast. Said was both an able commander and an economic genius, and it did not take him long to see that his East African empire was more worthy of his attention than the rocks and deserts in his little state of Oman on the western shores of the Persian Gulf. But first he had to reconquer it. He possessed efficient armed forces. The ships of his navy had been provided by Britain under the terms of a treaty made with him, and his army consisted of Baluchi mercenaries recruited from the borders of Persia and India. With these, he occupied Zanzibar and made effective his nominal control over the coastal towns from Warsheikh in the north to Lindi in the south, including the important cities of Mombasa and Kilwa, which had for long been practically independent. Under Said's influence, Zanzibar became the central market for the whole of the East African coast. After his introduction of the clove tree from the East Indies, the islands of Zanzibar and Pemba soon came to grow most of the world's supply of cloves. The plantations were invariably worked by slaves who were imported from the interior. In 1840, after a series of increasingly long visits to his African dominions, Said actually transferred his capital from Muscat to Zanzibar, where he was usually given the title of sultan. After his death in 1856, the scattered empire was divided, one son taking Oman, and another, Majid, becoming sultan of Zanzibar.

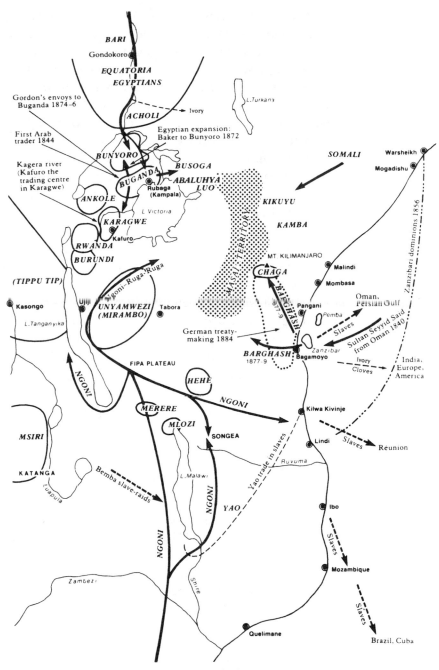

11. Eastern Central Africa, 1800–1884.

Sultans Said and Majid encouraged Arabs to settle in Zanzibar as plantation owners, and they also encouraged the coastal people to trade in the interior. The sultanate provided the background of security necessary for large-scale trade: debts could be collected at Zanzibar and contracts enforced. The financial arrangements for the trade were made by Indian merchants of Zanzibar and the coastal towns, who had strong commercial ties with their fellow countrymen across the ocean in India. They supplied credit to coastal traders to enable them to stock up caravans with goods and journey up-country, sometimes not returning with their purchases of ivory and slaves until several years later. In a letter dated 21 November 1872 (which was sent back to England with his body), Livingstone wrote of these Indian traders, 'The Banians have the Custom House and all the public revenue of Zanzibar entirely in their hands and by their money, arms, and ammunition and goods a large and cruel Slave trade had been carried on'.[2]

The Nyamwezi traders resisted the competition of the newcomers and were able to retain a near-monopoly of trade routes from central Tanzania to Katanga. But the coastal people were better organised and armed and had greater financial resources behind them. They were able to supply African rulers with guns and ammunition, which were beyond the means of the Nyamwezi traders. As the century went on, and as European armies were reequipped with more and more modern varieties of firearms, so more and more of the out-of-date models found their way on to the African market. By the end of the 1830s, Arab traders had penetrated to Lake Tanganyika and, in 1844, the first Arab visited the court of Buganda. So extensive was the Arab trading in the interior that it was said as a joke that 'when they pipe in Zanzibar, people dance on the shores of the great lakes'. Arabs established settlements at certain key points, such as Tabora in the Nyamwezi country and Ujiji on Lake Tanganyika. These were mainly commercial depots, but, in time, they grew to exercise a certain military and political control over the surrounding countryside. When Burton and Speke visited Tabora in 1858, the former wrote:

The Arabs live comfortably, and even splendidly. The houses, though single-storied, are large, substantial and capable of defence. Their gardens are

[2] Quoted in Zoë Marsh, *East Africa through Contemporary Records* (Cambridge, 1961), p. 44.

extensive and well planted; they receive regular supplies from the coast; they are surrounded by troops of slaves, whom they train to divers crafts and callings; rich men have riding asses from Zanzibar, and even the poorest keep flocks and herds.[3]

Generally, the Arabs obtained their ivory and slaves from the local rulers, who, armed with the imported guns, sent their warriors to hunt elephants and to raid the forests of neighbouring peoples, often capturing slaves in the process. In most of East Africa, however, slaving was more a by-product of the ivory rush than the primary object of the trade. Only the country around Lake Malawi was primarily a slaving region, where the powerful Yao chiefs raided the ill-organised and defenceless peoples of the eastern lakeshore. The Bemba, and later the Ngoni, did the same on the west. It was along the trade route from Lake Malawi to the coast that Livingstone noted some of the worst atrocities that he witnessed in all his long travels:

We passed a woman tied by the neck to a tree and dead. We saw others tied up in a similar manner, and one lying on the path shot or stabbed for she was in a pool of blood. The explanation we got invariably was that the Arab who owned these victims was enraged at losing his money by the slaves being unable to march...Today we came upon a man dead from starvation...One of our men wandered and found a number of slaves with slave-sticks on, abandoned by their master from want of food... We passed village after village and gardens, all deserted.[4]

Elsewhere, however, the emphasis was on ivory, although slaves were bought and sold at every stage along the trade routes. The Nyamwezi, for example, were great buyers of slaves, whom they employed in agricultural work while they themselves were absent on long trading journeys.

The Ngoni and Mirambo

The situation in Tanzania was complicated toward the middle of the nineteenth century by the incursions of the Ngoni from the south. Bands of warriors who had broken away from Shaka's Zulu kingdom (see Chapter 8) were swollen by the attachment of the remnants of peoples they had defeated on their long northward trek. They

---

[3] R. F. Burton, *Lake Regions of Central Africa* (London, 1860), vol. I, p. 328.
[4] *Last Journals*, ed. Horace Waller (London, 1874), vol. I, p. 70.

spread across much of western and southern Tanzania to the east and west of Lake Malawi, where they finally settled as ruling aristocracies. Far beyond the range of their settlement, their outlying raiders and their military tactics were absorbed into the new groupings of tribes that were taking place in Tanzania. Warrior bands, called *ruga-ruga* in Nyamwezi country, and *maviti* and *magwangwara* elsewhere, roamed the countryside, usually pillaging on their own account, but ready to be employed by ruthless warlords or Arab traders. Sometimes their raids caused their victims to combine against them. The centralised state of the Hehe, for instance, in south-central Tanzania, was formed in this way. On the other hand, a young Nyamwezi chief, Mirambo, actually took groups of Ngoni ruga-ruga into his service and used them to build up and extend his hereditary chiefdom in the western part of Unyamwezi. Mirambo became powerful enough, in the 1870s, to rival the Arab merchant princes. By 1880, he had gained control of the Ujiji trade route to Lake Tanganyika and was able to threaten even the route leading north-westwards to Buganda. It was with Mirambo, and not with his fellow Arabs, that Tippu Tip allied himself in his commercial exploitation of eastern Congo, which is described in Chapter 6.

The Interlacustrine Region

North of the Nyamwezi country, the trade with the rich interlacustrine region developed, from the 1840s on, mainly under the control of Swahili Arab merchants. The main trade route ran from Tabora through Karagwe, where there was a large Arab commercial settlement at Kafuro near the capital, to the Kagera River. Here it divided, a westerly branch leading off through the plains of eastern Ankole to Bunyoro, and an easterly branch following near the shoreline of Lake Victoria towards the capital of Buganda. The Tutsi kingdom of Rwanda, though still at the height of its power, would admit no strangers within its frontiers, and such outside trade as there was passed by Rwanda caravans to and from Karagwe. Ankole was nearly as hostile to foreigners as Rwanda. The big trading countries were Bunyoro and Buganda, for – in addition to her powerful armies – Buganda was the chief naval power of Lake Victoria. As the nineteenth century went on, fleets of the great Buganda canoes made of planks sewn together, with their high prows visible far over the water, came regularly to the southern shores of the lake, competing with the overland trade routes. In this way, Kabakas Suna and Mutesa, who reigned through the middle years of the century from about 1832 until 1884, steadily built up their stocks of cloth and guns and used them to arm and pay ever-more-efficient armies, which harried the Basoga to the east and the Bahaya to the south and nibbled more cautiously at the renewed military power of Bunyoro to the north-west.

It was not only from the south-east, however, that the outside world was forcing itself upon the interlacustrine states. As we saw in Chapter 3, the trading frontier of the Egyptian Sudan had been established since the 1840s in the Bari country to the south of the Nile swamps; by the 1860s, the Khartoum-based ivory traders were operating among the Acholi people of the northern province of modern Uganda. The Egyptians established their first contacts with Bunyoro by intervening in the succession struggle following the death of the ruler, Kamurasi, in 1869. In that year, the Khedive Ismail of Egypt sent the British explorer Samuel Baker to be governor of this 'Equatorial Province' of the Sudan. Baker tried unsuccessfully to occupy Bunyoro and had to be content with establishing forts along its northern edge. In 1873, however, he was succeeded by Charles Gordon, who had definite instructions to extend the Egyptian dominions to the Great Lakes. Thus, in 1874, Gordon's emissaries reached the court of Kabaka Mutesa of Buganda.

Mutesa knew enough of the outside world to guess what was afoot. An Egyptian garrison was detained by the Kabaka and given a taste of Buganda's power to hurt, and then allowed to retire unharmed. Meanwhile, Mutesa strengthened his links with the strangers from the east coast, buying more arms, listening to the Islamic teachings of his Arab friends, even learning to write the Swahili language in Arabic characters. His fears of the Egyptians were described by the Anglican missionary Alexander Mackay a few years later, in his biography which was written by his sister:

Egypt has always been an object of great suspicion in the eyes of the Baganda. Captain Speke, who formed Mtesa's acquaintance a dozen years before Stanley, tells how the king objected to his passing through Uganda to Egypt via the Nile . . . The Egyptian station of Mruli was regarded by Mtesa with very jealous feelings, and the Arabs lost no opportunity to fan the flame. Knowing well that with the presence of the white man the hope of their gains was gone, they told him that Colonel Gordon and the Turks (as they called the Egyptians) would soon come and 'eat the country'. The Baganda constantly had the word *Baturki* on their lips. Mtesa never wearied in narrating to Mackay all his intercourse with white men: how Speke brought Grant, and then sent Baker; how Colonel Long (Gordon's agent) came and was followed by Stanley. 'What do they all want?' asked Mtesa. 'Are they not coming to look for lakes, that they may put ships and guns on them? Did not Speke come here by the Queen's orders for that purpose?'[5]

It was almost certainly the presence of a second Egyptian delegation at his court at the time of the explorer Stanley's visit in 1875 which caused him to encourage Stanley to let it be known in Europe that he would like Christian missionaries to come and settle in his country. Mutesa was an exceptionally intelligent and open-minded man, and no doubt he was genuinely impressed by what his European visitors – first Speke (1862) and then Stanley – had told him of Christianity and European civilisation. As a statesman, he realised that if Buganda was really threatened by the Egyptian advance from the north, it would be wise to increase the number of his other foreign contacts, so as to be able to play them off against the Egyptians. Church of England missionaries from Britain, therefore, arrived in Buganda in 1877, and Roman Catholic missionaries from France in 1879, and, so long as the Egyptian threat lasted, both received a warm welcome. In the course of the next six or seven years, Christianity became so deeply embedded among a minority of the court circle in Buganda that it was able to survive a brief but terrible persecution at the hands of Mutesa's successor, Mwanga, in 1885–6.

Peoples and Trade Routes of Kenya

Right up to the colonial period, the main trade outlet of Buganda and the other interlacustrine states remained the south-easterly one, linking up with the trans-Tanzanian route at Tabora. It was difficult to set up a more direct route from Buganda to the coast at Mombasa because of the nomadic and warlike way of life of so many of the peoples, notably the Masai, in what became Kenya. The Masai did not merely attack strangers: throughout the nineteenth century, they fought almost continuously among themselves for control of the best

---

[5] J. W. H. Mackay, *The Story of the Life of Mackay of Uganda* (London, 1898), pp. 132–4.

pasturelands. Thus, the whole region of the Kenya highlands was in a perpetual state of unrest. Traders could only pass through this country at great peril to themselves and their goods, and no regular trading links could be set up by the Swahili Arabs with the densely populated lands of the Luo and the Abaluhya in the Kavirondo region to the north-east of Lake Victoria until several decades after they had taken over the Nyamwezi routes to the south and west of the lake. The equivalent among the Kenya peoples of the Nyamwezi were the Kamba, who lived some 300 km (180 miles) inland from Mombasa. They made trading contacts with the Kikuyu on one side and with the coastal peoples on the other as early as the 1830s, when a series of disastrous famines caused them to leave their homelands in search of food. The German missionary traveller Johann Krapf noted how 'The Swahili purvey to the Wakamba cotton fabrics (Americani), blue calico, glass beads, copper and brass-wire, red ochre, black pepper, salt and blue vitriol (zinc), and receive in exchange, chiefly cattle and ivory'.[6] The Kamba continued to monopolise trade between Kikuyuland and Mombasa until the 1880s, when the Arabs with their superior organisation and weapons drew off the Kikuyu trade into their own routes. The Arabs did not thrust into the hinterland of any part of the Kenyan or north Tanzanian coast until the 1860s, when they managed to open routes to the Chaga of the Kilimanjaro region. Thence they were able to work their way across the narrowest part of the Masai plain and on westwards to Kavirondo. By about 1880, these Arab traders in and hunters of ivory had reached the country to the west of Lake Turkana. Here, in the last unexploited ivory district of East Africa, they came into contact with Egyptians from the southern Sudan and with Ethiopians, all concerned with enriching themselves from the ivory trade.

The Summit of Swahili Arab Power in East Africa

We have seen that the most important development during the first three-quarters of the nineteenth century in East Africa was the commercial penetration of the whole region by the Swahili Arabs from

---

[6] J. L. Krapf, *Travels in Eastern Africa* (London, 1860), p. 353.

the east coast. And now, for a brief period in the late 1870s and early 1880s, it seemed that the commercial empire of Zanzibar might turn itself into a political one. In the eyes of the British consul-general at Zanzibar, Sir John Kirk, this was a development very much to be hoped for. Kirk had been in Zanzibar since 1864 and had built up a remarkable degree of influence, first with Sultan Majid and then with his brother, Sultan Barghash. Neither Kirk nor his masters in London wished for direct British intervention in East Africa. In their view, a friendly and easily influenced sultan of Zanzibar would be both the cheapest and the most effective means of achieving their two objectives: to end the East African slave trade and to prevent the intervention of other European powers in the area. In 1873, Barghash was persuaded to abolish the slave trade within his dominions, and from then onwards, so far as the British government was concerned, the wider the sultan's dominions, the better. Inspired by Kirk, Barghash engaged a British officer to enlarge and train his army, and in the late 1870s, he began to set up garrisons along the line of the main trans-Tanzanian trade route. As Kirk watched the growing interests of other European powers, especially of King Leopold of the Belgians, he spurred Barghash to greater efforts. The Arab traders in the far interior were encouraged to turn from commerce to conquest, and did so – first, Tippu Tip in the region round Lake Tanganyika; next, the Arabs who were settled round the north end of Lake Malawi; and, finally, the Arabs in Buganda. In 1887, a special representative of Sultan Barghash arrived in Buganda, where the previous year the Kabaka Mwanga had executed a number of Christians at his court. This representative plotted with the Muslim party in the kingdom to depose Mwanga in 1888, and then to seize power for themselves. A younger brother of Mwanga was declared to be Kabaka. This Muslim success, however, was short-lived. By 1890, Mwanga had regained power with the support of the Christian Baganda, in spite of his previous persecution of their religion.

The achievements of Tippu Tip and other Arab chiefs marked the summit of Arab power in East Africa; to the European missionaries living scattered about in the interior, this appeared in a very different light from that in which it had been conceived by Kirk at Zanzibar. Where Kirk had imagined a Zanzibar dominion recognised by the powers and responsive to British influence, the missionaries saw burning villages and starving refugees, and a new anti-European and anti-Christian attitude among the Arabs. The experience made them long for and, in some cases, work for European colonial occupation. In the event, however, Swahili Arab imperialism did not last long. Before any missionary condemnation of it had time to take effect, a handful of German adventurers had shown that the sultan's power in the interior of East Africa was nothing but a hollow sham. Neither Carl Peters nor his associates in the Society for German Colonisation had ever set foot in East Africa before 1884, but they had grasped the essential fact that a mere 50 or 60 km (30 or 40 miles) inland from the coast, there were African communities which owed no allegiance to the sultan of Zanzibar. They realised that the rulers of these communities could be persuaded without too much trouble to sign pieces of paper placing their lands under the protection of a European power. From that moment onwards, Kirk's plan was doomed. The European scramble for East Africa had begun.

Madagascar

King Nampoina's conquests at the end of the eighteenth and the beginning of the nineteenth centuries laid the foundations for the great Merina state. This must rank as one of the most remarkable political creations in the whole of Africa in the pre-colonial period. Nampoina's successor, Radama I (1810–28), transformed the warrior chiefdom into a nation comparable in many ways to the smaller states of Europe. He rounded off Nampoina's conquests, so that by the end of his reign, two-thirds of Madagascar was under Hova domination (see Maps 3 and 4). The rich kingdom of Betsileo, in the highlands around Fianarantsoa to the south of Tananarive, recognised the control of Radama. The Merina army was equipped with firearms, largely supplied by the British from the Indian Ocean island of Mauritius. Radama was advised on military matters by an unlikely trio – a Scotsman, a Jamaican, and a Frenchman. The king, however, did not confine his attentions to conquests and military reforms. In 1820, with royal permission, the first Christian missionaries, belonging to the British London Missionary Society, arrived in Imerina. The fruits of their efforts were astonishing – after seven years, it was estimated that 4,000 Hova could read and write their own language, and many had been trained to perform European trades.

The animist priests and the older Hova upper class naturally felt their positions threatened by the new religion and the young educated men, and there followed an almost inevitable reaction. Radama I was succeeded in 1828 by the first of the queens of nineteenth-century Imerina, Ranavalona. In 1835, she closed the London Missionary Society's schools and allowed only those foreigners to enter her kingdom who could contribute directly to its military and economic power. But the seeds of Christianity and of western education could not easily be uprooted. After a violent struggle for power at the death of Queen Ranavalona in 1861, a most remarkable man became prime minister – Rainilaiarivony, who remained in office until the coming of the French expedition in 1894. He made certain of his position by becoming the husband of three successive queens. Missionary work was resumed and, in 1868, Rainilaiarivony himself became a Christian. By the 1880s (by which time French Roman Catholic missionaries were also active), there had been a massive conversion to Christianity, and the proportion of Malagasy children at school was comparable to that in western Europe. Animist beliefs, however, did not wither away, and, indeed, continued to flourish, in many cases among converts to Christianity.

This continuation of traditional beliefs was one sign of the considerable strain that was building up within the Merina state. Its subject peoples resented the often harsh rule of the Hova aristocracy, and many of the Hova resented the huge personal power of the prime minister. Although the majority of Christians were converts of the London Missionary Society, and although Britain kept close diplomatic links with Imerina, a great amount of the external trade of Madagascar was in French hands. The Hova were proudly independent and had no wish to be under the 'protection' of either Britain or France. However, the French were determined to secure their commercial interests and, in 1885, after the first of the Franco-Malagasy wars, forced a treaty upon Imerina. As in the case of the Wichale Treaty between Italy and Ethiopia (see Chapter 10), the French and Malagasy versions of this treaty differed. The Malagasy considered that they had maintained their independence; the French thought that they had secured control over the external affairs of the island and had thereby set up a protectorate over it. As in the case of Ethiopia, the misunderstandings arising out of this treaty led to increased friction between France and the kingdom of Imerina.

EIGHT. Southern Africa, 1800–1885

The Conflict between Boer and Bantu

In tropical Africa, the basis for the early meetings between Africans and people from the rest of the world was trade. In South Africa, such encounters were usually over land. In tropical Africa, European and African merchants, even those engaged in the wretched slave trade, met on an essentially equal footing. They treated each other with a mixture of suspicion and respect. Europeans and Arabs were careful to acknowledge the authority of African rulers and to pay attention to the manners and customs of African peoples. In South Africa, the Europeans were present from the beginning not as traders, but as settlers. As their numbers grew and as they pushed inland from their first foothold on the Cape peninsula, they cast envious eyes on the land of the local people. During the seventeenth and most of the eighteenth centuries, this land was occupied by the San hunters and by the Khoi herdsmen. Thereafter, it was the much more densely settled land of the Bantu, who were agriculturalists as well as pastoralists. The only way the Boers could gain possession of the fertile land of the eastern Cape province was by conquest. Such a conquest might take the form of a party of frontier farmers, on horseback and armed with their hunting rifles, driving out the inhabitants of a nearby San or Khoi encampment or Bantu village. Or it might be carried out by the official forces of the colony, involved in a frontier war which was the consequence of the raids and counter-raids of Dutch and African farmers. Naturally, the conquerors felt superior to the conquered, and justified their actions on the grounds of their superiority.

The Boers' feeling of superiority is illustrated in an English traveller's account of a frontier farmer who was flogged and imprisoned by the British military authorities in 1798 for ill-treating a Khoi servant:

For the whole of the first night his lamentations were incessant; with a loud voice be cried, 'Myn God! is dat een maniere om Christian mensch te handelen'. (My God, is this the way to treat a Christian man.) His, however, were not the agonies of bodily pain, but the burst of rage and resentment on being put on a level with one of the Zwarte Natie [Black Natives], between whom and themselves the Boers conceive the differences to be fully as great as between themselves and their cattle.[1]

Here, we have the origins of the race attitudes characteristic of South Africa.

We have seen (in Chapter 2) that during the first thirty or so years after the Boers and Bantu met on what came to be known as the Eastern Frontier of the Cape Colony in the 1770s, a solution to the conflicts arising out of cattle-stealing and demands for more land might have been found if the two groups had been kept apart. An agreement to halt further expansion and the creation of a frontier properly defended by soldiers, like those which exist between modern states, might still have been possible. After the first or second decade of the nineteenth century, no solution along these lines had any real chance of success. The demands of people on both sides of the frontier for land could not be satisfied. The struggle for control of the land of southern Africa had to be fought out until one side or the other emerged as victor.

Shaka and the Zulu Nation

When the first clashes between white and black people took place along the Fish River, the population of the Nguni-speaking Bantu was increasing like that of the Boers. On the Bantu side of the frontier, there was less and less available land on which people could live

---

[1] Sir J. Barrow, *An Account of Travels into the Interior of Southern Africa in the Years 1797 and 1798* (London, 1801), vol. I, p. 398.

and graze their cattle. Cattle, which required a large area of pasture, were essential in the lives of the South African Bantu: they were the outward sign of their wealth and power, and no man could marry without handing over cattle to his bride's family. In earlier times, this pressure of man and beast upon the land would have been met by further expansion along the coast in a south-westerly direction, at the expense of the more thinly settled Khoi of the western Cape. This line of expansion was now blocked by the Boer farmers, who, as we have seen, were also hungry for fresh land. Thus, any Bantu people seeking to enlarge their territory could do so only at the expense of their neighbours, using military means. In the early years of the nineteenth century, two groups at the northern end of the Nguni country, the Swazi and the Zulu, militarised their social structure and embarked upon careers of conquest, with the result that most of South Africa was plunged into a period of destruction and violence known to Africans as the Time of Troubles (Sotho: *difaqane*; Zulu: *mfecane*.)

The Zulu were originally a small clan living in the territory of one of the Nguni rulers in Natal, Dingiswayo. Shaka, who was born in 1787, was one of the sons of the Zulu clan-chief. He quarrelled with his father and took refuge at the court of Dingiswayo, where he grew up to become a regimental commander. In 1816, after the death of his father, he was made chief of the Zulu clan by Dingiswayo. Two years later, Dingiswayo was murdered and Shaka took over the military empire that he had started to build up. Shaka proved to be a military leader of outstanding genius. He reformed the organisation, weapons, and tactics of Dingiswayo's *impi* (Zulu: regiments). The young warriors were formed into age regiments, and were not allowed to marry until they had completed their military service at the age of thirty, or even later. Adolphe Delegorgue, a French traveller in the 1830s, wrote of the transformation brought about by Shaka (the older spelling of his name was with 'Ch'):

Before Chaka, the Zulus wore sandals, and in their battles they hurled the *assagai* [Zulu: spear], as the Amakosa [Xhosa] still do. Above all, they charged in a mass, and without observing any orderly arrangement. Chaka formed regiments of a thousand men each. He did away with the sandal, in spite of the thorny nature of the vegetation, and ordered every warrior to take but one assagai, which was to be exhibited after a fight, stained by the blood of an enemy. The struggle could only be hand to hand. This new way of fighting, unknown to the neighbouring nations, greatly facilitated Chaka's conquests.[2]

Shaka experimented with the new assagai before making it the standard weapon of his impis; a trader, Henry Fynn, who first visited the great king in 1824, heard of the 'sham-combat' and recounted it in his diary, as an example of Shaka's thoroughness and of his ruthlessness:

Chaka disapproved of the custom of throwing the assagai. To substitute a different mode of attack, he assembled two divisions of his followers, who were ordered to supply themselves with a reed each from the river-bank, that he might be convinced of the effect which only one weapon would produce when used at close quarters. The two divisions then opposed each other, the one throwing their reeds, the other rushing on and stabbing their opponents. The result of this collision met with Chaka's entire satisfaction; few in the first division escaped being wounded, and several severely. Chaka then ordered six oxen to be slaughtered, and collecting the assagais of his followers, he ordered the shafts to be broken and used in cooking the meat. The prime parts were given, hot, to those who had been conspicuous for courage: the inferior parts, after being soaked in cold water, were given to those who had been seen to shrink in the combat.[3]

Shaka's impi, which in battle encircled the enemy like the horns of a buffalo, were so effective and so highly disciplined that they proved almost irresistible. The neighbouring Nguni chiefs were defeated and their lands used by the Zulu for grazing cattle. Many of the young men and women, however, were incorporated into the Zulu nation, which under Shaka and his successor Dingane, who murdered his royal brother in 1828, came to dominate most of the area of modern Natal. As we shall see, it was the existence of this aggressive and rapidly expanding kingdom in the rear of the Cape Colony's eastern frontier which made the policy of separation along the line of an agreed and stabilised frontier impossible to carry out.

The Time of Troubles: Mohesh and the Basuto

The indirect effects of the Zulu expansion were felt throughout southern Africa. In the hope of escaping from Shaka and his impi, fugitives from Natal streamed across the Drakensberg mountains. To find

[2] *Voyage dans l'Afrique australe* (Paris, 1847), vol. 2, p. 218.
[3] *The Diary of Henry Francis Fynn*, ed. J. Stuart and D. McK. Malcolm (Pietermaritzburg, 1950), p. 283.

room to settle, they had to become conquerors themselves, imitating the Zulu methods of fighting. Under their impact, the Sotho–Tswana peoples of the highveld clashed upon one another like an avalanche of stones rolling down a hillside. Thousands of displaced people wandered over the veld or sought refuge in the mountains. Some were driven out by famine to live by violence and pillage, and set out like the Zulu on campaigns of conquest. The brunt of the invaders' onset was borne by the Batlokwa, who were ruled by a redoubtable chieftainess called Mantatisi and later by her son, Sikonyela. Assimilating many of the refugees from Natal, Sotho peoples struck out against the Sotho–Tswana peoples of the western Transvaal and Botswana and threw them into utter disorder. Only after the middle of the century did the various Tswana peoples, such as the Bakhatla and the Bamangwato, reemerge as stable chiefdoms. One Sotho group, the Bafokeng or Makololo, were driven northwards by Mantatisi. Their leader, Sebetwane, is said to have appealed to his people in 1823 in the following words:

My masters, you see that the world is tumbling about our ears. We and other peoples have been driven from our ancestral homes, our cattle seized, our brothers and sons killed, our wives and daughters ravished, our children starved. War has been forced upon us, tribe against tribe. We shall be eaten up one by one. Our fathers taught us *Khotso ke nala* – peace is prosperity – but today there is no peace, no prosperity! What are we to do? My masters, this is my word: Let us march! Let us take our wives and children and cattle, and go forth to seek some land where we may dwell in tranquillity.[4]

Thereupon he led the Makololo northwards, in a running struggle with their great enemies, the Ndebele, to the east of them. Finally, about 1840, they settled on the upper Zambezi, after having overcome the Lozi people of the Barotse kingdom and made them their subjects. Their rule over the Barotse lasted only some twenty years, but this was time enough for their Sotho language to become the language of Barotseland.

In two other areas, refugees from the Mfecane were gathered together by very able chiefs who merged them into new nations strong enough to withstand pressure from the Zulu and, later on, even from

---

[4] Quoted in Edwin W. Smith, *Great Lion of Bechuanaland: The Life and Times of Roger Price* (London, 1957), p. 367.

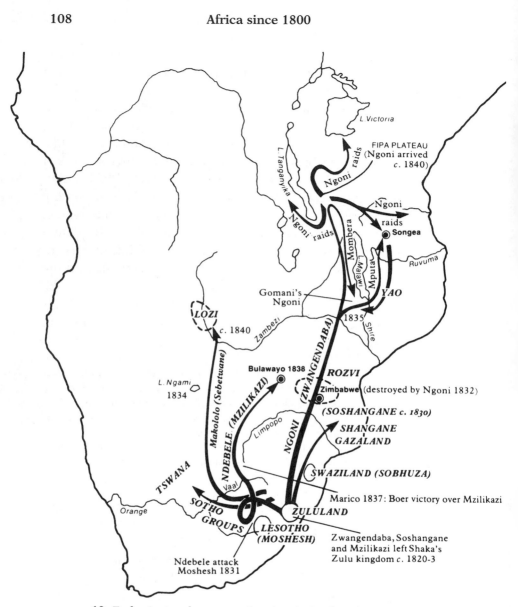

12. Early nineteenth-century migrations in South and East Africa.

the Europeans. One of these was the Swazi kingdom, created by Sobhuza and his successor Mswazi. The other was Lesotho. The creation of this kingdom was the life's work of Moshesh, one of the greatest leaders southern Africa has known. His character and the steps he took to build Lesotho were described by Eugène Casalis, the French

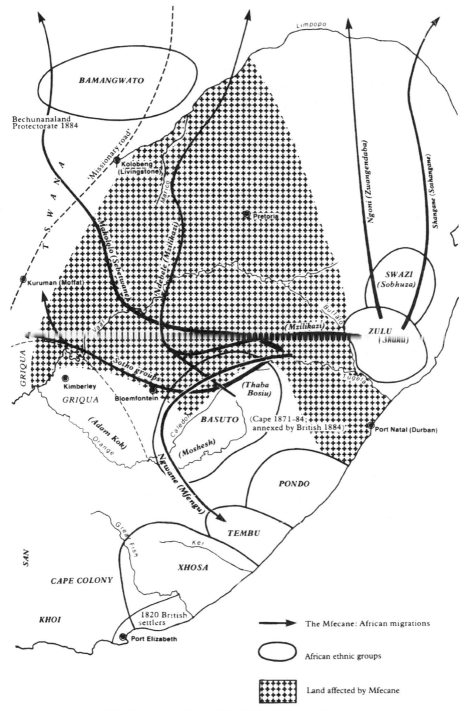

13. Southern Africa, 1800–1885: African migrations.

missionary who first entered the country in 1833 and who spent
many years as Moshesh's adviser on 'foreign affairs'. Casalis wrote
of Moshesh in the rather pompous language characteristic of many
Europeans at that time: 'Moshesh has an agreeable and interesting
countenance, his deportment is noble and dignified, his features be-
speak habits of reflection and of command, and a benevolent smile
plays upon his lips.' Casalis was told of the peaceful times before the
Mfecane:

At the time of Moshesh's birth (about 1790) the country of Basutos was extremely
populous. Disputes arose from time to time between the various communities,
but generally little blood was shed. The green pastures of Butobute, Moshesh's
home, and the steep hills where he and his companions hunted, are still celebrated in the national songs of the Basuto. At the moment when it was least
expected, these favourite sports were suddenly interrupted by disastrous invasions from Natal. Desolation was carried into the peaceful valleys of Lesuto,
fields remained uncultivated, and the horrors of famine were added to those of
war. Nearly all the influential men in the country were swept away by the tide
of war. Moshesh breasted the stream. Being of a very observant disposition, he
knew how to resist and how to yield at the right moment; procured himself allies,
even among the invaders of his territory; set his enemies at variance with each
other, and by various acts of kindness secured the respect of those even who had
sworn his ruin.[5]

In their struggles against both Zulu and Boers, the Basuto were aided
by the mountains of their country, which provided them with defen-
sive positions almost impregnable even by troops armed with rifles.
Moshesh's great tactical and diplomatic skill, which enabled the Basuto to exercise an influence quite out of proportion to their numbers
and military strength, is shown in the way he treated the Zulu off-
shoot called the Ndebele after they had failed to capture his mountain
fortress of Thaba Bosiu in 1831:

Accustomed to victory, the Zulus advanced in serried ranks, not appearing to
notice the masses of basalt which came rolling down with a tremendous noise
from the top of the mountain. But soon there was a general crush – an avalanche
of stones and a shower of spears, which sent back the assailants with more
rapidity than they had advanced. The chiefs who were seen rallying the fugitives,
and snatching away the plumes with which their heads were decorated, and
trampling them under foot in a rage, led their men again towards the formidable
rampart. But in vain. The next day the Zulus retired. At the moment of their

5 Eugène Casalis, *The Basutos* (1861) (Cape Town, 1965), pp. 15–16.

departure a Mosuto, driving some fat oxen, stopped before the first ranks, and gave this message. 'Moshesh salutes you. Supposing that hunger had brought you into this country, he sends you these cattle, that you may eat them on your way home.' Moshesh was never troubled by these people again.[6]

Some Zulu groups, whose leaders had quarrelled with Shaka, left Zululand to make their own conquests elsewhere. Soshangane took his people, the Shangane, into Gazaland in southern Mozambique, where they conquered and largely absorbed the Tsonga, who were the earlier inhabitants of that region. Next, Zwangendaba and his warriors swept northwards across the Limpopo and on to the Zimbabwean plateau, where they destroyed the old Rozvi kingdom of the Changamires, the rulers of the western plateau. Before long, however, Zwangendaba and his 'Ngoni' moved on, to settle finally in the highlands east and west of Lake Malawi. Some of the farthest-flung of these Ngoni impi, always gathering fresh recruits from the peoples they defeated, campaigned as far north as the southern shores of Lake Victoria and as far east as the Indian Ocean. As we saw in Chapter 7, they had a considerable effect on events in East Africa. Lastly, Mzilikazi led his Ndebele (Sotho: Matebele) Zulu across the Drakensberg and on to the highveld, in the wake of Mantatisi and Sebetwane's Sotho groups, until they were defeated near modern Pretoria by the invading Boers in 1837. The Ndebele then retreated north across the Limpopo and settled on the western part of the Zimbabwean plateau (Matabeleland), making many of the local Shona people, the former subjects of the Rozvi kingdom, into their tribute-paying subjects.

The Expansion of the Boers: The Great Trek

Refugees also fled from the Zulu armies into the eastern Cape Colony, increasing the frontier conflicts with the Dutch farmers, whose numbers were increased by 5,000 British settlers in 1820. The lawlessness on the frontier and the rough treatment by the Boers of their semi-servile labourers shocked the humanitarians and missionary societies in Britain. During the early years of the nineteenth century, these groups forced the British government to adopt a more

---

[6] Ibid., p. 63.

responsible concern for the non-white peoples of the British empire. The most outspoken of the Christian missionaries in South Africa was John Philip of the London Missionary Society. Mainly through his efforts, the Khoi and San of the Cape Colony were brought under the protection of the law in 1828. Later, after the abolition of slavery in 1833, he extended his campaign to include the former slaves. In the eyes of the Boers, the British government was more concerned with giving legal protection to their servants than with helping them to expand at the expense of the Nguni tribes. Every Dutch farmer's son considered it his birthright to possess a 6,000-acre ranch when he got married, and in this wasteful way the available land within the colony's borders was soon exhausted. In 1836, a large area of land on the eastern frontier, which had previously been annexed to the colony was returned to the Africans because the British government was not prepared to meet the expense of administering it. This was more than the Boers would endure, and many trekked (*trek*, Dutch: a journey, a migration) out of British territory and across the Orange River to the north. Anna Steenkamp, the sister of one of the leaders of the Great Trek, gave as one of their reasons for leaving the Cape

The shameful and unjust proceedings with reference to the freedom of our slaves: and yet it is not so much their freedom that drove us to such lengths as their being placed on an equal footing with Christians, contrary to the laws of God and the natural distinction of race and religion, so that it was intolerable for any decent Christian to bow down beneath such a yoke; wherefore we rather withdrew in order thus to preserve our doctrines in purity.[7]

Livingstone later commented: 'The Boers determined to erect themselves into a republic, in which they might pursue without molestation the "proper treatment of the blacks". This "proper treatment" has always contained the element of compulsory unpaid labour'.[8]

The Trekkers had learned from hunters and traders that fertile parts of Natal had been virtually depopulated by the Zulu and turned into grazing lands. They planned to infiltrate the Zulu lands by moving across the Transvaal and descending through the Drakensberg passes into Natal. By this means, they hoped to outflank the densely settled Nguni between the Fish River and Natal. At first, the

---

[7] Quoted in John Bird, *Annals of Natal* (Pietermaritzburg, 1888), vol. I, p. 459.
[8] *Missionary Travels and Researches in South Africa* (London, 1857), p. 29.

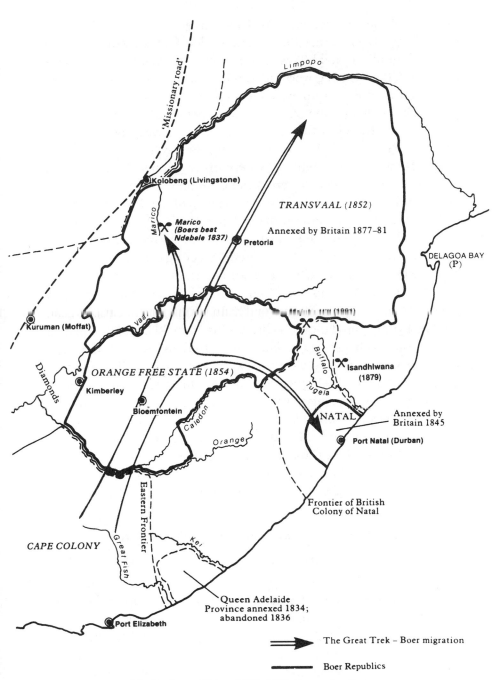

'Missionary road'

Limpopo

Kolobeng (Livingstone)

Marico

Marico
(Boers beat
Ndebele 1837)

Pretoria

TRANSVAAL (1852)

Annexed by Britain 1877–81

DELAGOA BAY
(P)

Vaal

Kuruman (Moffat)

Majuba Hill (1881)

Buffalo

Tugela

ORANGE FREE STATE (1854)

Diamonds

Kimberley

Bloemfontein

Caledon

Orange

Isandhlwana
(1879)

NATAL

Annexed by
Britain 1845

Port Natal (Durban)

Eastern Frontier

Great Fish

Kei

Frontier of British
Colony of Natal

CAPE COLONY

Queen Adelaide
Province annexed 1834;
abandoned 1836

Port Elizabeth

⟹ The Great Trek – Boer migration

▬▬ Boer Republics

14. Southern Africa, 1800–1885: Boer migrations.

Zulu king Dingane successfully resisted this encroachment. By 1839, however, the Boers under Pretorius had defeated the Zulu and had set up a republic in Natal. This action brought them into conflict once again with the British government, which would not allow the existence of a rival European state on the shores of the Indian Ocean. It also rightly feared the effects of Boer penetration into Natal on the encircled Nguni of the eastern Cape. Natal was, therefore, annexed by Britain in 1845. Frustrated in this way, most of the Natal Boers returned to the highveld, where other groups of farmers had already driven the Ndebele across the Limpopo. The British government half-heartedly followed the Boers north of the Orange river but, in 1852 and 1854, recognised the independence of, respectively, the Boer republics of the Transvaal and the Orange Free State.

In the middle years of the nineteenth century, therefore, South Africa consisted of two British colonies, the Cape and Natal; the two Boer republics; and many independent African kingdoms and chiefdoms, of which the Basuto and Zulu kingdoms were the largest. The total white population was little more than 300,000; the African population was between 1 million and 2 million. In 1853, the Cape Colony was granted a constitution with an elected parliament and, in 1872, full internal self-government, with ministers responsible to parliament. The franchise was non-racial; that is, representatives were elected by people of all races, provided they owned property of a certain value or received a certain amount in wages. This liberal political attitude of the Cape was not shared by the other Europeans in South Africa. In the Boer republics, only white people were recognised as citizens, and only white males exercised the vote.

The End of the Independent African States

The discovery of great diamond deposits near the junction of the Orange and Vaal Rivers in 1868 hastened the inevitable process whereby the self-governing African peoples and states lost their independence and were brought under European rule. Already in 1856–7, the situation had seemed so desperate to the Xhosa and Tembu living immediately to the east of the Cape Colony that they followed the prophecy of a girl, Nongquase. She stated that if, on a certain day, the cattle were killed and the grain destroyed, the tribal ancestors would drive the Europeans into the sea. The result, of course, was a disastrous famine, in which thousands died, while thousands more abandoned their land and went to seek work and food in the Cape. The opening of the diamond mines greatly increased the demand for labour, and Africans converged upon Kimberley from all over southern Africa. In the early days of the mining, the companies regularly paid these workers in guns and ammunition, and so thousands of Africans returned to their homes with firearms. This led to exaggerated fears on the European side of a 'united native rising'. Fortunately for the white men in South Africa, the wars that did break out were no such thing, but they were extremely destructive because Africans as well as Europeans were using firearms.

In 1871, the Cape government assumed control over the Basuto, who had been involved in a bitter land struggle with the Free State farmers. Next, in 1877–8, it finally broke the fighting power of the Xhosa and other Nguni tribes on the eastern frontier – though at a great cost in men and money. Again, in 1877, the British government took over the Transvaal, where the forces of a poverty-stricken Boer government could make no headway in the war which had broken out against the Bapedi under their chief Sekukuni. This involved the British (who in Natal had been friendly with the Zulu) in a quarrel between the Transvaal Boers and Cetshwayo, the nephew and successor of Dingane, over an area of grazing land. Cetshwayo was now provoked by Sir Bartle Frere, the British high commissioner in South Africa, to armed conflict. The Zulu defeated one British army at Isandhlwana before being crushed by the reinforcements which the British hurriedly sent into Natal. The following year – 1880 – saw the outbreak of a long war between the Cape government and the Basuto, sparked off by an attempt to disarm the Africans. The Cape had to be rescued from this disastrous war in 1884, when the British government took over direct responsibility for administering Basutoland. These were not the only troubles. Whites were also involved in clashes with some of the Tswana tribes and with the Korana (Khoi) people on the lower Orange River. In South-West Africa, the mutual enmity of the Herero (Bantu) and Nama (Khoi) peoples, both pastoralists in a dry land, was inflamed by the activities of European traders, who took sides in their disputes and supplied them with both firearms and liquor.

Just before the outbreak of all these wars and while they were in progress, attempts were made – in Britain by the colonial secretary, Lord Carnarvon, and in the Cape by Frere – to unite the white states in South Africa into a single large territory under one government. By the end of the 1870s, this attempt at confederation had failed. The Boers in the Orange Free State had never forgiven the British annexation of the diamond-bearing district of Griqualand West in 1871. At the end of 1880, the Transvaalers rose against the government imposed upon them by Britain three years previously, and in 1881 defeated a British force sent to put them down in an action at Majuba Hill.

The Road to the North

Much of the hostility between the British government and the Boers was due to the presence of the Christian missionaries, whose activities among the Africans were regarded by the Boers with great suspicion. Missions were well established within the colonial borders of the Cape and Natal, though they could make little headway among the still independent and warlike Nguni peoples, especially the Zulu and the Ndebele. They were more influential among the Sotho and Tswana groups, however. The Paris Missionary Society established a close relationship with Moshesh, as we have seen, and – although neither he nor his successor was converted – many thousands of the Basuto became literate and Christian. Robert Moffat of the London Missionary Society had worked among the Griqua (a group of mixed Khoi and European descent) and Tswana peoples at Kuruman, beyond the northern frontier of the Cape, since the 1820s. Here, Boer encroachment upon Tswana lands during and after the Great Trek added to the dislike of the missionaries for the Transvaal government and made them determined to keep open a way to the north which was free from Boer control. Livingstone began his career in Africa as a missionary and explorer, working to open up this 'missionary road' – the narrow strip of habitable Botswana between the Transvaal and Kalahari desert, which led northwards to Matabeleland and Barotseland. Through Livingstone's great journey from Barotseland to Luanda and from there across Africa to the Zambezi mouth (1853–6), European governments, traders, and missionaries were made aware of the possibilities for Christianity and commerce in the lands north of the Limpopo. The British government, in particular, realised the vital importance of the 'missionary road' between South Africa and the interior. As soon as the Germans annexed the South-West African coast in 1883, the British replied by declaring a protectorate over Botswana (known during the colonial period as Bechuanaland). This paved the way for Rhodes's occupation of Zimbabwe a few years later.

NINE. The Partition of Africa on Paper, 1879–1891

European Trading Interests in Africa before Partition

During the last quarter of the nineteenth century, events took place which changed the face of Africa and which can only be understood by tracing their origin and development outside Africa. In 1879, more than 90 percent of the continent was ruled by Africans. By 1900, all but a tiny fraction of it was being governed by European powers. By about 1914, the lives of almost all Africans were being deeply affected by the changes brought about by these foreign rulers. The European powers partitioned Africa among themselves with such haste, like players in a rough game, that the process has been called 'the scramble for Africa'. The motives for this partition, the reason why the European powers acted as they did, and when they did, are a part of European history rather than African history, and it is to these European affairs that we must now turn our attention.

We have to remember, first of all, that throughout the first sixty-five years of the nineteenth century, the only great powers in western Europe were Britain and France. Germany and Italy did not yet exist as separate and unified states. Of the lesser powers, Holland and Denmark actually abandoned their African possessions (trading posts on the Gold Coast) during the nineteenth century, leaving only Portugal as a minor competitor with France and Britain. We also have to remember that even France, despite its considerable military strength, lagged well behind Britain in the race for commercial and industrial development. Precisely because its manufactures were inferior or more expensive than those of Britain, France pursued a 'protectionist policy' – that is to say, it tried to reserve the trade of French colonies for its own merchants. In the Senegal from 1815, and from the 1840s in Guinea, the Ivory Coast, Dahomey, Gabon, and Madagascar, there were, therefore, French naval and commercial bases from which non-French traders were kept out. These areas were, however, quite small. In the British possessions, the same customs dues were charged to British and foreign traders alike. In fact, traders of all nations did the largest part of their business in Africa on stretches of the coast over which no European flag yet flew. So long as most of the trade was carried on near the coast, and so long as most of the coastline was free to all comers, Britain, at least, had no economic motive to annex large territories in Africa. Even France found that its protected settlements were more of a financial burden than they were worth.

The Development of Anglo-French Rivalry in West Africa

By the 1870s, however, a new situation was beginning to develop in West Africa. The trade was no longer exclusively a coastal trade. At the few key points where railways or river steamships could be introduced, European trade was starting to penetrate the interior. The French were thrusting deep into the Senegal valley, and it was known that their objective was to connect the Senegal and the upper Niger by a railway, which would attract the trade of a great part of the West African interior into French hands. Here was a development which must affect the British trading posts on the Gambia and which might in time affect the trade routes leading to Sierra Leone and the Gold Coast. Again, on the lower Niger, the penetration of the interior markets by British firms trading upriver in their own steamers had reached a stage at which, to go farther, it was necessary for them to come together and form a single company with a monopoly over the trade. Only by this means could the essential installations be afforded and a united front be maintained in dealing with the powerful Fulbe emirates of the interior. By 1879, George Goldie amalgamated the British firms trading up the Niger River, only to find himself facing competition from French traders. This he dealt with in a characteristically ruthless fashion by undercutting their prices at a loss to himself and so forcing them to sell out their interests to his own company. Thus, the French were left feeling that, for the future at least, their commercial companies must be given political support.

The Entry of New Powers

Already, in the early 1870s, Britain and France had considered partitioning West Africa into 'spheres of influence', in each of which only the firms of one country would be allowed to trade. It had been suggested by the French that the Gambia should be given to France in exchange for British control over the coastline from Sierra Leone to Mount Cameroun. The scheme had fallen through in 1875, but, had it not been for the intervention of other European powers, it would probably have been revived in the 1880s so as to leave the French in control of the upper Niger and the waterways leading to the Upper Guinea coast, and the British in control of the lower Niger and the coastlands of Lower Guinea. In the early 1880s, however, the slow movement towards an Anglo–French partition of West Africa, arising from the commercial penetration of the interior, was both speeded up and complicated by the appearance on the African scene of two new European powers which had not previously shown any great interest in Africa. The result of these interventions was to force all the European powers, including France and Britain, to look far beyond their immediate economic needs. What each power feared was that its rivals would keep the trade of their new colonies to themselves by enclosing them within high tariff (or customs) barriers. Therefore, each power felt compelled to enter the scramble for territory in order to reserve the largest possible sphere for its own future activities.

King Leopold and the Congo

The first of these newcomers was an individual rather than a nation state. It was Leopold II, King of Belgium, a little country situated uncomfortably between the European giants, France and Germany. The Belgian people did not share the expansionist dreams of their ruler. As early as 1861, Leopold had written, 'The sea bathes our coast, the world lies before us. Steam and electricity have annihilated

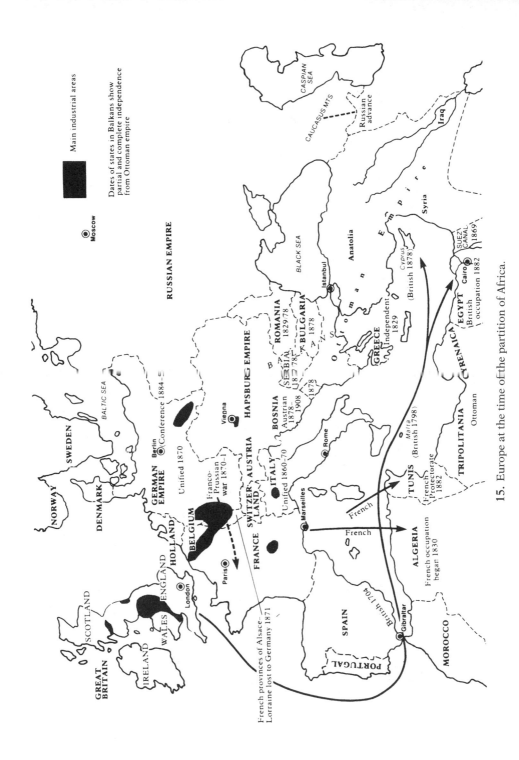

15. Europe at the time of the partition of Africa.

distance. All the non-appropriated lands on the surface of the globe (mostly in Africa) can become the field of our operations and our success'. Leopold was a master diplomat, a man of boundless ambition and, in his younger days, he had a genuine idealism – a belief in human progress and in the need to improve the conditions of less privileged peoples. As he grew older, his idealism was largely submerged by a growing love of wealth and power. As we saw in Chapter 6, Leopold's opportunity came when Stanley's schemes for the opening up of the Congo basin, which the explorer had formed after his descent of the river in 1877, were rejected by the British government. In 1879, Leopold took Stanley into his service. During the next four years, Stanley established road and river communications from the Congo estuary to Stanley Falls (Stanleyville, Kisangani). Leopold on the Congo, like Goldie on the Niger, was aiming at a commercial monopoly, which would attract all the trade of the Congo basin into his own river steamers and his own railway from Lake Malebo to the coast.

Leopold did not at this stage attempt to obtain treaties of sovereignty or legal possession from the African rulers of the lower Congo area. He relied on his own mastery of the lines of communication. The immediate effect of his operations, however, was to stimulate the competition of a rival French group, whose agent, Savorgnan de Brazza, returned to Europe in the summer of 1882 with a treaty signed by Makoko, chief of the Bateke country on the northern shores of Lake Malebo. This treaty placed his territory under French sovereignty. De Brazza toured France, stirring up imperialist sentiment so successfully that he persuaded the French government both to ratify his treaty with Makoko and to set in motion a large programme of treaty-making and annexation along the Nigerian coast. This, in turn, led the British government to join in the race for Nigerian territory and forced King Leopold to seek treaties granting sovereign rights in the lower Congo area. The scramble for West and Western Central Africa had thus begun in earnest.

Once he had started upon territorial annexation, King Leopold skilfully prepared the way for international recognition of his claim to rule the Congo basin. He persuaded the French government to support him by a secret promise that the territory should revert to France if he himself should prove unable to govern it. He also gained the support of the German chancellor, Bismarck, just at the moment when Germany herself was about to enter the colonial field. To English merchants, he held out tempting hopes of valuable contracts and, with their help, he broke down the British government's plan to bar his access to the Congo by recognising Portuguese claims of sovereignty over the river mouth. Finally, his American secretary, Sanford, persuaded the United States to join France and Germany in giving recognition to the Congo Free State.

Germany Enters the Scramble, 1883–1885

During the 1850s and 1860s, a great political and economic revolution had taken place in Germany, in which most of the independent states whose peoples spoke the German language became united around the north German state of Prussia, under the leadership of Bismarck. The basis of political unification was a customs union which enabled Germany to embark upon industrialisation. This combination of political amalgamation or unification and modern industrial growth resulted in the emergence of a great power in Europe. By the 1870s, the new Germany was able to rival France militarily and Britain industrially. The former rivalry led to the Franco–Prussian war of 1870–1, in which France was overwhelmed and lost the frontier provinces of Alsace and Lorraine to Germany. In both France and Germany, some political groups turned from this war to thoughts of colonial expansion: the French as a form of compensation for the humiliation of defeat, the Germans out of the realisation of newfound strength. For a long time yet, Bismarck personally refused to take any outward interest in the colonial question. It was left to merchant groups in the northern German ports to stir up a national demand for colonies. These groups succeeded so well, however, that from 1883 to 1885, Bismarck – suddenly changing his attitude – was able to take the diplomats of Europe by surprise in declaring German protectorates in four widely scattered parts of Africa–Togo: Cameroun (known to the Germans as Kamerun), East Africa, and South-West Africa.

Germany's bid for colonies was not based on any substantial interest that had built up in Africa beforehand. It was a simple assertion of her new position among the world powers. There is much truth in

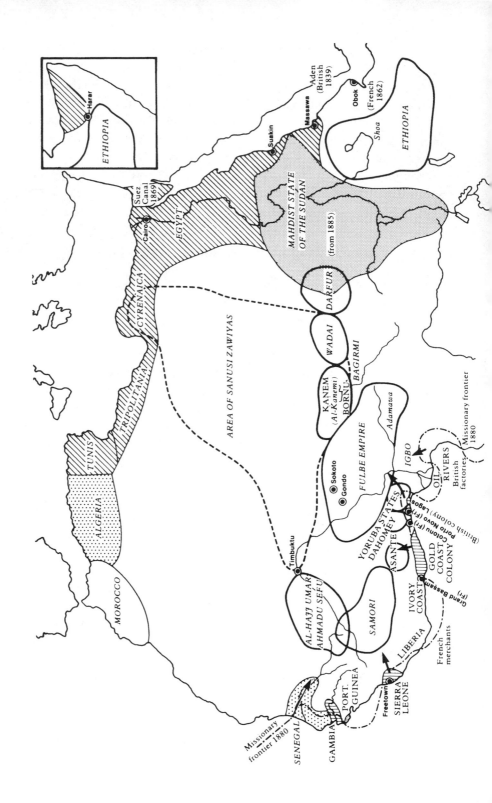

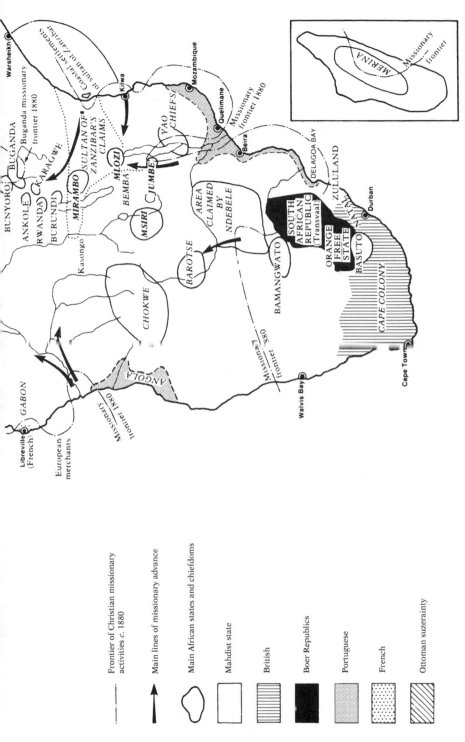

16. Africa on the eve of partition: African states and European settlements.

Frontier of Christian missionary
activities c. 1880

Main lines of missionary advance

Main African states and chiefdoms

Mahdist state

British

Boer Republics

Portuguese

French

Ottoman suzerainty

the view that Bismarck himself took part in the scramble mainly in order to dominate the international politics of the European powers which were connected with it. He wanted to turn French ambitions away from the recovery of her lost provinces, and the best way to do so was to involve her in rivalries with other powers for overseas territories. He, therefore, supported French claims in West Africa and the Congo basin and made his own African annexations in places which would threaten British claims rather than French ones.

It was now that Britain's peculiar position in Egypt became of such vital significance in the diplomacy of partition. The British occupation of Egypt, it will be remembered (see Chapter 3), had been planned as a joint Anglo–French operation to crush Urabi Pasha's revolt and to restore the authority of Khedive Tawfiq. It was originally intended to be only a temporary intervention and, therefore, nothing was done to alter the control of Egypt's finances by the International Debt Commission. British rule in Egypt was thus dependent at every turn on the goodwill of the commission, on which, since French opposition to the continued British occupation was certain, the German vote was of the utmost importance. Bismarck, throughout the vital years of the participation, supported British rule in Egypt. His price was British acceptance of Germany's new annexations and of his support of the claims of France and King Leopold to the north and south of the lower Congo.

It was Bismarck, therefore, who dominated the first round of the scramble, which came to an end at the Berlin Conference (1884–5). The conference prepared the way for newcomers to the African scene by requiring that claims to colonies or protectorates on any part of the African coastline should be formally notified to the other powers taking part in the conference, and by insisting that such claims must be backed by the establishment of an effective degree of authority in the areas concerned. This put an end to the British idea of informal empire. The conference also decreed that there should be freedom of navigation on the Niger and the Congo – thus, in theory frustrating British attempts to close the Niger against the French and the Congo against King Leopold. The years 1883–5, therefore, saw Britain checked, surprised, or forestalled in one part of Africa after another. The former large sphere of British influence in Lower Guinea was now broken up by a French protectorate in Dahomey

(Bénin) and two German protectorates in Togo and Cameroun. The Congo and the Gabon coast, where British trade had flourished for so long, was divided between France and King Leopold. The unity of the southern African coastal regions, so long dominated by Britain, was broken by a German protectorate in the south-west. The Merina kingdom on Madagascar had signed a treaty with France, despite the fact that British missionary influence had been an outstanding feature in the island since the 1830s. And the old area of informal empire exercised through the sultan of Zanzibar in East Africa was shattered by the German annexations in the interior from Dar es Salaam. As bases from which Britain could build afresh, there remained only Egypt, the scattered possessions in West Africa, and the self-governing Cape Colony and Natal in the south.

Lord Salisbury and the Restoration of British Initiative, 1885–1891

The revival of British fortunes in Africa, and their conversion to the new conditions of formal as opposed to informal empire, was largely the work of Lord Salisbury. Salisbury was prime minister of Britain from 1885 to 1892, and rivalled even Bismarck as a master of diplomacy. His first act was to open a way for northward expansion from the Cape Colony by declaring a protectorate over Bechuanaland (now Botswana), the primarily desert area between German South-West Africa and the independent Boer republic of the Transvaal (then known as the South African Republic). This action was to gain increased significance from the discovery in the following year (1886) of the vast gold deposits of the Witwatersrand in the Transvaal. Although these were in Boer territory, the exploiters were nearly all English-speaking capitalists from the Cape Colony and from Britain itself. These British exploiters were led by Cecil Rhodes, who had already made a fortune in the diamonds of Kimberley. He shared the common belief that 'a second Rand' would be found in the highlands north of the Limpopo River, and was determined that Britain should control this potentially rich area. Bechuanaland was his 'Suez Canal to the North', up which in 1890 there travelled the 'pioneer column' of white settlers who occupied Southern Rhodesia (now Zimbabwe). Salisbury disliked and distrusted Rhodes, but he was prepared to use

his great wealth and energy to help carve out a belt of British territories in the highlands between the Portuguese colonies of Angola
and Mozambique.

Salisbury's second action was to rescue for Britain what remained
of East Africa after the German annexations of 1884. In 1886, he
negotiated with Bismarck a division of the area into two 'spheres
of influence', following the present boundary between Kenya and
Tanzania. In 1890, by ceding to Germany the North Sea island of
Heligoland, he persuaded Bismarck to sign a comprehensive series
of boundary agreements, under which Germany recognised British
claims to Zanzibar, Kenya, Uganda, Northern Rhodesia (now Zambia), Bechuanaland, and eastern Nigeria. In the same year, Salisbury
concluded a treaty with France in respect of the western boundary
of Nigeria, in return for British recognition of the French protectorate over Madagascar (which the rulers of the island did not acknowledge), and in 1891 an agreement with Portugal in respect of
Nyasaland (now Malawi) and the two Rhodesias.

Thus, by the end of Salisbury's period of office in 1892, although
many interior boundaries remained to be drawn, the broad outlines
of the European partition of Africa had been sketched out. The cornerstone of Salisbury's African policy was the continued British occupation of Egypt. As he himself recognised, the consequence was
that Britain should give way to French claims for the predominant
place in West Africa. German claims, too, had to be admitted in
the four regions where they had been staked. The British West-
African possessions were confined to a modest extension from the
pre-partition footholds. The main British share in the partition had
to be found in a northward expansion of British South Africa through
Bechuanaland to the Rhodesias and Nyasaland, and in a slice of East
Africa stretching from Mombasa to the upper Nile. Salisbury realised
that Egypt, with British help, would soon be strong enough to undertake the reconquest of the Sudan from the Khalifa and that the
final extension of British power would take place in this direction.
Salisbury admitted in a memorandum to the British cabinet that the
slogan 'all British from the Cape to Cairo' was a rough expression of
his African policy as a whole.

It is important to remember that the outline partition accomplished by 1891 was, in large measure, a partition which existed only on paper. Despite the insistence of the Berlin Conference that claims to African coastlines must be supported by effective occupation, most of the claims recognised by the powers were, in fact, based on a few scraps of paper obtained by consuls and concession-hunters from African chiefs who had very little idea of what they were doing and whose authority usually extended over only a very small part of the areas claimed. There was not a single territory in Africa where anything like effective occupation existed at the time of the partition. The final division of territories reflected not so much the strength of European interests on the ground as the political power of the claimants in Europe. The partition was nevertheless important. It represented the deliberate intention of powerful European states to carry their influence into the innermost parts of Africa, as they had already done in much of Asia, in the Americas, and in Australasia. No one could doubt that they had the necessary power. The fact that they acted with so large a measure of mutual agreement that the partition did not cause an outbreak of war between them was probably of benefit to Africa as well as to themselves.

TEN. The Partition of Africa on the Ground, 1891–1901

European Conflicts in Africa

The first stages of the partition, when European states were laying claim to coastal regions and navigable rivers and were defining on paper the boundaries running inland from these first footholds, were accomplished with surprisingly little bloodshed and conflict. The reason for this was that very small numbers of European forces were used in Africa during this time. The first occupying groups consisted of small, mobile expeditions of European officers or chartered-company officials, accompanied by a few dozen lightly armed porters, scarcely distinguishable from the expeditions of the first explorers. Africa itself was so immense that these first little groups of Europeans seldom came into contact with each other. Their attitude to the African peoples had necessarily to be that of negotiators rather than conquerors. They entered into the local politics of every region that they came to, supporting the groups and factions which had some reason to be friendly and avoiding those which were hostile. In the later stages of the scramble, however, toward the close of the nineteenth century when forces were somewhat larger and when the final, interior frontiers were being claimed, meetings between rival European expeditions became more frequent. Collisions occurred between the occupying forces and those of the larger and more organised African states, which often fought desperately for their survival. Numerically, the armies of these states often outnumbered the European expeditions by many hundreds to one, but the superiority of European weapons was overwhelming. A single machine gun could put to flight a whole army of undisciplined men armed only with ancient guns and spears. As it raced toward its conclusion, therefore, the scramble produced increasing bloodshed. At first there were small incidents in West Africa, in the Congo, and in East Africa. Then came the French 'pacifications' of Madagascar and Morocco, the war between Ethiopia and Italy, and the reconquest of the Sudan. Finally came the deadly struggle in South Africa, in which white fought white.

The French Advance down the Niger

After the Berlin Conference, the French took steps to consolidate their possessions on the West African coast. By 1893, the colonies of the Ivory Coast and French Guinea had been officially established. In the same year, French troops entered Dahomey (Bénin) and deposed Behanzin, the last independent king of Dahomey. Dahomey became a French colony in 1900. The main French expansion in West Africa, however, took place from the basin of the Senegal River. Here, by 1879, the French advance up the river had brought them into contact with the empire of Ahmadu Sefu, the son of al-Hajj Umar (see Chapter 5). Indecisive clashes between General Gallieni's Senegalese troops and Ahmadu's forces continued for many years, but Ahmadu's empire broke up once its military power had been destroyed. The French entered the upper Niger valley and captured Bamako in 1883. A more determined opposition to French penetration was put up by Samori, a Muslim Mandingo from the interior borderlands of Guinea and the Ivory Coast. In a series of conquests begun in the early 1870s, this warlord had succeeded in uniting under his rule most of the peoples in the vast area between the sources of the Niger and the upper Volta basin. Samori became the hero of the fiercely independent southern Mande peoples in his relentless opposition to the French. Although his homelands around Bissandugu were occupied in 1891, he was not finally defeated and exiled by the French until 1898.

Samori's resistance delayed, but could not halt, French penetration down the Niger. Timbuktu was taken in 1894 and Say in 1896. Beyond Say, the French advance was blocked by the British in Hausaland. Once in control of the upper and middle Niger, therefore, they

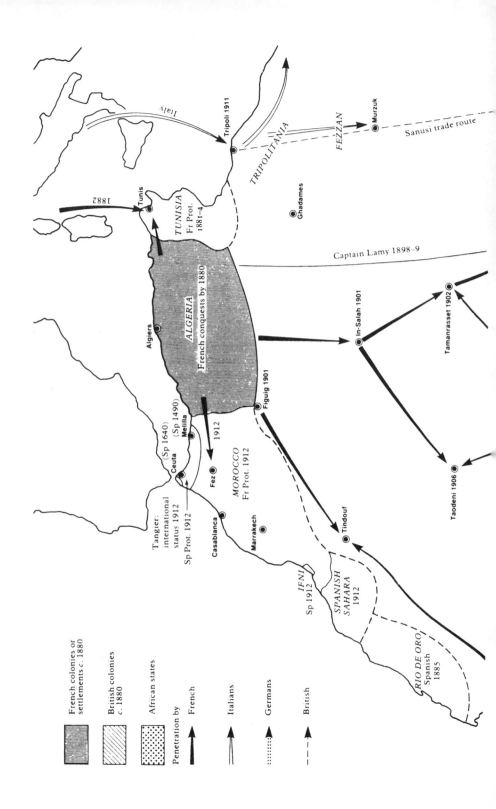

French colonies or settlements c. 1880

British colonies c. 1880

African states

Penetration by
French
Italians
Germans
British

Italy

1882

Tunis

TUNISIA
Fr Prot. 1881–4

Tripoli 1911

TRIPOLITANIA

FEZZAN

Murzuk

Sanusi trade route

Ghadames

Captain Lamy 1898–9

ALGERIA
French conquests by 1880

Algiers

In-Salah 1901

Tamanrasset 1902

Figuig 1901

1912

(Sp 1640)
(Sp 1490)
Ceuta
Melilla

Tangier:
international
status 1912

Fez

MOROCCO
Fr Prot. 1912

Sp Prot. 1912

Casablanca

Marrakech

Taodeni 1906

Tindouf

IFNI
Sp 1912

SPANISH
SAHARA
1912

RIO DE ORO
Spanish
1885

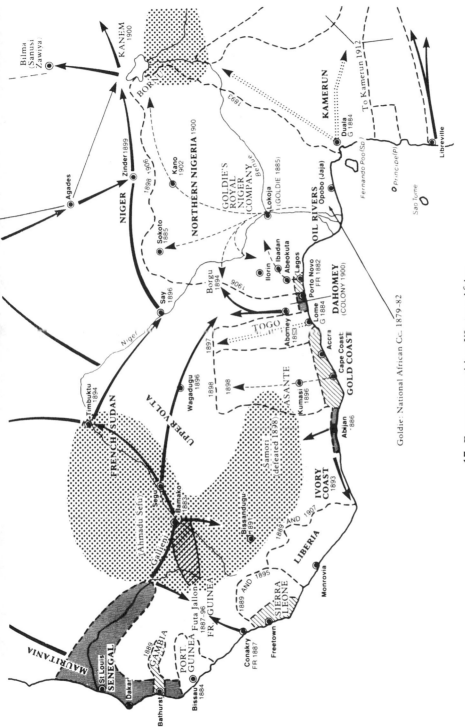

17. European partition: Western Africa.

turned their attention to filling in the gaps between the Niger valley and their possessions on the coast. This task was completed by the turn of the century. It was at this stage that frontier incidents with rival British expeditions in the Nigerian and Gold Coast interiors became frequent.

British Expansion in the Gold Coast and Nigeria

We have seen (Chapter 9) that Britain was prevented by the wider pattern of the diplomatic partition of Africa from pressing claims to a large consolidated area of West Africa. All it could do was to extend, by effective occupation on the ground, its existing footholds in Sierra Leone, the Gold Coast, and Nigeria. In the Gold Coast, the local situation depended on relations between the coastal 'colony' and the Asante empire, whose outlying dependencies were detached from their allegiance by treaty-making expeditions as a preliminary to the military occupation of Asante itself in 1896. In 1898, the Northern Territories, part of which had been tributary to Samori, were declared a protectorate in order to forestall expansion by the French from the north.

Britain's occupation of Nigeria was more complicated and took place from three different spheres. The first was from Lagos, where the small island colony expanded into a protectorate covering most of Yorubaland. The second was from the Oil Rivers, where British consuls supported the Liverpool firms in breaking the power of the African middleman chiefs like Jaja of Opobo as soon as the chiefs tried to make treaties with other European nations. The third was from Nupe and southern Hausaland. Here, Sir George Goldie's National African Company, which in 1886 became the Royal Niger Company, had powers under its Royal Charter to administer justice and maintain order. Goldie secured the friendship of much of Hausaland by a treaty made with the sultan of Sokoto in 1885. Nupe and the emirate of Ilorin, however, were invaded and overrun by the Royal Niger Company's army, the West African Frontier Force. Goldie's officers, notably Captain Lugard, were involved in incidents with the French, who were advancing down the Niger and up from the coast into Dahomey. Borgu was occupied only after a French expedition there had been forced to withdraw. These military operations against a rival European colonial power soon proved too expensive and too dangerous for a private company. In 1898, the British government brought the charter to an end, and two years later (1900) took over the control of northern Nigeria. British expansion continued in the direction of Bornu and Lake Chad. Kano was occupied in 1902.

The French in the Central Sudan: Rabih

The French moved into the central Sudan from three directions: from the Niger valley, from Gabon, and from Algeria. By about 1900, expeditions from all three were converging on Lake Chad. Goldie's Royal Niger Company prevented the French from occupying any but the northern desert fringes of Hausaland as they moved eastwards from Say on the Niger. In Gabon, the French government had begun to occupy the interior after the Berlin Conference and, by the late 1890s, was in a position to start pushing northwards towards the Shari River basin. Finally, in the wake of Captain Lamy's pioneer trans-Saharan expedition of 1898–9, the French began to occupy the principal oases: Tuat, Tamanrasset, Aïr, and Zinder. The nomadic Tuareg of the surrounding deserts, however, remained practically unaffected by the French presence until after the Second World War.

The final resistance to the French occupation of the central Sudan was put up by the Sanusi order from its fortified zawiyas in the Bilma region and, above all, by Rabih, an Arab soldier from Sennar. He had earlier served the Egyptian government in the Bahr al-Ghazal. After refusing to submit to the Mahdi, he had set off westwards with his armed followers. He failed in an attack against the sultanate of Wadai in 1887, but, by 1892, he had conquered Bagirmi and much of eastern Bornu. Here, he set up a slave-raiding state, which disposed of its booty along the Sanusi trade routes leading to Tripoli and Benghazi. As the French closed in on Rabih from all sides, he fiercely resisted their advance. He was finally defeated and killed in 1900.

The Reconquest of the Sudan: Fashoda

Before the French had defeated Rabih, the British in Egypt had reconquered the Mahdist state, which appeared to be threatened both by the Italians in Eritrea and by the French advance from the Congo. To forestall such moves, an Anglo-Egyptian military force, trained by the British commander Kitchener, moved into the Sudan in 1896. In 1898, this force defeated the Mahdist armies at the battle of Omdurman, in which 20,000 Sudanese were killed. Khartoum then fell to Kitchener. A week later, news reached him that a French force of African soldiers led by Commandant Marchand had installed itself at Fashoda, some 300 km (180 miles) farther south, after an incredible march from Gabon, which had lasted nearly two years. Kitchener hastened up the White Nile with a much larger force. The hostile camps faced one another for several months, while telegraphic messages flashed to and fro between the Sudan and Europe. In the end, the French gave way, and Marchand hauled down his flag – but not before France and Britain had been brought to the brink of a major war.

A brief mention can be made here of the last two territories in northern Africa to be seized by the European powers. In 1911, Italy launched an unprovoked, but not unexpected, invasion of the Ottoman province of Tripoli, and the next year pushed from there into Cyrenaica. Here, the Italian armies met bitter opposition from the bedouin tribesmen who belonged to the Sanusi order. Their resistance continued until the 1930s (see Chapter 14). At the western end of North Africa, Morocco escaped European control until 1912, not because of the sultan's ability to oppose it, but because the European powers quarrelled among themselves over which of them should occupy his kingdom. Their disagreements twice brought Europe within reach of war. Finally, the two powers most concerned – France and Spain – partitioned Morocco, Spain taking the smaller northern portion. Germany was bought off by being given extra territory in Cameroun. A French protectorate was declared over the main portion of the kingdom, the sultan remaining as the nominal head of his country.

East Africa and the Congo Basin

In East Africa and the Congo basin, the Arabs put up the main opposition to the occupation forces of the Germans, the British, and the Belgians. This opposition did not come openly from the sultan of Zanzibar. His capital would have been an easy target for the guns of European warships, and he therefore had to submit gracefully to the declaration of a British protectorate over the islands of Zanzibar and Pemba in 1890 and to the partition of his mainland territories. These were divided between the British and the German chartered companies, which were beginning to occupy what is now Kenya, the mainland of Tanzania, and Uganda. In 1886, the mainland territories of the sultan were declared by an international commission to extend only 16 km (10 miles) into the interior. The Germans then bought the coastal strip adjoining their treaty areas for a lump sum, while the British company leased the coastal strip of Kenya for an annual payment. That is why, throughout the colonial period, the red flag of the sultan continued to fly over Mombasa, Malindi, Lamu, and other Kenya ports. It may also be the reason why there was no Arab revolt in the British coastal sphere.

The active opposition from the Swahili Arabs came from two directions. The first was from the German part of the coast. The second was from the former slave- and ivory-traders scattered over the interior from Lake Malawi in the south, around both sides of Lake Tanganyika, and up into Uganda in the north. The movement probably stemmed from the attempt of Sultan Barghash to consolidate his mainland dominions on the eve of European partition. With its central leadership withdrawn, however, it exploded in a series of local uprisings, which the Europeans dealt with one by one. The sharpest of these struggles, though also the shortest, was that in 1888–9 between the Germans and the east-coast Arabs under their leader, Abushiri. Longer and more intermittent was that between the British and the Arabs of northern Nyasaland, which began in 1887 and was finally settled ten years later. King Leopold's officials fought their campaigns against the Arabs of eastern Zaire between 1891 and 1894. In Uganda, as in Nyasaland, Arab opposition to European penetration, though strongly influenced by the German occupation of the coast, began while the only Europeans in the area were missionaries. This opposition was an aspect of the local political situation. The local Christians supported the entry of European influence; the local Muslims opposed it. In the kingdom of Buganda, the Christian factions prevailed and made Buganda the principal ally of the British in their occupation of the region as a whole. The Arabs and the local

Muslim faction retreated into the neighbouring kingdom of Bunyoro, which remained the centre of resistance to British rule. It was
finally conquered by the British with the help of Buganda levies in a
series of campaigns which lasted from 1894 until 1899 (see Chapter
12).

The one country in East Africa which successfully resisted European attempts at occupation was Ethiopia. The European nation
involved in this attempt was Italy, which had entered late into the
scramble. Italy had occupied a part of the Eritrean coast of the Red
Sea in 1883, and in 1886 had participated in the division of the sultan of Zanzibar's mainland possessions by staking a claim to the
eastern Somali coast. In 1889, immediately after becoming emperor,
Menelik signed with the Italians the Treaty of Wichale. This treaty
defined the boundary between Ethiopia and Italian Eritrea. It also
stated in its Amharic version that Menelik's government might, if
it wished, use Italian diplomatic channels for its contacts with the
outside world. The Italian version of the treaty used a slightly more
definite expression, implying that Menelik had agreed always to conduct his external affairs through Italian channels. It does not seem
that the Italian negotiators deliberately intended to deceive Menelik –
certainly, they never intended to create a protectorate. Nevertheless,
it was on the basis of this phrase that the Italian Foreign Office two
years later notified the powers which had taken part in the Berlin
Conference of Italy's claim to a protectorate over Ethiopia. Italy now
attempted to enforce this invalid protectorate upon Menelik, and
disputes between the two sides resulted in the war of 1896. The Italian army was decisively defeated at Adowa, one of the first battles
of modern times in which a non-European army beat one officered
by, and partly consisting of, Europeans. Menelik turned from his
victory over the Italians back to his lifelong interest, which was the
extension of his kingdom to the south. Some of this country had paid
tribute to the Ethiopian kings of the late medieval period and had
been lost since the Oromo invasions of the sixteenth century. Menelik's conquests, however, reaching to Lake Turkana in the south and
to the ancient kingdom of Kaffa in the south-west, more than doubled the dominions which had come to him by inheritance and mar-
riage. They made Ethiopia almost a participant in the scramble for
Africa.

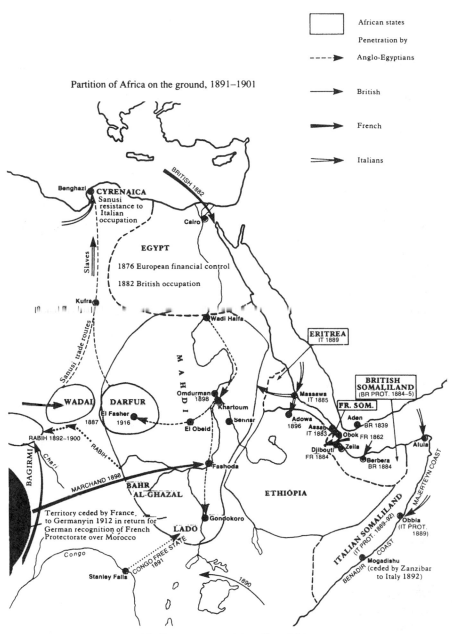

Partition of Africa on the ground, 1891–1901

African states

Penetration by

Anglo-Egyptians

British

French

Italians

Benghazi **CYRENAICA**
Sanusi
resistance to
Italian
occupation

BRITISH 1882

Cairo

EGYPT

1876 European financial control

1882 British occupation

Slaves

Kufra

Wadi Halfa

Sanusi trade routes

ERITREA
IT 1889

**BRITISH
SOMALILAND**
(BR PROT. 1884–5)

FR. SOM.

M A H D I

Omdurman
1898

WADAI   **DARFUR**
El Fasher
1887   1916

Khartoum

Massawa
IT 1885

Adowa
1896

Aden
BR 1839

Aden

El Obeid   Sennar

Assab
IT 1883

Obok
FR 1862

RABIH 1892–1900

RABIH

Djibouti
FR 1884

Zella

Alula

BAGIRMI

Chari

MARCHAND 1898

Fashoda

Berbera
BR 1884

**BAHR
AL-GHAZAL**

ETHIÓPIA

ITALIAN SOMALILAND
(IT PROT. 1889–92)

MAJERTEYN COAST

Territory ceded by France
to Germany in 1912 in return for
German recognition of French
Protectorate over Morocco

Gondokoro

LADO

Obbia
(IT PROT.
1889)

Congo

CONGO FREE STATE
1891

Stanley Falls

1890

Mogadishu
(ceded by Zanzibar
to Italy 1892)

BENADIR COAST

18. European partition: East Africa.

The French Conquest of Madagascar

In the late 1880s, the Merina kingdom began to break up under the pressure of French commercial and diplomatic influence. The prime minister, Rainilaiarivony, would not admit that the 1885 treaty gave France protectorate rights over the island. The French considered it did. Acting under what they understood were the terms of the treaty, the French in 1894 sent a large military expedition to Madagascar. This expedition entered Tananarive the following year and removed the prime minister. A definite treaty of protection was forced upon the queen. This foreign interference was the signal for one rebellion after another throughout Madagascar. Pagans turned upon Christians, blaming the new religion for the troubles which had come upon the island. The people of the old Betsileo kingdom rid themselves of the hated Hova domination. French military actions against these rebellions only made matters worse. At one time, Tananarive was the only place the French could hold. In 1895, General Gallieni came from his campaigns in West Africa to conquer (or 'pacify', as this action used to be called) Madagascar, which was declared to be a French colony. Nine years of bitter fighting passed before all the peoples of Madagascar had been forced by Gallieni and his second-in-command, Lyautey, to accept French rule. The Merina monarchy was overthrown – the last queen, Ranavalona III, exiled in 1897. The French administered the island as a unit, thus completing the work of unification begun by Nampoina more than a century before.

Rhodes and Central Africa

The occupation of Central Africa was left by the British government very largely to Rhodes and his British South Africa Company. The company was incorporated by Royal Charter in 1889 and was empowered to develop the region between Bechuanaland and the Zambezi, which was later to bear Rhodes's name. In 1891, the company was allowed to extend into the lands north of the Zambezi which became Northern Rhodesia (Zambia). South of the Zambezi, Rhodes's agents had extracted concessions from Mzilikazi's successor, Lobengula, on the strength of which a body of farming and mining settlers was sent in 1890 into Mashonaland, where they founded

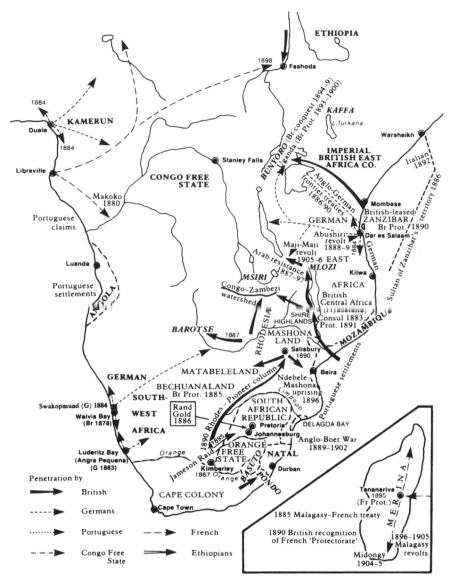

19. Southern Africa: the European partition – Britain, France, and Germany.

the Southern Rhodesian capital at Fort Salisbury. Farther north, Rhodes's agents raced those of King Leopold to secure possession of Katanga. The result of this scramble had, in fact, been decided beforehand by the international agreement of 1885, which fixed the

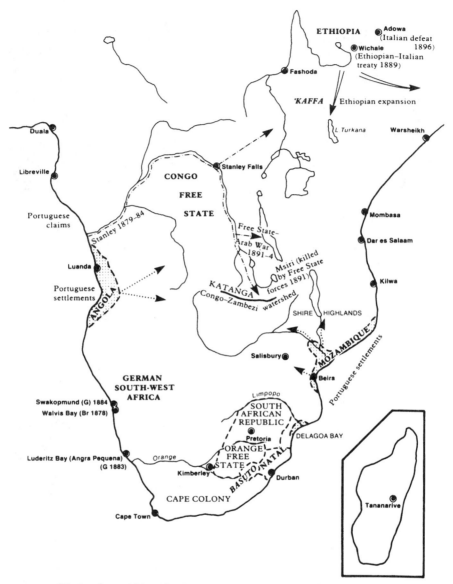

20. Southern Africa: the European partition – Leopold and Portugal.

Congo–Zambezi watershed as the limit of King Leopold's territory. Most of Msiri's kingdom (see Chapter 6), therefore, passed to
Leopold. Msiri himself was shot by a Belgian officer in a brawl arising from the treaty-making. The lands on the Zambezi side of the

watershed became British and later proved to include a substantial part of the rich Copperbelt. The only part of Central Africa excluded from the company's sphere was Nyasaland (Malawi), where British missionaries and traders, who were hostile to the British South Africa Company, had been active since the later 1870s. This part of the country became a protectorate under the direct control of the British government in 1891.

The early years of the colonists' settlement in Southern Rhodesia were a time of constant fighting. There were unofficial wars between the settlers and the Portuguese on the Mozambique border. The settlers had to conquer the Ndebele, who soon became thoroughly resentful of their presence in neighbouring Mashonaland. It is not pleasant to read how the colonists deliberately provoked the conflict with the Ndebele, but the war was probably an inevitable consequence of the European settlement. Lobengula died shortly after his regiments had been defeated in 1893. The seizure of land and cattle by the victorious settlers provoked both the Ndebele and the Mashona to make a last attempt to drive them out in 1896, when the Africans' will to resist the white man was finally broken by the machine gun.

The Anglo-Boer War

Rhodes was prime minister of the Cape Colony from 1890 to 1896. In addition, he directed the activities of the British South Africa Company in the territories to the north. Rhodes had visions of uniting the whole of southern Africa, including the Boer republics, as a self-governing dominion under the British flag. He talked of 'equal rights for all civilised men south of the Zambezi'. It would seem that what he meant by this was primarily an alliance between Boer and Briton to develop the wealth of the country and to promote more white immigration. The Boer leader, Paul Kruger, president of the Transvaal, had very different ideas. He wanted a South Africa dominated by the Boers, who would retain their own language, Afrikaans (which had grown out of the Dutch of the original settlers), their old-fashioned pastoral way of life, and their refusal of political rights to Africans or to Cape Coloured peoples. Although glad of the wealth from the Witwatersrand gold mines, Kruger was well aware that they were

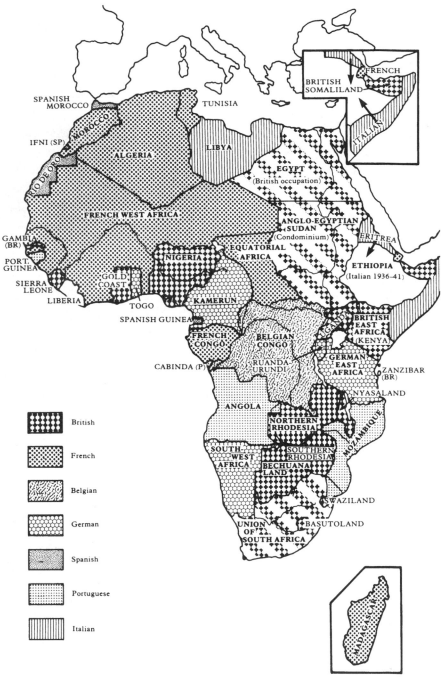

21. Africa: the final stage of partition, 1914.

being developed mainly by British immigrants into the Transvaal, who might soon become a majority of the white population. While taxing them heavily, therefore, he denied them the vote. On the other hand, he used the wealth with which they had provided him to build up his defences and his railway links with the outside world.

Rhodes tried to persuade the disgruntled immigrants (Afrikaans: *uitlanders*) to stage a revolution and topple Kruger's government. A raid on the Transvaal from Bechuanaland in 1895, led by Rhodes's henchman Jameson, was a total failure, and no uprising occurred. The raid ended Rhodes's political career, but elements in the British government which had been implicated in the plot were now determined on a decision with the Transvaal. The British high commissioner in South Africa, Sir Alfred Milner, deliberately incited the Transvaal to war. This broke out in 1899, and the Orange Free State stood beside its sister republic. The Boer armies – and after they were beaten, the irregular commandos – fought the whole might of Britain with tenacity and courage for more than two years. Destruction was widespread, and casualties on both sides were very high. Before peace finally came, the Boers had been inspired with an even greater bitterness against Britain and British institutions than they had had before. For the time being, however, the whole of South Africa was in British hands.

ELEVEN. Colonial Rule in Tropical Africa: (1) Political and Economic Developments, 1885–1914

The colonial period in tropical Africa lasted for about seventy years. The first thirty years of this period may be called the years of establishment, the next thirty the years of active development, and the last ten the years of retreat. In this chapter, we deal with the years of establishment mainly from the point of view of the colonial governments. In the next chapter, we shall try to look at the same years mainly from the point of view of the African peoples, and to consider the changes which the colonial period introduced into everyday life.

The Policies of the Colonial Powers

Once Africa had been divided between them, the European governments lost much of their earlier interest in the continent. There were few parts of Africa which were expected to produce immediate wealth. The European nations had partitioned Africa mainly in order to ensure that they would not be excluded from regions which might prove valuable in the future. Possession was what mattered to them, not development.

At the end of the nineteenth century, European states took a much narrower view of the functions of government, even within their own frontiers, than they do today. European states of those days had, for example, no public health services or old-age pensions and no public housing other than the workhouse. In most European countries, state education was still a recent introduction, and it was not yet

146

provided for all children. Taxation was much lower than it is today. Government spending was jealously controlled by the elected representatives of the voters, who were still, for the most part, the wealthy members of each community.

It is not surprising, therefore, that it was felt in Europe that the main duty of governments in the new African colonies was to maintain law and order, and to do so without expense to the European taxpayer. Education on the one hand, and economic development on the other, were left almost entirely to the private enterprise of Christian missions and commercial companies. Even the work of government was sometimes delegated to chartered companies, which were empowered to recruit their own officials and police forces, to collect taxes, and to administer justice. Where European governments assumed direct responsibility for the government of their new colonies, the most strict economy was practised. Officials were few in number; military and police forces consisted of ill-trained and poorly armed local recruits commanded by a few European officers.

Such governments were at first obliged to seek allies among their new subjects by entering into the web of intertribal politics and by aiding the friendly groups in their struggles with their traditional enemies. Unfriendly groups were often left severely alone for as long as possible. If action against such groups proved necessary, the small colonial forces, aided by their native allies, often burnt the villages of the resisters and seized their cattle. Such raids were continued until the authority of the colonial government was recognised. Only as local revenues were slowly built up from customs duties and head-taxes could colonial governments afford to employ regular civil services and police forces which could effectively occupy and administer the whole of the territories under their rule. In most African colonies, this position had barely been reached by the time of the outbreak of the First World War in 1914.

The gravest obstacle in the way of any kind of economic development of the new African colonies was the lack of any pre-existing system of wage labour which could be employed for public works such as building, road-making, and porterage. In these circumstances, nearly all colonial governments made extensive use of forced labour and, in practice, this often meant turning a blind eye to local institutions of slavery and tribute labour so that 'chiefs' could supply the labour demands of the colonial administrators. In nearly every instance, this led to abuses. Nevertheless, in most African colonies, a surprising amount was achieved during this period and a foundation laid for the period of active development which was to follow. By 1914, the construction of railways and feeder roads had opened most of tropical Africa to some kind of wheeled traffic, with the result that cash crops could be grown and marketed profitably. The great number of small, tribal sovereignties which had been such a barrier to almost every kind of progress had been amalgamated into approximately forty separate territories, most of which were capable of growing into modern states with sufficient resources to stand on their own feet. The greatest benefit – and that which impressed itself vividly on the memories of most Africans who had experienced the pre-colonial period – was the relative peace and security imposed by all the colonial governments, even the harshest and most arbitrary ones. It was, above all, 'the colonial peace' which freed energies for new activities and which made possible not only economic development, but also the spread of the universal religions of Christianity and Islam and the beginnings of modern education and learning. It is against this general background that we must now consider the various types of colonial government which emerged in different parts of tropical Africa during the period between partition and the First World War.

West Africa: The Realm of the Peasant Producer

The distinguishing feature of this region was that the peoples of the coast had been trading for more than three centuries with the peoples of Europe. Among them, the demand for European goods had become so deeply ingrained that, after the abolition of the slave-trade, they had made the most strenuous efforts to develop for themselves cash crops which could be exchanged for the imports which they had come to regard as necessities. This meant that colonial governments in West Africa had one supreme advantage over governments in other parts of the continent. They could begin to build up their revenues by taxing an established trade. Even a light customs duty on imported spirits and firearms could yield them the revenue out of which to pay their first small bodies of officials and military forces. It could provide them with a basis on which they could borrow money. It was this fact, far more than any climatic differences from other parts of Africa, which caused colonial governments to seek to establish their revenues by building up peasant production rather than by trying to attract concessionaire companies or private settlers with gifts of land. They had inherited an economic system on which they could build. Most colonial administrations in Africa would have liked to build their economies on peasant production. In West Africa, conditions enabled them to do so. At the beginning of the colonial period, even in West Africa, it was only a small part of the region that was affected by the growth of a cash economy. The basic economic activities of the majority of people still consisted in producing food crops, housing materials, fuel, and clothing, mostly for their own consumption. Although this involved a considerable amount of local trade and even some long-distance trade, the way of life was still of the kind called by economists a 'subsistence economy' as opposed to a 'cash economy'. It has been estimated that in 1900, such activities accounted for about 90 percent of Nigerian production and 75 percent of that of the Gold Coast. Yet, in spite of the predominance of the subsistence economy, the beginnings of a cash economy were in existence and provided a growing-point for the future.

French West Africa

The most consistent pattern of colonial rule was that developed by the French in their West African possessions. This was not the result of any imperial plan thought out beforehand. It was due to the fact that the seven younger colonies of Soudan, Mauritania, Upper Volta, Niger, Guinea, Ivory Coast, and Dahomey were all in a sense extensions or offshoots of the old colony of Senegal. Access to the first four of these was, at first, mainly through Senegal. In all of them, the occupation was carried out by military forces, of which the backbone was the Senegalese army trained by Faidherbe and Gallieni in the course of their struggles with al-Hajj Umar, Ahmadu Sefu, and Samori in the region between the upper Senegal and the Niger Rivers (see Chapters 5 and 10). The fighting with Samori continued until 1898. Because the French had become so accustomed to fighting for the occupation of their territories, they were less willing than the British to negotiate with those African rulers who might have been open to such an approach. The kingdom of Dahomey, the Mossi states of Wagadugu and Yatenga, and other important states were broken up. The French administrative units (called *cercles*) which replaced them were more uniform in size and more directly controlled – first by military officers and later by civilian officials – than their counterparts in British territories.

The economic policy of the new French West African colonies was likewise based on the example of the Senegal, where Faidherbe and his successors had made the colonial administration self-supporting by encouraging the African population to grow ground-nuts on their own farms. This meant that the Senegalese peasants had a crop which they could sell for cash, with some of which they could pay the head-tax imposed by the government. As the French armies advanced into the interior, the civilian administration set up in the newly conquered districts at once sought to introduce similar cash crops. Particularly high hopes were set on the development of cotton-growing in the Niger basin. As in all other parts of the African interior, however, the biggest obstacle was the lack of transport. The first railway, built by the military as a strategic link between the upper Senegal and the upper Niger – although adequate for the movement of troops and supplies – proved useless for commercial cargoes.

The railway terminals could only be reached by small steamers of shallow draught, and even they could only make the journey at certain seasons of the year. The difficulty of navigation on the Senegal was overcome only with the completion of the line from Dakar to Kayès in 1924. The uncertainties of navigation on the upper Niger remain to this day. In some coastal parts of Guinea, the Ivory Coast, and Dahomey, there was some early development in palm-oil, cocoa, and other forest produce. Here again, the opening up of the interior had to await the building of railways, and this was not begun until the early years of the twentieth century. Indeed, the railways were only starting to make significant progress by about 1914. The earliest cash earnings of the people of Soudan and Upper Volta were in fact those of migrant labourers who went to seek work in the ground-nut areas of Senegal and the palm-oil and cocoa districts of the Gold and Ivory Coasts.

It was the problem of economic self-support which led the French to federate their West African territories in a single unit, in which the richer and more accessible regions could help to support the poorer and more remote. In 1895, the governor of Senegal had been given supervisory powers over his colleagues. This had been mainly in order to secure military coordination at a time when French armies were fighting with Samori around the interior frontiers of Soudan, Guinea, and the Ivory Coast. Under French laws passed in 1902 and 1904, at the beginning of the great period of railway-building, all the West African territories were grouped under a government–general situated at Dakar. This government–general consisted of the governor–general, his officials, and advisory councils. It took an important share of the customs duties levied in all the coastal colonies. With this revenue, the government–general negotiated loans for railways leading to the interior. This meant, in the early days, that Senegal and Dahomey were between them contributing three-quarters of the federal budget of French West Africa, although to the great benefit of the region as a whole.

British West Africa

The British West African territories presented, at the beginning of the period, a rather confused appearance. Not only were they geographically separated from one another, but their longer and more divided history also had left them under three different kinds of government. As explained in the previous chapter, there were the four Crown Colonies of the Gambia, Sierra Leone, the Gold Coast Colony, and Lagos. In eastern Nigeria, there was the Oil Rivers Protectorate, administered by the Foreign Office. And, finally, in northern Nigeria, there was the territory administered under charter by the Royal Niger Company. These differences, however, were not as important as they appeared. The Royal Niger Company, as we have seen, surrendered its charter in 1898. In 1900, Northern Nigeria became a British protectorate, the same year as eastern Nigeria was taken over by the Colonial Office. Thereafter, the British West African colonies came to resemble more closely than any others in Africa their French neighbours. They resembled them, above all, in the fact that they were economically based on the production of cash crops by African peasants. They resembled them further in that the prosperity of the coastal regions was used to build up administration in and communications

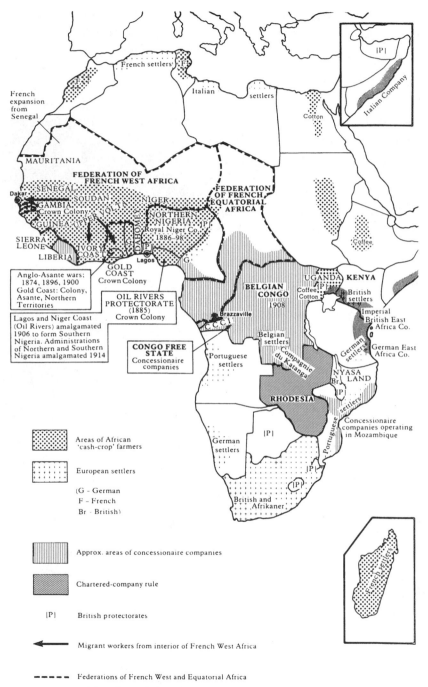

French settlers' F

French
expansion
from
Senegal

Italian   settlers

Cotton

|P|

Italian Company

MAURITANIA

**FEDERATION OF
FRENCH WEST AFRICA**

**FEDERATION
OF FRENCH
EQUATORIAL
AFRICA**

SENEGAL
Dakar
GAMBIA   SOUDAN
Crown Colony   NIGER
GUINEA   UPPER VOLTA
DAHOMEY
NORTHERN
NIGERIA
Royal Niger Co.
1886-98 |P|

SIERRA
LEONE
IVORY
LIBERIA   COAST
Lagos
GOLD   G
COAST
Crown Colony

Coffee

Anglo-Asante wars:
1874, 1896, 1900
Gold Coast: Colony,
Asante, Northern
Territories

OIL RIVERS
PROTECTORATE
(1885)
Crown Colony

UGANDA KENYA
Coffee |P|
Cotton   British
settlers

BELGIAN
CONGO
1908

Lagos and Niger Coast
(Oil Rivers) amalgamated
1906 to form Southern
Nigeria. Administrations
of Northern and Southern
Nigeria amalgamated 1914

Brazzaville

Imperial
British East
Africa Co.

**CONGO FREE
STATE**
Concessionaire
companies

C C C |

Belgian
settlers

German
settlers

German East
Africa Co.

Portuguese
settlers

Belgian
settlers

Compagnie
du Katanga

NYASA
LAND
Br
|P|

RHODESIA

Concessionaire
companies operating
in Mozambique

Areas of African
'cash-crop' farmers

German
settlers

|P|

European settlers

(G - German
F - French
Br - British)

British and
Afrikaner

|P|

|P|

Approx. areas of concessionaire companies

Chartered-company rule

|P| British protectorates

French settlers

Migrant workers from interior of French West Africa

- - - - - Federations of French West and Equatorial Africa

22. Africa: colonial economies and administrations.

with the interior. Moreover, though geographically much smaller, the British West African territories had more than double the population – and perhaps three or four times the wealth, of the whole of French West Africa. And, so, despite the lack of a federation between them, they developed more rapidly than the French territories.

The Gold Coast moved fastest. Here, the great political problem was the continued unity and strength of the Asante nation, which had largely recovered from its defeat of 1874. Two more serious military campaigns in 1896 and 1900 were fought before Asante would submit to the authority of the British colonial government. Even before the final defeat of the Asante, deep mining for gold by British companies had begun in Adansi and in parts of southern Asante which had been annexed by Britain after the war of 1874. Mining provided the impulse for the construction of the first railway in the colony, which reached the gold-mining district of Tarkwa from Sekondi by 1901. At the end of the nineteenth century, gold exports from the Gold Coast were actually falling, from a value of some £80,000 in 1897 to £22,000 in 1901. After the railway reached Tarkwa, the value rose rapidly: £97,000 in 1902, £255,000 in 1903, £1,165,000 in 1907, and £1,687,000 in 1914. Within a few years of its extension to Kumasi in 1903, to ensure military and political control over Asante, the second great significance of the railway proved to be its opening up of the forest region, first to rubber-tapping and then to cocoa-farming. In 1901, the value of cocoa exported from the colony was £43,000; it was £95,000 in 1902, £515,000 in 1907, and £2,194,000 in 1914. By that year, cocoa amounted to 49 percent of all exports, and cocoa alone was already paying for all the Gold Coast's exports. The exportation of timber, worth £169,000 in 1907, also resulted from the building of the railway. Cocoa, gold, and timber made the Gold Coast, by 1914, the most prosperous of all the African colonies.

In Nigeria, as in the rest of West Africa, it was the peasant producers of the coastal regions who, by the customs duties levied on their imports even more than by their direct taxes, provided the revenues out of which colonial administration and a modern system of communications were gradually extended over the interior. The Lagos protectorate in the south-west and the protectorate of Southern Nigeria (the old Oil Rivers) in the south-east were amalgamated in 1906 as the self-supporting colony of Southern Nigeria. The North, meanwhile, with its vast population, remained cut off from access to world markets save by the long and precarious line of river communications on the Niger and the Benue. The colonial administration there, despite continuing grants-in-aid from the British Treasury, was able to maintain itself only by making the utmost use of the existing Fulbe system of government. Under British overrule, the Fulbe emirs continued to police, tax, and administer justice to their Hausa subjects, while accepting advice from British residents posted at their courts. The system worked, but it was scarcely progressive. Even Lugard, the first governor of the North (1900–6), who was responsible for the system, realised that Northern Nigeria could be modernised only when it had been politically amalgamated with the South and linked by railways with the coast. Lugard returned to Nigeria in 1912, and two years later (1914) became governor–general of the whole territory. By this time, the differences between north and south had hardened too much to be easily eliminated. Nevertheless, the administrative unification of the country marked a great step forward.

The Realm of the Concessionaire Company: France and King Leopold in the Congo Basin

The region of Africa drained by the Congo and its tributaries was, as we have already seen, a very different one from West Africa. At its heart was the equatorial rain forest, inhabited sparsely by Africa's most isolated and, therefore, least developed peoples. The denser and more complex societies of the area lived around the rim of the river basin. Their former trading links had been in some cases northwards to Libya and Egypt, in some cases eastwards to the Zanzibar coast, in some cases westwards to Portuguese Luanda. Before the coming of river-steamers in the 1880s, little trade had passed by water through the forest centre to the Congo mouth. Along the Western Central African coast from Mount Cameroun to Luanda, the trade established in the nineteenth century had been disrupted by the activities of the Free State officers on the lower Congo and of the French in Gabon. There was no worthwhile exchange of European manufactures against African produce on which the colonisers could build, as they had been able to do in West Africa. No government could support itself by levying customs on the trade passing through Boma or Libreville, still less raise a loan for the building of railways round the Congo cataracts or south from the upper Kasai to Katanga. The finance required for such projects was 'risk capital', which had to be attracted by the possibility of large long-term gains in order to offset the lack of immediate returns. In these circumstances, the time-honoured solution was that followed in railway development in North and South America – private capital was attracted by grants of land and mineral rights in the area to be opened up.

Such was, in fact, the origin of the system of concessionaire companies which was to become the distinguishing feature of the colonial history of this region. In 1886, King Leopold made the first contract of this kind with the Compagnie du Congo pour le Commerce et l'Industrie (CCCI), under which the company agreed to build a railway around the lower Congo rapids from Matadi to Leopoldville, in exchange for which it could claim 1,500 hectares (slightly more than 14 square kilometres) for every kilometre of line constructed. Thus, the lower Congo railway alone involved the alienation of nearly 8,000 square kilometres. No sooner was it completed in 1898, than similar contracts were made with two other companies. These organisations undertook to build railways from the upper Congo to Lake Tanganyika and from the limit of navigation on the Kasai to the heart of Katanga. A variation on the railway concession was that given in 1891 to the Compagnie du Katanga. This was at the time when Rhodes was threatening to overrun Katanga from the south and when King Leopold could not himself afford to undertake the effective occupation of the region. He, therefore, chartered the Katanga Company to do so in exchange for one-third of the vacant lands and mineral rights in the area.

All the land conceded in this way was, in theory, 'waste land', the villages of the Congolese and the land actually under cultivation by them being excluded. But because land was useless without labour, every form of pressure was put upon the local inhabitants to work for the concessionaire companies. The worst abuses occurred during the period from about 1895 to 1905, when the invention of pneumatic rubber tyres for bicycles and motorcars was causing a great demand for rubber. In the long term, this demand was met by the development of rubber plantations in South-East Asia. While the boom in wild rubber lasted, however, very large profits indeed were made by the concessionaire companies in the Congo. In theory, these companies employed – but in practice compelled – their Congolese neighbours to tap rubber in the forests, usually for token rewards. The profits secured in this way aroused the greed of King Leopold, who took over and managed himself large areas of Crown land. Other areas he leased to private companies on a profit-sharing basis. The system proved so attractive that it spread into French Equatorial Africa. Here, the French government saw in it a means of reducing the large annual deficits which had been accumulating since the beginning of colonial rule. In both territories, the worst abuses of the system were brought to an end between 1906 and 1910, when the end of the wild-rubber boom coincided with an outcry by international public opinion. In 1908, King Leopold was forced to cede the Congo to Belgium. In an effort to provide a more direct administration and to cut down expenses, France in 1910 joined the four territories of Gabon, Middle Congo, Oubangui-Chari, and Chad into the federation of French Equatorial Africa. This was modelled upon the government–general of French West Africa. Its capital was at Brazzaville. Both the French and Belgian governments, however, had contracts with the concessionaire companies which they could fulfil only by leaving the companies in possession of large areas of land and with commercial monopolies over still larger regions. The Belgian Congo was further burdened with an enormous debt which King Leopold had incurred by borrowing money on the Congo's account and spending it on his palaces and other public buildings in Belgium. The interest alone on this debt at one time absorbed nearly a fifth of the country's revenue.

Certainly, the foundation of colonies in the Congo basin presented a very different problem from that faced in West Africa. The region was a very poor one, and the people who lived in it had practically no sources of income that could be taxed to pay for the expenses of government and of modern communications. The only possible way to create such wealth was to reorganise the labour of the people. In a very crude manner, the concessionaire companies did achieve this end.

The Realm of the European Settler: Britain, Germany, and Portugal in East and Central Africa

Like the Congo basin and unlike West Africa, the new colonies of East and Central Africa had at the time of their occupation no trade, other than the declining trade in ivory, on which colonial revenues could be built. Unlike the Congo territories, however, these colonies in East and Central Africa were mostly crossed by the chain of high-land country running from the Kenya highlands south-westwards towards the Cape. Here were some lands fairly sparsely occupied by African pastoralists, on which Europeans could settle as farmers. To colonial governments in search of revenue, a policy of limited white settlement by Europeans who would act as employers and organisers of African labour appeared as an attractive solution.

The German government was committed in principle to promoting settlement for its own sake. Germany at the end of the nineteenth century had a large and growing rural population, and German peasants had been emigrating in the hundreds of thousands to the United States for many years. One of the main aims of the promoters of the colonial movement had been to enable such emigrants to settle in German lands overseas. In German East and South-West Africa, Cameroun, and Togo, settlers were encouraged to make claims. Land was set aside for them, particularly in the areas destined to be opened up by railways.

The British government in London had no such fixed inclination to favour European settlement. In Southern and Northern Rhodesia, settlement was promoted by the British South Africa Company. This was done for two reasons. First, the idea agreed with the ideals of Cecil Rhodes, that the highlands of Central Africa would make an excellent home for English-speaking farmers. The second was that land grants were a means of rewarding the occupiers, who would otherwise have had to be paid out of company funds. But, in Nyasaland, where a protectorate government was established in 1891, and in Uganda and Kenya, when these countries were taken over from the Imperial British East Africa Company in 1894–5, governors were left by the British government to solve their own problems in their own way. It is remarkable that the Uganda Railway, completed from Mombasa to Kisumu on Lake Victoria by 1901, was paid for by the imperial government out of an interest-free loan, which was later written off as a gift. In Uganda, after five years of mainly military activity, the colonial government settled its account with its Baganda allies by signing a special agreement with them in 1900. This turned the Baganda chiefs into a land-owning aristocracy and gave the Buganda state a degree of recognition which would have made a policy of European settlement almost impossible to carry out. The Baganda responded to the situation by taking up the cultivation of cotton on a scale which soon made the country independent of grants-in-aid. Kenya, on the other hand, and also Nyasaland, were thought to present revenue problems which could only be solved by encouraging settler plantations.

The scramble for Africa among the more powerful European nations infused new life into the ancient Portuguese colonies of Angola and Mozambique. New settlers were encouraged to leave Portugal to become farmers in the interior of these colonies. The Portuguese looked upon this colonisation by settlers more as a means of controlling their huge African possessions than as a means of developing them. In many parts of Angola and Mozambique, the settler landowner was more like a one-man concessionaire company than was his British or German opposite number. On his estate, he collected taxes and administered summary justice to his African tenants, from among whom he recruited both his labour and his private police force. This was feudal Europe of the Middle Ages surviving in twentieth-century Africa.

The Europeans who settled in East and Central Africa during the period up to 1914 were very few in number – some 10,000 in what is now Zimbabwe; some 3,000 each in what are now Zambia, Kenya, Tanzania, and Namibia; probably not many more in Mozambique and Angola; and only a few hundred in Malawi and Uganda. Several thousand Frenchmen settled in the highlands of Madagascar and formed the largest group of French *colons* in Africa outside the Maghrib. Numerically, the European settlers were much less significant than the Indians, who settled in the wake of the colonial occupation as artisans and petty traders all over East Africa and in parts of Central Africa as well. The Indians settled in the towns and villages and lived by their own labour. The Europeans, on the other hand, settled in competition with the Africans, on the land, and lived

as employers of African labour. Even so, only small areas were directly affected, and most of the areas of dense African population – for example, those around Lake Victoria and Lake Malawi – were untouched. Indeed, throughout the greater part of all these countries, African communities lived their lives and were ruled by the colonial administrators on much the same lines as in West Africa. Unlike West Africa, however, instead of being encouraged to add cash crops to the subsistence crops grown on their own land, the Africans were encouraged to earn the money they needed to pay their taxes by working, usually as migrant labourers, on European farms. Like the concessionaire company in the Congo basin, the European farmer settler of East and Central Africa was at this time chiefly important for the part he played in reorganising African labour by bringing some of it into the market economy. Politically and socially, as we shall see in the next two chapters, the European settler introduced much more confusion into tropical Africa than the concessionaire company. Whereas the company thought mainly of its profits, the settler was apt to think mainly of his children and grandchildren and of the position they would occupy in society. This posed a problem which grew steadily more important during the years after the First World War. It had then to be decided whether these parts of tropical Africa were to be developed in the interests of the settlers or of the indigenous inhabitants. The result was a series of uneasy compromises, which we shall examine in Chapter 13.

TWELVE. Colonial Rule in Tropical Africa: (2) Social and Religious Developments

The Impact of Colonial Rule

The impact of colonial rule on African societies varied greatly, not only from one territory to another, but also from one part of a territory to another. To some extent, the reasons for this sprang from their social organisation or the way in which they made their living. For example, specialised pastoralists, like the Masai in Kenya or the Herero in South-West Africa, found it much more difficult to adapt themselves to the wishes of colonial governments than most of the peoples who lived by agriculture. Then again, warrior groups, like the Ndebele of Southern Rhodesia or the Ngoni of Northern Rhodesia and Nyasaland – themselves the colonialists of an earlier period, found it more difficult to work and pay taxes than their former subjects, the Mashona and the Chewa. Much more important than the sociological reasons, however, were the sheerly accidental circumstances under which each group in a particular territory made its first contacts with the colonial government.

There were people who gained from colonial rule. In nearly every territory, there were 'favourite peoples', those who by good luck or good judgement made common cause with the colonial power and received privileged treatment as a result. To such peoples, the colonial period brought at first no shame, but, on the contrary, extended frontiers, enhanced prestige, and a sense of prosperity and achievement. In Northern Rhodesia, for example, the Barotse – who,

under the influence of the missionary Coillard had written to ask for British protection – received special treatment from the British South Africa Company. Because of their readiness to sign treaties and concessions, they were recognised as the overlords of a wide surrounding region. By signing away the land and mineral rights of the peoples supposedly subject to them, they were able to protect their own country from most kinds of European interference.

In German East Africa, it was the Swahili people of the coastal towns who were the most favoured by the German colonial government. The urban Swahili were the first to experience the tactless and oppressive rule of the officials of the German East Africa Company. In 1888, a rebellion was organised against them by Abushiri, an Arab sugar planter in the Pangani district, who recruited his followers from the former armed guards of the interior caravan trade. The result was serious enough to cause the German government to revoke the Company's charter and to undertake the suppression itself with the aid of 600 Sudanese mercenaries recruited in Egypt. Thereafter, the troops were moved into the interior, and a form of civilian administration was devised for the coastal towns which was conciliatory to Muslim feelings and made use of traditional leaders. The system proved so successful that the Germans decided to concentrate their whole educational effort on the establishment of Swahili-speaking schools, in the coastal towns. From these schools, there gradually emerged a highly privileged class of Swahili policemen, clerks and interpreters, who assisted the German administrators and accompanied them as they extended their activities from the coastal districts into the interior. These people understood the new system of government and were able to turn it to their own advantage in a variety of ways.

In Uganda, it was the Baganda who filled this intermediate role between the British and the other peoples of the protectorate. Baganda armies fought alongside the British in many early campaigns and received their reward in the extension of Buganda's boundaries at the expense of its neighbours. Far beyond even these extended boundaries, the Baganda accompanied the expanding protectorate administration and were employed for a time as chiefs in nearly every district in the country. Buganda got in first with every colonial improvement. The new roads radiated from Buganda; the first schools and hospitals were built there; it was there that the first cash crops – coffee and cotton – were grown.

In Nigeria, to take one more example, there were two privileged groups: the Fulbe ruling class in the north and the already educated townsmen of the coast – Yoruba from Lagos, Efik and Ijaw from the city-states of the Delta, Ibo from the river ports of the lower Niger. The Fulbe were early resisters who swiftly came to terms with their conquerors and, in consequence, found their system of government supported, extended, and made more profitable than it had been before. The success of the coastal people was more like that of the Swahili. They were the clerks, the merchants, the schoolmasters, who accompanied the British administrators as they moved inland, and who helped to transform the institutions of the Yoruba city states and the Igbo village communities into a pattern acceptable to the colonial government.

These then were the people who gained from colonial rule. Those who suffered from it were, by contrast, those who, through ill-luck or ill-judgement, or simply from an excess of patriotism, challenged the colonial power and found themselves disastrously overthrown. In Madagascar, many of the people who had long been hostile to the Hova ruling group seized the opportunity of its decline in power at the time of the French invasion. They rose against the Hova and the French. However, the rebellions were put down with a heavy hand by the French. The condition of many of these groups was no better under colonial rule than it had been under Hova domination. In Southern Rhodesia, first the Ndebele and then the Mashona very understandably rose in an attempt to drive out the white colonists, who were visibly settling down in their land and taking it over for their own use. The result of the war of 1893 and revolts of 1896–7 was that most Ndebele and Mashona found themselves driven off the land they had previously grazed or farmed, and herded roughly into 'reserves'. Here, they had to start life afresh, often without their cattle, often without even the support of their old social groupings, which had been broken up as a result of warfare and flight. A still worse fate befell the Herero of Sout-West Africa, who in 1904 rose against the German settlers who had been infiltrating into their land. Two-thirds of the Herero were exterminated in the course of the German counter measures. The Herero country was declared the property of the state, and the survivors were forbidden to keep cattle, since they no longer possessed any land on which to graze them. A handful of refugees escaped into Bechuanaland. The remainder passed into European employment.

Nowhere else in tropical Africa were settlement and resistance quite so unfortunately combined. North of the Zambezi, the areas required for European settlement were very small, and the earlier inhabitants of those areas were either left where they were or, at worst, moved only a few miles. The largest displacement was that of the northern Masai from the central part of the Kenya highlands, and this was brought about by agreement, not by force. The groups which suffered most by the colonial occupation were not those who lost a small part of their land to settlers. Rather, they were those who, for one reason or another, found themselves opposing instead of supporting the spread of colonial power. The Banyoro of Uganda are a particularly unhappy example of this. These people opposed the British mainly because the British were supported by their traditional enemies, the Baganda. Between 1890 and 1897, Bunyoro became a place of retreat for Arab and Swahili traders, for Muslim Baganda, and for all those who opposed the pro-British, Christian parties dominating the Buganda scene. These refugees included the rebellious Kabaka of Buganda, Mwanga. Advised by their Baganda allies, the British came to regard Bunyoro as ready for conquest. When this had been carried out with the assistance of Baganda levies, the British deposed the ruler in 1899, carved off the outlying districts of his kingdom, and gave them to Buganda. For ten years or so, the British even forced the Bunyoro government to employ a number of Baganda chiefs in key positions. The result of all this was a feeling of helplessness and frustration, which lasted right through the colonial period and which made Bunyoro the last district in Uganda to adopt any of the useful innovations that came with British rule. Bunyoro had its Tanzanian counterpart in the kingdom of Uhehe, its Zairean counterpart in the Lunda kingdom of Mwata Yamvo, its Nigerian counterpart in the kingdom of Benin, its French West African counterpart in the kingdom of Dahomey, its Ghanaian counterpart in the kingdom of Asante, and so on.

The basic question in the social and religious history of any particular African people at the beginning of the colonial period was
whether it was swimming with the tide of advancing colonialism
or against it. Eventually, no doubt, *all* African societies suffered a
great blow through the loss of sovereignty, as the colonial governments progressively established the effectiveness of their overrule.
In African societies, as in all others, the ultimate sanction behind
authority was that of religion. The religious sanction began to be
undermined as soon as the authority ceased to be absolute. Though
the ordinary man in the ordinary village might continue to live his
life much as before and to be ruled for all practical purposes by
the same village headman, it could only be a matter of time before
he realised that there had been a change in the ultimate authority
which controlled his life. Sooner or later a murder would be committed, and the accused and the witnesses would be taken, not to the
chief's court as of old, but to the court of the colonial power, with
its strange procedures and punishments. Sooner or later the European district officer would appear on tour, with the local chief very
much a subordinate in his train. There would be demands for labour
to build roads, for porters to carry luggage or building materials or
trade goods. There would be talk of taxes to come, payable first in
kind, but later only in the unfamiliar pieces of minted coinage. It
might be necessary to obtain this money by working for others or by
trading in markets far outside the tribal area. Against these demands
the tribal authority offered no protection and, therefore, its divine
sanction was slowly undermined.

Christian Missions and Western Education

At this point in time, the Christian missionary or, in some parts of
tropical Africa, the Muslim missionary, was fortunately available to
help build up again what had been broken down. As we have seen,
the missionary had entered most parts of tropical Africa ahead of
the colonial governments. At any time up to 1914, and in most places
long after, he would have been a much more familiar figure, in the
rural areas at least, than the government official. With the coming of
the colonial period, his activities took on, almost everywhere, a new

lease of life. It is a remarkable and often overlooked fact that the colonial expansion of the nineteenth century provoked among the young men and women of Europe a response not only from those who wished to rule, but even more from those who wished to serve, in the backward places of the world. Missionary societies of every denomination experienced a boom in recruitment and in financial support, with the result that missions all over tropical Africa were able to be strengthened very greatly during the years between 1890 and 1914.

The object of all missionaries was to bring African people into membership of the churches to which they themselves belonged. At this period, they at last began to be outstandingly successful in doing so. All over the previously animist parts of tropical Africa, from about the seventh parallel of north latitude southwards, Africans flocked to join the churches – and not only to join them, but also to serve them actively as evangelists and catechists and ordained ministers. Only where Islam was already well established – in Senegal and Guinea, in Soudan and Niger, in Northern Nigeria and the Chad territories, in the northern Sudan and in Somalia, and in the coastal belt of East Africa – did Christian propaganda encounter any serious resistance. Only in these areas did Islam itself carry out a comparable expansion, spreading from its town bases into the surrounding countryside and consolidating itself through the development of Koranic schools and religious brotherhoods. In southern Nigeria, Yorubaland, poised between the Muslim north and the Christian coastlands, experienced both movements simultaneously.

The main means used by all the Christian missions in their evangelism was to found networks of village schools in which children of all ages could be given a very simple education in reading, writing, and arithmetic alongside the religious instruction leading to baptism and church membership. These 'bush-schools', as they were called, were not impressive places architecturally. This description, written in Northern Rhodesia in 1912, would have been typical of much of Africa: 'The school consisted of a fence of grass, 6 feet high, surrounding a big tree, a few poles laid across short, forked sticks for seats, and a mass of wriggling, youthful humanity'. A little later, a school like this would probably have developed into a building of the kind so well described by Bishop Kitching in northern Uganda, which served as a school on weekdays and a church on Sundays. Kitching wrote:

Imagine a rough shed, built of mud and wattle and thatched with grass. Very likely it is leaning sideways and is propped up with extra poles at varied angles. A few gaps left in the mud serve for windows and doorways. At one end the floor is raised a few inches by way of a chancel, and a pole or bamboo runs across as a Communion rail. At each side a mud-walled enclosure does duty as reading-desk and pulpit. On the inside of the roof hang innumerable hornet's nests, and possibly a few bats. On the walls, suspended from little pegs, are sheets displaying the alphabet, or rows of syllables, some of them nibbled by intrusive goats or fretted by the ubiquitous termites. Look in at about 8.30 in the morning, and you will see groups of readers of mixed ages and sexes, seated on the floor in front of the sheets, saying over the letters or syllables in a sing-song voice. Somehow they get the syllables memorised, and are promoted to reading consecutive print.[1]

Such were the beginnings of western education in tropical Africa. The first instructors were, of course, European missionaries, but the brighter pupils who emerged from the system were given further training as catechists and teachers. As a result, education soon developed into a popular movement, in which foreign missionaries occupied only the supervisory positions and in which most of the teaching and evangelistic posts were held by Africans. These educated people constituted a new and very real kind of leadership rivalling that of the traditional chiefs. In the Africa of 1900–14, these mission teachers were the men and women who understood and felt at ease in the new world of the colonial period. To the tribal beliefs of their parents, they had added a faith which they knew to be shared by people of all colours and all climates. Their religion taught them that all men had the same capacity for improvement in this life and salvation in the next. They were not, therefore, cast down by the changes which confronted them, but rather regarded them as opportunities to be seized. The development of the colonial administrations, of commercial and mining companies, and of European plantations – all increased the demand for clerks and skilled craftsmen, especially for those who knew a European language. The mission school soon emerged as a clear avenue for advancement, along which the ambitious could

---

[1] A. L. Kitching, *From Darkness to Light* (London, 1935), p. 31.

escape from the narrow discipline of village life into a wider world of well-paid urban employment.

The Birth of Nationalism

Part of the significance of the Christian missions was that, in their religious as well as their educational work, they were introducing Africans to the wider, western world into which they were now entering. They were showing them how they could succeed in that world. They were helping to make them into good colonial citizens. At the same time, however unconsciously, the missionaries were teaching the Africans to weigh up and criticise the influences of Europe *from within*. During the earliest years of the colonial period, opposition to colonialism had been the opposition of the least westernised groups, whose leaders simply wanted to drive out the Europeans and restore the situation which had previously existed. From the mission schools, however, there was beginning to emerge, even before 1914, a new kind of opposition to colonialism. This opposition did not aim to restore the pre-colonial situation. On the contrary, the aim of the mission-educated Africans was to capture the political and religious institutions introduced into Africa from the West. This they meant to do either by taking over these institutions from the inside and gradually replacing their European masters, or by imitating them from the outside and establishing similar alternatives to the colonial institutions.

These mission-educated Christians were, in fact, the first real African nationalists. Some of them believed that the way forward lay in joining the churches planted by the missions and in seeking the best employment they could get in the service of colonial governments and commercial companies. They hoped that one day, their children or grandchildren would rise naturally into the controlling positions. Others already believed that this hope was vain and that it would be necessary for Africans to found their own independent churches and to prepare for an ultimate and revolutionary challenge to the colonial authorities. Either way, these new nationalists were thinking in modern terms – not in terms of a reversion to tribal beliefs and tribal organisations, but in terms of Christian churches under African leadership and of African successor states based on the existing colonial territories and governed along western rather than along traditional African lines.

A pamphlet written in 1911 by a Nyasaland African called Charles Domingo gives a perceptive picture of the outlook of the more radical of these early nationalists. Domingo wrote:

There is too much failure among all Europeans in Nyasaland. The three combined bodies – Missionaries, Government and Companies or gainers of money – do form the same rule to look upon the native with mockery eyes. It sometimes startles us to see that the three combined bodies are from Europe, and along with them there is a title Christendom. And to compare and make a comparison between the Master of the title and his servants, it provokes any African away from believing in the Master of the title.

If we had power enough to communicate ourselves to Europe, we would advise them not to call themselves Christendom, but Europeandom. Therefore the life of the three combined bodies is altogether too cheaty, too thefty, too mockery. Instead of 'Give', they say 'Take away from'. There is too much breakage of God's pure law as seen in James's Epistle, chapter five, verse four.[2]

As one can see, Charles Domingo was not a highly educated man. His ideas were simple ideas. His use of English was far from perfect. But what is interesting about him is that he was judging the Europeans he had met according to their own professed standard of moral judgement, namely the New Testament. He evidently did not doubt that the Epistle of James represented 'God's pure law', nor did the people for whom he was writing. The conclusion he drew from the failure of Europeans to practise their Christianity was not that Africans should abandon it, though he realised that was a danger, but that they could and should practise it better under their own leadership. Charles Domingo and those like him all over tropical Africa at this time represented the *most* westernised element in the colonial societies. Even on the equator, most of them dressed in all the elaborate finery of early-twentieth-century Europe. In every aspect of their lives, they were the pioneers of European taste and customs. The independent churches founded at this period were mostly even more European in their ritual and procedure than the mission churches. Yet, for all their imitativeness, these early African nationalists had

[2] George Shepperson and Thomas Price, *Independent African* (Edinburgh, 1958), pp. 163–4.

learned one thing above all others from their mission education: they wanted to run their own lives for themselves.

Although historians now know that opinions such as these were forming under the surface, they were not, in the years before 1914, much in evidence to Europeans who lived or worked in Africa at the time. Only in the coastal towns of West Africa, where some well-to-do merchant families had been educating their children in the western tradition for two or three generations, were there newspapers owned and edited by Africans which made a habit of exposing colonial abuses. Here, too, there was a sprinkling of Africans like Sir Samuel Lewis, who had risen to the top level of the colonial civil service of Sierra Leone, or James Johnson, the Yoruba bishop of the Anglican Niger Delta Pastorate, whose opinions were far too powerful to be ignored. Otherwise, the colonial governments, the missionaries, the settlers, and the commercial companies appeared to be in complete control of their several spheres. Almost everywhere, the first military stage of colonial occupation had been succeeded by civil administration. Modern communications had penetrated to most districts. Cash crops were being widely grown. Migrant labourers were moving freely over long distances to various kinds of European employment. Taxes were being paid. At last, grants-in-aid from the governments of the European countries were being steadily eliminated. Most Europeans imagined that the foundations of empire were being laid down for a thousand years to come. To the extent that they were aware of the mission-educated Africans – the slowly developing intelligentsia – they wrote them off as an unrepresentative and unimportant minority. Even so great an administrator as Lugard referred to them contemptuously as 'trousered blacks', from whose exploitation the uneducated majority must be protected for a long time to come. The eyes of the colonial administrations were fixed on the traditional chiefs and the old social hierarchy, whose influence they were unconsciously doing so much to destroy by their patronage. They ignored the new men and women, on whom the future of Africa was really to depend.

THIRTEEN. The Inter-War Period, 1918–1938

The War and the Mandates System

The First World War, fought between 1914 and 1918, marked an important turning point in the history of the tropical African territories. Before the war these colonies had been backwaters, each connected with the mainstream of world events only through the single channel linking it to one or another of the colonial powers. There had been little overall policy. Each colony had been thought of as a separate problem, and mainly as a problem of economic self-support. After the war, things moved faster. Most African colonies were by now sufficiently established to be able to think of more than mere survival. Their revenues were beginning to show modest surpluses over the bare cost of law and order. Colonial governments were able for the first time to contemplate expenditure on education, on health, on agricultural and veterinary services, and on economic development of various kinds. After the war, too, colonial powers started to take their colonial responsibilities more seriously. They tried to work out consistent policies for the African colonies. They developed within their colonial ministries important specialist departments and advisory services designed to assist all the colonial governments under their control. This increasing centralisation did much to break down the previous isolation of individual territories.

The war also made the colonial powers somewhat responsible to international opinion. The former German colonies were divided among the victor nations. Britain took most of the former German

East Africa as Tanganyika Territory, and Belgium the remainder as Ruanda–Urundi. South Africa took the former German South-West Africa, and France and Britain each took adjoining parts of Cameroun and Togo (the British called their part 'Togoland'; the French, 'Togo'). The changes were not outright annexations in the manner of the original partition. In the hope of avoiding further conflicts, the victorious powers had set up an international authority, the League of Nations. Largely on the initiative of the American president Woodrow Wilson, it was agreed that those powers taking over German colonies should do so as 'mandatories' of the League. Those undertaking the task were required to recognise that the interests of the population concerned must have equal weight with those of the administering power. In spite of the lead taken by Wilson, the U.S. Congress would not agree to America joining the League. This gravely weakened the organisation from the very start of its life. Nevertheless, with strong British support, the establishment of a Mandates Commission of the League went forward. The mandatories agreed to govern their territories as 'a sacred trust of civilisation' until such time as they were 'able to stand on their own feet in the strenuous conditions of the modern world'. Annual reports on each of the mandated territories had to be sent to the League at its headquarters at Geneva in Switzerland and, in the Mandates Commission of the League, it was possible for international opinion to have some influence on the policy of the mandatory powers.

The Dual Policy in British Africa

In practice, it turned out to be the mandatory powers themselves who tended to dominate the Commission's meetings. This was significant because it showed that these powers were not merely concerned with defending their actions in the mandated territories, but were also seeking a defensible policy of colonialism which could be applied to all their overseas possessions. Foremost among these practical thinkers about colonialism was Lord Lugard, who had ended his career as colonial administrator and had become the principal British representative on the Mandates Commission. In 1922, he published a book called *The Dual Mandate in British Tropical Africa*, which

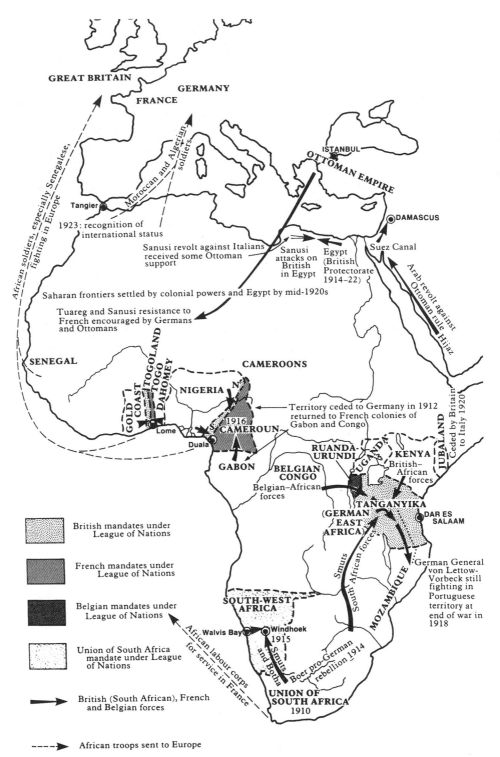

23. Africa and the First World War.

inspired a whole generation of colonial administrators and was accepted as a guide by politicians and civil servants in Britain. Lugard started from the doctrine that a colonial power had a double responsibility: on the one hand to the colonial peoples under its rule and on the other hand to the outside world. To the colonial peoples, it owed material and moral advancement leading ultimately to self-government. To the outside world, it had the obligation to see that the natural resources of its colonies were developed and that they found their way onto the world market. Lugard argued that, properly balanced, these two obligations need not conflict with one another. To secure a proper balance, it was necessary to ensure that in the economic field as well as in that of government, the colonial peoples were encouraged to do as much as possible for themselves.

In the field of government, Lugard prescribed a general adoption of the system of indirect rule, which he had first evolved in Northern Nigeria and later adapted to the differing circumstances of the South. Indirect rule meant government through the traditional chiefs. In Lugard's words, a colonial official 'would consider it as irregular to issue direct orders to an individual native ... as a General commanding a division would to a private soldier, except through his commanding officers'.[1] At the same time, indirect rule was not just a system for concealing the exercise of power by the colonial government. It was basic to Lugard's thinking, although not always to that of his followers, that the traditional local government of the chiefs should be progressively modernised. The aim was that it should be able to take on more and more responsibility, especially financial responsibility for the raising and spending of public funds. Under indirect rule, taxes were collected by the chiefs, who passed on most of the money to the colonial government for national use. The chiefs were, however, allowed to keep a proportion of the taxes for their own 'Native Treasuries' and to spend the money on local needs and largely at their own discretion. This expenditure included the salaries of local government employees, such as clerks, messengers, and policemen, and also local public works, such as offices, courthouses, dispensaries, markets, country roads, and footpaths. Lugard looked forward to

---

[1] Lugard's Amalgamation Report, 1919, p. 14, cited in Margery Perham, *Lugard: Years of Authority 1898–1945* (Oxford, 1960), pp. 469–70.

a time when the smaller traditional chiefdoms would federate with their neighbours to form larger units. In this way, he imagined that a class of people would eventually emerge with the experience necessary to take responsibility at a national level.

In economic development, Lugard was once again insistent that the largest possible place should be left free for the enterprise of Africans in their own countries. He recognised, of course, that large-scale and long-term economic investment, such as that required for railways and harbours, was clearly beyond the scope of local communities. Equally, he thought that projects of this kind were too important to be left to outside private enterprise; therefore, in these matters he was a strong and early advocate of state ownership. In other kinds of large industry, such as mining, he saw a legitimate field for outside enterprise, though he stressed that not only colonial governments but also local 'Native' governments should receive an interest in the profit. In the field of agricultural production, however, he was a firm opponent of the outside enterprise that was seeking to establish plantations for tropical produce in the West African countries. These European companies used arguments such as those put forward in 1924 by Lord Leverhulme when he said, 'The African native will be happier, produce the best, and live under the larger conditions of prosperity, when his labour is directed and organised by his white brother who has all these million years start ahead of him'.[2] Lugard in the 1920s regretted the policy of white settlement in East Africa, which he had himself advocated in the 1890s. He saw it had the effect of obstructing African enterprise of the kind which had flourished so successfully under the West African system of peasant production. That Lord Leverhulme's United Africa Company was refused permission to acquire plantations in any of the British West African colonies was due very largely to Lugard's influence.

The Dual Policy in East and Central Africa

Obviously, the part of tropical Africa where the dual policy was hardest to apply was in East and Central Africa, from Kenya south to

---

[2] Speech, cited in Michael Crowder, *The Story of Nigeria* (London, 1973), p. 264.

Rhodesia. Here Europeans had been encouraged to settle, and here they were now claiming the right to take an increasing share in government. In Rhodesia, this process had indeed gone too far to be stopped. When, in 1923, the British South Africa Company asked to be relieved of its governmental responsibilities, effective power was transferred to the 33,000 white settlers. North of the Zambezi, however, the British government was already by this time showing signs of its change of heart. The policy adopted in 1918 of encouraging demobilised army officers to settle in Kenya had led, within three years, to an acute labour crisis. During this crisis, the colonial government had instructed its administrative officers to put pressure on the chiefs to direct their subjects into European employment. This led to such an agitation by missionaries and by the administrative officers themselves that public opinion in England was aroused. When the settlers pressed for further political powers in 1922–3, they were resisted. In July 1923, the British government issued a White Paper stating that

Primarily Kenya is an African territory, and His Majesty's Government think it necessary definitely to record their considered opinion that the interests of the African natives must be paramount, and that if and when these interests and the interests of the immigrant races should conflict, the former should prevail. As in the Uganda Protectorate, so in the Kenya Colony, the principle of Trusteeship for the Natives, no less than in the Mandated Territory of Tanganyika, is unassailable.[3]

The following year (1924), the British government sent an all-party parliamentary commission under the chairmanship of one of Lugard's greatest admirers, William Ormsby-Gore (later Lord Harlech), to investigate the guiding principles of British policy in East Africa. In its report, the commission reaffirmed that there need be no conflict between the interests of the settlers and those of the native inhabitants. White settlement should not be allowed to hold back the education of Africans or their training in economic skills, especially training in the best use of their own land. Though it did nothing to attack settlement, the Ormsby-Gore commission envisaged a great expansion in the functions of colonial governments, in the building up of health services, education services, and agricultural and veterinary

---

[3] *Indians in Kenya Memorandum* (HMSO, London, 1923), p. 6.

services. All these measures were directed toward the African population of the territories. It was this report which helped to set British policy in East Africa in line with that pursued in the West.

Education in the British Colonies

In 1925, Ormsby-Gore, now under-secretary of state for the colonies, summoned the governors of the West and East African colonies to London. He ordered them to pursue a much more active policy of education by entering into partnership with the Christian missions of all denominations and by subsidising the mission schools on condition that they conformed to the proper standards of efficiency. This did not result in a great increase in the total number of African children attending school, which remained at about a third of those of school age. But, of those who did attend, the great majority now stayed at school for at least four years. And, from this time onwards, there were government inspectorates in every colony. Subsidies were given only on condition that teachers were trained and that the prescribed syllabuses were followed. In Muslim areas, like Northern Nigeria, local-authority schools were set up and staffed by government-trained teachers. As a result, during the fourteen years from 1925 to 1939, the standard of primary education was much improved, and the effects were felt over the whole field of employment. The higher standards were noticed in government – and especially in local government – in the churches, in commerce, in industry, and in every walk of life where a little clerical skill and a little knowledge of the world was needed.

More revolutionary still, however, was the progress made in secondary education. Here, the numbers involved were very small indeed. Nigeria was probably the only country in British Africa which in 1939 had more than a dozen secondary schools. In most countries, the output was between 100 and 200 students a year. Nevertheless, it was these few hundreds of secondary school students who demonstrated that tropical Africans were capable of filling a wide range of posts of skill and responsibility, for which it had previously been thought necessary to import Europeans. With the exception of a few West Africans from well-to-do families who had been educated abroad, it was from this generation that there emerged the first professional men and women. There were doctors and veterinary surgeons, the first agricultural and forest officers, the first managers of retail stores, the first secondary schoolteachers, and, above all, the first educated chiefs and local government officials. Not all of these secondary school students, however, consented to fill the occupations intended for them by the colonial authorities. It was in this generation that most of the leaders of the nationalist revolution received their secondary education: Kenyatta, Banda, and Azikiwe toward the beginning of it; Nkrumah, Tafawa Balewa, and Oginga Odinga toward the end of it. It is probably true that, had the colonial governments and the Christian missions not provided the means of secondary education during this inter-war period, there could have been no successful nationalist revolution until long after the Second World War.

The French Policy of Association

If it was Lugard and Ormsby-Gore who laid the foundations of British colonial policy between the wars, their French equivalent was Albert Sarraut, minister of colonies in 1920–4 and 1932–3. Sarraut's outlook was very different from that of the Englishmen. It was less respectful of the African personality and, yet, at the same time more fraternal toward the African. Sarraut never talked of 'allowing the African to develop along his own lines'. His dominant thought was rather that France and its African colonies must be kept as united in peace as they had been in war. The key to his plan was the rapid economic development of the colonies, to provide France with raw materials and with markets for French manufactured goods. 'Our colonies', he wrote, 'must be centres of production, and no longer museums for specimens'. Assimilation of Africans into French culture remained the ultimate objective, but no special effort was made to hurry it on. In 1936, apart from the four coastal *communes* of the Senegal with their 80,000 black *citoyens* (citizens with full political rights), only about 2,000 out of 14 million French West Africans had received French citizenship. The immediate emphasis was on 'association', meaning the collective association of the French colonies with France. Economically, the French empire was to become as centralised as it already was administratively. There was no thought that any of the colonies would ever become independent. African chiefs were merely the 'agents' of the French administration, and there was no intention at all of allowing their powers to grow. Indeed, the top-grade chiefs, the *chefs de canton*, were really officials of the French administration. They were normally chosen from among the more efficient clerks and interpreters in the government service rather than on any hereditary principle.

It was, above all, in education that French policy differed from British. Although a few mission schools received government subsidies for exceptional efficiency, nine-tenths of the formal education given in French Africa between the wars was given by the state. Moreover, all teaching was in French. The aim of education was neatly defined by one governor–general of French West Africa as 'instruire la masse et dégager l'élite' (give primary education to the masses and win over the elite). Primary education was given in 're-gional schools', of which there were by 1937 about eighty scattered over French West Africa. There was a very much smaller number in French Equatorial Africa. Secondary education was limited to filling the needs of the government service. Nearly all of it was given in three first-class institutions in Dakar. The best-known of these institutions, both academically and for its output of later nationalist leaders, was the teacher-training college called the Ecole William Ponty.

In the Congo, the Belgians pursued between the wars a policy which resembled the French policy insofar as rule was direct rather than indirect. In 1919, the colony was being administered in no fewer than 6,000 separate chiefdoms (*chefferies*). By 1934, this had been re-duced by amalgamations to some 2,500, but even at this figure the African chief in the Belgian Congo was scarcely even the equivalent of the French chef de canton. Like his opposite number in French West Africa, he was strictly the agent of the colonial government. In the Belgian colonial service, as in the French, administrative dis-tricts were much smaller than in most British territories, and the administrative staff was larger. Control, therefore, was correspond-ingly closer. In education, the Belgians, like the British, preferred to subsidise mission schools rather than to organise a state education service. Unlike the British, however, they subsidised only 'national', that is to say Roman Catholic, missions. Even more severely than the French, the Belgians limited schooling to primary education only.

Their stated aim was to bring forward the inhabitants of the colony at a uniform pace, and so to prevent the exploitation of the many by the few. Actually, as it turned out, the result was to leave the country with few effective leaders at independence and with not nearly enough educated people to operate the machinery of government.

Colonialism and Nationalism

Although by the 1920s the tropical African colonies of all the European powers were being run at least partly in the interests of their African inhabitants, developments were still dominated by European governors, administrators, and commissions of inquiry. No important decisions were made by Africans and, in a sense, there were fewer Africans of importance in this period than there had been in the period before 1914, when a few of the old leaders still survived from the pre-colonial period. By the 1920s, most of these older men were either dead or in retirement. Their places had been taken by men who owed their promotion to Europeans and who tended to be the 'trusties' of the colonial administrations. A small but important number of educated men and women were leaving the secondary schools, but they were still young and inexperienced, and they held as yet only minor jobs in government and commerce. A very few were able to study in Europe and America and became doctors and lawyers; however, on their return to Africa, they were often not given the status merited by their qualifications. Most such people considered that their attainments deserved greater rewards. Out of these individual grudges emerged a more general dissatisfaction with the way their countries were being governed.

The earliest political associations were formed, naturally, in West Africa, where the coastal people had been in contact with Europeans for centuries and where a tiny minority had enjoyed western education for several generations. In Sierra Leone, the leading freed-slave families and in Senegal, the Creoles (descendants of marriages between French men and African women) had taken part in local politics since the middle of the nineteenth century. In the Gold Coast and in Lagos, small associations had sprung up during the early twentieth century among the lawyers, doctors, and businessmen. As early as 1918, a Gold Coast lawyer, J. E. Casely Hayford, founded the

National Congress of British West Africa, which spread to Nigeria in 1920. The Congress demanded that Africans should participate in the government. For the most part, however, the activities of these early politicians were confined to local affairs, and they had little influence on the colonial governments. In French West Africa, political consciousness centred upon the four coastal communes of Senegal, where the 80,000 citoyens had as early as 1914 elected a black Senegalese, Blaise Diagne, to the Chamber of Deputies in Paris. In 1917, Diagne became the under-secretary of state for the colonies of metropolitan France, and this helped to set the fashion that politically conscious Senegalese should join the political parties of France. From about 1936 onwards, increasingly left-wing governments were elected in France. Socialists and communists were now able to obtain appointments in the colonies, especially in the education service. As a result, considerable numbers of French West Africans joined the French socialist and communist parties.

In the field of Pan-African politics, student organisations in Britain and France were the chief means of turning local and individual grievances into a true spirit of nationalism. Much of the inspiration of these organisations came from the writings and activities of American and West Indian Negroes, such as Edward Blyden, W. E. DuBois, and Marcus Garvey, who stressed the similarities in the conditions of black people on both sides of the Atlantic. Under their influence, Africans began to think in terms of taking over control of the political units which the colonial powers had created and of uniting them after the manner of the United States of America or the Union of Soviet Socialist Republics. Foremost among the student organisations was the West African Students' Union, founded in 1925 in London by the Nigerian Ladipo Solanke. The Italian invasion of Ethiopia in 1935 added fuel to the growing fire of nationalist feelings. The decisive event in the history of nationalism in British West Africa was undoubtedly the return in 1935 of Nnamdi Azikiwe from his studies in America and his launching – first in the Gold Coast and then in his native Nigeria – of a popular press. This was the most essential step in getting the political ideas of pan-Africanism accepted by a mass audience. Soon after his return, Azikiwe helped to send to America eight Nigerians and four Gold Coasters, all of whom grew into key figures of the post-war nationalist revolution. The most prominent of this group was a young Gold Coast teacher named Kwame Nkrumah.

Most of the West African politicians were men who had broken away from their tribal backgrounds. They organised their activities in a European way, using newspapers and popular agitation. These caused riots at times, but were essentially non-violent. In East Africa, discontent with European rule still assumed a mainly tribal form. The history of nationalism in Kenya, for example, is largely the history of Kikuyu dissatisfaction and resistance. The numbers of the Kikuyu were increasing rapidly. Their natural path of expansion out of the forests around Mount Kenya was blocked by the European settlers. Many became squatters and farm labourers on European estates, while others left the land and joined the growing numbers of unemployed in Nairobi. In 1922, a clerk in government service, Harry Thuku, started a political association which drew attention to these problems. He was sacked from his job and arrested, whereupon a large crowd assembled in Nairobi and was fired upon by the police. Thuku was banished to the remote Northern Frontier District, but political groups spread widely among the Kikuyu. When, in the late 1920s, some missionary societies attempted to interfere with Kikuyu initiation customs, many teachers left the mission schools and formed an Independent Schools Association. Jomo Kenyatta first came to prominence as secretary of the main Kikuyu party, the Kikuyu Central Association, before he left to study and work in Britain in the 1930s. When Thuku was released from detention in 1931, he formed a moderate party which quarrelled bitterly with the Kikuyu Central Association. The Kikuyu were thus unable to present a united front to the government and the settlers – and this, of course, suited the Europeans very well.

Although between the wars Kenya appeared to be almost the only troubled territory in tropical Africa, the apparent calm that prevailed in other colonies was deceptive. During the early 1930s, the whole momentum of colonial economic and social policy suffered a grave setback due to the world slump of 1929–31, which had a disastrous effect on the prices paid for primary products and, therefore, on the revenues of all colonial governments. Huge cuts had to be made in all public services, including even basic administration and security. In some territories, the number of government employees was reduced by more than half. In the view of some historians, this was the moment when colonial rule began to unravel, especially in the urban centres that were just beginning to grow into towns. During the later 1930s, with the gradual return of economic buoyancy, some of the lost ground was recovered, but there is no doubt that, under the surface, African society was changing rapidly, and not in the way Lugard had hoped for. The 'trousered blacks' rather than the long-robed chieftains were setting the pace. Africa was seething with new ideas and new ambitions, making ready to exert its will in opposition to the rule of European governments. Still, without the added ferment of the Second World War, it is very doubtful if the authority of the colonial governments would have been challenged until very much later than it in fact was.

FOURTEEN. North and North-East Africa, 1900–1939

The Pan-Islamic Movement

By 1914, North Africa and the Muslim lands of the Horn of Africa were all in European hands. Only Ethiopia clung to a precarious independence. The variety of political and social conditions in this region was staggering. The contrast between Somali pastoralists on one hand and the wealthy citizens of Cairo on the other was extreme. Yet, they possessed a common faith and a single cultural tradition which set them apart from most of the people of tropical Africa. The European powers had to adapt their policies and their methods of administration to the institutions of Muslim society. These were too deeply rooted to be set aside. Warfare and political conflict loomed larger over these countries throughout the colonial period than in any other part of Africa. Resistance to the loss of independence was inflamed by the intense religious hostility long felt by Muslims for the Christian peoples of Europe. As a result, revolts led by shaikhs and holy men continued until the 1930s, by which time nationalist opposition organised on modern political lines had developed. Nationalism, here as elsewhere, was influenced by European political ideas absorbed in colonial schools and metropolitan universities. Throughout this region, it was influenced also by the pan-Islamic reform movement.

The pan-Islamic movement was a reaction against the relentless encroachment of Christian Europe upon the lands of Islam. It began among groups of educated Turks in the Ottoman empire in the

1860s and the 1870s. The movement owed something to the example of the unification of Italy and Germany, which was taking place about that time. The ideas spread to Cairo, Damascus, and other Arabic-speaking cities of the Middle East. The central argument of the pan-Islamists was that the only way the Muslim world could survive in the face of European aggression was for all Muslims to sink their political and local differences and to unite against the common foe. Political unification could only be brought about through a thorough rethinking of the principles and practices of the Muslim religion. Al-Azhar University in Cairo became the main centre for the teaching of pan-Islamic ideas, in spite of the British occupation of Egypt after 1882. To al-Azhar came students from all over the Muslim world, including the Maghrib and the Sudanic lands. These students returned to their homes inspired by the reforming movement.

French Rule in the Maghrib

By the beginning of the twentieth century, Algeria had already been ruled for many years as if it were a part of France, whereas in Tunisia and Morocco the governments of the bey and the sultan survived the establishment of the protectorates. They were, however, increasingly staffed with French officials. All three countries were poor, suffering from perennial droughts, poor soils, and, above all, difficulties of communication caused by the mountainous interior. The French now tackled these problems with determination, especially that of communications. By the 1930s, it was possible to travel from Marrakech to Tunis by train, and Maghribi roads were the best in Africa. The growth of Casablanca offers an outstanding example of development under French rule. In 1900, it was a tiny fishing village. Even before the establishment of the protectorate in 1912, the French had constructed an artificial harbour, with rail links to the iron and phosphate mines of the interior. By 1936, it had a population of a quarter million. Moroccans flocked to Casablanca (as Algerians did to Algiers and Oran) to work in the factories and port installations, the more poorly paid among them living in shanty-towns on the outskirts of the city.

In all three countries, Frenchmen were encouraged to settle as colons. In Algeria, by the turn of the century, there were more than

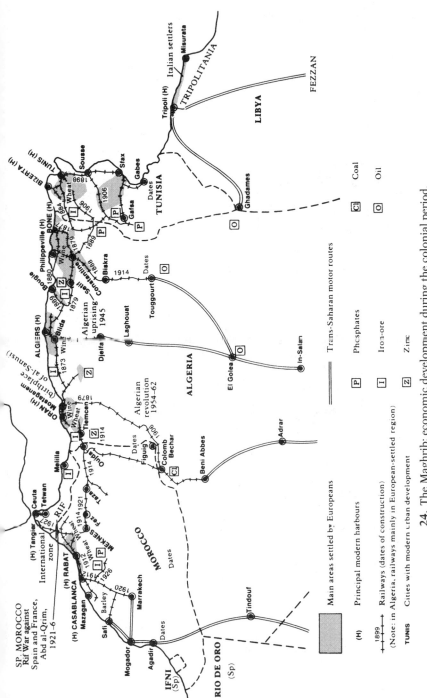

24. The Maghrib: economic development during the colonial period.

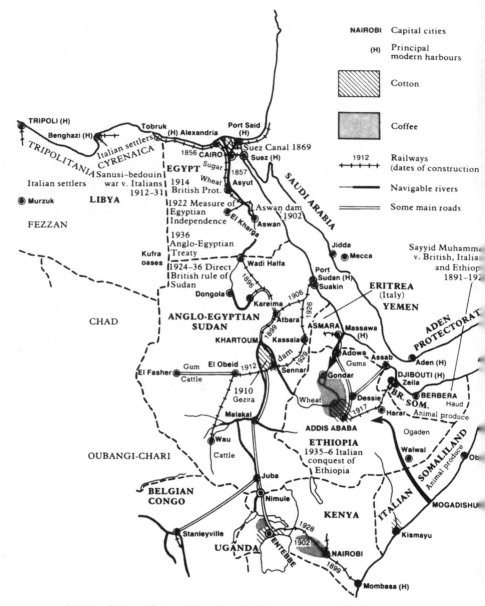

25. North-East Africa under colonial rule: economic and political development.

500,000, and by 1936 they had grown to nearly 1 million. In the same year, there were more than 200,000 colons in Morocco and nearly as many in Tunisia. Undoubtedly, most of the economic development which took place under French rule was attributable to these immigrants, though their presence in such numbers caused grave political and social difficulties. Not only did they occupy much of the land, but in every town, they also competed for jobs with the indigenous Muslim population. The Muslim population too was growing rapidly: in Algeria alone, it doubled itself, rising from 4.5 million to more than 9 million during the first half of the century. With the best land and the highest-paid jobs in European hands, the Muslims tended to become poorer as their numbers increased. By the 1930s, many thousands of Maghribis had migrated to France in order to earn a better livelihood.

The colons of Algeria remained, in the fullest sense, citizens of France. They elected their own deputies to the National Assembly in Paris and exercised a steady pressure on French politics. Theoretically, the same rights of citizenship could be granted to educated Muslims but only if they abandoned Muslim for Christian law, which few of them cared to do. The colons, needless to say, did nothing to encourage them. In 1913, a French writer summed up the settler point of view as follows: 'In a conquered country almost the only kind of co-operation that can occur between the two races is one in which the conquered work for the conquerors'.

Morocco: Lyautey and Abd al-Qrim

The territory which differed most from Algeria was Morocco. This was partly because French rule there did not begin until 1912. It was mainly because of the outstanding character of its first resident–general, Marshal Lyautey, who held the office for thirteen years, from 1912 until 1925. Lyautey was a colonial ruler of the highest order. He understood and respected the traditional institutions of North African Islam, and was determined that they should be preserved with dignity. At the same time, he had a sure grasp of economic affairs, and the rapid modernisation of the Moroccan economy was largely his work. When he came to Morocco, he found it 'submerged in a wave of anarchy'. In particular, he had to take on the task of pacifying the tribes of the bilad as-siba (see Chapter 4). For centuries, no sultan of Morocco had been able to subdue these tribes. Perhaps Lyautey's greatest achievement was the bringing of law and order to areas that had never previously been controlled by the central government of Morocco, and by means more humane than forceful conquest. His principle was 'to display force in order to avoid using it'. His policy of combining French interests with those of the sultan and the tribal *caids* (chiefs) was similar to Lugard's work in Hausaland, and suffered from the same defects.

In the early 1920s, Lyautey's pacification was rudely interrupted by the Rif War. The Berbers of the Rif mountains in the northern zone of Morocco rose against the inefficient and often unjust Spanish military government. Brilliantly led by a former *qadi* (Muslim judge) called Abd al-Qrim, they defeated a Spanish force in 1921 and followed this up by pushing the Spaniards into the coastal towns. Abd al-Qrim proclaimed a 'Republic of the Rif'. The term was modern, but he had a thoroughly old-fashioned ambition – to become sultan and found a new dynasty in Morocco. Abd al-Qrim's military successes made him the hero of the Muslim world. This gave him the false confidence to extend his operations into the French zone. By doing so, he brought down the whole might of the French army against him. France and Spain, in the words of an American observer, 'had enveloped the Rif in a wall of steel, employing every device of scientific warfare against the embattled tribesmen'. Once this had happened, further resistance was futile. In May 1926, Abd al-Qrim

came riding astride a mule into the French lines. At one point he was crossing a stream in which French soldiers were bathing. As soon as they saw who he was, they came rushing towards him. Though naked, they saluted him in correct military fashion, and expressed their great admiration for his qualities as a soldier and a leader.[1]

The French exiled him to the island of Réunion, but, years later, he returned to play a part in the Moroccan nationalist movement.

In 1925, Lyautey submitted his resignation to the French government in protest against the delays in sending him the reinforcements which he had asked for during the crisis of the Rif War. To his surprise

[1] Rom Landau, *Moroccan Drama* (London, 1956), p. 128.

and grief, his resignation was accepted. It is said that he boarded his ship at Casablanca with tears streaming down his face. His successors, who were lesser men than he, soon pushed the old ruling classes into the background, giving them no further opportunity to modernise the traditional institutions. In 1927, when the old sultan died, the French arranged for a young prince, Sidi Muhammad, to accede to the throne of Morocco. The French imagined that they could educate the young sultan to rule entirely according to their wishes. They could not have been more mistaken for, after the Second World War, Sidi Muhammad became the leader of the Moroccan nationalist movement. The French also attempted to play off the Berbers against the Arabs: the result was to unite them in opposition to French rule.

The Beginnings of Nationalism in the Maghrib

Nationalism in the Maghrib was a reaction against the realities of French rule, which were at variance both with the theory of assimilation in Algeria and with the terms of the protectorate treaties in Tunisia and Morocco. As early as 1920, Lyautey had forecast that 'a young generation is coming along which is full of life, and which needs activity. Lacking the outlets, which our administration offers them so sparingly, they will find another way out, and will seek to form themselves into groups in order to voice their demand'. In Morocco and Tunisia, it was possible to foresee the emergence of free, reformed, Muslim states. Moroccans looked back with pride over a long and glorious past. Their sultan claimed descent from the Prophet Muhammad and was the spiritual as well as the temporal leader of the country. The young Sidi Muhammad did not abandon his outward show of subservience to the French until after the Second World War, but his sympathies were known long before. The foundations of the nationalist movement, however, were laid by others. One summer's evening in 1926, ten young men met in a garden in Rabat, sipping mint tea under the boughs of a mulberry tree. They were addressed by an eighteen-year-old student, Ahmad Balafrej, who was one day to be prime minister of Morocco. 'Without freedom', he said, 'the darkness of the grave is more comforting to the spirit than the light of the sun'. The ten agreed to form a secret association to oppose French rule by any and all means. Nearly twenty years of preparation by journalism and political organisation were to be necessary before early movements like this one were able to combine in 1943 as the Istiqlal Party, or Party of Independence. The Istiqlal Party garnered the support of the sultan and a large section of the Moroccan people.

In Tunisia, the beginnings of democratic political organisation stretched far back beyond the colonial period to the middle of the nineteenth century, when, as we saw in Chapter 4, the Destour (Constitution) Party was formed to curb the power of the Ottoman bey. The Destour Party remained active during the early years of French rule, but represented mainly the wealthy citizens of the capital. In 1934, however, Habib Bourguiba broke away from the old party to found the Néo-Destour, composed of younger, more radical groups, with a modern secular policy. Bourguiba proclaimed that 'The Tunisia we mean to liberate will not be a Tunisia for Muslim, for Jew, or for Christian. It will be a Tunisia for all, without distinction of religion or race, who wish to have it as their country and to live in it under the protection of just laws'. But in 1934, Bourguiba and his supporters had still a long struggle ahead of them. Being generally sympathetic to France and French culture, they wanted to negotiate Tunisia's independence in a friendly way. The French and Italian settlers in Tunisia were opposed to such an independence, as were the French civil servants who staffed the Tunisian administration in large numbers. Above all, the French military chiefs were determined that Tunisia should remain French. They saw Tunis and the naval station of Bizerta as a necessary base for the coming war against Fascist Italy. Until after the Second World War, therefore, the French dealt with the Néo-Destour by imprisoning its leaders, by banning its newspapers, and finally by outlawing the party and closing its offices.

In Algeria, nationalism had to contend with an even more difficult situation. The political structure of the country had been entirely refashioned by the French. Most educated Muslims had been to French schools and spoke French better than they spoke Arabic. Yet, the privilege of French citizenship was in practice denied to them. There was little surviving from the past on which they could build. In 1934, Ferhat Abbas wrote despairingly, 'Men who die for a patriotic ideal are honoured and respected. But I would not die for an Algerian fatherland, because no such fatherland exists. I search the history books and I cannot find it. You cannot build on air'. The sense of an Algerian nationhood was born only during the bitter war fought with France between 1954 and 1962, in which the more moderate nationalists of the 1920s and 1930s, like Ferhat Abbas, were swept aside by younger, more extreme leaders. Nationalism in Algeria could hardly make a beginning until nationalism in Tunisia and Morocco had all but gained the victory.

The British in Egypt and the Sudan

After the British occupation of 1882, Lord Dufferin, who had been ambassador in Istanbul, was sent to Egypt to report on a possible system of government. He advised that the country could not be administered from London with any prospect of success: 'Any attempt on our part to do so would at once render us objects of hatred and suspicion to its inhabitants'. Unfortunately for both countries, this warning went largely unheeded. As allies of the Ottoman sultan, who was still the nominal sovereign of Egypt, Britain could not annex the country outright. The khedive and his ministers continued outwardly to govern the country. In reality, the British consul–general in Cairo held absolute power in Egypt. Lord Granville, the British foreign minister, wrote, 'It is essential that in important questions affecting the administration and safety of Egypt, the advice of Her Majesty's Government should be followed, so long as the provisional occupation continues. Ministers and Governors must carry out this advice or forfeit their offices'. Compared with other African countries, Egypt was highly developed both socially and economically. Nevertheless, the British carried out many improvements, especially in irrigation. The Aswan dam was completed in 1902. It stored sufficient water to irrigate the Nile valley year-round and, for the first time in 5,000 years, Egyptian agriculture became independent of variations in the annual Nile floods. In other fields, however, the problem was not the lack of modernisation, but the fact that modernisation had outstripped the financial resources of the country. Indeed, the foremost aim of Lord Cromer, who as consul–general from 1883 until 1907 held the position of supreme power, was to simplify the elaborate government of the khedives, and so to lighten the burden of taxation upon the peasant fellahin.

Material benefits, however, did not endear the British to the Egyptians, and discontent soon developed into nationalist demands for their withdrawal. Already by the 1890s, most Egyptian politicians were nationalists and, from then on, Anglo–Egyptian relations ran round in a vicious circle. The nationalists had only one demand: that the British should quit Egypt. The British replied that they could not do so until a strong and financially stable government had been established. This was impossible because the nationalists would not cooperate with the khedive and the British to form one. Thus, a growing gulf of misunderstanding and hostility separated the rulers from the ruled. In 1914, when Turkey sided with Germany in the First World War, and when Britain as a counter-measure declared a protectorate over Egypt, this gulf grew wider. Egypt became the base for all British military operations in the Middle East. Egyptians suffered real hardship from the foreign troops who were quartered among them. These troops requisitioned their labour, their animals, and their produce for military purposes. They voiced their resentment against Wingate, the high commissioner for the protectorate, in a popular song:

Woe on us Wingate, Who has carried off our corn, Carried off our cotton, Carried off our camels, Carried off our children, Leaving us only our lives, For love of Allah, now leave us alone.[2]

Egyptian resentment erupted into open revolt in 1919, when Britain and France failed to keep their promises to grant independence to the Arab provinces of the old Ottoman empire. Britain, now realising that she could only hold the country by force, decided to give way to Egyptian demands. But so suspicious had Egyptians become of British intentions that no politician was prepared to risk his reputation by signing a treaty with the occupying power. In 1922, therefore, Britain issued a one-sided declaration, granting Egypt a modified form of independence. British forces still remained in the country, but, under a new constitution, the khedive was recognised

---

[2] George Young, *Egypt* (London, 1927), p. 228.

as king, and the parliament was to be elected under a universal male franchise.

One of the immediate results of self-government in Egypt was to show how unreal was the joint rule of Britain and Egypt over the Sudan under the so-called condominium arrangement. The Sudan had been 'reconquered' in 1898 by the Egyptian army with the aid of British troops. The annual deficit in the Sudan's budget, which had persisted from then until 1913, had been met from the Egyptian, and not from the British, Treasury. For twenty-five years after the reconquest, Egyptians had held all but a hundred or two of the most senior posts in the army and the civil service. Nevertheless, all real power in the Sudan was exercised by the British governor–general and by the senior British administrators and military officers. British power was exercised on the assumption that the Sudan was a separate country from Egypt, with interests of its own which were more important than those of Egypt. For example, education in the Sudan was launched along English lines, very distinct from the largely French tradition prevailing in Egypt. More sinister still from the Egyptian point of view, the British were planning to use the Nile waters for a great irrigation project in the cotton-growing district of the Gezira, south of Khartoum. This scheme was undoubtedly beneficial to the Sudan, but it emphasised to every Egyptian that the waters of the Nile – the lifeline of Egypt – were in the control of another power. In fact, Egypt, which had ruled the Sudan in the nineteenth century, had been squeezed out of it by Britain in the twentieth.

This resentment over the Sudan led, in 1924, to the assassination by an Egyptian nationalist of the governor–general of the Sudan, Sir Lee Stack, when he was passing through Cairo on leave. The British reaction to the incident was severe. King Fuad was given twenty-four hours in which to order the withdrawal of all Egyptian officers and army units from the Sudan, and there followed a replacement of nearly all the Egyptian civil officials by British or Sudanese. From this time, the Sudan took on more and more the appearance of an ordinary British colony. 'Indirect rule' became the order of the day, and with it there grew up a new concern for the non-Muslim population of the southern Sudan. The British came to distrust the educated Sudanese emerging from the northern schools. They were felt to be disloyal to the government and sympathetic to Egypt. Just as the

Egyptians had been excluded from the government of the north, so the northern Sudanese were now excluded from the government of the south, with the result that the two halves of the country grew farther apart instead of closer together. The north was accessible to the outside world, and most of the economic development took place there. The south, although protected from northern and Islamic influences, remained equally isolated from the economic and social developments which might have enabled it to stand on its own feet. The results of this policy were to prove disastrous when, on Sudanese independence, a mainly northern government had to undertake the administration of the south.

Meanwhile, in Egypt, political power was alternating between the Wafd Party and the court party of the king. The Wafd Party was led by Zaghlul Pasha, a moderate nationalist, who had been forced by the circumstances of the 1919 rebellion to take up a hostile attitude to the British. By the 1930s, disillusionment with the intrigue and corruption of the professional politicians had become general. Rich Egyptians – many of them of the old Mamluk, Turkish class – seemed to get richer, while the lot of the urban workers and the fellahin grew harder. The mood of the country in 1935 was expressed by the young Gamal Nasser, then still a pupil at secondary school, who wrote in a school essay, 'The nation is in danger, and the disputes among the Parties are being fomented by Imperialism, the Palace, and the Party leaders themselves. Thus they hope to keep the country divided and busy with the race for lucrative posts, so that the Egyptians shall forget that they have a right to freedom'. In their frustration, many young people turned to political groups actively hostile to parliamentary democracy. The most influential of these was the fiercely nationalistic Muslim Brotherhood. This body aimed at reestablishing a truly Muslim state in which the great extremes of riches and poverty would disappear.

In 1936, after years of fruitless negotiations, Britain and Egypt signed a treaty, the fundamental provision of which was that British troops were to be confined to the Canal Zone. Although an attempt was made to solve some of the problems of the Sudan, no real understanding on this territory was possible. Britain and Egypt agreed to administer the Sudan in the interests of the Sudanese. Egyptian army units rejoined the Sudan garrison, and the virtual exclusion of Egyptian civilians from the Sudan was brought to an end. The Egyptians had to face the fact that, as a result of the Anglo–Egyptian estrangement, the sense of Sudanese separateness from Egypt had gone too far to be undone. This, no less than the temporary return of British military government to Egypt during the Second World War and the emergence of a western-supported Jewish state in Israel, determined that in the long term Egyptian nationalism would continue to grow in hostility toward the West.

The Italian Spheres of Influence: Libya

The remaining parts of Arabic-speaking Muslim Africa were those subject to Italian domination, of which the most turbulent throughout this period was Libya. We have already seen (see Chapter 10) how in 1911–12 Italy conquered the Ottoman provinces of Tripolitania and Cyrenaica. The elimination of the Turks, however, merely gave the Italians possession of the coastal towns. They soon came up against the real rulers of the interior, the shaikhs of the Sanusi zawiyas described in Chapter 4. These zawiyas were by now established in all the tribal territories of the nomadic bedouin of Cyrenaica and the Fezzan. The shaikhs, though still primarily religious leaders, had come to be regarded by the bedouin Arabs as their natural representatives in all their dealings with the outside world. The shaikhs had usually cooperated with the Turkish officials, who had been their fellow Muslims. When the Christian Italians conquered Tripoli and Benghazi, they moved into solid opposition. What had been mainly a religious movement now became a nationalist and political one. In 1912, the head of the Sanusi brotherhood, Sayyid Ahmad, moved his headquarters from the Kufra Oasis into southern Cyrenaica, and during the next six years concentrated all his energies on organising armed resistance to the Italians. His efforts were supported by Muslims throughout the Middle East. Gifts of money and arms flowed in from unofficial committees in Egypt, Turkey, Syria, and the Hijaz. When Italy entered the First World War in 1915 on the side of the Allied Powers, Turkey, which was fighting on the side of Germany and Austria, began to give him official support. When the Allied Powers emerged victorious from the world struggle, Sayyid Ahmad retreated to Istanbul, retaining his position as head of the

Sanusi brotherhood but relinquishing his temporal power in Cyrenaica to his nephew, Sayyid Idris, who was to become – twenty-five years later – the first king of Libya.

Between 1918 and 1922, Idris entered into a series of only half-sincere agreements with the Italians, in which he undertook to recognise Italian sovereignty in exchange for a large measure of autonomy in the bedouin areas. In 1922, the Fascist Party of Benito Mussolini seized power in Italy and denounced these agreements. The Arab leaders of Tripolitania and Cyrenaica thereupon met in conference and recognised Idris as amir of all Libya, and Idris – having accepted – withdrew to Egypt in anticipation of the expected military action of the Italians. This was launched at the end of the year. From then onwards, for nine years, the Libyan bedouin fought a war which, on a smaller scale, can be likened to the Algerian War of 1954–62. There were never more than 1,000 bedouin under arms, but with the secret support of the entire civil population, they engaged the continuous attention of an Italian army of 20,000. They forced the Fascists to adopt methods, such as aerial bombardment and the isolation of the civilian population in concentration camps, which sickened the whole of the civilised world. The main organiser of this phase of Libyan resistance was a Sanusi shaikh, Sidi Umar al-Mukhtar, whose capture and public execution by the Italians in 1931 brought military operations to an end. Italy thus enjoyed only eight years of undisputed rule before its North African empire was submerged in the Second World War, from which the Libyans under Idris emerged with their right to independence recognised.

The Italian Spheres: Somalia and Ethiopia

We saw in Chapter 10 how the first round of Italian imperialist expansion in North-East Africa was brought to a halt in 1896 by the decisive victory of the emperor Menelik at Adowa. In the peace treaty that followed this battle, Italy managed to retain its foothold on the Red Sea coast in Eritrea. It also had its protectorate treaties signed in 1889 with the Majerteyn Somali sultans of Alula and Obbia, and its lease from the sultan of Zanzibar of the Benadir ports of Brava, Merka, Mogadishu, and Warsheikh. This lease was changed in 1905 into an outright purchase. Until 1905, the Italian government did little to build on these earlier foundations. Eritrea centred upon the declining port of Massawa, from which the Ethiopian trade was being increasingly diverted to the new harbour of Djibouti in French Somaliland. A railway from Djibouti to Addis Ababa was begun in 1896 and completed in 1918. In Somaliland, the Alula and Obbia protectorates were left to themselves other than occasional visits by Italian gunboats. The Benadir ports were ineffectively administered by two Italian commercial companies, the first of which went bankrupt in 1896, the second in 1904.

In these circumstances, the first outburst of Muslim Somali resentment against Christian imperialist domination fell not upon the Italians, but upon the British. The small British protectorate on the southern shores of the Gulf of Aden was home to a great religious leader of the nomadic Somali, Sayyid Muhammad Abdile Hassan. He was known to his British opponents as 'the mad mullah'. Born in 1864 in the region inland from Berbera, Sayyid Muhammad gained an early reputation for piety and learning. During his early travels as a wandering shaikh, he visited Mogadishu, Nairobi, and parts of the Sudan. In all these places, he became aware of the threat to Islam of the expanding forces of western Christendom. When Sayyid Muhammad returned home in 1891, he began to preach resistance to the British and was declared by them to be an outlaw. He retreated with his followers into the Haud and the Ogaden, the unadministered no-man's-land between Ethiopia on the one hand and British and Italian Somaliland on the other. From the Haud and the Ogaden, Sayyid Muhammad launched attacks on the three neighbouring governments. British, Italian, and Ethiopian troops were continuously and expensively engaged in expeditions against him until his death in 1920. Sayyid Muhammad wrote a great number of letters to friends and enemies. His letters to the British were frequently most expressive in their defiance. In one of them he wrote

If the country were cultivated or if it contained houses or property, it would be worth your while to fight for it. But the country is all jungle [he meant that it was uncultivated], and that is no use to you. If you want bush and stones you can get these in plenty. There are also many ant-heaps, and the sun is very hot. All you can get from me is war and nothing else.[3]

---

[3] D. Jardine, *The Mad Mullah of Somaliland* (London, 1923), p. 185.

It was from Sayyid Muhammad that the 3 million or 4 million nomadic Somali, until then conscious only of their clan loyalties, derived their first sense of a wider national unity. Today, he is rightly
regarded in Somalia as the father of Somali nationalism. However,
unlike the founder of the Sanusi movement, whom he so much resembled, Sayyid Muhammad left no successor. On his death, Somali
resistance to the British and Italians ceased. Normal colonial governments were developed in British and Italian Somaliland.

The centre of political interest in North-East Africa now switched
to the renewed plans of the Fascist government of Italy to conquer
the kingdom of Ethiopia. This conquest had been long prepared, but
it could not be put into operation until Italian troops were freed from
the bitter war against the Sanusi in Libya. The excuse for the attack
was found in the disputed frontier between Somalia and Ethiopia
in the Ogaden. Here, the Italians intrigued with the Somali clans
who lived within Ethiopian territory and gradually advanced their
military posts far across the undemarcated border. At last, in December 1934, the expected clash occurred between an Ethiopian
escort patrol accompanying a boundary commission and the garrison of an Italian military post at a place called Walwal. The emperor Haile Selassie appealed to the League of Nations. Haile Selassie
had been crowned in 1930, although he had been the real ruler of
Ethiopia since 1916, under his old name of Ras Tafari. In the League
of Nations, Britain and France supported his cause but did not show
sufficient determination to prevent the Italian aggression. In 1935,
therefore, Mussolini's armies marched up the already prepared military roads from Massawa in the north and Mogadishu in the
south-east. With their vastly superior weapons, they completed their
conquest by May 1936. The emperor was forced to become a refugee
in England. The Italian East African empire – made up of Eritrea,
Ethiopia, and Somalia – had become a reality, after being the dream
of many Italians since the time of partition of Africa. It was, however,
to last only five years.

The effects of Mussolini's militaristic colonialism of the 1920s and
1930s were widespread. Although it has been argued that Italy was
only doing in a more ruthless way what other European countries
had done in the rest of Africa twenty or thirty years earlier, both the
place and the timing in fact made a vast difference. By the 1920s

and 1930s, the other colonial powers had gone far in reforming their colonial policies in the interests of the governed. Britain, especially, had recognised the ultimate right of colonial subjects to govern themselves. In Libya and in Somalia, Italy had turned the clock back. In Ethiopia, she had committed naked aggression against an internationally recognised state which had shown considerable ability in modernising itself without any outside interference. This was the first occasion on which the peace-keeping activities of the League of Nations had been tested, and they were found wanting. Adolf Hitler, who had recently come to power at the head of another Fascist movement, in Germany, was not slow to read and respond to the lesson. In the year of Mussolini's victory over Ethiopia, Hitler set out on the path of aggression which was to lead directly to the Second World War. German troops invaded the Rhineland, the zone between France and Germany which had been demilitarised after the First World War. In the introduction to his history of the Second World War, Winston Churchill drew attention to the influence of Mussolini's action in Ethiopia. He wrote, 'If ever there was an opportunity of striking a decisive blow for a generous cause it was then. The fact that the nerve of the British government was not equal to the occasion, played a part in leading to a more terrible war'. Within Africa, the Italian conquest of Ethiopia was seen by every politically conscious African as a colonialist crime which finally impugned the whole system. Haile Selassie, during his long exile in England, represented the imprisonment of a whole continent.

FIFTEEN. South Africa, 1902–1939

South Africa was the first African country to experience the social stresses resulting from the transformation of an agricultural into an industrial economy. The pace of change between 1900 and the outbreak of the Second World War was faster – and on a larger scale – than in any other part of the continent. By 1939, the concentration of mines and factories on the Witwatersrand was comparable to the industrial regions of Europe and North America. In the centre of the Rand stood Johannesburg, the largest city in Africa except for Cairo. From the Rand, gold flowed to the banking houses of the world, binding South Africa into the web of international finance and commerce. Yet, the fruits of this material prosperity were unevenly distributed. Only gradually did even all the white people reach a high standard of living. Africans, because of their colour, were excluded from all but a meagre share. Political change in no way kept pace with economic advance. The white rulers were restricted by attitudes and policies which had taken root in the nineteenth century or even earlier. They seemed incapable of any fresh approach to the racial tensions which became sharper as more and more Africans were integrated into the expanding economy.

South Africa after the Boer War

After defeating the South African Republic (Transvaal) and the Orange Free State in the Anglo–Boer War, the British felt guilty at the way in which they had bullied the two small Boer republics.

They tried to conciliate the defeated enemy by yielding, amongst other things, to their demands on the political status of the Africans. Concession to the Boers was considered to be more urgent than protection of African interests. One of the clauses of the Peace of Vereeniging (1902) gave the white people in the conquered Transvaal and the Orange Free State the right to decide whether or not to extend the parliamentary franchise to Africans. When Britain granted self-government to the two territories in 1906 and 1907, political power passed once again into Boer hands, and non-whites were permanently excluded from the vote.

The debate on African rights now shifted from Britain to the four colonies themselves. The political leaders of these colonies wanted to set up a union. They hoped by this means to put an end to the disputes which had caused the war and to promote the economic and political development of South Africa as a whole. At the heart of the whole idea of union was the necessity evident to every white politician of developing a single policy toward the Africans. As the future Boer leader and statesman Jan Smuts had written in 1892,

The race struggle is destined to assume a magnitude on the African continent such as the world has never seen, and the imagination shrinks from contemplating; and in that appalling struggle for existence the unity of the white camp will not be the least necessary condition – we will not say of obtaining victory, but of warding off (or, at worst, postponing) annihilation.[1]

If union was to be achieved, three traditional white attitudes toward Africans had somehow to be reconciled. The first was the Liberal tradition of the Cape. The second was *baaskap*, the uncompromising inequality practised in the Transvaal and the Orange Free State. The third was the policy of protective segregation which British governors had tried to adopt in parts of Natal and the Cape, and also in the three protectorates of Basutoland, Bechuanaland, and Swaziland. In addition, there was the problem of evolving a common policy toward the Indians, of whom there were by 1900 around 100,000 in Natal and 10,000 in the Transvaal.

Cape Liberalism was the tradition inherited from the British colonial government of the Cape Colony, which accepted as citizens those

---

[1] W. K. Hancock, *Smuts*, vol. I (Cambridge, 1962), p. 30.

Africans and other coloured people who conformed to white standards. Under this system, educated Africans who owned or leased property of a certain value could register as parliamentary voters. In 1909, Africans formed 4.7 percent of the Cape electorate. Cape leaders defended this system not only on grounds of idealism, but also on grounds of expediency. Merriman, a distinguished liberal politician, argued that the colour-blind franchise was a 'safety valve', for 'to allow no African vote at all would be building on a volcano'. Sauer, another Cape leader, in 1904 expressed more genuinely liberal beliefs when he said, 'I do not believe that where representative institutions exist a class that is not represented will ever receive political justice, because after all it is material interests that will eventually prevail, and therefore the class having no political power will suffer'. The Cape Liberals were supported by many educated Africans, who were anxious to preserve their hard-won privileges (such as exemption from the pass laws). They felt they could no longer identify themselves with the mass of tribal Africans, from whom they had grown apart. For nearly thirty years, John Tengo Jabavu was the mouthpiece of these enfranchised Africans. As early as 1884, he had launched, with white financial backing, the newspaper *Imvo Zabantsundu* (African Opinion), stating that 'the time is ripe for the establishment of a journal in English and Xhosa, to give untrammelled expression to the feelings of the native population'. But *Imvo's* criticism of white rule was very mild, and Jabavu's faith in the political future of the white Liberals became toward the end of his life (he died in 1921) rather pathetic.

Baaskap was the simple exercise of white domination, which had been evident from the earliest days of Dutch settlement on the Cape frontier. The Boers brought this attitude along with them when they trekked northwards, in the 1830s, and had written it into the constitution of the South African Republic (Transvaal), which proclaimed, 'There shall be no equality in State or Church between white and black'. The miners from England and elsewhere who flocked to South Africa after the discovery of diamonds and gold quickly adopted the baaskap attitude. They protected their high wages by an industrial 'colour bar' which prevented Africans from performing skilled work. Baaskap led to the intermingling of the races of South Africa, not to their separation. The Boers wanted as much African land as they could get. Like the miners, they thought of the Africans only as cheap labour which had no need of land of its own.

The physical separation of whites and Africans had been attempted in the Cape, first by the Dutch and later by the British colonial government. It had broken down because of the impossibility of controlling the frontier. By the end of the nineteenth century, the frontier problem had been replaced by that of the various pockets of land or 'reserves' into which Africans had retreated before the white advance. Separation found a new wave of support among missionaries and administrators. This led to the demarcation of the Transkeian Territories by the Cape government. In addition, the British protectorates of Basutoland, Bechuanaland, and Swaziland were established. A commission set up after the Boer War by the British high commissioner, Lord Milner, reported in 1905 in favour of the widespread application of separation throughout South Africa. The Cape politician Merriman remarked that such a policy was at least a century too late to be practicable. The advocates of baaskap, on the other hand, who opposed separation in 1905, were to adopt it some thirty years later. By then, there was proportionately less land available on which Africans could lead a separate existence because the African population had greatly increased.

The differing attitudes toward the Indian population shown in Natal and the Transvaal were particularly revealing of the nature of racial feelings in general. In Natal, where the economy turned on sugar, Indian 'contract labourers' had proven since about 1860 to be disciplined and uncomplaining workers on the plantations, and those who wished to settle permanently at the end of their contracts were encouraged to do so. Some of these immigrants then turned to trading and other service industries and, in this guise, began to penetrate the Transvaal, especially in the years following the South African war. There, they were at once regarded as dangerous competitors by the less skilled Dutch and British workers on the Witwatersrand, and legislation was quickly introduced to prevent the further immigration of Indians and to register all those already there. It was in an attempt to secure the repeal of this 'Black Act' that Mahatma Gandhi developed his technique of *satyagraha*, or 'loving firmness', which he was to practise with such momentous consequences in British India. Gandhi suffered his first sentence of imprisonment in 1908 for his peaceful refusal to register as an Indian immigrant in the Transvaal.

1910: Union

In the negotiations which led up to union, the white people of the two northern colonies and Natal proved themselves more determined to prevent the spread of liberalism than the Cape delegates were to promote it. At the National Convention of 1908–9, a compromise was reached by which the first Union Parliament was to be elected on the existing colonial franchises. This meant that qualified Africans in the Cape would retain the vote, whereas Africans in Natal, the Transvaal, and the Orange Free State would have no political rights. It was further agreed that not even in the Cape should any African be able to stand as a parliamentary candidate. The Cape delegates did succeed in entrenching the franchise provisions in the constitution, so that they could only be amended by a two-thirds majority of both Houses of the Union Parliament sitting together. This was not a very secure safeguard, however, and the compromise as a whole was certainly felt as a bitter blow by the educated Africans. For once, even Jabavu joined forces with his more militant compatriots in trying to resist the form of union decided upon by the National Convention. One of the many meetings called by Africans at this time 'noted with regret that the contemplated Union is to be a Union of two races, namely the British and the Afrikaners – the African is to be excluded'. Only one white Liberal, W. P. Schreiner, supported these African protests. Alone in his community, he felt that human rights were more important than union:

To embody in the South African constitution a vertical line or barrier separating its people upon the ground of colour into a privileged class or caste and an underprivileged inferior proletariat is as imprudent as it would be to build a grand building upon unsound and sinking foundations. In our South African nation there must be room for many free peoples, but no room for any that are not free, and free to rise.[2]

A delegation which included both Schreiner and Jabavu went to London, but failed to persuade the British government to change the

[2] W. P. Schreiner to J. C. Smuts, 2 August 1908, *Selections from the Smuts Papers*, vol. 2, ed. W. K. Hancock and Jean van der Poel (Cambridge, 1966), p. 450.

proposed Union constitution in any way. The Union of South Africa was established on 31 May 1910. The British government maintained that it could not interfere with the decisions of the National Convention. It declared, however, that the three protectorates of Basutoland, Bechuanaland, and Swaziland would not be transferred to the new South African State until it had become clear how the racial provisions of the constitution would work in practice.

Though Jabavu soon reverted to his alliance with the white politicians of the Cape, other more politically conscious Africans launched in 1912 the (South) African National Congress (ANC), as a Union-wide body to protect African interests. Solomon Plaatje, a highly cultured Tswana journalist and writer, became the secretary–general of the Congress. The first legislation denounced by the Congress was the Natives Land Act of 1913, which prevented Africans from acquiring land outside their own areas. Of this Act Plaatje wrote, 'Awakening on Friday morning, June 20th 1913, the South African Native found himself a pariah [outcast] in the land of his birth'. Javabu wrote in favour of the Act, because it had been introduced by Sauer, one of the Cape Liberals in the government. This proved the end of the old man's influence among his fellow Africans. His failure was but one sad facet of the failure of the liberal cause in general. Liberalism became hopelessly compromised by the discriminatory legislation of the Union government. The attitudes that prevailed in South Africa were summed up by an Afrikaner historian fifty years later when he said,

Particularly significant was the fact that the act and 'compromise' of Union enabled the ex-Republics of the Transvaal and the Free State to indoctrinate the rest of the Union with their traditions and ideals. This was eminently true of the two great principles which counted as corner-stones of the national existence of the Afrikaner people: republicanism, and the practice and theory of the inequality between white men and black men.[3]

Smuts and Hertzog

Smuts, who served under General Botha until 1919 and then became prime minister of the Union, was a man of great learning, with profound insights in the fields of religion, philosophy, and science. In 1917, he became a member of the British War Cabinet in the

[3] D. W. Krüger, *The Age of the Generals* (Johannesburg, 1961), pp. 9–10.

war against Germany, and from then until his death in 1950, he was looked upon as a statesman of world renown. He was a close friend of Sir Winston Churchill during the Second World War and one of the founders of the United Nations Organisation. Yet, on the racial problem, which surely would have benefited from the application of such a penetrating mind, he lacked any constructive ideas. In 1906 he had written to Merriman,

I sympathise profoundly with the native races of South Africa, whose land it was long before we came here to force a policy of dispossession on them. And it ought to be the policy of all parties to do justice to the natives and to take all wise and prudent measures for their civilisation and improvement. But I don't believe in politics for them ... When I consider the political future of the natives in South Africa, I must say I look into shadows and darkness; and then I feel inclined to shift the intolerable burden of solving the problem to the ampler shoulders and stronger brains of the future. Sufficient unto the day is the evil thereof.[4]

This timidity pervaded the first ten years of the Union's history. Meanwhile, the racial problems were becoming more difficult, and the younger generation of white people seemed no more capable of solving them. The African policy of Botha and Smuts was muddled and indecisive. It consisted of a further dose of baaskap, of colour bar and pass laws, coupled with a half-hearted attempt to put into practice some of the recommendations of Milner's commission on the subject of separation.

In 1922, white mine-workers struck and seized control of the Rand after the mine-owners threatened to employ Africans as skilled workers at lower wages than the whites enjoyed. Smuts had to use soldiers to put down this 'rebellion'. This led to his defeat in the 1924 election by a combination of the Labour Party, which represented the views of the rebellious white miners, and the Afrikaner National Party. This new party had been formed by General Hertzog in 1913. Although he was one of the main architects of apartheid, Hertzog was one of the most honest of the white politicians. He rightly said that it was the fear of being overwhelmed and swept aside by the vastly superior number of Africans that was at the root of the white attitude: 'The European is severe and hard on the Native because he is afraid of him. It is the old instinct of self-preservation. And the immediate

[4] Hancock, *Smuts*, vol. I, p. 221.

outcome of this is that so little has been done in the direction of helping the Native to advance'. His policy was to remove this fear by physically separating the races, so as to create two South Africas: one white, the other African. Hertzog believed that when Africans were deprived of political and other rights in the Union as a whole, they should be given compensation in the form of more land and of some measure of local self-government.

Hertzog never abandoned his Afrikaner principles. He stood for the primacy of the Afrikaans language in South Africa and for the abandonment of any deference to British policy in international affairs. Nevertheless, he welcomed a reconciliation of the Dutch and British elements in the white population. When the world economic crisis of 1929–33 produced a demand among the white electorate for a 'national' government, composed of the leaders of the two main parties, Hertzog was prepared to enter a coalition with Smuts. In 1934, most of Hertzog's Afrikaner National Party joined with most of Smuts's South African Party to form the United Party, which was to remain in power till 1948. Smuts's side of the compromise was to support the Natives Representation Act, introduced in 1936, which brought to an end the registration of qualified Africans as voters on the common roll with whites in the Cape province. Hertzog's side of the compromise was to modify his anti-British line, both inside South Africa and in relation to the Commonwealth. Among Smuts's followers there was one – the brilliantly clever and deeply religious Jan Hofmeyr – who spoke against the 1936 Act. Hofmeyr said,

By this Bill we are sowing the seeds of a far greater potential conflict than is being done by anything in existence today. We have many educated and semi-educated Natives in South Africa. Many of them have attained to, and many more of them are advancing towards, European standards. They have been trained on European lines. They have been taught to think and act as Europeans. We may not like it, but those are the plain facts. Now what is the political future for those people? This Bill says to these Natives 'There is no room for you. You must be driven back on your own people'. But we drive them back in hostility and disgruntlement, and do not let us forget this, that all this Bill is doing for these educated Natives is to make them the leaders of their own people, in disaffection and revolt.[5]

---

[5] Alan Paton, *Hofmeyr* (Cape Town, 1964), pp. 227–8.

Although Hofmeyr was a cabinet minister in the governments of Hertzog and Smuts, his words were received in stony silence. Much more significant than Hofmeyr in South African electoral terms were the nineteen 'Purified Nationalists', led by D. F. Malan, who refused to follow Hertzog into the coalition. These followers of Malan advocated still sterner measures to ensure the survival of the white man in South Africa. In 1934, they were not very important politically. But in racially divided communities, where a minority race holds power, 'the enemy is always on the Right', that is, the racial extremists. The future in South Africa lay with those nineteen members, whose successors, in 1948, were to sweep the United Party from power and introduce yet another round of racialistic legislation.

The African Predicament

By 1939, the economic and political grievances of the African population in South Africa were already so great that a revolution would not have been at all surprising. The material prosperity of the country depended on the gold mines; the gold mines depended on African labour. Yet, African workers in the mines, as also in the growing number of industrial jobs, received about an eighth of the wages paid to white men. They were supposed to have their homes in the 'reserves' and to come and work in the white towns as migrant labourers without their families. The social and moral harm caused by this frequent disruption of family life was generally ignored by the white employers. Yet, the land left to the Africans was totally inadequate to support them. In 1913, Africans, who formed nearly three-quarters of the population, possessed only 11 percent of the land of South Africa, and this amount was only with great difficulty increased to 13 percent by the late 1960s through government purchase under Hertzog's legislation of 1936. Many Africans had long before this abandoned the impoverished reserves to live permanently in slums on the outskirts of the white towns. By 1936, more than 1 million (22 percent) Africans had become urban dwellers. Another 2 million were working on white farms, completely subject to their masters. They received wages so low that it was only just possible for them to pay their taxes. The prices of most things that Africans bought went up by 50 percent between the two world wars, yet African wages remained nearly stationary. Africans had no means of increasing their wages or improving their conditions of work. Their wages were fixed by law. It was a criminal offence for them to combine in strike action. Their every movement was controlled by pass laws, which required that all Africans outside the reserves must carry a variety of permits. As early as 1919, a Johannesburg newspaper, *The Star*, had commented that 'the Native is crowded off the land, denied a permanent foothold in urban areas, exploited at every point, badgered from pillar to post, and under disabilities of all kinds, whether he stays at home or seeks work away from it'.

Nevertheless, African reactions to these conditions of discrimination and restriction were still very far from revolutionary. During the inter-war years, the African National Congress had little influence or authority even among Africans. It continued to hold its conventions annually on the outskirts of Bloemfontein, but, in 1938, it still had fewer than 4,000 members. Much more significant through most of this period was the Industrial and Commercial Union (ICU), founded in 1919 by Clements Kadalie, an ambitious clerk from Nyasaland. At one time, the ICU could boast a membership of 200,000. But the ICU became unwieldy. Its central organisation was weak, and it was unable to operate effectively among the all-important mine-workers. The employers' control over the African mine-workers was extremely strict. Like its rival, the African National Congress, the ICU was rent by dissensions between communists and more moderate leaders. It failed to influence the government in labour matters, just as the ANC failed to divert Hertzog from his goal of territorial separation.

Even in 1940, Africans were still remarkably restrained and tolerant toward the white society in which, economically, they were becoming ever more integrated. This was due partly to the fact that South Africa was by far the richest country in Africa, and African wages, low though they were compared with those received by the whites, were still higher than in most of the continent. More money was available in South Africa to spend on African education, which, at the secondary level at least, was of a high standard. Africans, therefore, demanded no more than to receive a greater share in the wealth of the country and to be considered as citizens in their own land. Their nationalism was subdued – markedly so in comparison with the strident Afrikaner nationalism which was growing up at the same time. Many young Africans were hopeful about the future. There was still room for political adjustment between the races, and if the white people had earnestly desired to create a multiracial nation, they could still have done so. But, as we have seen, the opinion of white South Africans was in fact moving rapidly in the opposite direction. To secure election by a white constituency, an ambitious politician had to go one step further than his rivals on the racial issue, and always in the same extreme direction. Therefore, although all seemed peaceful enough on the surface, the sands of goodwill were in fact fast running out.

South-West Africa

We noted in Chapter 13 that the German colony of South-West Africa became a League of Nations mandated territory administered by South Africa. The country was, in fact, governed as if it were part of the Union, and local resistance was put down by force. In 1922, the Bondelswarts, a Nama group who had lost much of their land to the Germans, opposed the levying of a dog tax. Dogs were of great importance to them for herding and hunting. A police force was sent against them, and their village was bombed. The police commented, 'The effects of the lesson taught in this short campaign will have an indelible impression not only on the minds of those who resorted to the use of arms in defiance of lawful authority, but on other native tribes in this territory as well'.

Land-hungry white South African farmers eagerly bought the cheap farms in the country, the government providing funds to enable them to purchase stock and equipment. By 1935, there were 32,000 settlers in the territory (some of them Germans who had stayed on), and nearly one-third of the land was in their possession. Much of the rest was desert. The Africans were forced to live in reserves and to labour for the white man to get enough money to pay their taxes. They had merely exchanged one hard master – the Germans – for another.

SIXTEEN. The Last Years of Colonial Rule

The Second World War was a turning point in the modern history of Africa. Before it broke out, the pace of change in Africa since the establishment of colonial rule at the end of the nineteenth and the beginning of the twentieth century had been steady and unhurried. After the war, the momentum increased until it became uncontrollable.

In 1939, the whole of Africa was under some kind of European rule. The Italians were in occupation of Ethiopia. British troops remained in Egypt, in the Suez Canal Zone. Even Liberia was, in practice, dominated by the American Firestone Rubber Company. The Union of South Africa was an independent dominion within the British Commonwealth, but its African and Asian populations enjoyed less freedom than the inhabitants of the colonial territories. Everywhere, colonial rule appeared to be firmly rooted. Every colonial territory had police and military forces adequate for all ordinary situations. Although the numbers of armed men were almost incredibly small – Nigeria, with a population of 20 million, was garrisoned by only 4,000 soldiers and a similar number of armed police – with modern fast communications, reinforcements could have been brought quickly from overseas to deal with any special emergency. But, for twenty years or more in most colonies, there had been no such emergencies. Colonial governments had come to be regarded as too strong to be successfully challenged.

Nevertheless, the concept of trusteeship in colonial policy had begun to produce some practical results during the twenty years since the end of the First World War. Trusteeship was linked with the policy of indirect rule in the British African territories. It had everywhere given African communities some say in the management of their own affairs at the local level and through their traditional authorities. In the West African colonies, a start had even been made in the Africanisation of the central institutions of the colonial governments. A handful of Africans were at last being recruited as administrative officers, and some African members were included in the legislative councils and assemblies which advised the governors. Just after the war, a former British colonial officer-turned-writer expressed the opinion that 'We shall not disappear tomorrow, nor the day after tomorrow, but the governor of each British colony is in fact presiding over the liquidation of that colony – as a colony. It is to become a self-governing dominion'.[1] The French policies of cultural assimilation and economic association were designed to make France and its colonies interdependent. No Frenchman seriously thought that any colony would ever achieve a political status independent of France. A few Africans, however, were rising to positions of power in France itself and were preparing to carry French political party organisation back into the French African territories.

The flaw in all colonial policies was the denial of scope for the political abilities and ambitions of the educated elite. In the British territories, indirect rule gave status and often considerable power to hereditary chiefs and other members of the traditional ethnic aristocracies. But it left the new educated professional class without either political influence or social recognition. Under the French system, the educated Africans could rise higher in the government service, but only at the price of complete identification with France and French culture, which involved cutting their ties with their fellow Africans. The first generation of educated Africans – men like Casely Heyford in the Gold Coast, Blaise Diagne in Senegal, Herbert Macauley in Lagos, or Tengo Jabavu in the Cape Colony – while pressing for a greater participation in central government by the educated elite, accepted the existing gulf between educated and uneducated, between the traditional rural society and the modern urban one.

---

[1] W. R. Crocker, *On Governing Colonies* (London, 1947), pp. 66–7.

None of them tried to build up a mass following, and probably they would not have succeeded had they done so. Among the second generation of educated Africans, there were a few like Azikiwe, who understood that major reforms would not come until the educated had made political contact with the uneducated. Others younger still, like Nkrumah and Senghor, were in 1939 engaged in their European or American studies, and would return with the same lesson ever more firmly in their minds. But, had it not been for the Second World War and for the profound change in the balance of world power that followed, it is very doubtful whether even Nkrumah's generation would have lived to see African independence, let alone whether they themselves would have brought it about. The educational policies of both France and Britain had made it certain that independence would come to Africa within the twentieth century. The fact that it came in the 1950s and 1960s, rather than in the 1980s and 1990s, was due primarily to the five-year struggle around the globe.

The 1939–1945 War and Its Aftermath

The war greatly increased the number of Africans who were politically conscious. Soldiers from all over Africa were recruited by Britain and France. They went into action in Ethiopia, North Africa, and Italy, and against the Japanese in Burma. Most of the Africans who became soldiers had never before left their native lands or even their own home districts. On active service, despite the dangers and the hardships, they were well fed and clothed, and comparatively well paid. They learned to see their own countries in perspective from the outside and to appreciate that conditions there left much to be desired. Many of them learned to read newspapers, to listen to wireless bulletins, and to take an interest in international affairs. Among the first news of great events to reach them was that of the fall of France and of the occupation of its heartland by Germany in May 1940. Belgium and Holland were likewise occupied and their governments were in exile in Britain. All this was a great blow to the prestige of the colonial powers. Again, at quite an early stage of the war, soldiers from both East and West Africa took part in the reconquest of Ethiopia from the Italians, and the significance of the return of the emperor Haile Selassie to his throne was not lost upon them. Nor did they long remain ignorant of the fact that the South-East Asian empires of Britain, France, and Holland had collapsed before the Japanese onslaught of 1942 like straw huts in a storm, leaving the great British Indian empire under the threat of invasion from the east. In Africa itself, the political dissensions which had so weakened France at the beginning of the war were soon transferred to the French African colonies. In 1940, most of the French colonial officials had sided with the Vichy government of German-occupied France, although the governor of Chad, Félix Eboué, by birth a Negro from French Guyana, had from the first supported the Free French resistance movement led by General de Gaulle. By 1943, the whole of French Equatorial Africa had joined de Gaulle, and Eboué had become the governor–general at Brazzaville. Only after much intrigue and infighting did the governments of French West Africa and Madagascar gradually follow suit. This dissension among Frenchmen lowered their prestige in the eyes of their African subjects. In the Maghrib countries, the civil war between Free France and Vichy was even more intense. The Maghribis, being closer to the American armies fighting in the Mediterranean theatre, looked to the United States with its anti-colonial traditions as a potential liberator. After meeting President Roosevelt at Casablanca in 1943, Sultan Sidi Muhammad of Morocco began openly to support the nationalist cause.

When the war ended in 1945, the world of 1939 had changed almost beyond recognition. Italy, Germany, and Japan had been in turn defeated, but at a terrible cost to the victors, especially those whose territory had been occupied and ravished, but also Britain, which had spent all its reserves and run deeply into debt in fighting the war in the west alone for two years before the United States joined in. Even though Britain and France remained in nominal control of vast empires, it was clear that political, economic, and military leadership had passed from the western European countries to the two superpowers, America and the USSR, both of which were in principle committed to the anti-imperial cause. Although the initial threat to those empires was bound to be felt in Asia, where education and political consciousness were so much further developed than in Africa, the more distant future of Africa was sure to be affected. Indeed, it is now known that in confidential exchanges between the

American and British governments during the closing years of the war, it had been agreed that the African colonies of the European powers could realistically be prepared for independence by the end of the twentieth century. During the years immediately after the war, successive French governments came gradually to accept this view.

Meanwhile, in 1947, Britain took the momentous step of liquidating its Indian empire. The subcontinent was partitioned between India and Pakistan, which became independent states within the Commonwealth. Ceylon did the same. Burma, on becoming independent, did not even join the Commonwealth. These countries between them were inhabited by well over 500 million people, about one-seventh of the world's population. Much of the area had been ruled by the British since the eighteenth century, and many ancient civilisations had flourished there before the British came. To the indigenous traditions of learning, there had been added a powerful stream of western education, beside which the primary and secondary schools of colonial Africa appeared the merest trickle. In all these countries, university graduates existed in the tens of thousands. They had long filled the learned professions and occupied all but the very highest positions in the state. Political parties of a modern nationalist kind had been growing up through half a century and were actively supported by hundreds of thousands or even millions of people. To the British, therefore, it did not seem that there was any essential contradiction between withdrawing from South Asia and continuing for another half-century to govern its African colonies. To politically conscious Africans, however, as also to the colonial peoples of South-East Asia, the end of the British empire in India was the event which, above all others, exploded the mystique of imperialism everywhere.

It was from the South-East Asian region, where Indonesia obtained independence from the Dutch in 1951 and where the communist guerrillas of Ho Chi Minh drove the French from Indo–China in 1954, that the so-called Afro-Asian liberation movement soon afterwards began to hasten events in colonial Africa. It was at this period also that American influence, operating mainly through the United Nations Organisation, became of decisive importance. The UN had in 1945 taken over responsibility for supervising the administration of the former Mandated Territories of the League, known henceforward as Trusteeship Territories, sending regular commissions

to inspect them and maintain pressure on their governments to develop them. The UN Charter also included a comprehensive statement of the rights of all peoples to freedom and justice. This was
adopted largely as a result of American pressure and against the
wishes of the colonial powers. When the smaller countries, such as
those in Latin America, took their seats in the UN, they fell in enthusiastically with the attitude of the United States. However, it was the
adherence of the new Asian states which most radically changed the
voting balance in the UN. There was now a large majority of lesser
powers, which demanded the speedy end of colonialism everywhere.
The leader of these newcomers was, of course, India, whose government was then developing the idea of 'positive neutralism' between
the capitalist and communist sides in the Cold War. But, the first
big conference of these non-aligned nations was held at Bandung
in Indonesia in 1955, with communist China also taking part. The
only African countries then independent were Egypt, Ethiopia, and
Libya, but observers were sent by the main nationalist movements
in the Sudan, the Gold Coast, South Africa, and Algeria. The conference declared in its manifesto that 'Colonialism in all its manifestations is an evil which should be speedily brought to an end', and
it called upon the colonial powers to grant freedom and independence to colonial peoples. The sense of solidarity among Asian and
Middle Eastern countries had now spread to nationalist activists all
over Africa south of the Sahara, who knew that henceforward they
had friends to support them in their struggle. For Asian countries,
Bandung marked the end of the transition from colonial rule to independence. For Africans, it marked the beginning of the last, decisive
phase in the revolutionary movement.

Development: The Last Phase of Colonialism

Despite all the changes in the world scene, the colonial powers –
Britain, France, Belgium, and even Portugal – entered with enthusiasm on a final period of rule in Africa, which they all imagined would
last for at least fifty years, although in the event it was destined to last
less than half that time. There were several reasons for this final burst
of activity. First and foremost, the demand for tropical produce, and
the prices paid for it, had risen sharply during the war, and remained

high for more than a decade afterwards. Moreover, colonial governments had learned during the war to take a much larger share of
African farmers' earnings by forcing them to sell their export crops
to state marketing corporations at prices far below what they would
fetch if they were sold on the world market. For the first time in
their history, therefore, colonial revenues were buoyant. It looked
as though a significant expansion of the public services in education, health, and agricultural and veterinary services, as well as all
kinds of desirable public works, could now be set in train. More than
this, however, the colonial powers themselves were now for the first
time prepared to spend a small part of their own taxpayers' money
on development aid to the colonies. The motives for this new gen-
erosity were mixed. On the one hand, it was a response to the fact
that colonialism was under international attack. It was, therefore,
more necessary to show that the colonies were benefiting from the
association. But on the other hand, there was, in the wartime and
post-war situation, a sense in which the tropical colonies were proving for the first time to be of real value to the colonial powers. These
were all in debt to America. They needed to import American goods,
and yet they themselves were producing little that America wished
to buy. The dollar was thus a 'hard currency', while the pound and
the franc were 'soft currencies'. The tropical colonies were producers
of the primary products that America wished to buy, and the resulting dollars could be shared out within the franc and sterling currency zones instead of being credited directly to the colonies where
they had been earned. The system meant, in effect, that the dollar-
earning colonies were compelled to take a high proportion of imports
from their metropolitan powers at a time when they might have preferred to buy American. At all events, the operation was beneficial
enough to the colonisers to make them invest their own money in
colonial development which might enhance the productivity of their
colonies.

So far as British Africa was concerned, a Colonial Development
and Welfare Act had been introduced as early as 1940, but, in the circumstances of war, it could be little more than a declaration of intent.
However, when seeking its renewal in September 1944, the colonial
secretary, Oliver Stanley, wrote to the chancellor of the exchequer in
the following words:

I believe that the time when we must take action ... is now upon us. The end of the fighting in Europe will, I am convinced, be the psychological moment at which to announce our intention to make fully adequate provision for the assistance from His Majesty's Government which will be necessary for a dynamic programme of Colonial development. It is the moment at which to demonstrate our faith and our ability to make proper use of our wide Colonial possessions. It is also the moment when the minds of administrators in the Colonies will be turning even more definitely towards planning for the future, and when a clear call from here will give them faith in the permanence and adequacy of our policy ... I make no pretence ... that this is going to be profitable transaction on a purely financial calculation. The overriding reason why I feel that these proposals are essential is the necessity to justify our position as a Colonial Power.[2]

Between 1946 and 1955, £210 million from funds provided by the Act, from private investment, and from money raised by the colonial governments themselves was spent on development plans in the British territories. Before the war, French colonies had been even poorer than the British colonies. Therefore, when money began to pour in, the change was even more startling. Investment came from private sources and from a government fund set up in 1946. This fund, which was known by the acronym of its French title as FIDES, provided official aid on a scale even larger than the British. The development plans of the nine West African territories alone totalled £277 million for the period 1946–55.

This new flow of money, both from expanding internal revenues and from external aid, revolutionised the activities of colonial governments during the post-war period. From this time, every colony had its planning staff and its development programme. Among the more spectacular projects were the hydroelectric installations on the Nile at Jinja in Uganda, at Kariba on the Zambezi between Northern and Southern Rhodesia, on the Volta River at Akasombo in the Gold Coast, and at Fria and Kimbo in Guinea. The main purpose of these projects was to supply power for industrialisation. Industries supported in this way included cotton-spinning in Uganda, the extension of copper-mining in Northern Rhodesia, a variety of factories in Southern Rhodesia, the smelting of bauxite into aluminium, as well as a whole range of light industries in the Gold Coast and Guinea.

---

[2] Oliver Stanley to Sir John Anderson, 21 September 1944, cited in Wm Roger Louis, *Imperialism at Bay 1941–1945* (Oxford, 1977), pp. 102–3.

The largest project of all was the Inga scheme for damming the lower Congo, which was designed to supply half as much electricity as was then produced in western Europe. Its implementation was halted by the crisis that followed the independence of the Belgian Congo, and thereafter was only partially resumed.

Hydroelectric power for industrialisation was, however, only one particularly striking feature of the development programmes with which every colonial government was concerned after the Second World War. Central to every programme was the expansion and diversification of agricultural production. This was directed not only to the production of cash crops, but also to the production of food for local consumption, especially by the growing populations of the new towns. Agricultural and veterinary services extended their operations into almost every administrative district. Strenuous efforts were made to educate farmers to adopt improved methods, such as the rotation of crops, contour-bunding to prevent erosion in hilly areas, consolidation of scattered holdings, and introduction of better tools and simple machinery. Pastoralists who had hitherto bred cattle largely for prestige, concentrating on numbers rather than on the yield of milk and meat, were persuaded to accept scientific breeding methods and to produce regularly for the market. This meant using co-operative creameries and abattoirs in the grazing districts instead of moving large herds on the hoof to distant selling points. Again, fish-marketing corporations were set up in many countries, and refrigerated vans began to visit the fishing communities of the seaboards, lakes, and rivers to buy their produce and distribute it to the towns. All these activities demanded in turn a corresponding revolution in transport. The old dirt roads of pre-war Africa could no longer stand up to the weight of traffic that now passed over them. A very large proportion of most development budgets was spent on reconstructing and tarring the main trunk roads.

Progress in Education

It was soon realised by all colonial governments in the post-war period that if one limitation on development was money, another and more serious one was the shortage of educated people. Because there had been so few secondary schools in colonial Africa before the war, a large number of Europeans had to be employed to operate the new development plans. These people were expensive. They had to be induced to come to Africa by high salaries, subsidised housing, and frequent home leave with free travel. On the political side, these new 'invaders' of Africa undid much of the good which they contributed with their skills. Their presence widened the gap between Europeans and Africans. It created the impression that the colonial grip on Africa was tightening, and it intensified political unrest and made all government activities suspect to the people. Education, therefore, soon became the cornerstone of every development plan.

At the end of the war, the vast majority of schools were still those of the Christian missions. Nearly all of them were primary schools, and most of them provided only four years of education in one or another of the African languages. The first priority for advancement was to extend the four-year period to six, the two additional years being devoted largely to the study of a European language. The main problem, therefore, was to train enough primary-school teachers who had the necessary qualifications in English or French. The most significant educational development of the 1940s was the establishment throughout colonial Africa of primary-teacher training centres, which in their early days were essentially schools of English or French. The problem of access to a 'language of wider communication' had to be solved before it was possible to press on toward the provision of a more adequate number of secondary schools. Before the war, these had been very few indeed. Most territories had only two or three such schools, and they had been staffed mainly by European teachers. Now these schools had to be multiplied, which could only be done very gradually, by bringing in more teachers from abroad and by employing the fortunate few Africans who had passed through the existing schools. Whereas the reform of primary education had involved only the addition of two more years, six new years of education were required for a secondary school. Even if a school was able to add a new class every year, therefore, a full secondary school could not be established in less than six years. In fact, most schools took much longer than this to grow. Although the 1950s saw a great increase in the number of secondary schools, most of them were dismissing their pupils after only three or four years. This was still the state of things when most African countries attained independence.

The secondary-school output determined the possibilities for higher education. Nevertheless, the British government, at least, did not allow the secondary-school bottleneck to hold up the foundation of universities in colonial Africa. A commission set up in 1943 reported two years later that the development of universities was 'an inescapable corollary of any policy which aims at the achievement of colonial self-government'. During the four years after 1945, four university colleges were established: at Ibadan in Nigeria, at Achimota in the Gold Coast, at Khartoum in the Sudan, and at Makerere in Uganda. The university college at Salisbury in Southern Rhodesia was added in 1953. At all these places, fearfully expensive European staffs were built up, while the output of graduates climbed slowly from a hundred to two or three hundred a year. In French Africa, the first university to be founded was that at Dakar in 1955, just three years ahead of Senegalese independence. In the Belgian Congo, the universities of Lovanium and Elizabethville narrowly predated the political independence that came in 1960. In retrospect, it can be clearly seen that higher education arrived too late for graduates to have any chance of capturing the political initiative in independent Africa. Indeed, there were not nearly enough of them to supply the bare needs of modern administrative and social services, let alone those of an emerging private sector in industry and commerce. Higher education in colonial Africa had been planned to serve the needs of the 1990s, rather than the 1960s. Nevertheless, the foundations had been laid, on which independent nations could try to build insofar as their economic resources allowed.

It was perhaps in their steady support of educational development at the higher levels that the British and French governments showed their awareness of how close they were to decolonisation and their good faith in preparing for it. Belgian policy in the Congo was, in contrast, to put nearly all government support into the multiplication of primary schools. Defending this policy, Pierre Ryckmans, who had been governor–general of the Congo from 1934 until 1937, and who then became the Belgian representative on the United Nations Trusteeship Council, wrote in 1955:

Everyone who knows the Congo is convinced that Belgian rule is indispensable there, and that the end of it would be the end of all that we have built up during three-quarters of a century. We have preferred to give primary education to the mass of children, and to organise secondary education later, as soon as available resources allow. French West Africa has a thousand young people studying in France, while we have just a handful studying in Belgium. But we have ten times more children than they have in primary schools. I sincerely believe that in thirty years' time we shall have in the Congo at least as many university graduates, and at least as many high-school graduates, and infinitely fewer illiterates than do our French neighbours in West Africa, even though the first university in the Congo opened its doors only last year. But will thirty years of peaceful progress be given us?[3]

Ryckmans answered his own question with a cautious affirmative: he was 'full of hope'. Four years later, both he and his government were proved sadly mistaken when the Congolese were quite unprepared for the responsibilities of an independence which was thrust upon them rather than for which they had struggled for.

Preparing for Democracy

During the time that remained to them after the war, the field in which colonial governments were most active was that of local government. In the British territories, indirect rule was quietly abandoned as too gradual for the world situation. There was clearly not going to be time in which to allow African systems of local government to evolve 'along their own lines'. Democratic local government had to be attained within a very few years. The only thing to do was to follow western models. Every chief was soon surrounded by an elected council. The supervision of many local services was entrusted to these councils, where previously they had been administered autocratically by the chief or the European district commissioner. The English county council was the model followed increasingly in British territories, while the French aimed to reproduce the system of communes which were the principal units of representative local government in France. In the employment of the district councils and communes, many Africans learned to take administrative

---

[3] Pierre Ryckmans, 'Belgian Colonialism', *Foreign Affairs*, October 1955, cited in Joan G. Roland, *Africa: The Heritage and the Challenge* (Greenwich, Conn., 1974), pp. 205, 211.

responsibility in ways that were not yet open to them in the service of the colonial central governments. Many future national politicians gained their political training through membership on elected local councils.

When it came to the creation of representative institutions at the colonial level, British and French policy still showed hesitations and contradictions. So far as the British were concerned, the intention to decolonise was not in doubt. Oliver Stanley, the wartime colonial secretary, had stated in June 1943, 'We are pledged to guide colonial peoples along the road to self-government within the British empire'. No one yet knew whether this meant the full sovereign independence of every individual colonial unit, large or small. There were many people in Britain who hoped that federations of West, East, and Central African territories would emerge. But the immediate course seemed clear: to repeat the pattern of constitutional development followed earlier in the European-settled lands in Canada, Australia, and South Africa. Political power would gradually be devolved to the legislative councils which had already been set up in all the colonies. At the same time, the membership of these councils would be widened by increasing African representation through the nomination of the governors and the chiefs. Later, the legislative councils would become even more representative by giving the vote to a wider and wider circle of the people in the colonies.

Such a plan raised no special difficulties in relation to West African colonies, where all the British people were temporary residents only. The complications arose on the eastern side of Africa, where from Kenya all the way to Southern Rhodesia, there lived small communities of British settlers who thought of themselves as permanent residents of these countries. They had already been afforded varying degrees of privilege in their government, and the advance of the African majority populations would mean the end of their privileged position. To understand their attitude, one has to remember that South Africa had gained independence with a franchise virtually limited to white people, and that in 1923 Southern Rhodesia, with a much smaller proportion of whites to blacks, had gained internal self-government on the same basis. British views had changed greatly since 1923. All the same, the British governments of 1945–55 felt they had an obligation to protect the settlers of eastern and central Africa from a too rapid transfer of power to the African majorities. Britain, therefore, spent ten years experimenting with a variety of so-called multiracial constitutions in these areas. The typical multiracial constitution was one in which each racial group elected a certain number of representatives to the legislature. In this way, the various groups were more or less evenly represented, regardless of their actual size. The hope was that a democratic moderation would emerge from the balancing of one group against another. Few Africans could see any justice in such a system. Nevertheless, the multiracial constitutions probably did perform a useful function in providing a transitional stage between white-settler privilege and majority rule.

French hesitations and contradictions turned less upon the number of Frenchmen resident in any particular one of their African territories than upon the future relations of the French overseas territories to France. Right up to 1960, the French plan for decolonisation envisaged little more than local autonomy for the ex-colonies within a centralised imperial system represented first by the French Union and later by the French Community. Whereas the French Union had been intended to include all the French overseas territories, in Indo-China as well as in Africa, the French Community was limited to Africa south of the Sahara and to those small island territories which had accepted full integration with metropolitan France. Algeria was included within the Community only while it remained a part of France. Tunisia and Morocco were never members. In practice, however, French Africa from 1945 to 1955 was passing through a phase of decolonisation very similar to the 'multiracial' period in British East and Central Africa. In French West and Equatorial Africa and Madagascar, legislative assemblies were being developed both at the federal and at the territorial levels. During this transitional stage, half of the seats in these assemblies were elected by the *citoyens de plein exercise*, which was to say, in effect, by the locally resident French population.

Except in the Belgian and Portuguese possessions, the rulers of colonial Africa from the Sahara to the Zambezi realised by about 1955 that they had entered into the last phase of European colonisation. Yet, French and British colonial governments played their parts in this final act of the colonial drama with unprecedented vigour and enthusiasm. Development money was being poured into the tropical

African colonies. Agriculture and industry were being actively stimulated, and education was being given a decisive push forward. Local government was being made quickly and surely more democratic. Central government was also being made more representative, though less rapidly and less certainly. The colonial rulers were preparing to leave. There was no more time for further political experiments. Therefore, western models were increasingly being used for the development of political institutions. All over British Africa, speakers in their traditional wigs and knee-breeches presided over the rectangular debating chambers of the Westminster model, in which 'government' and 'opposition' sat facing each other. All over French Africa, assemblies sat in semicircular chambers on the Paris model, in which the 'left wing' merged imperceptibly into the 'right wing', without a dividing 'floor'. These were the 'old bottles' imported hastily from Europe to contain the 'new wine' of African nationalism. They did not prove to be very successful. As soon as the Africans took complete control of their own affairs, they changed them almost beyond recognition. But, like the multiracial constitutions which preceded them, they provided a framework for the transition from dependence to independence.

SEVENTEEN. The Road to Independence: (1) North and North-East Africa

A s we saw in Chapter 14, nationalism in the Muslim north of Africa had developed much earlier than in Africa south of the Sahara. Egypt, indeed, had been self-governing since 1922. Yet, it was not until forty years later – after all of West Africa and most of eastern Africa had become independent – that the final emancipation of this region was completed by the withdrawal of the French from Algeria. North Africa's emergence from colonialism was thus a much longer drawn out and more piecemeal process than that of the regions to the south. And, although it became in its final stages increasingly linked with the rest of the Pan–African freedom movement, its origins were different and must be separately treated. The countries of the Horn of Africa likewise took special paths to independence, which fit more easily with those of the lands to the north of them than with those farther to the south.

Egypt and the Sudan

The key country of the whole North African region was, as ever, Egypt. Although a British garrison remained in the Canal Zone in accordance with the terms of the 1936 treaty (see Chapter 14), the wartime occupation of the rest of the country ended in 1946, leaving Egypt free to resume the political independence it had enjoyed before the war. Egypt had, by far, the largest population and, by far, the most developed industry and commerce of any of the North African countries. It was also the intellectual capital of the Arabic-speaking world.

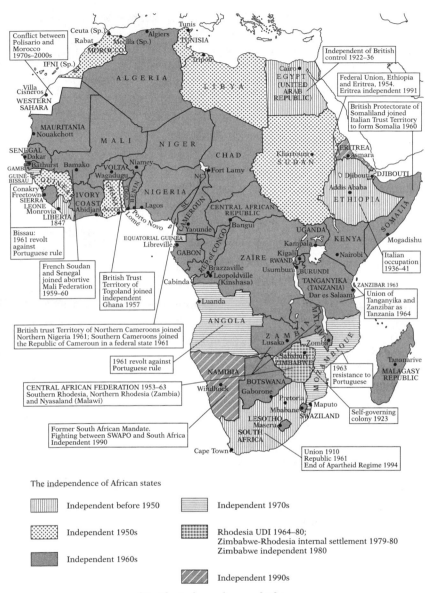

Conflict between Polisario and Morocco 1970s–2000s

Independent of British control 1922–36

Federal Union, Ethiopia and Eritrea, 1954. Eritrea independent 1991

British Protectorate of Somaliland joined Italian Trust Territory to form Somalia 1960

Bissau: 1961 revolt against Portuguese rule

French Soudan and Senegal joined abortive Mali Federation 1959–60

British Trust Territory of Togoland joined independent Ghana 1957

Zanzibar 1963

Union of Tanganyika and Zanzibar as Tanzania 1964

Italian occupation 1936–41

British trust Territory of Northern Cameroons joined Northern Nigeria 1961; Southern Cameroons joined the Republic of Cameroun in a federal state 1961

1961 revolt against Portuguese rule

1963 resistance to Portuguese

CENTRAL AFRICAN FEDERATION 1953–63 Southern Rhodesia, Northern Rhodesia (Zambia) and Nyasaland (Malawi)

Self-governing colony 1923

Former South African Mandate. Fighting between SWAPO and South Africa Independent 1990

Union 1910 Republic 1961 End of Apartheid Regime 1994

The independence of African states

Independent before 1950

Independent 1970s

Independent 1950s

Rhodesia UDI 1964–80; Zimbabwe-Rhodesia internal settlement 1979-80 Zimbabwe independent 1980

Independent 1960s

Independent 1990s

26. The independence of Africa.

The two universities of Cairo had between them a student population of 20,000. It was there that Arabic-speaking students from the
Maghrib met those from Libya, Sudan, and Somalia and formed the
same kind of associations as other African students from the English-
and French-speaking colonies south of the Sahara were forming in
London and Paris at the same period. But whereas students from
sub-Saharan Africa generally felt themselves to be outsiders – if not
actually foreigners – in the metropolitan imperialist countries, those
from North Africa who studied in Egypt knew that they were in an
entirely congenial milieu. For those North African nationalists whose
primary loyalty was still to Islam, Egypt was both a place of refuge
and a nursery of revolt.

Egypt itself was still in 1946 a land of immense social inequalities
and vivid economic contrasts. Although the country looked large on
the map, nearly all of its 20 million people were crowded into the
Nile valley and delta and the Suez Canal Zone. In these habitable
areas, the population density was among the highest in the world,
one agricultural region having as many as 2,650 people to the square
mile. Cairo was already a huge city of more than 2 million people, by
far the largest city in Africa at the time. Alexandria had more than
1 million, and several other towns had populations of more than
100,000. Nevertheless, more than 80 percent of Egyptians were
country-dwellers, and by far the greatest number were small farmers
(fellahin), who tended to fall deeper into poverty and malnutrition
as their holdings grew smaller by subdivision. Those who owned
their own land mostly held tiny patches of 1 acre or less. The rest
paid rent to landowners, and were often even worse situated. More
than a third of the cultivable land of Egypt was owned by the great
pashas, many of them descended from the Mamluks and Circassians
of Ottoman times or else from the family and favourites of Muhammad Ali. Most of the commerce of Egypt was in the hands of a non-
Egyptian merchant class, often Greeks whose ancestors had been
in Egypt for centuries. Modern industry and services tended to be
owned by foreign companies from western Europe and the Levant.
At the top of the social hierarchy perched King Farouk, the descendant of Muhammad Ali, who lived the life of an extravagant playboy.
The whole situation was, therefore, one which contained many of
the necessary ingredients for revolution.

It was clear that the traditional rulers of such a society would adopt the classic tactic of trying to divert internal discontent into the channel of external aggression. Already in 1944, they had joined with other Arab countries in forming the Arab League, the earliest and most persistent objective of which was to prevent the emergence of a Jewish state in Palestine as soon as Britain fulfilled its declared intention of laying down its Mandate. In 1947, the United Nations duly decreed the partition of Palestine between Israel and Jordan. In 1948, the armies of the Arab League went to war against Israel and were humiliatingly defeated by the one-year-old state. Egyptians especially felt this blow to Muslim prestige, which showed up the corruption and inefficiency of the monarchy and the politicians. Frustrated in their attempts against Israel, the politicians now responded by turning the hatred of the foreigner against the continuing British presence in the Canal Zone and in the Sudan. At first, in covert defiance of the 1936 treaty, armed bands of Egyptians were encouraged to attack British troops and installations. Then, in 1951, the Egyptian government unilaterally declared the 1936 treaty to be at an end. British reprisals against Egyptian terrorist attacks led to an outburst of popular feeling in Cairo, in which British and other foreign property was destroyed. Six months later, on 23 July 1952, a group of young army officers seized power. They were led by Colonel Gamal Abdul Nasser, but used an older man, General Neguib, as a figurehead in forming a Revolutionary Command Council, which quickly swept away the discredited monarchy and parliament.

One effect of the deterioration in Anglo–Egyptian relations had been to cause Britain, from about 1951 onwards, to set a course toward rapid independence for the Sudan, for not to have done so would have been to drive the very real forces of Sudanese nationalism into the arms of the Egyptians. From the British point of view, a hostile Egypt had better be countered by a friendly Sudan. Strangely enough, the new rulers of Egypt were thinking on parallel lines. It happened that Neguib and Nasser had both served in the Sudan, and had there come to appreciate the strength of Sudanese nationalist feeling. They realised that a friendly Sudan, even if independent of Egypt, was preferable to a hostile dependency. The new Egypt, therefore, accepted the British proposals, made in 1952, that the Sudanese people should hold elections under a constitution providing internal self-government for a period of three years before deciding upon complete independence or union with Egypt. When the time came, in January 1956, the Sudan voted to become an independent republic outside the Commonwealth.

Meanwhile, in 1954, Neguib had been ousted as President of Egypt by Nasser, under whose rule Egypt's relations with the western countries went from bad to worse. Nasser lost no time in identifying himself with independence movements in the rest of Africa and, in 1955, he personally attended the conference of non-aligned nations at Bandung which issued the rousing manifesto against 'colonialism in all its manifestations' discussed in Chapter 16. Internally, Nasser's Egypt was the first country in Africa to put radical socialist policies into practice, by limiting severely the amount of land which an individual could own and by redistributing the large estates among the peasants. Externally, he succeeded in ridding Egypt of the last traces of European domination. Britain agreed to withdraw its troops from the Canal Zone, leaving the canal to be operated as before by the Anglo–French company that had built it. Nasser then turned to his plan for extending the area of irrigated land in Egypt by building a huge new dam across the Nile at Aswan. This was to have been financed mainly by American and British aid. America, however, became increasingly annoyed by his non-aligned policies and, in 1956, withdrew its offer of financial assistance. Nasser responded by nationalising the Suez Canal, announcing that he would finance the 'high dam' from its profits.

The governments of Britain and France reacted with exasperation to Nasser's latest move and determined to deal him a blow that would bring him to his knees. In their anger, they failed to reckon with the international disapproval that such action would provoke, and they even failed to consult with their principal ally and creditor in the United States. Instead, they set up a dishonest charade by getting Israel to attack Egypt along the line of the Suez Canal, so that they could then intervene to separate the warring parties and make safe the waterway for the commerce of the world. On this pretext, British and French forces landed near Port Said in September 1956 and reoccupied the Canal Zone, hoping that a swift victory would bring about the fall of Nasser. In the event, they found that their surreptitious action was almost universally condemned. In the United

Nations, the Soviet Union was supported by most of the smaller countries in demanding a withdrawal; and, in the United States, President Eisenhower informed the British and French governments that there would be no further support for their still shaky currencies. Under this pressure, Britain and France had no option but to withdraw their forces and to face public and lasting humiliation. It was not Nasser but the British prime minister, Sir Anthony Eden, who was forced to resign on grounds of ill health, and the British people who had to endure the discomforts of petrol rationing because of the damage caused by their own forces to the Suez Canal. The affair provided a sweeping victory for Nasser, which greatly enhanced his standing in other African states and in the Muslim countries of the Middle East. In 1958, Egypt formed a political union with Syria known as the United Arab Republic. Although the union proved short-lived – it collapsed in 1961 – Egypt retained the new name for some time. One result of the Suez crisis was that the Soviet Union, by providing finance for the Aswan dam and other projects, and by arming Egypt, obtained a foothold in a region of great strategic, political, and economic importance. In Cairo, the Egyptian intelligentsia referred to the Soviet ambassador humorously as 'Cromersky'.

Meanwhile, the Sudan, which had finally achieved its independence from both Britain and Egypt in the year of the Suez crisis, was experiencing a rough start to its new existence. The Muslim and Arabic-speaking population of the north, which dominated the country politically and economically, was divided within itself into a number of religious, tribal, and class interest groups which did not fit easily into the Westminster pattern of parliamentary government hastily installed by the British on the eve of their departure; there was relief only when, in 1958, the army officers led by General Abboud seized power from the politicians. The military hand at the centre of government, however, did nothing to solve the more fundamental division between the north and the south of the country. This was something which really went back to the days of slave- and ivory-hunting in the nineteenth century, when Muslim Egyptians and northern Sudanese together raided the black, animist peoples of the south. The British-dominated condominium government had done nothing to heal this rift, administering the north and the south in separate compartments, and concentrating its efforts at economic development almost entirely in the north. This policy was reversed only in 1949 – far too late to have any appreciable effect before the country began its mad scramble to independence in 1953. The south's first political party was founded only in that year, and fears of northern domination of the independent government were already rampant. These fears were fully borne out when, in 1954, Sudanese civil servants were appointed to replace the departing English. Out of 800 senior posts, only 6 were filled by southerners. The first open conflict occurred in the middle of 1955, a few months before independence, when the government decided to transfer soldiers from the north to the south and vice versa. Southern troops mutinied in Torit and elsewhere in Equatoria province. The mutinies were quickly put down, with considerable loss of life, but many of the disgruntled southern soldiers decamped into the bush and engaged in sporadic attacks on government posts and installations. The Khartoum government vacillated between attempting to appease the southerners and imposing a centralised Islamic and Arabic-speaking administration upon them. In 1962, there was a prolonged strike in the Christian mission schools in the south and, during the next two years, all foreign missionaries were expelled. Many Christian schools were replaced by Koranic ones and, in some districts, officials refused to recognise any but Muslim names. The local army unit, the Equatoria Corps, mutinied, led by their anti-Muslim and anti-communist missionary educated officers, and these troops formed the core of the *Anyanya* ('snake poison') sucessionists who rose in open revolt in 1963. The government's response to the now widespread rebellion was to send more troops, but the hostility of the people and the nature of the country made military suppression of the guerrillas impossible. The government held the few towns, and the roads connecting them, while the rebels controlled much of the countryside. It was to be the earliest and also the most persistent of independent Africa's civil wars.

States of the Horn

For a brief five years, from 1936 until 1941, the main territories of the Horn of Africa – Ethiopia, Eritrea, and Somalia – had been brought under a single rule as Italian East Africa. For a still briefer period at the beginning of the war, the Italians added by conquest the territory of British Somaliland. French Somali Coast (the modern Djibouti) escaped Italian conquest by virtue of a governor who supported Vichy France. When the British in turn conquered the Italian East African empire in 1941–2, British military administrations were installed in all the territories except Ethiopia, which was recognised as an independent state under the rule of the emperor Haile Selassie, who had returned under the protection of a British expedition from the Sudan to take part in the liberation of his country. This was in reality much more than a simple restoration. The Italians had done much to modernise the country, and the new empire inherited, for example, a network of engineered roads and telecommunications connecting the capital with the provincial centres. Moreover, whereas the old empire had been, in terms of international standing, an anomalous survival from the pre-colonial period, the new empire, restored and recognised by the entire international community, was seen by many, both inside and outside Africa, as the herald of a new postcolonial Africa – a state of respectable size, with a basic framework of modern institutions, yet governed by a traditional aristocracy with venerable roots in the African past.

After the war, there were intensive deliberations at the United Nations about the future government of North-East Africa. Haile Selassie argued for retaining the broad structure of the Italian empire by closely associating both Eritrea and Somalia with Ethiopia. Eventually, in 1950, the former Italian Somalia became a United Nations Trust Territory, which was placed under Italian administration for a ten-year period, while the British continued to rule northern Somaliland as a colony. At least three different plans were proposed for Eritrea, with its population of 1 million, divided almost equally between the mountain-dwelling Tigreans, who were Ethiopian Christians, and the Afar and Danakil of the coastal plain, who were Muslims. The Arab countries wanted Eritrea to be independent; the British wanted it partitioned between Ethiopia and Sudan; the Ethiopians wanted to annex the whole. At length, in 1952, the Ethiopian view prevailed, though under a federal constitution which gave the Eritreans a considerable say in their own affairs. Ten years later, Eritrea was more tightly integrated by imperial decree, a change which antagonised many Eritreans. Opposition to Ethiopia

developed in two rival movements – the Muslim Eritrean Liberation
Movement and the Eritrean People's Liberation Front, both of which
received help from outside sources, including radical Arab states and
countries of the eastern bloc.

After reassuming the reins of power at the end of the Second World
War, the emperor Haile Selassie continued to rule Ethiopia very
much as he had done during the 1920s and 1930s. As the number of
western-educated Ethiopians grew, so the forms of a modern bureaucracy were gradually established with the help of foreign advisers
drawn from several developed countries. But the inner network of
real power remained in the hands of the emperor's extended family
and their spouses, who were strategically disposed in every institution and region and who reported directly to the palace rather than
to the official ministries. Nevertheless, some aspects of Ethiopia's
economy and administration were modernised. Large amounts of
aid flowed in from the western countries. From 1953, the United
States became the main supplier of aid and military equipment, and
from the mid-1960s, this aid was much augmented in order to coun-
terbalance the Soviet supply of armaments to neighbouring Somalia.
As ruler of an ancient African state which had preserved its independence through all but five years of the colonial period, Haile Selassie
was able to play a major part in the Pan–African politics of the 1960s,
not only mediating disputes between the newly independent states
and advising them in diplomatic procedures, but also training the
freedom fighters sent to him by resistance movements in those territories still under colonial rule. In 1962, for example, he hosted the
first conference of PAFMECA (the Pan–African Freedom Movement
of East and Central Africa), which was attended, on the eve of his
arrest and long imprisonment, by the young Nelson Mandela, as a
secret emissary of the African National Congress (ANC) of South
Africa. 'Here', writes Mandela, 'for the first time in my life, I was wit-
nessing black soldiers, commanded by black generals, applauded by
black leaders, who were all guests of a black head of state. It was a
heady moment. I only hoped it was a vision of what lay in the future
of my own country'.[1] Following that conference, Mandela toured
the newly independent countries of North and West Africa. Rabat in
Morocco he described as 'the crossroads of virtually every liberation

[1]   Nelson Mandela, *Long Walk to Freedom*, New York, 1994, p. 256.

movement on the continent', where he met freedom fighters from Mozambique, Angola, Algeria, and Cape Verde. However, it was to Ethiopia that he returned to undergo a course of military training in preparation for his intended role as commander of the military wing of the ANC known as Umkonto we Sizwe. It is small wonder that in the following year, Haile Selassie was able to persuade his fellow heads of state to site the headquarters of the newly founded Organisation of African Unity (OAU) in Addis Ababa.

The decade of Italian Trusteeship in Somalia was generally judged to be enlightened and generous. A wide-ranging education programme was implemented, which trained administrators and technical personnel. In 1954, an Institute of Law and Economics was opened under the auspices of the University of Rome, which later developed into the University of Mogadishu. The Italians encouraged local participation in the territorial government and, by the middle of the decade, most senior administrative positions were in Somali hands. Without doubt, the deliberate and rapid decolonisation of Italian Somalia was greatly helped by the fact that all the inhabitants of the country spoke a single language and felt themselves to be a nation. Most African countries had to undergo a process of nationalist unification, for which some delaying tactics by the colonial power was absolutely necessary. With the Somali, the problem was rather that the sense of Somali nationalism existed over a wider region than the Trust territory. It extended clearly over the whole of British Somaliland, where the colonial government – although less active than the Italian Trusteeship administration in its preparations for decolonisation – at least did nothing to prevent the future unification of the two territories. Albeit in a hurried and disorganised way, British Somaliland was brought to independence five days before the Italian territory and, on 1 July 1960, the legislative assemblies of the two countries met in joint session at Mogadishu and constituted themselves into the National Assembly of the independent and sovereign Republic of Somalia.

Six years before this event, in 1954, in a move fraught with danger for the future, Britain had returned to Ethiopia the Ogaden district, comprising the low plateau on the eastern side of the Ethiopian mountains which provided vital seasonal grazing for the nomadic Somali. After independence, the chief concern of the Somalia government was to promote the unification of all the Somali-speaking

lands and, in particular, to regain control over the Ogaden. The irredentist spirit was flaunted by the new Somali flag, which displayed a
five-pointed star representing the five sections of the divided Somali
people, of which those in the Ogaden, Djibouti, and Kenya were under white colonial rule. Before the independence of Kenya in 1963,
the British authorities, while recognising the nationalist sentiments
of the Somali-speaking population there, announced that the Northern Frontier District (NFD) was to remain an inalienable part of
Kenya. The British were, in fact, much more concerned to placate
the strongly expressed views of Kenyatta and other Kenyans than
to accommodate Somali claims. The Somali government, therefore,
broke off diplomatic relations with Britain and encouraged Somali
insurgents in the NFD to wage a guerrilla war with Kenya, which
lasted for more than four years. Likewise, border skirmishes developed along the frontier between Somalia and Ethiopia and erupted
into large-scale inconclusive fighting from 1964 onwards. Soviet assistance in building up the Somali army had already begun before
this, but it was only after the military coup of 1969, which installed
General Siad Barre as head of state, that Soviet involvement in Somalia increased on a massive scale and began to be a fundamental
factor in all of the countries of the Horn.

Libya and the Maghrib

Between Egypt and the French-ruled Maghrib lay the sprawling
country of Libya, which had formed part of the African empire of
Italy. Libya's road to independence, like that of Ethiopia, Eritrea,
and Somalia, was determined primarily by the results of the Second World War. The British, during their North African campaigns
of 1942 and 1943, had entered into close and secret relations with
Sayyed Idris, the temporal head of the Sanusi brotherhood which
had organised the bedouin resistance to the Italians during the 1920s
and 1930s (see Chapter 14). From his place of exile in Egypt, Idris
directed the Sanusi nomads of the western desert to help the British
forces fighting the Italians and, in particular, to protect an important line of communication for military supplies which crossed the
Sahara from the Free French colony of Chad. Following the expulsion of the Italians from Libya in 1943, Idris returned to his country

with full British support for his claim to be its ruler. There were still a number of problems which had to be solved before he could be recognised as king of a united and independent Libya, however. While the Italians had found their main difficulty in extending their rule from the settled, mainly Berber populations of the coastal cities to the nomadic Arab pastoralists of the interior, Idris now encountered the reverse problem of making the rule of the bedouin acceptable to the more sophisticated and cosmopolitan people of the coast. While the problem was being resolved, the country remained, with the consent of the United Nations, under the administration of its wartime conquerors. The two northern provinces of Cyrenaica and Tripolitania remained under a British administration which, while strongly favouring the claims of Idris, was anxious to retain control until those claims were firmly established. The southern province, that of the Fezzan, had been occupied during the war by the Free French from Chad, who were in no hurry to move out of the frontier region, since the Sanusi brotherhood was as strong in Chad as in Libya and might all too easily inspire an irredentist movement in the French colony. In 1949, therefore, the UN began to play a hastening role, sending its own commissioner to work out a constitution acceptable to the country as a whole. At last, in 1951, a constituent assembly drawn from all three provinces declared Idris king of Libya, and the new state began its independent existence in December of that year. For more than a decade following, Libya remained a poverty-stricken backwater, heavily dependent on British and American aid and on the military agreements which Idris had made with the western countries. Its economic situation was transformed only in 1965, when the discovery of large oil resources under the desert suddenly converted Libya into the wealthiest country in Africa in terms of income per head of population. Only then was the stage set for the emergence of Colonel Gadhafi as one of the most influential and flamboyant military dictators of the postcolonial world.

The Maghrib was divided during the colonial period into Algeria, which was administered as a part of France, and the two flanking protectorates of Morocco and Tunisia. There was no essential difference between the state of nationalist opinion in the three countries. The vast majority of all their populations were solidly Muslim and Arabic-speaking. Their leaders looked to Cairo and the Arab League for support in their struggle and were also affected by developments toward independence in Libya, Sudan, and Somalia. The difference between them was mainly one of strategy, which arose from the differing degrees of French commitment. It was obvious to all that if France would adopt delaying tactics in the protectorates, in Algeria it would fight to the bitter end.

In Morocco, the sultan had made himself the central figure of the nationalist movement. He refused to give his consent to French laws banning the Istiqlal and other nationalist parties. In a desperate attempt to overcome the resistance to their rule in Morocco, the French sided with the nomadic pastoralists of the Atlas mountains, who were traditionally hostile to the sultanate. In 1953, the French deposed Muhammad V, and exiled him first to Corsica and later to Madagascar. The tribal kaid Thami al-Glawi was made sultan in his place. This act made Muhammad V the popular hero of Morocco and more than ever the symbol of the country' s hopes. Unrest broke out with the formation of an Army of Liberation by the nationalist groups. The French were forced to admit defeat and to agree to the principle of independence for Morocco. In November 1955, Muhammad returned to his country and was reinstated as sultan. A broadly representative delegation, including the Istiqlal, negotiated with the French, and Morocco became independent in March 1956. A similar agreement was made with the Spanish government in respect to the northern zone. Thus, after only forty-four years under European control, Morocco became once more a united independent kingdom.

As soon as Morocco became independent, King Muhammad's government began to stake claims to parts of neighbouring territories which it had ruled at various times in the past. In 1957, it invaded the Spanish colony of Rio de Oro, which stretched along a 600-mile fogbound coastline opposite the Spanish Canary islands. This attempt was firmly repulsed by the Spaniards, but it did not prevent Morocco from claiming large parts of the adjoining French colony of Mauritania. This claim was undermined when the French gave independence to Mauritania in 1960, but Morocco still refused to recognise Mauritanian independence until 1969. In 1973, a nationalist movement with the name Polisario emerged among the indigenous Saharan people of Rio de Oro, whereupon the Spanish government agreed that the future of the territory should be decided by a referendum.

Morocco now went to the UN and the International Court of Justice to press its claim. The Court upheld the validity of Morocco's historic claims, but nevertheless supported the right of the Saharan people to self-determination. In 1975, Muhammad's successor, Sultan Hassan, led a 'Green March' of 350,000 Moroccan civilians to liberate the Rio de Oro in the name of Islam. Spain, in the dying days of the Franco regime, gave up the unprofitable struggle and, in 1976, pulled out, leaving the territory partitioned between Morocco and Mauritania. Polisario was ignored in the deal, and many of the Saharans fled to Algeria. Polisario continued its struggle and, aided by Algeria, established a government called the Saharan Arab Democratic Republic (SADR), which succeeded in evicting the Mauritanians from their part of the country in 1979. But the fighting between Polisario and Morocco continued sporadically and inconclusively throughout the 1980s, with Polisario controlling much of the interior desert and Morocco the few towns and the phosphate deposits in the northern coastal region. Polisario organised its refugee camps with great efficiency and introduced excellent educational facilities, for girls and women as well as for boys. Within its own territory, the SADR had one of the highest literacy rates in Africa.

What had started as an adventure by King Hassan for largely domestic and dynastic reasons had become for Morocco a national cause which could not now be jettisoned. Development money was poured into Moroccan-occupied Western Sahara, and its economy and administration were increasingly integrated with those of Morocco itself. Polisario was supplied with military hardware by Algeria, and also by Libya and the Soviet Union. Morocco was of great strategic importance to the United States in the politics of the Cold War. In the Arab world, too, most governments supported King Hassan. An OAU plan for a referendum in 1981 was rejected by both sides, and it was only with the ending of the Cold War that the issue of the Western Sahara declined in international importance to the extent that the UN was able in 1990 to negotiate a cease-fire, pending a future referendum.

In Tunisia, it seemed at first that France would pursue a more conciliatory policy toward emerging nationalism than it had done in Morocco. Habib Bourguiba, the founder of the Néo-Destour party (see Chapter 14), returned to his country after four years of self-imposed exile, and the following year he felt able to state that 'with independence accepted in principle, there are no more problems'. But such optimism was misplaced. Increasing resistance to constitutional change came from the French and Italian settlers in the country. It came also from the French governor–general of Algeria, who feared the effect on that country of having an independent Tunisia as neighbour. In 1952, Bourguiba was arrested, and disturbances broke out which the French were unable to control. By 1954, moreover, France was fighting a full-scale war against the nationalists in Algeria, and had neither the will nor the military forces to break a serious revolt in Tunisia. As in Morocco, therefore, France chose to give way to the nationalist movement. In 1955, Bourguiba was released. Tunisia became independent in March 1956, at the same time as Morocco. But relations with France became strained once more in 1961 when, at the time of the Evian negotiations between France and the Algerian nationalists, Bourguiba demanded the evacuation of French troops from the military base at Bizerta. Violent fighting broke out and continued until France agreed to complete the evacuation by June 1962. By that time, a large proportion of the European community in Tunisia had left the country. After the Bizerta crisis, Tunisia and France became more closely aligned again. There was substantial French investment in the development of Tunisia's varied agricultural resources, which ensured a measure of economic and social stability in the newly independent state.

In Algeria, the first outbreak of nationalist violence occurred within a few days of the end of the Second World War, when police fired upon a procession at Sétif. Enraged Muslims turned upon the French settlers, and the French replied with ruthless retaliation. More than 100 Europeans and many thousands of Muslims were killed. This grim experience gave many Algerians their first intimations of nationhood. In 1946, Ferhat Abbas, who in 1934 had doubted the existence of an Algerian fatherland (see Chapter 14), was able to write, 'The Algerian personality, the Algerian fatherhood, which I could not find among the Muslims in 1934, I find there today. The change that has taken place is visible to the naked eye, and cannot be ignored'. But the French, nevertheless, ignored this growing Algerian nationalism. For eight years, from 1945 until 1953, France had been fighting – and losing – a bitter war to reestablish her control over her richest and most populous colonial territory in Indo–China, where the terminal military disaster at Dien Bien Phu was felt to be a national humiliation of catastrophic proportions. The effect of the Indo–Chinese war on French policy elsewhere was, on the one hand, to speed up thoughts of decolonisation in Black Africa and the North African protectorates, but on the other hand to be totally unyielding about Algeria, where 1 million *pieds noirs* had relations all over the mother country. No French ministry in the long series of weak governments which followed one another at frequent intervals from 1945 to 1958 could face the unpopularity of abandoning what was still, constitutionally, a part of metropolitan France. The Muslim uprising there of 1954 was influenced by events in Morocco and Tunisia. In a real sense, the French only withdrew from these protectorates with the object of being better able to hold Algeria.

In October 1954, the Algerian nationalists formed themselves into an organisation called the *Front de la libération nationale* (FLN). Three weeks later, the revolt was launched on 1 November, All Saints' Day, a date which had been deliberately chosen for its significance to the Catholic pieds noirs. The war lasted for nearly eight bitter years and was conducted in classic guerrilla style. The FLN fighters never numbered more than about 40,000, but they were supported and supplied by a vast civilian population. Their surprise attacks on the farms and installations of the pieds noirs were deadly enough to strain the resources of the French army, which at the height of the insurgency numbered 200,000 troops. There were times when the rebels seemed to be almost vanquished, but they regrouped in the safe havens provided by the Tunisians and always returned to the attack. The Egyptian triumph in the Suez Canal crisis was a great encouragement to them, and helped to keep open their supply lines for Russian and Chinese arms. The Suez crisis also paved the way for the return to French politics of General de Gaulle. The French people needed a strong ruler to rescue them from disastrous overseas adventures, and they were at last prepared greatly to increase the presidential powers. During his election campaign, the general promised victory in Algeria. He visited Algeria, ending all his speeches with the phrase 'Vive l' Algérie française!' No sooner was he in power, however, than he started to pursue his *'politique de l'artichaut'* – his artichoke policy – of stripping off, leaf by leaf, the strong combination of right-wing generals, embattled settlers, and reactionary administrators who had defied the peace-making efforts of all his predecessors. These die-hard Frenchmen had set up the *Organisation armée secrète* (OAS), which from 1961 onwards waged a campaign of terror in Algeria and in France. A cease-fire was finally arranged with the FLN at Evian in 1962, by which time older leaders like Ferhat Abbas had been pushed aside by younger, more radical men. The crucial issue of full independence from France remained unresolved until the last minute, but was finally conceded. More than 18,000 French soldiers and some 10,000 pieds noirs, and an estimated 1 million Algerians, had died in the war. The conflict had had elements of tragedy. In spite of the oppression and hatreds engendered, the relationship between France and Algeria, between Algerians and Frenchmen, had been exceptionally close, and the revolt when it came was almost like a violent quarrel between members of a family. In some respects, at least, the rift took a surprisingly short time to heal.

After a short period of civil war, during which most of the 1 million French settlers left the country, Muhammad Ben Bella emerged as the strongman of independent Algeria and became the country's first president. He was a popular but impulsive leader, with a liking for abstract and authoritarian solutions for his country's problems. The FLN as an organisation did not survive the end of the fighting. Political power in Algeria tended to polarise around the leaders of powerful civil or military influence groups. Under the leadership of Ben Bella, Algeria achieved a prominent position in the Pan–African movement and in the affairs of the Organisation of African Unity. As one of the few African countries to gain independence by violent revolution, it was only to be expected that Algeria would adopt sweeping socialist policies to cope with the many problems left by the long war with France. Ben Bella was an outspoken critic of all manifestations of neo-colonialism and was particularly hostile to the European minority governments of southern Africa. He aligned himself closely with Russia and with its communist allies, especially Cuba. Yet despite embittering memories of the recent struggle, Algeria retained many links with France. Several thousand French technicians were employed in the exploitation of the oil of the Algerian Sahara, and thousands of young Frenchmen served for short periods as teachers in Algerian schools in lieu of military service in France.

In spite of his international prestige, however, Ben Bella's position within Algeria soon became less secure. The civil war which had followed the winning of independence had left wounds in many parts of the country, particularly among the freedom-loving Berbers of Kabylia, whose attempts at opposition had been ruthlessly crushed by Ben Bella. Many other Algerians resented his dictatorial methods. There was also the fact that he had spent most of the Algerian war in a French jail and consequently had never really won the confidence of the former fighters of the FLN, who disliked taking orders from one whom they regarded as a non-combatant. It was the former commander of an FLN army group who later became Ben Bella's minister of defence, the dour and puritanical Colonel Boumédienne, who, feeling his own position threatened by the president, staged an almost bloodless coup d'état in 1965, which toppled him from power. The new government represented a compromise for Algerian politics. It contained members of Ben Bella's former administration, as well as army leaders and representatives of other sectional interests. Internal problems were given more attention than under the regime of his predecessor, and Algeria henceforward pursued a less extreme and less expensive foreign policy. The coup d'état led to the indefinite postponement of a much-heralded conference of the Afro–Asian countries, which was to have been a second Bandung and which was to have been held in Algiers in June 1965. China and other countries of the extreme left refused to attend, claiming that there were too many deep divisions among the Afro–Asian states for such a meeting to produce useful results. Within Africa, the mantle of extremist interventionism was soon to pass from Algeria to the more erratic shoulders of Gadhafi's Libya.

EIGHTEEN. The Road to Independence: (2) Africa from the Sahara to the Zambezi

The roots of Black African nationalism reach in many directions back into history. One powerful impulse was the growing ethnic awareness of the descendants of the African slaves in the New World, which was proclaimed by activists such as Marcus Garvey with his slogan 'Africa for the Africans', and Edward Blyden, who settled in Liberia in 1850, with his idea of the African personality. Even more influential was the Pan–Africanist doctrine of William DuBois, who organised Pan–African Congresses in the 1920s and 1930s. Many Africans from British colonies who were studying in Britain and the United States were caught up in the excitement of these ideas and schemes. Another powerful strand in the web of African nationalism was that stemming from European socialism and communism, which, especially after the Russian Revolution, were vehement in denouncing the colonial system. Africans who went to Europe discovered in socialism, and in particular in Marxist communism, techniques of political action which appeared well suited to their needs, a call to heroism in a world struggle, and a promise of future freedom and prosperity. And in Europe, of course, there was the pervasive and heady example of nationalism in practice, an example which was already spreading through colonial lands in Asia like wildfire.

To see how these complex strands were woven together to produce the political activity that resulted in independence, we can look for an example at the early career of Kwame Nkrumah, which is so well told in his autobiography, *Ghana*. Nkrumah was born, probably in 1909, the son of a goldsmith of the Nzima tribe in the south-western corner of the Gold Coast. Nzima people had long been active in the commerce of the west coast. Nkrumah was educated at a Roman Catholic mission school and then at the great secondary school at Achimota, near Accra. He thought of the priesthood and eventually became a mission teacher, but this did not satisfy his ambitions. In 1935, with the help of an uncle working in Lagos and with the encouragement of the Nigerian nationalist, Dr Azikiwe, he went to the United States. There he spent ten years, first studying and then teaching at Lincoln University in Pennsylvania. He read widely and has said that the writings of communists and socialists did much to influence him in his revolutionary ideas and activities, 'but of all the literature that I studied, the book that did more than any other to fire my enthusiasm was the *Philosophy and Opinions* of Marcus Garvey'. In 1945, Nkrumah left America for London and there met for the first time the West Indian journalist George Padmore, who became one of his closest friends and advisers. The two men played a prominent part in the Fifth Pan–African Congress held at Manchester in that year. The majority of delegates at this congress were Africans, although it was presided over by DuBois, then seventy-three, the 'Grand Old Man' of the movement. In Padmore's words, DuBois 'had done more than any other to inspire and influence by his writings and political philosophy all the young men who had forgathered from far distant corners of the earth'.[1] The congress adopted strongly worded resolutions condemning colonialism: 'We are determined to be free. We want education. We want the right to earn a decent living, the right to express our thoughts and emotions, to adopt and create forms of beauty. We demand for Black Africa autonomy and independence. We will fight in every way we can for freedom, democracy and social betterment'. At the congress, and later in London, Nkrumah worked closely with Jomo Kenyatta and had meetings with Africans from the French territories, such as Senghor and Houphouët-Boigny. At this stage, most of the political activity among Africans took place in London or Paris, and not in Africa itself. It was then that the foundations of a continent-wide movement were laid. 'The political conscience of

---

[1] George Padmore, *Pan-Africanism or Communism?* (London, 1956), p. 161.

African students was aroused, and whenever they met they talked of little else but nationalist politics and colonial liberation movements' (Nkrumah).

The Gold Coast: The Breakthrough

Until 1947, the Pan–African movement, although it had won the allegiance of the young African intellectuals studying abroad, had achieved little or nothing in Africa itself. Only Dr Azikiwe's newspapers, which were read by a small group of educated people throughout British West Africa, did something to prepare the ground for a more radical approach to politics. The colonial governments, to the extent that they had even heard of Pan–Africanism, thought of it as mere 'students' talk'. The African leaders whom they recognised, and to whom they were preparing to make limited political concessions, were men of an older generation who had done well under colonial rule – the chiefs, lawyers, businessmen, and rich farmers. It was men of this sort who in 1947 founded the United Gold Coast Convention (UGCC) in an attempt to face 'the problem of reconciling the leadership of the intelligentsia with the broad mass of the people' (Nkrumah). These were men of substance and experience. They were Gold Coast patriots, too. They looked forward to independence in the shortest possible time – some of them thought in about ten years' time. They even realised that, to keep up pressure on the colonial government, it would be necessary to organise widespread support among the people. But they did not themselves know how to do so. They had their own professions to pursue. Politics to them was a spare-time occupation, as it was for most politicians in Europe. In western European countries, the only full-time political organisers were the paid agents of the political parties, who did not themselves stand for election. This was why the UGCC leaders in 1947 invited Nkrumah to come home and be their general secretary. Here, they thought, was a man who knew the techniques of organisation and who would take the rough work off their hands.

No sooner had Nkrumah arrived back in the Gold Coast than he began to pursue an activist policy designed to seize the initiative from the colonial government. He started to reform the inefficient party organisation:

I found on going through the minute book, that thirteen branches had been formed throughout the country. In actual fact just a couple had been established and these were inactive. I saw at once the urgency of a country-wide tour. The results of this were most successful, for within six months I had established 500 branches in the [original] Colony alone. I issued membership cards, collected dues and started raising funds.[2]

The leaders of the UGCC became involved in violent demonstrations by ex-servicemen in Accra. The six top men of the party, including Nkrumah, were placed in detention by the government. This was the beginning of the split between Nkrumah and the UGCC. Nkrumah welcomed such violent activities; his colleagues had second thoughts about their value in achieving independence. The British government responded to the disturbances by inviting an all-African committee under Sir Henley Coussey to make recommendations for constitutional reform. The other five leaders of the UGCC joined the committee: Nkrumah alone was not invited.

The Coussey constitution, which was accepted by the British government, was a real landmark in the history of British moves toward decolonisation in Africa. It was implemented by the new governor, Sir Charles Arden-Clarke, as soon as he took up his duties in 1949. It provided for an all-African legislative assembly, directly elected in the more developed parts of the country and indirectly elected elsewhere. An executive council or cabinet was formed, with eight ministers chosen from the assembly and three more to be nominated by the governor from the ranks of the European civil service. It was, in fact, the constitution under which Nkrumah was to begin his rule, first as leader of government business and later as prime minister, from 1951 till 1954. In 1949, however, Nkrumah had just founded his own Convention People's Party (CPP) in opposition to the UGCC. He denounced the Coussey constitution as 'an imperialist fraud', demanding instead 'self-government now'. He followed up his claim with a campaign of 'positive action'. This was a movement of strikes and boycotts, designed to create a sense of struggle throughout the country. For their part in the positive-action campaign, Nkrumah and other CPP leaders were arrested and condemned to imprisonment on various charges of incitement, libel, and sedition. They remained

---

[2] *Ghana* (London, 1959), p. 61.

in prison for a year, while the colonial government proceeded with its preparations for a general election in February 1951. This was won by the CPP, led during Nkrumah's enforced absence from the scene by K. A. Gbedemah. This electoral victory of the CPP was the result of such political efficiency that the party won the respect and admiration of the formerly very hostile colonial government. Arden-Clarke, therefore, decided to release Nkrumah and to invite him to form a government. Nkrumah, for his part, agreed to abandon his claim for 'self-government now' and to work for a period under the Coussey constitution. This gave the CPP ministers the great advantage of learning to operate the machinery of government from the inside before taking on the full responsibilities of independence. On Arden-Clarke's side, this bargain, struck in February 1951, committed the colonial government to working, for only a brief transitional period, with the representatives of a radical party with a great popular following. The CPP was very different in its aims and leadership from the moderate, middle-class people to whom the colonial government had previously hoped to hand over power. The government in Britain – and, indeed, the outside world as a whole – watched in amazement the steadily growing friendship between these two very different men as they steered the Gold Coast toward independence. Nkrumah tells in moving terms how he received from Arden-Clarke the news of the date – 6 March 1957 – fixed by the British government for the Gold Coast's independence under the new name of Ghana:

He handed me a dispatch from the Secretary of State. When I reached the fifth paragraph the tears of joy that I had difficulty in hiding blurred the rest of the document. After a few minutes I raised my eyes to meet those of the Governor. For some moments there was nothing either of us could say. Perhaps we were both looking back over the seven years of our association, beginning with doubts, suspicions and misunderstandings, then acknowledging the growth of trust, sincerity and friendship, and now, finally, this moment of victory for us both, a moment beyond description.

'Prime Minister,' the Governor said, as he extended his hand to me, 'this is a great day for you. It is the end of what you have struggled for.'

'It is the end of what *we* have been struggling for, Sir Charles,' I corrected him. 'You have contributed a great deal towards this; in fact I might not have succeeded without your help and co-operation. This is a very happy day for us both!'[3]

[3] Ibid., p. 282.

The Sequel to Ghana in British West Africa

So far as the rest of British West Africa was concerned, the decision to decolonise followed automatically from the decision to do so in the Gold Coast. In Nigeria, the course toward independence was firmly set by a new constitution which came into operation in 1951. This was the same year as Arden-Clarke's bargain with Nkrumah. That the process of independence took three years longer to achieve in Nigeria than in the Gold Coast was due to the special problems created by the differences in education, wealth, and outlook among the three regions of Nigeria. The Northern region was largely Muslim and Hausa-speaking. The traditional Fulbe ruling class still exercised the predominant influence. The mainly Yoruba-speaking Western region was traditionally organised into a number of states ruled by kingly chiefs, while the Eastern region consisted largely of Igbo-speaking people who had never been bound together into powerful political units. The problems created by these differences could not be solved by setting up a unitary state covering the whole of Nigeria. This the 1951 constitution partly tried to do, and it was proved to be unworkable. Dr Azikiwe, who had become chief minister of the Eastern region, was especially critical of the attempt to minimise regional powers. The problems of Nigeria could only be settled by the compromise solution of a federal system of government. This more complicated structure took longer to develop than the unitary government of independent Ghana. A new constitution came into force in 1954. Under it, Nigeria became a federal state, with clearly defined powers granted to the federal government and all other powers given to the regional governments. Each region had to become internally self-governing before the territory as a whole could become independent. The most backward region politically was the North. When, however, this immense region came to play its full part in Nigerian affairs, it dominated the territory politically. No federal government could be formed without members of the Northern People's Congress Party, and the first federal prime minister, Sir Abubakar Tafawa Balewa, was a northerner.

The strains and stresses produced by the interactions of regional interests in Nigeria delayed the granting of full independence until 1960. The major problem in Sierra Leone and, especially, in the

Gambia, was the very opposite to Nigeria's. Both territories were very small and, consequently, relatively poor. Nevertheless, the process started in the Gold Coast could not be halted. Sierra Leone became independent in 1961 and the Gambia in 1965. The Gambia is one of the smallest countries in Africa. It is merely the narrow strip of land along the banks of the Gambia River and is completely surrounded by the French-speaking state of Senegal. The granting of independence to the Gambia raised the question as to whether a country of this size could be viable as a sovereign state, but events proved, in South-East Asia and elsewhere, that mini-states could be extremely successful economically; the Gambia, although not as well-off as some of these states, was to benefit from its size and position.

The Independence of French West Africa

The difference in attitude toward the growth of nationalism between French- and English-speaking West Africans may be seen in a comparison between the life of Senghor and that of Nkrumah. French Africans were at first concerned more with the cultural than with the political aspects of colonialism. English-speaking nationalists, it has been said, wrote constitutions, while their French-speaking contemporaries wrote poetry. Léopold Sédar Senghor was born in 1906 in a coastal village south of Dakar. His prosperous Catholic parents sent him to schools in the colony and later to Paris. The poems he wrote while in France are full of homesick memories of his childhood days. From 1935, after becoming the first African *agrégé* (qualified secondary-school teacher) in France, he taught in French *lycées* (grammar schools). On the outbreak of the war in 1939, he joined the army and was captured by the Germans, who tried unsuccessfully to persuade him to turn against France. His years in Paris had brought Senghor into contact with a wealth of political and literary ideas. He knew many outstanding French West Indians and became the close friend of Aimé Césaire from Martinique, who was to become, like himself, a poet and a politician. Before directly tackling political problems, these young men felt the need to produce a creed, or statement of cultural values. Between them, Senghor and Césaire created the concept of *négritude*, 'the affirmation', as they described it, 'of the values of African culture'. In 1947, Senghor and a fellow Senegalese, Alioune Diop, founded *Présence Africaine* in Paris, a magazine devoted to the renewal of these values. Meanwhile, Senghor was turning to practical politics. After the war, he returned to Senegal as a socialist politician and took part in the events which led up to the formation of the French Union in 1946. He refused to attend the Bamako conference of that year which founded the Rassemblement Démocratique Africaine (RDA). He rightly believed that the new party would be dominated by communists. Instead, Senghor led a popular political movement in Senegal and was elected as a deputy to the French Assembly. Under his influence, many young Africans devoted themselves seriously to writing, poetry, and the arts. This engagement of some of the best minds in French West Africa with cultural affairs partly explains why, in the early 1950s, these territories were not so politically conscious as their English-speaking neighbours.

Support for Senghor's party extended into Upper Volta and other territories, where it came into direct collision with the RDA. The main issue between the two parties from 1955 onwards was that between the federal policy of Senghor and the territorial policy of Houphouët-Boigny. Houphouët, who was born in the Ivory Coast in 1905, went to France for the first time when he was elected a deputy in 1945. Previously, he had been a medical assistant, a prosperous cocoa farmer, and a local chief. He had entered politics as the spokesman of a farmers' association. Although a highly sophisticated man, he retained a good measure of the peasant's 'down-to-earth' common sense. He became the first president of the RDA. After the breakaway of the RDA from its communist alliance in 1950, he held cabinet posts in several French governments. After the war, the Ivory Coast had become the richest of the French West African territories, providing more than 40 percent of the Federation's exports. Houphouët argued that in the federal Union, supported by Senghor, the Ivory Coast would always be subsidising its poorer neighbours. As a minister in the French government, therefore, he was influential in preparing the Loi Cadre (Outline Law) of 1956. Under the Loi Cadre, France retained control of foreign policy, defence, and overall economic development. All other aspects of government became the responsibility, not of the existing federal governments of French West and Equatorial Africa, but of the twelve individual colonies of which they were composed. The Loi Cadre was deeply influenced by the approaching independence of the Gold Coast and Nigeria. France understood that the French Union – a plan for a kind of superstate – would need to be replaced by something much looser and more like the British Commonwealth. But, partly thanks to Houphouët, the autonomy offered was to units so small (in population, if not in size) that their practical dependence on France was bound to remain very great. Senghor unsuccessfully opposed these constitutional changes, which he considered would result in splitting up West Africa into too many small, weak states. In this opposition he was supported by Sékou Touré of Guinea, a prominent figure in the RDA.

Sékou Touré was born in 1922 and was, therefore, a much younger man than either Senghor or Houphouët-Boigny. Although he was a descendant of the famous Samori, his family was poor. His first visit to France had been as a delegate to the Communist Trades Union Conference in 1946. Sékou Touré soon became the leading trade unionist in French West Africa. In 1956, he led a breakaway movement from the French parent body of the Union, although he still held communist views, and formed a new Federation of African Trades Unions, free from outside ties. While most of his contemporaries concentrated upon increasing their influence in Paris, Sékou Touré realised that it was in Africa that the foundations of real power were to be laid. He favoured the retention of the federal government at Dakar. In 1958, it looked as though a regrouping of political parties was about to take place, with Sékou Touré leaving the RDA and joining Senghor. At this moment, however, General de Gaulle came to power in France as a result of the revolt of the French army in Algeria in May 1958. De Gaulle established a new constitution in France, the Fifth Republic. He offered the colonial peoples the choice between autonomy (self-government) as separate states within a French Community, which now replaced the earlier Union, or else immediate independence, with the severance of all links with France. In the referendum held in September 1958, all the colonies of French West and Equatorial Africa voted acceptance of de Gaulle's proposals for autonomy except for Guinea, whose people followed Sékou Touré in voting 'No'. Sékou Touré was bitterly disappointed with the failure of French West Africa to achieve independence as a federation. He considered that the new Community was little more than a disguise for the continuing domination of France.

When Guinea decided to become independent, France immediately stopped all economic aid and withdrew its civil servants and technicians. Faced with an economic collapse, Sékou Touré turned to the Soviet Union and to other communist countries for assistance. Nkrumah offered him at once a loan of £10 million, and the two statesmen declared the formation of a union between their two countries. This was a gesture of solidarity, however, rather than a real constitutional measure. But, as a gesture, it was effective, for the other territories, which had voted 'Yes' in the referendum, began at once to readjust their positions. Senegal and French Soudan came together to form the Mali Federation and, in 1959, demanded and obtained complete independence while remaining members of the Community. The Ivory Coast joined in a looser grouping, the 'Entente Council', with Dahomey, Upper Volta, and Niger, each member of which demanded its individual independence of France. By November 1960, all the French West and Equatorial African territories had become independent, as had the Malagasy Republic (Madagascar). After a matter of months, the Mali Federation divided again into its two parts, French Soudan now taking to itself the name of Mali. The Community, as de Gaulle had envisaged it, was a dead letter, although French aid – and, therefore, French influence – remained very great.

It is often maintained by critics of decolonisation that the French deliberately pursued a policy of balkanisation by breaking up the two Federations and granting independence to their twelve constituent colonies. The Federations had been largely devices set up by the French for the poorer colonies to be subsidised by the richer, and as the leaders of these latter – Houphouët-Boigny of Ivory Coast and Léon M'ba of Gabon – saw independence in the offing, they were no longer prepared to have their countries continue in this magnanimous role.

The United Nations Trusteeship Territories in West Africa followed the same broad path as the colonies proper. British Togoland decided by plebiscite to join Ghana in 1957, while French Togo became an independent republic in 1960. The history of Cameroun during the decolonisation was the stormiest of all West African countries. Civil war between communist and anti-communist groups broke out in 1956 and had not been completely resolved when the territory became independent in 1960. In 1961, plebiscites were held in British

Cameroun. The northern part voted to remain within Northern Nigeria. The southern part, however, voted for union with its French-
speaking neighbour. Thus, the Federal Republic of Cameroun
combined for the first time areas which had been under different colonial rules and defied the language gulf which separates the
English- and French-speaking states of West Africa.

Nkrumah had always made it clear that, once Ghana had achieved
its independence, it would be his main objective to lead the rest of
Africa to independence and unity. Accordingly, in December 1958,
he invited representatives of nationalist movements in twenty-eight
territories still under colonial rule to meet at Accra for the first All-
African People's Conference. Nkrumah was at that time at the height
of his influence. He was the undisputed leader of the Pan–African
movement. At the conference, however, he deliberately shared the
limelight with Tom Mboya of Kenya, who proved to be a brilliant
chairman. This was the first real demonstration that East Africa
was beginning to play a significant part in the African revolution.
A few months before, Mboya and Julius Nyerere of Tanganyika had
formed the Pan–African Freedom Movement of East and Central
Africa, which sent its own delegate to Accra. Kenya and Tanganyika
were both, according to Mboya, 'facing a rough patch in the independence struggle' and felt the need for Pan–African support. The Accra
conference set up a body to direct and assist anti-colonial struggles
and planned to establish other regional organisations on the same
lines as PAFMECA. Some African leaders, previously unknown to
one another, came away from Accra with a new sense of solidarity and purpose. In particular, Patrice Lumumba returned to the
Belgian Congo tremendously impressed by the contacts he had
made. The Belgians later admitted that the Accra conference
'brought decisive results for the Congo. There Lumumba got the support which he needed to implement his demand for independence'.

East Africa: Mau Mau and Multiracialism

The 'rough patch in the independence struggle' alluded to by Tom
Mboya was largely the result of the uncertainty of British policy toward East Africa during the years 1948–58. The British government
was slow to understand that the appeal and compulsion of African

nationalism were bound to spread from one end of the continent to the other. It knew that the East African territories were economically much poorer, and educationally more backward, than the West African countries. Britain, therefore, assumed that nationalism in East Africa would be correspondingly slower to develop. Moreover, British thinking about its East African policy was complicated by the settler problem. It was considered that the presence of the settlers demanded that some alternative should be found to the normal pattern of one man/one vote democracy. This alternative was to be along the lines of the 'multiracial' type of constitution which we described in Chapter 16. It was thought that this stage of political development would need to last for at least twenty years. This meant for as long ahead as anyone needed to think.

This distinction between the preparedness of West and East Africa for independence seemed to most European minds to be fully justified when, in 1951, there broke out in Kenya the violent insurrection by some Kikuyu people, known as Mau Mau. No observer of the situation denied that the Kikuyu had exceptional grievances. Their numbers had grown steadily throughout the colonial period and, yet, the land into which they might have expanded was occupied by settlers' farms. As the East African Royal Commission of 1955 reported, 'Throughout our inquiry we were impressed by the recurring evidence that particular areas were carrying so large a population that agricultural production in them was being retarded, that the natural resources were being destroyed, and that families were unable to find access to new land'. In the face of this land shortage, large numbers of Kikuyu were driven to seek inadequately paid jobs in the towns, or else on the European farms. In the towns, many were unemployed and took to living by crime. These poverty-stricken and land-hungry people looked with understandable envy and resentment on the settlers' estates. These were large, well tended, and rich. Many of them included large areas of uncultivated land.

The Mau Mau rebellion began with the murder of a few British farmers. Their cattle were mutilated and other acts of violence carried out. All these demonstrations were intended to instil such terror into the settler community that most would leave the country. Similar events had taken place in Ireland during the nineteenth century. There, the landlords had been Englishmen, and the Irish peasants

poor and landless. In Kenya, the government responded by arrest-
ing Jomo Kenyatta and other well-known Kikuyu leaders. They were
charged with organising the revolt and were condemned to long
terms of imprisonment. Kenyatta strenuously denied the accusation.
Certainly, his removal from the scene had no obvious effect on the
course of events. The active insurgents were comparatively few in
number. They had their bases in the almost impenetrable forests
high up the slopes of Mount Kenya and the Nyandarua range. From
these forests, they ventured forth in small bands in the dead of night
to swoop on outlying farms, to attack the soldiers who had been sent
against them, and, very frequently, to take bloody reprisals against
fellow Kikuyu suspected of cooperating with the government. The
British would not give way in the face of such tactics. The fact that
the enemy was unseen made a resort to counter-terrorism almost inevitable. The Kikuyu peasantry were rounded up from their scattered
homesteads and made to live in villages which could be defended and
policed. People suspected of collaborating with the insurgents were
roughly interrogated in the attempt to get information. The detention camps for captured insurgents used brutal methods to break
the psychological resistance of their inmates – that is, their cling-
ing to ideas that the government considered dangerous. Such is the
nature of all secret warfare. By the end of 1955, the back of the revolt
had been broken, at a cost to Britain of more than £20 million and
some hundred British lives. The casualties of the civil war between
insurgents and collaborators among the Kikuyu were officially estimated at 3,000, but were reckoned by some reputable observers at
ten times that number. Nothing like this had ever happened in West
Africa. It was akin to the war in Algeria between the nationalists and
the French. Obviously, not much progress toward self-government
was possible in Kenya while the struggle lasted. On the other hand,
the Mau Mau revolt did serve to demonstrate that small bodies of
British settlers – like those in Kenya, Tanganyika, Nyasaland, and
Northern Rhodesia – were incapable of defending themselves. It also
showed that the multiracial constitutions in these countries would
be effective only as long as British force was available to underpin
them.

Immediately, the most important effect of the Mau Mau revolt on
political development in Kenya was to prevent the emergence (until

after independence) of a single mass party. While the insurrection lasted, the colonial government, fearing that it would spread to the whole country, permitted political organisations on a regional basis only. By the time the emergency was over, regionalism had developed so far that a deep rift had opened between the Kikuyu and the Luo politicians on the one hand and those of the Kalenjin and coastal Bantu peoples on the other. When regional politics were again permitted, two rival parties emerged: the Kenya African National Union (KANU) and the Kenya African Democratic Union (KADU). Because of their mutual distrust, Kenya, which might have been the first, proved in fact to be the last of the East African countries to achieve independence.

Although for different reasons, Uganda was almost as deeply divided as Kenya. There were three contending interests in the territory. The first was the exclusiveness of the kingdom of Buganda. Buganda feared to lose its privileged position in the territory, which it owed to the settlement established by the colonial power. Most of the Buganda politicians found it difficult to work with those from other parts of the country. Secondly, there was the moderate nationalism of the other traditional kingdoms of the south and west. They resented the privileges and aloofness of Buganda, yet felt that they, too, had much to lose from rapid change. Thirdly, there was the less hesitant radicalism of the north and east, where the socialist Uganda People's Congress soon found its main support. The alliance which eventually brought about the independence of Uganda was one between the first of these three interests and the third. This, however, was slow to emerge. So Uganda, despite the absence of a settler problem, was by no means in the forefront of the nationalist struggle in East Africa.

The pacemaker on the eastern side of Africa turned out, surprisingly enough, to be Tanganyika, which economically and educationally lagged far behind its two northern neighbours. Also, political consciousness had been much slower to emerge in Tanganyika during the early years of the African revolution. Yet, between 1956 and 1959, Tanganyika not only pushed through from the backward ranks of colonies to the front, but also actually set the pattern for all the British territories from Kenya to the Zambezi. Without any doubt, Tanganyika's sudden success was due to the fact that the Tanganyika

African National Union (TANU), founded by Julius Nyerere in 1954, was by far the most efficiently organised mass party to emerge anywhere in Africa since Nkrumah's CPP. Within three or four years of returning to Tanganyika from his studies in Edinburgh, Nyerere had created a nationwide party structure, with active branches in almost every district in the country. He was helped, as he said himself, by the fact that the population was divided among more than 120 tribal groupings, none of which had been large enough – or central enough – to predominate. Nyerere was helped, too, by the Swahili language. As a result of the Arab penetration of the nineteenth century and the educational policies of the German and British colonial governments, Swahili was understood throughout the length of the land. Finally, because so little in the way of political organisation had been attempted before, he was able to start with a clean slate.

From the first, the weight of Nyerere's attack was directed against the 'multiracial' conception of constitutional advance. As the United Nations Mission of 1954 stated in its report, 'The Africans of this country would like to be assured, both by the United Nations Organisation and by the Administering Authority, that this territory, though multi-racial in population, is primarily an African country and must be developed as such'. During the next four years, Nyerere strove by a remarkable moderation to show that, although TANU stood for government by the African majority, non-Africans would have nothing to fear from such a government. Nyerere preached this doctrine with such success that in the elections of 1958, held under the existing 'multiracial' constitution, all of the contested seats were won either by TANU candidates or by those non-Africans who received TANU support in exchange for an undertaking to collaborate with TANU when elected. The result of the elections coincided with the appointment of a new governor, Sir Richard Turnbull, who saw, as Arden-Clarke had seen in the Gold Coast in 1951, that the turning point in the country's development was at hand. In October 1958, Turnbull announced that, when self-government was attained, Tanganyika would be ruled by its African majority. Nyerere enthusiastically welcomed this statement, saying,

We have always waited for a Governor of this country even to indicate that it was the government's policy that, when self-government is eventually achieved, the Africans will have a predominant say in the affairs of the country. Now the Africans have this assurance, I am confident that it is going to be the endeavour of the Africans, if non-Africans have any fears left, to remove them quickly.

Under the guidance of Nyerere and Turnbull, who worked together in the same spirit as Nkrumah and Arden-Clarke, Tanganyika fairly scampered out of the colonial era. Full independence was achieved in December 1961, after an apprenticeship of little more than three years. This was in a country with a population larger than Ghana's, but with less than a tenth of the number of university and secondary-school graduates.

Obviously, once the multiracial system had been abandoned in Tanganyika, it could no longer be seriously defended in Kenya or Uganda. Nor could it be defended in Nyasaland or Northern Rhodesia, the two northern territories of the Central African Federation which had been formed in 1953 (see Chapter 19). The new trend in British policy as a whole was recognised when, early in 1959, Iain Macleod succeeded Alan Lennox-Boyd as colonial secretary. Whereas Lennox-Boyd's policy had been to strive for every additional year of colonial rule that could be gained, Macleod's was to free Britain from responsibilities in Africa with all possible speed. The 1960 Kenya constitution which bears his name provided for an African majority in the Legislative Assembly. 'At one swift blow', said a leader of the settlers, 'power was transferred to the Africans'. Further political changes in Kenya, as also in Uganda, were delayed only by disagreements among the Africans themselves. In Kenya, not even the release of Kenyatta in August 1961 could break the deadlock between KANU and KADU. When the country became independent in December 1963, it was under a compromise constitution which provided for considerable regional autonomy. In Uganda, Milton Obote, the founder of the Uganda People's Congress, succeeded in 1962 in making an alliance with the royalist Buganda Kabaka Yekka Party. This alliance at last carried the country to independence with the Kabaka of Buganda as head of state.

Britain completed its decolonisation of East Africa in December 1963 by granting independence to Zanzibar under a constitution which left the Arab sultan as head of state. The government was formed by an obviously precarious alliance between the political party directed by the old Arab ruling minority and the smaller of two parties representing the African majority of the population. In the event, this new government lasted less than two months before being violently overthrown by a communist-inspired revolution. Here at least, the British were to blame for moving out too soon, before ensuring the transfer of political power to a stable regime.

The Belgian Congo

While East Africa was hurrying along the path to independence, an even more sudden and perilous emancipation from colonial rule was taking place in the Congo. Until 1957, the Belgians had continued to rule their huge colony as if it were completely isolated from the changes taking place elsewhere in Africa. When, in 1956, a lecturer at the Colonial University in Antwerp, Dr A. A. J. van Bilsen, published a 'Thirty Year Plan for the Political Emancipation of Belgian Africa', he was attacked in Belgium as a dangerous revolutionary. Van Bilsen based his timetable on the perfectly correct notion that 'in the Congo and Ruanda-Urundi the formation of an élite and of responsible, directing *cadres* is a generation behind the British and French territories'. Yet, four years after van Bilsen had made this statement, the Belgian authorities who had attacked him for his imprudent haste had left the Congo to fend for itself. On the eve of the independence of the Congo in 1960, the Belgian prime minister implicitly acknowledged his country's failure: 'if we could have counted at this moment on proper organisations at a provincial level, the political solutions for the Congo would have been greatly facilitated'.

The independence of the Congo was, in fact, far from being a triumph of African nationalism. It was, rather, a result of Belgian irresolution and of the inability of a small country like Belgium to stand up to international pressures. The first crack in the wall of Belgian paternalism came in 1957, when Africans first took part in municipal elections. Joseph Kasavubu, who had built up a position of political leadership among the Bakongo people of the lower Congo, was returned as mayor of one of the Leopoldville communes (municipalities). This was typical of what happened elsewhere. An American observer wrote, 'Almost every party formed in the Congo had its origin in a tribal group, and since there were many tribes, there were many parties. Local interests were paramount and never ceased to be a powerful factor in politics'. Patrice Lumumba, who emerged at the same period as a political leader in Stanleyville, was the only Congolese politician who had a clear vision of the importance of creating a single, nationwide party. To succeed, he would have needed not only time, but also some prolonged resistance from the Belgian colonial government in order to force other Congolese politicians to see the necessity for such a party. This resistance, however, was not forthcoming.

In August 1958, de Gaulle visited Brazzaville, just across the river from Leopoldville, to proclaim autonomy within the French Community for the four colonies which had formed the Federation of French Equatorial Africa. Naturally, this provoked unrest on the Belgian side of the Congo River. Many of the little tribal parties began to demand independence for the Belgian Congo. Strikes and disorders broke out and, in January 1959, less than a month after Lumumba's return from the Accra conference, a serious riot occurred in Leopoldville. Mobs of unemployed people sacked European shops and mission schools. The situation in the capital was brought under control in less than a week, but the blow to Belgian prestige was great. During the year that followed, it became evident that law and order in many parts of the country were on the verge of breakdown. Some of the most dangerous situations were the result of tension between rival groups of Congolese. In Kasai province, for example, a civil war threatened between the Kasai Baluba, who worked on the oil-palm plantations, and the Benelulua, who regarded the Baluba as intruders into their country. Again, in the mandated territory of Ruanda–Urundi, an extreme state of tension was developing between the Batutsi ruling class and the Bahutu majority of the population. The Batutsi had maintained their social and political predominance under both German and Belgian rule, and their object, like that of the settlers in Rhodesia, was to gain political independence for the territory before the introduction of a universal franchise destroyed their ascendancy. The Belgians reacted to the steadily growing defiance of the Batutsi by suddenly switching their support to the newly formed Bahutu political movement, but they were unable to control the situation which resulted. All over the country, but especially in the north, the Batutsi were massacred by their former subjects, their houses burnt, their possessions looted, while the Belgian administration looked on, unable or unwilling to intervene. By the end of 1959, therefore, Belgian Africa presented a very different picture from that of 1956. It is true that the disorders had all been local ones. It is also true that to a larger power than Belgium, these disorders would not have appeared impossible to suppress. But to Belgium, in the words of a government spokesman, they presented a terrifying alternative: 'to try to organise independence as quickly as possible, or to accept responsibility for the bloodshed which any delay would probably bring about. A colonial war entails heavy financial losses, which a small nation cannot afford. We are fearful lest another Algeria might develop in the Congo'.

At the beginning of 1960, therefore, the Belgian government summoned a group of Congolese political leaders to a 'Round Table Conference' in Ostend. Several of the Africans who took part have stated that they went to Belgium expecting to settle for a five-year transitional period leading up to independence. They would have been willing to accept this. But Belgium was by this time disillusioned with the Congo. It was not prepared to take the responsibility of continuing to govern the country while Congolese political parties united themselves or while Congolese civil servants were trained to take over administrative duties from the Belgians. Above all, Belgium was not prepared to send any more troops to suppress the disorders that would certainly grow worse. While the conference was meeting, a cry went up throughout the country of 'Pas un soldat au Congo' ('Not a single soldier to Congo'). The Congolese negotiators at the Round Table Conference found no resistance against which they could bargain, no strength that would force them to unite. They came away with a date for independence which was less than six months away: 30 June 1960.

In May 1960, there were held the first national elections ever to take place in the Belgian Congo. The results were indecisive, but a few days before the end of Belgian rule, Lumumba, after lengthy negotiations, succeeded in forming a government with himself as prime minister and Kasavubu, his chief rival, as president. Even the independence ceremonies were a disaster. A paternal speech from King Baudouin provoked the bitter reply from Lumumba, 'Nous ne sommes plus vos singes' ('We are no longer your monkeys'). Six days later, the Congolese army – the Force Publique – mutinied. 'It all started', said Lumumba, 'when General Janssens, the Belgian Commander, refused to promote Congolese to the rank of officer'. The soldiers turned on the Belgian officers and their families, whereupon Belgian troops intervened to protect Europeans and their property. With the collapse of law and order, all the old hatreds and humiliations came bubbling to the surface. Africans avenged themselves on Europeans, and different peoples within the Congo fought each other. The worst inter-African conflict took place in Kasai, where the tensions between Baluba and Benelulua now broke out into open warfare. The political struggle between the regionalists and the centralists, which was so much a feature of this period of African history (in Kenya and French West Africa, for example), became charged with danger in the Congo. Kasavubu of the Bakongo, Kalonji of the Baluba, and Tshombe in Katanga all wanted to set up a loose federal structure, in which real power would reside with the provincial and tribal groups. Lumumba, on the other hand, tried to work for a strong, centralised state. On 11 July, Tshombe withdrew Katanga from the Congo and declared its independence. This move received the backing of the Union Minière, the huge company which controlled the Katanga copper mines. The Congolese government thereby lost the greater part of its revenues. Lumumba called upon the United Nations for military help to halt the disintegration of the country and to rid the country of the Belgian troops which had intervened in the mutiny. The UN thereupon entered the most critical operation in its history. Wisely, it called for most of its contingents of soldiers to be sent from the African states. But when these forces did not do exactly as Lumumba wished, he turned to the Soviet Union for assistance. The chaotic situation in Congo became a matter for worldwide concern, introducing the rivalries between communism and capitalism into the heart of the African continent. This made the African states more determined to follow a neutral path, but the 'Congo crisis' produced deep divisions in their ranks, as we shall see in subsequent chapters. As early as 1960, Nkrumah remarked prophetically, 'Once we admit our impotence to solve the question of the Congo primarily with our African resources, we tacitly admit that real self-government on the African continent is impossible'.

The calling in of the Russians proved the downfall of Lumumba. Hitherto, Belgian and other western influences had been confined to a veiled support of Tshombe's secessionist movement in Katanga. Henceforward, these influences, with American backing, began to intervene in the affairs of the central Congolese government. Lumumba was overthrown by an alliance between the army, led by Colonel Mobutu, and many of the regional politicians, headed by Kasavubu. The Russians were expelled. Lumumba escaped from UN protection in Leopoldville, but was captured by Congolese soldiers on his way to Stanleyville and later handed over to Tshombe in Katanga, where, on the outskirts of Elisabethville, he was murdered in January 1961, although his death was hushed up for several weeks. Faced with the problem of the central government's bankruptcy, the UN at last began to intervene more forcefully to break the secession of Katanga. The UN secretary–general, Dag Hammarskjöld, was himself a casualty of the tragedy in the Congo, being killed in an air crash near Ndola, Northern Rhodesia, in September 1961, on his way to negotiate with Tshombe. It was only in 1963, however, after much heavy fighting, that this province was occupied and reunited with the Congo state. By this time, it was the UN that was bankrupt. A number of its richer member states, including Russia and France, had refused to contribute to the Congo operations. Those who did contribute (Britain and America especially) were suspected of paying the piper in order to call the tune; that is, of using the UN in order to achieve their own aims. The UN had no option but to withdraw from the Congo. Left to itself, the central government could not hope to hold the all-important Katanga region by force. The unity and the solvency of the country could only be maintained by admitting Tshombe and his supporters to the central government on their own terms.

Meanwhile in Rwanda, and to a lesser extent in Burundi, tension between the Batutsi and the Bahutu continued to grow. Attempts to join the two little countries into one independent state failed, and they went their separate ways. The UN supervised the final stages of the transition to independence. In Rwanda, the previously subservient majority of the population overthrew with fearful violence the Batutsi monarchy and proclaimed a republic. In Burundi, the monarchy survived but was constitutionalised. Both states achieved independence in 1962. In Rwanda, this at first served merely to intensify the harrying of the Batutsi, most of whom were driven as refugees into neighbouring countries. Tension and conflict between the two social groups (and between northern and central Bahutu) then became endemic and continued through the first three decades of Rwandan independence. The reverse, but otherwise similar, situation plagued Burundi. The monarchy was overthrown in 1966 by prime minister Micombero, who proclaimed himself president. Micombero's policy to enforce minority Batutsi domination led to the terrible tragedy of the Bahutu rebellion of 1973.

Madagascar

As we have seen in previous chapters, Madagascar has had in many ways a history distinct from that of the African mainland. The population of the island is largely non-African, the language entirely so. At least since the beginning of the nineteenth century, there has been little coming and going across the Mozambique Channel. During the colonial period, when it was under French rule, Madagascar was a kind of halfway house between the French territories in West Africa and those in South-East Asia and the Pacific. From the time of the Second World War, however, the isolation of Madagascar from the rest of Africa began at last to be broken down. During the war, the island experienced the occupation of British forces, many of them African. After the war, Malagasy students began to go in some numbers to France. There they encountered French-speaking students from the West African territories, to whom they felt more akin than to the South-East Asians. Most important of all, perhaps, was the fact that the timing of Madagascar's struggle for independence coincided with the African revolution rather than with the Asian one. The first modern political party with independence as its object was founded in 1946. This party had its first trial of strength with the French in the following year, when a famine caused by the mismanagement of the government-controlled Rice Board gave rise to a violent rebellion. The revolt sprang up all over the island, among many different groups, including the formerly dominant Hova, as a spontaneous reaction to colonial rule. The ferocity of the French military action against the rebels led to a still more widespread insurrection, which took nearly a year to repress. Many aspects of the Malagasy rebellion were similar to the earliest anti-colonial rebellions, such as the Maji-Maji outbreak in German East Africa in 1905–6. The Maji-Maji rebels thought that the German bullets would be harmlessly turned into water. Similarly, during the Malagasy rebellion,

When the rebels, armed only with pointed sticks, went in to attack troops armed with rifles and machine-guns, they advanced in step in serried ranks shouting 'Rano, Rano', which means 'Water, Water', as a magical formula intended to turn the bullets into water as they left the guns. Even some of the French soldiers began to have doubts and to panic when their fire proved ineffective through faulty aiming or the use of old cartridges.[4]

After the great rebellion, Madagascar entered upon an unusually smooth transition from colonial rule to self-government and then to independence. Much of the credit for this is due to the moderation of one remarkable personality, Philibert Tsiranana, who, in common with many other African leaders, began his career as a teacher. He was opposed to the rebellion and, after its repression, used all his gifts to heal the deep scars. His Social Democratic Party cooperated with the French in implementing reforms introduced under the Loi Cadre of 1956, and some of the Malagasy who had been sentenced by the French to long terms of imprisonment for instigating the rebellion became ministers in his cabinet. In the de Gaulle referendum of 1958, he was supported not only by the Malagasy, but also by many of the 80,000 French settlers on the island. When the country became independent in June 1960, Tsiranana became the first president. The only serious opposition to his government came from the Hova people of the highlands around the capital. These former rulers of the island were still the best educated and the most sophisticated group. They were mainly Protestant, while the majority of the population was Roman Catholic. These religious and social tensions took time to be resolved. Nevertheless, Madagascar became an important and unequivocal member of the community of African states. It played a leading part both in the Union of French-speaking states, the Afro–Malagasy Joint Organisation (OCAM), and in the Organisation for African Unity. Madagascar also responded to the economic overtures made by South Africa. The Malagasy, ancient colonists from across the Indian Ocean, had at long last been assimilated into the mainstream of African affairs.

[4] O. Mannoni, *Prospero and Caliban* (London, 1956), p. 59.

NINETEEN. The Road to Independence: (3) Central Africa

A t the time when the British colonies in West and East Africa were advancing toward political independence, the British government decided, in 1953, to create a constitutional arrangement for its Central African territories which set them apart from its other African lands. The protectorates of Northern Rhodesia and Nyasaland, which had few resident Europeans, were joined with Southern Rhodesia, which had been effectively controlled by its white settlers since 1891, to form the Central African Federation. It was hoped that this would grow into a powerful, multiracial state, big enough to act as a counterweight to the power of white-dominated South Africa. One of the many compromises built into the Central African Federation was a division of ultimate responsibility between the metropolitan country and a locally based settler government. After ten years, the Federation broke upon the rock of this unresolved conflict. Westminster could not resist the tide of African nationalism in the two northern territories, whereas Salisbury was determined to hang on for a much longer time.

Along either side of the Central African Federation, and controlling its main lines of access to the Atlantic and the Indian Ocean, lay the Portuguese colonies of Angola and Mozambique. For thirty years after the Second World War, the Portuguese empire in Africa proved an exception to the rule that a colonial system based in Europe could not resist the onslaught of African nationalism. The reasons for this exception were, first, that Portugal was one of the poorest countries of Europe. It had few industries and a standard of living not much higher than many African countries. Unlike those of other colonial powers, its colonial interests were considered to be not marginal but central to its economic existence. Second, the Portuguese state was a dictatorship. The Portuguese people, accustomed to authoritarianism at home, were unmoved by authoritarian rule in the colonies. Dr Salazar, the Portuguese prime minister from 1932 until 1968, consistently played upon feelings of national pride and glorified the achievements of the Portuguese imperial past as an inducement to future greatness. In 1943, he wrote: 'The rich extensive colonial lands, underdeveloped and sparsely populated, are the natural complement for metropolitan agriculture. In addition they will take care of Portugal's excessive population'. Large numbers of Portuguese continued to migrate to the African territories. By the late 1960s, there were more than 250,000 settlers in Angola and 130,000 in Mozambique. The African populations were 5 million and 8 million, respectively. Commercial agriculture and mining remained firmly in European hands.

Portugal's racial policy was, in theory, similar to the French policy of assimilation. The status of citizen, however, conferred few political rights either in Portugal or the colonies. To become a citizen, an African had to comply with a whole range of educational and economic qualifications so difficult for an African to obtain that only a small number succeeded. In 1950, there were only 30,000 *assimilados* in Angola and 25,000 in Mozambique. The vast majority of the population were classed as *indigenas* (natives), whose main function in the eyes of the administration was to provide labour. In 1943, a colonial minister said, 'If we want to civilise the native, we must make him adopt, as an elementary moral precept, the notion that he has no right to live without working'. The economic development of the colonies greatly benefited Portugal itself and, by the early 1960s, about 25 percent of the national budget was derived from Africa. In 1951, the colonies were theoretically incorporated into Portugal as 'overseas provinces', but the inferior status of the African indigenas continued.

The Central African Federation

During the war years, both Southern and Northern Rhodesia had experienced boom conditions. The demand for copper – a vital component in many kinds of armaments – soared and good prices were obtained by the Northern Rhodesian mining companies, which were reflected in the wages paid to miners, and especially to the white miners, who consolidated their monopoly of the skilled jobs. A number of manufacturing industries were established in Southern Rhodesia, and its agricultural production – particularly of tobacco, cattle, and maize – increased. Southern Rhodesia was used by the British as a training area for Royal Air Force pilots, and after the war, considerable numbers of British ex-servicemen settled in the country with their families. The white population in 1954 was 80,500; by 1960, it had reached 220,000, compared with an African population of some 4 million. The great majority of these whites lived in the towns, particularly in Salisbury and Bulawayo, where they were joined by a large influx of Africans from the rural areas. The settler-dominated Southern Rhodesian government had divided the country along racial lines. Urban Africans were forced to live in separate townships, while the Land Apportionment Act of 1930 had allotted half of all the land, including most of the best land, for white occupation. Whites had a monopoly of most jobs down to the level of skilled artisan, and were paid at much higher rates than Africans.

During the 1920s and 1930s, many white Rhodesians had imagined that their country might become a fifth province of the Union of South Africa, but, after the victory of the National Party in the South African elections of 1948, English-speaking Rhodesians felt alienated from such a solution to their security problem. Sir Godfrey Huggins, the long-serving prime minister of Southern Rhodesia, now joined forces with Sir Roy Welensky, the trade-union boss of the white miners of Northern Rhodesia, in reviving an old scheme for the union of the two Rhodesias. They knew that they would have no chance of success with the British government unless Nyasaland was also included, since it was economically dependent on the other two territories. They argued that, although in Northern Rhodesia and Nyasaland the European communities were even smaller than in Southern Rhodesia, it would be preferable to control these predominantly African lands, difficult though this might be, than to have them as independent neighbours. The settlers hoped that a large Federation would soon become a fully amalgamated Dominion, free from British control. They also wanted the economic benefits which were expected to result from federation, and the opportunities for further white settlement which this would create.

The economic growth of the Federation was, as expected, rapid. New industries were developed in Southern Rhodesia, and towns increased in size – especially the federal capital at Salisbury. One of the world's largest dams was constructed on the Zambezi at Kariba, to provide cheap electricity for the copper mines of Northern Rhodesia and the industries of Southern Rhodesia. Africans shared less in the expansion than Europeans. In 1961, the average annual income of wage-earning Africans was still only £87, and many Africans were not even wage-earners. Nyasaland, in particular, had reason to be dissatisfied because all that it gained economically from the federal government was a small annual subsidy in recognition of its function as a labour reserve.

In Southern Rhodesia, African nationalist opposition to white rule dated back to the 1940s and 1950s, when labour movements were formed, including a union of railway workers led by Joshua Nkomo. Ndabaningi Sithole and Robert Mugabe were both leaders of a teachers' association. In 1957, a revived African National Congress (ANC) came into being under Nkomo, but was banned by the Whitehead administration two years later. By 1961, a new party, the Zimbabwe African People's Union (ZAPU), had emerged, again under Nkomo's leadership. In 1963, Nkomo attempted to set up a government in exile in Dar es Salaam. In response to this, Sithole founded the Zimbabwe African National Union (ZANU) within Rhodesia. Thus was created the initial critical split in the nationalist movement. ZAPU was largely supported by Nkomo's Ndebele people and had its local base in Bulawayo, whereas ZANU had big Shona support and operated from Salisbury. In Northern Rhodesia and Nyasaland, African nationalist activity likewise predated the establishment of the Federation, but it was the imposition of federation that gave nationalism in the two territories its focus and its sense of urgency.

Within ten years, the two contending forces of settler intransigence and African nationalism had destroyed the new state. Despite all their talk of partnership between the races, the European politicians who controlled both the federal and the Southern Rhodesian parliaments were determined to maintain European supremacy. 'Political control', wrote Huggins in 1956, 'must remain in the hands of civilised people, which for the foreseeable future means the Europeans'. Welensky, for his part, likened 'partnership' to the relationship between a horse and its rider. African resentment towards the federal government came to a head in 1959, soon after the return to Nyasaland of Dr Hastings Banda after an absence of more than forty years. Demonstrations, strikes, and riots led to the declaration of states of emergency in both Nyasaland and Southern Rhodesia, and to the detention without trial of many African nationalist politicians. The federal government maintained that opposition came only from a handful of 'extremists'. Many people in Britain shared this belief. But it was rejected by the Devlin Commission which inquired into the Nyasaland troubles:

> The government's view is that these nationalist aspirations are the thoughts of only a small minority of political Africans, mainly of self-seekers who think their prospects of office will be worse under Federation; and that the great majority of the people are indifferent to the issue. We have not found this to be so. It was generally acknowledged that the opposition to Federation was there, that it was deeply rooted and almost universally held.

The 1959 emergencies marked the dividing line in the fortunes of the Federation. Early the following year, the Belgians decided to pull out of the neighbouring Congo and, by this time, the British government had lost faith in the multiracial experiments in Tanganyika and Kenya. Harold Macmillan, the British prime minister, during his 1960 African tour, was critical of the lack of progress toward genuine partnership in the Federation. He ended his tour in Cape Town, where he delivered his famous 'wind of change' speech before the South African parliament:

> We have seen the awakening of national consciousness in peoples who have for centuries lived in dependence on some other power. Fifteen years ago this movement spread through Asia. Many countries there of different races and civilisations pressed their claim to an independent life. Today the same thing is happening in Africa and the most striking of all the impressions I have formed since I left London a month ago is of the strength of this African national consciousness. The wind of change is blowing through the continent, and whether we like it or not this growth of national consciousness is a political fact, and our national policies must take account of it.

Macmillan's speech surprised and annoyed white South Africans, and north of the Limpopo it marked a further stage in the decline

of the Federation. The Monckton Commission, which was sent to
look into its workings, reported that for Africans, partnership was a
'sham'. The commission recommended that, if all else failed, the territories should have the right to secede. Iain Macleod, the colonial
secretary who had been responsible for departing from the multiracial idea in Kenya (see Chapter 18), decided that the Federation
should not stand in the way of the two northern territories attaining
African majority rule. Under Banda's leadership, Africans in Nyasaland achieved this in 1961. The Northern Rhodesian settlers, with
Welensky's help, delayed a similar development in that country for
two years longer. By 1963, however, Kenneth Kaunda, who had built
up a great reputation for statesmanship, led Northern Rhodesia to
this position. He and Banda made it clear that they would take the
earliest opportunity of withdrawing from the Federation.

In Southern Rhodesia, the picture was equally bleak for supporters of the Federation. In 1961, African nationalist leaders rejected a
new constitution which would have given them a limited voice in the
government and, in 1962, the white electorate voted the Rhodesian
Front, a new right-wing party under the leadership of Winston Field,
into power. This party was committed to the maintenance of white
rule in the country. The British government now appointed R. A.
Butler as a special minister to preside over the dismantling of the
Federation and, on the last day of 1963, it came to an end. Nyasaland
became independent as Malawi in July 1964, and Northern Rhodesia followed suit as the Republic of Zambia in October of the same
year. Southern Rhodesia reverted to its earlier status as a British
colony enjoying internal self-government, but with the immense advantage of retaining control over most of the armed forces of the
former Federation, including some modern aircraft. The Rhodesian
Front government used increasingly harsh methods to break up the
nationalist movements. It banned both of the major African political
parties, placing the leaders, including Nkomo and Sithole, under restriction without trial. During 1965, both groups began to reorganise
in the safety of Lusaka.

Throughout 1963 and into 1964, Field tried to negotiate independence terms with the Westminster government and failed. In April
1964, he resigned and was replaced by the tougher and more resilient
Ian Smith, who continued negotiations with the British Labour

government which came into office in October 1964. Finally, on 11 November 1965, Smith's government made a Unilateral Declaration of Independence (UDI), the opening paragraph of which intentionally echoed the American Declaration of Independence of 1776:

> Whereas in the course of human affairs history has shown it may become necessary for a people to resolve the political affiliations which have connected them with another people and to assume among other nations the separate and equal status to which they are entitled . . .

These and other sentiments in Smith's declaration must have seemed bitterly ironic to the African majority of Rhodesians. White Rhodesia's UDI failed to secure the recognition of any other country in the world. Nevertheless, thanks to the practical cooperation of South Africa and Portugal, it was able to survive for more than ten years.

The Colonial Wars in Angola and Mozambique

In February 1961, barely six months after the independence of the Congo, serious rioting occurred in Luanda, the capital of Angola, when armed members of the Movimento Popular de Libertação de Angola (MPLA) tried to free political prisoners from the city's prison. The following month, a much more serious revolt broke out in northern Angola, by supporters of the União das Populações de Angola (UPA), which had been formed in 1958 by Holden Roberto. The UPA operated from bases in the Congo, where Roberto was much influenced by Patrice Lumumba. The party was largely supported by Bakongo people, who lived on both sides of the frontier. In 1962, the UPA merged with another party to form the Frente Nacional de Libertação de Angola (FNLA).

The revolt in northern Angola was an extremely grave event. More than 6,000 'loyal' Africans were killed by the nationalist guerrilla forces, as well as some 2,000 whites – the largest number of European civilians killed in any single African territory during the anti-colonial struggles. Totally unprepared for the outbreak of hostilities on this scale, the Portuguese had to rush 50,000 troops from Portugal. These were largely successful in suppressing the uprising by the end of 1961, but only after about 50,000 Africans had been killed in savage fighting. This was, however, but the first stage of the Angolan war of liberation and, in 1962 and 1964, similar nationalist insurrections broke out in Portuguese Guinea and Mozambique, respectively.

Portuguese colonial policy was attacked in the United Nations by all countries except South Africa and Spain. A UN subcommittee, which was not allowed to enter Angola, reported at the end of 1961:

> The Portuguese authorities face a historic choice, whether to continue to rely on the use of force, with its inevitable miseries, or to respond to world opinion and take measures to build a new relationship with the people of Angola. What is needed is readiness to understand the new forces in the world.

Portugal, however, showed few signs of understanding these forces. After the outbreak of the revolt in Angola, reforming legislation was rushed through by the government, by which the status of indigenas was formally abolished, and all the inhabitants of the colonies became Portuguese citizens. The local legislative councils were given slightly increased powers. Yet the Portuguese resolve to remain an imperial power was undiminished. In particular, further migration to the colonies was encouraged. 'We believe it necessary', said the overseas minister, 'to continue the settlement of our Africa by European Portuguese who will make their homes there and find in Africa a true extension of their country'. Such measures, he said, 'prove the sureness with which we contemplate the future, the serenity with which we face the difficulties of the present, and our faithfulness to the course of history'.

In Portuguese Africa, as later in Rhodesia and South Africa, the greatest difficulty faced by nationalist movements which were forced to operate from outside their own countries was that of maintaining cohesion between the different exiled groups, especially when these derived their support from different outside patrons. In 1962, the FNLA set up a government in exile in Kinshasa, with Roberto as prime minister and an Ovimbundu, Jonas Savimbi, as foreign secretary. This was an attempt to widen support for the party from the Bakongo of the north to include the peoples of the centre and the south, and it received strong, although covert, assistance from the United States. Later the same year, Agostino Neto, the newly elected president of the MPLA, established a rival government in exile, which operated from Brazzaville in the Congo Republic, and looked for outside help mainly to the Soviet Union and its allies. In

1964, Savimbi quarrelled with Roberto and left Kinshasa to found his own party, the União Nacional para a Independência Total de Angola (UNITA), with its base in the far south of Angola, near the frontier with South-West Africa, where he managed to attract outside help from countries as widely separated in ideology as China and South Africa. All of these party 'governments', as they became better organised, tried to set up enclaves of African rule within the borders of Angola. By the later 1960s, the MPLA was active in the mountain region to the north-east of Luanda, while the FNLA built up its bridgehead among the Bakongo and also tried to penetrate the eastern-central region from bases in Zambia. UNITA kept to its southern sphere of influence. All three movements were successful in attracting some rural populations to recognise their authority in raising taxes, running bush schools and clinics, and training centres for their armed followers. The Portuguese, however, with their superior weapons and mobility, had little difficulty in holding the major towns and the roads which connected them and in protecting the mines and plantations on which the economy of the country depended. The price they had to pay was the continued deployment of around 50,000 troops. On a much smaller scale, the same could be said of the revolt in the tiny West African colony of Guinea.

By the early 1970s, however, it was the rebellion in Mozambique that was causing the Portuguese the greatest problems. The Frente de Libertação de Moçambique (FRELIMO) was formed in 1962 in Dar es Salaam by the amalgamation of three earlier-established parties, under the presidency of Eduardo Mondlane. Mondlane was born in southern Mozambique and studied in the United States. Later, he worked for the UN in New York and then taught at an American university. In its early years, FRELIMO was supported mainly by the Makonde and Nyanja peoples of the far north of the country near the Tanganyika border. Many of these peoples had fled from the Portuguese into Tanganyika, and these were the first recruits into the FRELIMO army. In 1964, FRELIMO started to make attacks southwards across the Rovuma against Portuguese military installations on the Makonde plateau. The guerrillas tried to move southwards along the coast, but could make little progress because of the traditional hostility of the Makua. Instead, in 1965, they spread their operations into the Niassa district bordering on Malawi and, by 1968, had infiltrated as far south as Tete on the Zambezi. Until this time, the scale of the revolt had been quite small, but with the penetration of Tete it began to look serious.

In 1966, the Portuguese announced plans for a dam and hydro-electric power station on the Zambezi River between Tete and the Zambian frontier, where the river flowed for nearly 80 km (50 miles) through the Cabora Bassa gorge. Work started in 1969, and the dam was completed in 1974. The Cabora Bassa scheme had far-reaching implications for southern Africa. In effect, it amounted to a declaration by Portugal that her occupation of Mozambique was a permanency. Naturally, therefore, FRELIMO tried to impede and harass the dam's construction. For their part, the Portuguese, with some South African military or police support, vigorously defended the project. Mondlane, who had led FRELIMO so resolutely, did not live to see the successful outcome of his insurrection. Early in 1969, he was killed by a parcel bomb, rumoured to have been sent by Portuguese agents, while working at his office desk in Dar es Salaam. He was succeeded as president of FRELIMO by Samora Machel, the army commander in the field. If Machel's forces could not actually prevent work on the dam, they made themselves widely felt over the Tete district and, in 1973, they moved their guerrilla operations still farther south into Manica, where they seriously disrupted the rail and road links between Beira and Rhodesia. So critical was the military position that in March 1974, it was decided to airlift 10,000 more troops to Mozambique to join the 60,000 already there. It was the intensification of the fighting in Mozambique that broke the back of the Portuguese resolve. Many individuals in the army and in industry now considered that the country's best chance of economic recovery lay in associating with the European Economic Community rather than in pursuing pipe dreams of an African empire. On 25 April 1974, officers of the Movimento das Forças Armadas overthrew the Caetano regime which had succeeded that of Salazar in 1963, and the new government of General Spinola announced that Portugal would grant some form of self-government to all its overseas possessions. Within a few months, Guinea (Bissau) achieved full independence, but the situation in Angola and Mozambique was more complex.

After the April coup, the Portuguese had to adopt the unfamiliar role of peacemaker between the three nationalist parties in Angola.

Finally, after a meeting at Alvor in Portugal, a provisional government was set up to prepare the way for independence in November 1975. But during the intervening period, the three movements each consolidated their military and political positions, FNLA occupying the north, MPLA at last gaining a firm foothold in Luanda and its Mbundu hinterland, while UNITA built up its support among the Ovimbundu of the central-southern region. By June 1975, the transitional government had collapsed. Outside powers now openly intervened, not to bring about a peaceful solution, but to make the situation even more dangerous. The United States and China provided support to FNLA and UNITA, while the Soviet Union backed MPLA. By the middle of 1975, if not earlier, Cuba had sent instructors to the MPLA forces. In August, South African troops occupied the hydroelectric installations near the South-West African border, to protect them from attacks by MPLA and SWAPO – the nationalist movement of the African peoples of South-West Africa. South African advisers now moved into southern Angola to support UNITA forces. At the end of October, a South African mobile column rapidly advanced north, capturing Benguela and Lobito and reaching as far as the Cuanza River south of Luanda. Meanwhile, FNLA forces, including some European mercenaries, and with Zairean support, had advanced from the north to within striking distance of Luanda. By the middle of November, however, massive amounts of Russian and Cuban equipment had arrived at Luanda, including heavy tanks and artillery, along with some 15,000 Cuban troops. These soon imposed a decisive defeat on the FNLA attackers from the north. South Africa had failed to obtain U.S. and other western support for its military presence in Angola; so, after receiving an undertaking from the MPLA government that there would be no interference with the hydroelectric plant on the Cunene River, it was decided to withdraw. UNITA's forward positions rapidly crumbled before the Cuban advance and, although it managed to maintain just enough of a presence to keep the Benguela railway out of action, most of Angola was for a time controlled by Neto and the MPLA.

In Mozambique, the Portuguese military government had originally planned to hold a referendum to decide the territory's future. It soon became apparent, however, that the morale of the Portuguese forces – white and black – was too low to control the situation for even a few months. There were strikes in the docks at Beira and Lourenço Marques, and rural uprisings directed against plantations owned by whites. Portugal's new rulers accordingly gave up the attempt to negotiate a constitutional settlement and, in mid-1974, signed the Lusaka Accord with Machel, which left FRELIMO in full control of the country. In spite of some resistance by Portuguese settlers, mainly in Lourenço Marques, independence was achieved in June 1975.

Following the apparent victory of Neto's MPLA in Angola and of Machel's FRELIMO in Mozambique, both countries were governed along rigid Marxist lines, with much emphasis placed on the mobilisation of the whole population to create new socialist societies, free of both their colonial and much of their older African inheritance. In both countries, most of the European settlers fled during the early months of independence. Both governments, however, showed themselves to be pragmatic in so far as their external relations were concerned. The MPLA honoured the understanding not to interfere with the Cunene power stations, but nevertheless provided assistance to the SWAPO guerrillas who were infiltrating South-West Africa from Angola. In 1978, South African forces retaliated by raiding the SWAPO base at Cassinga, some 200 km (150 miles) inside Angola, and such raids continued into the 1980s. Again, while accepting support from Russia and Cuba, Angola retained its commercial agreement with the American Gulf Oil Company to exploit the oil of Cabinda. Mozambique, for its part, provided full support to the Rhodesian nationalist forces which operated from bases in Mozambique in launching their offensives inside Rhodesia, in reprisal for which Mozambique had to suffer many destructive raids by Rhodesian government troops. On the other hand, Mozambique maintained correct diplomatic relations with South Africa and tolerated the continued recruitment of large numbers of Mozambican migrant workers for the South African gold mines, and itself employed South African staff to run the railway and harbour facilities of Maputo, which was the new name for Lourenço Marques.

By the late 1970s, events were proving how hollow had been the victories of both the MPLA and FRELIMO. The socialist policies pursued by the Angolan and the Mozambican leaders were proving equally disastrous on the economic side and, in both countries, civil war was once again becoming widespread. In Angola, the forces of UNITA had been defeated but not broken. Under Savimbi's capable leadership, and with much South African and some Zambian help, the movement recouped its losses and was able to continue its struggle against the Luanda government. In this struggle, much depended on the future of South-West Africa. The MPLA did not feel secure enough to get rid of the Cubans and come to terms with Savimbi until South-West Africa had become independent of South African garrisons. But South Africa, covertly backed by the United States, would not grant independence to South-West Africa without at least a promise of Cuban withdrawal. In Mozambique, a shadowy 'anti-Marxist' guerrilla movement called RENAMO (The Nationalist Resistance Movement of Mozambique), which was initially recruited and trained by the white government of Ian Smith, began attacking FRELIMO forces and disrupting local services. After 1980, patronage of RENAMO passed to South Africa, although through agencies over which the South African government probably had little control, and its operations became more widespread and more destructive than before.

From Rhodesia to Zimbabwe

As was to be expected, the Rhodesian UDI produced a crisis with worldwide ramifications. Here, almost at the end of the long story of African liberation movements, was a minority of 250,000 white Rhodesians asserting their right to rule in independence over more than 4 million Africans. Yet, no country in the outside world was prepared to intervene by force of arms – certainly not Britain, which was still in international law responsible for Rhodesia. The British government refused to recognise the declaration and successfully prevented its recognition in all other capitals of the world. Working through the UN, it went on to organise a series of financial and commercial sanctions, which were agreed to by most governments, but which were not always enforced by those governments upon their own citizens. South Africa and Portugal refused to operate sanctions at all, and there is no doubt that this was what mainly enabled Rhodesia to survive. Above all, oil – the one external commodity really vital to the Rhodesian economy – continued to reach the country.

In the meantime, however, more militant action was being launched against Rhodesia from the outside. Between 1967 and 1970, ZAPU, together with the African National Congress of South Africa, organised a number of guerrilla incursions into the Zambezi valley from Zambia. Then, late in 1972, ZANU started an offensive into north-eastern Rhodesia from the FRELIMO-held enclaves in Tete district. As the scale of guerrilla attacks increased, so did that of the regime's counter-insurgency measures, which were helped until 1975 by South Africa. These included the construction of security fences along the border with Mozambique, the herding of the local population into 'protected villages', and the designation of 'no-go' areas, where anyone breaking the curfew could be shot on sight. Early in 1973, Smith closed the border with Zambia in retaliation for Kaunda's support of the ZAPU guerrillas. The coup in Portugal in April 1974 implied that Mozambique would soon be an independent state hostile to Rhodesia, which thus became considerably more isolated.

From about 1974, guerrilla activities were conducted by armies which were distinct from the political parties which formally controlled them – ZAPU's Zimbabwe Independence People's Army (ZIPRA) and ZANU's Zimbabwe African National Liberation Army (ZANLA). In 1975, Robert Mugabe left Rhodesia for Mozambique, where he played an important part in directing the war, working closely with President Machel. By 1976, guerrilla activities had escalated into outright war fought on a number of fronts and, by 1979, the nationalist forces had succeeded in penetrating deep into Rhodesia, almost as far as Salisbury itself. South Africa became increasingly concerned by the scale of the conflict and changed its policy from one of support for the white government into one designed to promote the emergence of a 'friendly' black government installed in an independent Zimbabwe. As early as 1974, the South African prime minister, Vorster, tried without success to negotiate with the nationalist leaders, and the next year he even joined forces with President Kaunda of Zambia to put pressure on the Rhodesians. In 1976, Ian Smith made one attempt to achieve an 'internal settlement' by holding talks with Joshua Nkomo: when they failed, Nkomo left Rhodesia for Zambia. Later that year, the American secretary of state, Henry Kissinger, visited southern Africa and, as part of a wider mission, met all the main actors in the Rhodesian drama. Astonishingly, he obtained Smith's agreement in principle to settle for African majority rule within two years, but the only response of Nkomo and Mugabe was to escalate the fighting and to form a Patriotic Front to unite the efforts of ZAPU and ZANU. At length, in 1978, Smith concluded an internal settlement with the 'moderate' African element, led by Bishop Muzorewa, Sithole, and Chief Chirau, with whom he agreed to share power, pending one-man/one-vote elections in April 1979. By this time, the strains of the mounting struggle were clearly beginning to tell upon the European population. Whites were emigrating in significant numbers, even though compelled to leave most of their property behind them when they did so. Of those who remained, many were by now conscripted at least for part-time service in the defence forces. Despite strenuous attempts to Africanise the army, it became increasingly doubtful how wholeheartedly such forces would fight against their fellow countrymen in the guerrilla movements. And the Rhodesian economy showed signs of disintegrating under the burden of war.

Thus, when Bishop Muzorewa emerged victorious from the election of April 1979, it was apparent that, even though Rhodesia had taken the momentous step to a mainly black government, there would be no lasting peace and no international recognition until the nationalists in exile had been accommodated. Lord Carrington, who became British foreign secretary in May 1979, at once addressed himself to this problem. Essentially, it was a matter of persuading Muzorewa and his colleagues to submit themselves to a fresh election, to be held after a brief period of resumed British rule, during which the exiles would be permitted to return to the country and join fully in the election campaign. Equally, it was necessary to persuade the exiles to drop their military activities in favour of political action and to trust in the fair conduct of the election. Carrington's initiative received much support at the routine meeting of Commonwealth prime ministers at Lusaka in August. Leaders of the front-line states joined in putting pressure on the various parties to attend a constitutional conference in London, which in the event dragged on from September until December. Just before Christmas, it was judged that sufficient mutual trust had been achieved for Lord Soames to be sent as governor, with wide powers but no force other than a contingent of military 'monitors' 1,400 strong, to supervise the reabsorption of some 25,000 guerrilla fighters and the conduct of the election which followed only two months later.

The result of the election of February 1980 was probably a surprise to all who took part in it. Of 100 seats in the new parliament, Muzorewa's party won three and Sithole's party none. Of the exiles, Joshua Nkomo's party, which had enjoyed the hospitality of Zambia and the material support of the Soviet Union, won twenty seats, all in Matabeleland. The overwhelming victory, with fifty-seven seats, went to Robert Mugabe's ZANU/PF, the party with a reputation for uncompromising Marxism, which had been hosted in exile by Machel of Mozambique. The remaining twenty seats were reserved for whites, and all went to the Rhodesian Front. If there was momentary dismay felt in western countries, this was certainly reciprocated in those of the Soviet bloc, whose satellites were not even invited to the independence celebrations which followed on 18 April. Meanwhile, Mugabe's early speeches and public statements had been reminiscent of those of Jomo Kenyatta when he assumed power in the Kenya of 1963. Reconciliation was the keynote. Pragmatism rather than dogma was to be the guiding light. Black and white would walk into the future arm-in-arm and with full confidence.

TWENTY. The Long Road to Democracy in Southern Africa

During the years between 1945 and 1980, while the rest of Africa was making the transition from colonial rule to independence under African governments, the principal country of southern Africa was moving firmly in the opposite direction. The reason was not that the 9 million or so Africans who lived there were any slower in developing political consciousness than those living in countries farther north. To the contrary, missionary education in South Africa went back to the middle of the nineteenth century, and by the middle of the twentieth, there were black professors, black doctors, black clergy, black journalists, and a host of other professional people who were at least as able as their contemporaries in other African countries to see the significance of the United Nations Charter and the coming withdrawal of the British from India. Black South African delegates had attended the Fifth Pan–African Congress in Manchester in 1945 and were in touch with the emerging political leaders of tropical Africa like Nkrumah and Kenyatta. By December 1945, the African National Congress (ANC) of South Africa had formally and publicly demanded one-man/one-vote and freedom of movement, residence, and land-ownership. Its officials were already lobbying at the United Nations, and even presenting petitions from the Africans of South West Africa asking for a UN trusteeship to replace the League of Nations Mandate.

What made the difference in South Africa was the existence of a white community of some 4 million, by far the largest and longest

established in the whole continent, which had long controlled the
whole civil and military apparatus of the state and was independent
of any outside power. The white South Africans, especially those of
Dutch descent, had long ago lost touch with relatives in Europe, and
they took it for granted that their children and grandchildren would
remain in Africa and continue to enjoy the same political and economic privileges as themselves. Until the Second World War, these
privileges had not needed to be very forcefully asserted. Up to this
time, all the rest of Africa, and much of southern Asia, had been ruled
by much smaller white minorities than their own, and South Africa,
like Rhodesia, had been regarded as an honorary member of the
colonial club. Any differences in the way Africans were governed in
South Africa were regarded as matters of method and timing rather
than of fundamental ideology. But when, in 1945, Britain announced
the intention of withdrawing from its Indian empire, and when the
independence of some West African territories began to be talked of
as none too distant, white South Africans were quick to see that their
privileges would either have to be surrendered or else defended by
the use of more and more coercion.

    Internally, the war had brought important changes in South Africa.
Considerable numbers of young white men, mostly from the English-
speaking community, had joined the armed services and fought in
campaigns in North Africa and Europe. Africans, Coloured people, and Indians had joined the non-combatant medical and labour
services. The civilian jobs of the white soldiers, which had been
mostly in industry and commerce, were taken partly by 'poor white'
Afrikaners who had been pushed off the land and partly by Africans
migrating from the rural areas. Thus, Afrikaners consolidated the
important position they already occupied in the industrial sector of
the economy, while many Africans moved into skilled or semi-skilled
jobs from which they had previously been debarred. The war years
witnessed an immense growth of mining, but even more of manufacturing industries. South African factories became major suppliers of small arms to the Allied forces. As a result, the size of the
labour force increased – and almost entirely from the non-white population groups. The new factories and the increased mining activities were nearly all in the established urban centres – Johannesburg
and its satellites in the Transvaal, and the ports of Cape Town, Port

Elizabeth, and Durban. The number of people of all groups living in South Africa's burgeoning cities vastly increased.

After 1945, the wartime government led by Jan Smuts appeared uncertain and vacillating in the face of the mounting political and economic pressures. By turns liberal and authoritarian, they adhered to no clear-cut policy to deal with South Africa's problems. Smuts realised that something would have to be done to alleviate the misery of South Africa's huge African urban population and the bitterness and confusion brought about by discrimination. In the 1948 elections, Smuts's United Party was narrowly defeated by the National Party, led by D. F. Malan, some of whose supporters had succeeded in frightening voters with the allegation that certain of Smuts's ministers were in favour of granting full political equality, which would result in a 'coffee-coloured race'. The determination to remain dominant, and the corresponding fear of being 'swamped' by the African majority, was one which motivated nearly all whites. Only a handful believed in – and worked for a free and equal society. Most whites clung to the notion of baaskap, and most were prepared to see the government of their choice using force to maintain it. At the theoretical level of political science, apartheid emerged among Afrikaner intellectuals of the late 1930s and 1940s. At its most ideal, the doctrine looked forward to a South Africa that would be geographically divided between the white race and the various African 'nations' – Xhosa, Zulu, Sotho. Among most whites, however, apartheid was little more than a dignified name for baaskap. As the Nationalist prime minister Strijdom put it, 'Call it paramountcy, baaskap or what you will, it is still domination. I am being as blunt as I can. I am making no excuses. Either the white man dominates or the black man takes over'. Indeed, the early National Party governments showed little interest in implementing the main proposals of the apartheid programme. Instead, they smothered the non-white people of South Africa with a mass of restrictive and discriminatory legislation, withdrawing rights, drastically limiting choice, and rigidly defining inequality. The meagre political rights of the Cape Africans and Coloured people, entrenched in the Union Constitution of 1910, were removed – those of the Coloured people in the course of a long and bitter constitutional conflict between 1951 and 1956 and those of the Cape Africans in 1959.

Every aspect of the lives of Africans, Coloureds, and Indians was affected by the torrent of legislation. A list of even some of these Acts of the white parliament indicates their range and scope. The Prohibition of Mixed Marriages Act 1949 and the Immorality Act 1950 prohibited members of different races from having any intimate relations. The Population Registration Act 1950, which made race a legal as well as a biological concept, was particularly insulting in defining a Coloured person in purely negative terms, as 'a person who is not a white person or a native'. The Abolition of Passes and Co-ordination of Documents Act 1952 made it compulsory for all African men (and later women) to carry a 'reference book', a new term for the old 'pass', and established a countrywide system of influx control to regulate the movements of Africans and to restrict their entry into the urban areas. The Group Areas Act 1950 and its amendments, and the Separate Amenities Act 1953, attempted complete physical and social separation of the races by the removal of Coloured people, Indians, and Africans to the outskirts of cities and towns, rigid segregation in sport and other recreations, the use of separate facilities on trains and buses, and of separate seats in public parks, all of which led to a rash of 'Whites Only' signs across the length and breadth of the land. The Native Laws Amendment Act 1957 consolidated the control over Africans in urban areas, which had first been attempted in the 1923 Urban Areas Act. The amended Industrial Conciliation Act 1965 legalised job reservation for whites and precluded Africans from the process of industrial conciliation over wages. The Suppression of Communism Act 1950, the Criminal Law Amendment Act 1953, and the Unlawful Organisations Act 1960 aimed at the total suppression of all but the tamest opposition, and were almost unequalled for their harshness in the democratic countries of the western world. Only a few legislative measures of the National Party (NP) governments in the 1950s were overtly ideological. The most important of these were the Bantu Education Act 1953 and the Extension of University Education Act 1959, which took African primary and secondary education out of missionary control and created separate and inferior institutions of university type for non-whites. These Acts made education an instrument of government policy in attempting to reshape and control men's minds. H. Verwoerd, then minister of native affairs, said of the 1953 Act,

Racial relations cannot improve if the wrong type of education is given to the Natives. They cannot improve if the result of Native education is the creation of frustrated people who, as a result of the education they receive, have expectations in life which circumstances in South Africa do not allow to be fulfilled immediately, when it creates people who are trained for professions not open to them.

The long succession of NP governments did not tamper with the Westminster model of parliamentary democracy. Elections were held regularly, and opposition parties were allowed to function within the safe confines of the all-white electorate. The party's steadily growing electoral successes were an indication both of the support which it had built up among some English-speaking electors as well as among the great majority of Afrikaners. In 1974, the NP held 82 percent of the seats, the highest proportion gained by any one party in South African history. The official opposition, the United Party (UP), failed to find an alternative policy to that of the government and slowly broke up. The Liberal Party was much more outspoken in its criticism of the regime, and individual members of it were prosecuted under the government's repressive laws. In 1965, the government introduced the Prohibition of Political Interference Act, which made it illegal for anyone to belong to a racially mixed political party, whereupon the Liberals decided to disband. Another liberally inclined movement, the Progressive Party, was founded in 1959, and this slowly captured the liberal wing of the United Party. By 1975, it had become the Progressive Reform Party, which won seventeen seats in the elections. The rump of UP members divided into two smaller parties. Meanwhile, within the NP there emerged a group of right-wing Afrikaners who considered that the party leaders were insufficiently resolute in their racial policies. During the 1960s, the party became divided between a so-called enlightened group of *verligtes* and the hardliners, or *verkramptes*. The verligtes were in favour of 'positive apartheid', including a policy of detente and dialogue with black African states, while the verkramptes were concerned to uphold baaskap. In 1969, the extreme verkramptes formed a new party, the Herstigte Nasionale (Reconstituted National) Party. The HNP never won any seats in parliamentary elections, but its political activities, combined with those of the verkramptes who remained within the NP, acted as a powerful brake on the government's verligte tendencies.

As was only to be expected, following the sheer mass and brutality of government legislation, the 1950s saw political activity by non-whites on an unprecedented scale. There were widespread multi-racial demonstrations against the government's determination to do away with the Coloured people's franchise. These were joined by white groups such as the short-lived ex-servicemen's Torch Commando and the more durable women's Black Sash movement. Then, in 1952, the African National Congress (ANC) – led by Albert Luthuli, Oliver Tambo, Nelson Mandela, and Walter Sisulu – swung into a concerted campaign of passive resistance to various discriminatory rules and regulations, including the carrying of passes. Already in 1951, the government had armed itself with the Suppression of Communism Act, which left the minister of justice to decide which persons or organisations were communist. In 1953, it enacted further repressive legislation, enabling it to declare a state of emergency, to arrest people for passive resistance and hold them without trial, and to ban people to specific rural areas. This inspired many white radicals, not all of whom were communists, to side with the African opposition, as did the main Coloured and Indian groups. They formed a Congress Alliance, which in 1953 held a Congress of the People at Kliptown near Johannesburg. There a Freedom Charter was adopted, opening with the words 'We, the people of South Africa, declare for all our country and the world to know . . . that South Africa belongs to all who live in it, and that no government can justly claim authority unless it is based on the will of all the people'. The government's reaction was to charge 156 leaders of the Congress Alliance with high treason. However, the trial was bungled and, after four years of legal wrangling, all the accused were acquitted.

Meantime, important changes were taking place within the main African opposition movement. The ANC split between those who supported the multiracial ideal enshrined in the Freedom Charter and those who pursued more specifically African aims. The latter group, led by Robert Sobukwe, formed the Pan–Africanist Congress (PAC) in 1959. Despite the arrest of most of the leaders, mass demonstrations continued, the most successful being a bus boycott at Alexandria in the Transvaal. In 1960, the PAC launched a further campaign of passive resistance to the pass laws, and this led to the most tragic of all the confrontations between the white government and the African people opposing it. On 21 March 1960, police fired on a peaceful and unarmed crowd at Sharpeville in the southern Transvaal, killing seventy-two people and wounding some 186, including women and children. A few days later, 30,000 Africans marched into the centre of Cape Town from their 'location' at Langa some miles away. Some of them were killed by police-shooting at Langa.

Sharpeville immediately became the signal for worldwide condemnation of the South African regime, and the government was clearly shaken both by the strength of the African opposition and by the international reaction to the killings. Nevertheless, three days later, a state of emergency was declared, most of the leading opposition leaders were arrested, and both the ANC and the PAC were proclaimed unlawful organisations. Both of these organisations now realised that they had come to the end of the road which led through peaceful non-violent resistance, and both turned reluctantly to violent methods. The ANC mounted the Umkonto we Sizwe (Spear of the Nation) to sabotage government installations, while the PAC was involved in Poqo, which aimed to terrorise whites. The decade of peaceful demonstrations was characterised by Albert Luthuli, who was elected president of the ANC in 1952, and who was banned to a remote corner of Zululand for launching a defiance campaign in 1959. He was honoured internationally by a Nobel Peace Prize, and was grudgingly suspended from his banning order so that he could travel to Norway to receive it. He died in 1967 and, toward the end of his life, he wrote the following moving reflection:

Who will deny that thirty years of my life have been spent knocking in vain, patiently, moderately and modestly, at a closed and barred door? What have been the fruits of moderation? The past thirty years have seen the greatest number of laws restricting our rights and progress, until today we have reached a stage where we have almost no rights at all.

The non-violent defiance campaigns and demonstrations were largely urban affairs, organised by a middle-class African elite. Given the increasingly tight control exercised by the security forces, it became a major problem for the ANC and PAC leaders to mobilise mass support. In rural areas, however, different kinds of resistance movements emerged, which were independent of the ANC and PAC and much more difficult for the government to deal with. The most widespread and prolonged of these occurred in various parts of the Transvaal, and also among the Pondo people of the Transkei. Here, after three years of bitter conflict, the government declared a state of emergency and launched a full-scale war against the Pondo. Many people were killed, and many more injured before open resistance came to an end. The state of emergency remained in force throughout the setting up of a Bantustan in the Transkei and, indeed, was continued by the Matanzima government there.

The crushing of open resistance in Pondoland, together with the massacre at Sharpeville, marked a turning point in the history of South Africa. With some members of the outlawed ANC and PAC turning to violent resistance, the government had the occasion to operate even more draconian repression. In 1962, the security police captured Nelson Mandela, who had been operating underground for more than a year-and-a-half, and in July 1963, the rest of the ANC Umkonto leadership at their secret headquarters at Rivonia Farm near Johannesburg were rounded up. The ensuing trial ended with Mandela and eight others receiving life sentences. The six black accused were sent to join Robert Subukwe, the leader of the PAC, on Robben Island, a bleak rock set in the rough seas off Cape Town. Meanwhile, a veritable reign of terror destroyed the underground African opposition, as well as less dangerous organisations like the radical Indian, Coloured, and white movements, and created such an atmosphere of repression that even the respectable Liberal Party, as we have seen, felt obliged to give up the struggle.

During most of the thirty years of National Party rule, the South African economy expanded rapidly and brought great prosperity to the state and to the white population which dominated it. The bases for what could almost be called an economic miracle were the immense natural resources of the country; the ability of the skilled whites to support a fast-growing manufacturing sector; and the availability of a large, cheap, and strictly controlled labour force. South African economic growth between 1948 and the early 1970s was one of the highest in the world, rivalled only by that of Japan and certain peculiarly fortunate mini-economies like that of Singapore. Because of the very wide disparity in wages between white and black, the prosperity was not equally shared. Whites enjoyed one of the highest standards of living in the world, and it was this standard that they were prepared to defend by force if necessary. From the mid-1970s onward, partly as a result of the great increase in the price of oil, the economy started to fall back and to experience high inflation; 1976–7 was the year with the lowest growth since 1945. Foreign investors and foreign companies operating in South Africa were beginning to come under pressure from the international community, at least to pay equal wages to all their employees in South Africa, and the question of sanctions was frequently discussed. A further result both of the downturn in the economy and in the change from labour- to capital-intensive industrial processes was the growth of unemployment. It was estimated that in 1979, there were 2 million unemployed Africans, out of a total African labour force of around 8 million. Following the policy of separate development, many of the African unemployed were repatriated from the cities to their notional rural homelands, where they helped to increase the desperate poverty caused by a rapid growth in the African population.

The fundamental step in the implementation of separate development was the turning of the African reserves – the lands left to the natives after the massive expropriation of land by Europeans in the nineteenth century – into Bantustans or Homelands. The first move in this direction came with the Promotion of Bantu Self-Government Act of 1959, which provided for the setting up of 'territorial authorities' in 'national units', based on the lands occupied by the main tribal or language groups. The premise of the whole apparatus of separate development was set forth in the preamble to the Act, which said, 'The Bantu peoples . . . do not constitute a homogeneous people, but form separate national units on the basis of language and culture'. After more than two centuries of conflict, interaction and close integration into South Africa's urban economy, this premise was of doubtful validity. Moreover, the fact that the 13 percent of the country's total area which constituted the African reserves could not begin to accommodate the African population of 1960, let alone the numbers of anything up to 50 million expected by the end of the century, did not deter the regime, which set about its apparently impossible and contradictory task with verve. The ten Homelands were Transkei and Ciskei (Xhosa), Kwazulu (Zulu), Qwaqwa (Southern Sotho), Lebowa and South Ndebele (Northern Sotho), Bophuthatswana (Tswana),

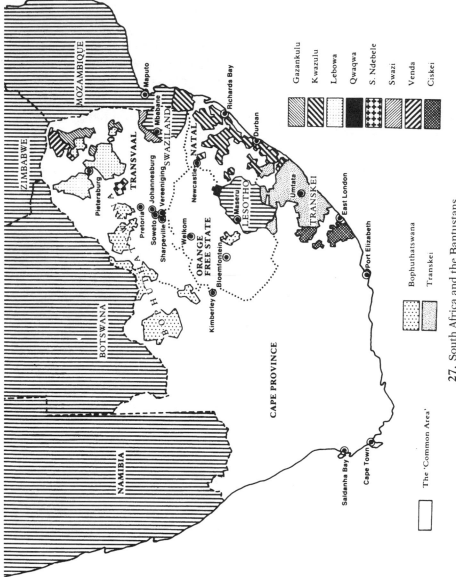

Gazankulu

Kwazulu

Lebowa

Qwaqwa

S. Ndebele

Swazi

Venda

Ciskei

Bophuthatswana

Transkei

The 'Common Area'

ZIMBABWE

MOZAMBIQUE

NAMIBIA

BOTSWANA

TRANSVAAL

Maputo

Mbabane

SWAZILAND

NATAL

Richards Bay

Durban

Pietersburg

Pretoria

Johannesburg

Soweto

Vereeniging

Sharpeville

Welkom

Newcastle

ORANGE
FREE STATE

Maseru

LESOTHO

Bloemfontein

Kimberley

Umtata

TRANSKEI

East London

Port Elizabeth

CAPE PROVINCE

Saldanha Bay

Cape Town

27. South Africa and the Bantustans.

Gazankula (Shangaan and Tsonga), Venda, and Swazi. None of these Homelands occupied continuous blocks of territory; even the largest, the Transkei, had white lands jutting right into it. This territory received a measure of self-government in 1963. Elections were held, the voters including not only those Xhosa resident in Transkei, but also all people of Xhosa origin, many of whom had lived in the urban areas for generations and had no ties with their notional homelands. A minority of the 'popular' vote, together with the support of the appointed chiefs in the new Transkei parliament, enabled Kaiser Matanzima to form an administration. He was one of a number of traditional leaders who were prepared to support the policy of separate development.

One of the more controversial figures to emerge in the 1970s was Chief Gatsa Buthelezi of Kwazulu. He used his position to criticise the racial inequalities perpetuated and reinforced by the South African government. He would not allow Kwazulu to go beyond a limited degree of autonomy, and continued to oppose the political fragmentation implied in separate development. His example was followed by the leaders of seven more of the ten Homelands. Transkei received its formal grant of independence in 1976 and was followed by Bophuthatswana in 1977. Neither state was recognised by any other country, and both were refused membership in the UN and the OAU. In Transkei, the Emergency laws which had been in operation since 1960 were incorporated into a new Public Security Act passed by the Matanzima government in 1977, which also set up a Transkei Intelligence Service to take over the functions of the South African Bureau of State Security (BOSS). However, the initial good relations did not last long. A dispute over the status of the Xhosa who lived outside the Transkei grew so bitter that, in 1978, the Transkei broke off all relations with South Africa. Although the rift was later papered over, cordial relations were never restored.

In 1979, more than 9 million Africans – double the entire white population of South Africa – lived outside the Homelands, in the so-called white areas. Of these, 4 million lived and worked on the white-owned farms, while 5 million lived in the urban areas. These urban Africans were those subject to the greatest pressure of the discriminatory policies under which they had to live out their daily lives. Inflation, poverty, social disruption, employment insecurity, an increasing crime rate, a high level of violence – together with the constant threat of deportation to distant and unknown 'homelands' – all combined to make people desperate and humiliated. The largest urban area was Soweto, the huge African city to the south-west of Johannesburg. A high proportion of the population there consisted of schoolchildren and teenagers. Compared with Africans in the rural areas, these children had received a modicum of education, enough to raise their expectations and to make them aware of their grievances. The immediate cause of the outbreak of violent resistance among them in June 1976 was the decision of the white authorities to impose Afrikaans as the medium for teaching in secondary schools, but behind it there lay the general dissatisfaction of youngsters with the whole content of Bantu education. Compared with the excellent facilities provided for white children, Africans had every reason to feel deprived. In 1975–6, an average of R644 was spent on every white school pupil, compared to R42 on every black one. The reaction of African youngsters was frustration, rage, and hatred. The school strikes spread rapidly. Soon, most of the other African urban areas in the Transvaal were affected and, by August 1976, the unrest had spread to Port Elizabeth, the Ciskei, and the western Cape. The police responded brutally but effectively and, by 1977, several hundred persons had been killed. Amongst a few other minor concessions, the government quietly dropped its Afrikaans language proposals.

Although nothing else equalled the impact of the school strikes, the closing years of the 1970s witnessed an intensification of some other forms of African resistance, and it was at this time that the repressive force of the South African government acquired its ugliest profile. African university students had in 1969 broken away from the National Union of South African Students to form the South African Students Organisation (SASO). This was soon followed by the emergence of a new political party, the Black People's Convention (BPC). Although both SASO and BPC encouraged other non-white groups to participate, they played a leading role in the development of a specific Black Consciousness or Black Power movement. The two organisations staged pro-FRELIMO rallies in 1975. When the school strikes added to these disturbances, the government of B. J. Vorster pulled out all the stops. All leading Africans and some of their white supporters were rounded up and detained under the various security laws. One of those held in custody was Steve Biko, the founder of SASO and one of the most respected and influential of the new generation of African leaders. Biko was arrested in Grahamstown in August 1977 and held and interrogated at Port Elizabeth prison. He was transferred to Pretoria jail for further interrogation and died there on 12 September. Although the magistrate at the inquest found that 'no one was criminally responsible' for Biko's death, the evidence suggested that he had died of injuries received during interrogation. Between 1976 and 1979, fifty or more persons were known to have died while in detention under South Africa's security legislation. When another well-known hardliner, P. W. Botha, took over as prime minister from B. J. Vorster in 1978, there were few people in South Africa who suspected that he would begin the laborious process of modifying and ultimately dismantling apartheid. Yet, so it was to prove.

The Protectorates and South-West Africa (Namibia)

From the 1880s, Basutoland and Bechuanaland, and from the end of the Anglo–Boer war Swaziland, were ruled by Britain as protectorates. They were administered by colonial civil servants working under a British high commissioner who was also the governor–general of the Union of South Africa. This was a divided authority which reflected the peculiar situation of the three small countries, which were landlocked, completely or partly surrounded by South Africa and economically dependent upon it. The constitution of the Union provided for the eventual incorporation of the protectorates, and South African governments periodically demanded that this should take place – the last occasion being as late as 1963. Britain resisted these demands on the grounds that transfer required the consent of the people concerned. Instead, the protectorates were gradually developed toward self-government along the same lines as the tropical African colonies. The hope was that perhaps this might help to bring nearer the sharing of power between the races in South Africa itself. Political parties were, therefore, encouraged to grow up in each country, which represented the different tribal affiliations of each, as well as the slight differences about the attitude which they should adopt toward their powerful white neighbour.

In Bechuanaland, the Bechuanaland Democratic Party, led by Seretse Khama, the chief of the Bamangwato people, won the pre-independence election of 1965 and carried the country through to independence in the following year, when its name was changed to Botswana. Seretse became president and soon emerged as one of Africa's foremost statesmen. Botswana was one of the few African states to retain a multiparty system. The exploitation of big diamond, cupro-nickel, and other mineral resources enabled it to be less dependent on South Africa than its two sister states, although it still relied heavily on South Africa for its external communications. In 1977, an all-weather road was constructed to the northern tip of Botswana, where at Kasungulu on the Zambezi it shared a short common frontier with Zambia; here, a ferry crossing provided a slender link with the black African states to the north. After Seretse's death in 1980, his vice-president, Quett Masire, became head of state and continued the cautious policies of his predecessor. In 1989, the World Bank reported that Botswana had the best record of any African country in maintaining an annual increase of 12 percent in gross national product for more than a decade on end.

Basutoland became an independent kingdom in 1966 and changed its name to Lesotho. It was governed by the Basutoland National Party (BNP), under the leadership of Chief Leabua Jonathan, who not only retained close economic links with South Africa, but also for a time played along with the South African policy of 'détente' with neighbouring black African states. In 1970, the BNP lost an election to its main rival, the Basutoland Congress Party, whereupon Chief Jonathan, with the connivance of the South African government and with the help of a small paramilitary police force of South African and British mercenaries, staged a coup. The king, Moshweshwe II, was banished for a time and, after his return, played little part in politics. Thus, Lesotho became in effect a one-party dictatorship, although, as time went on, Chief Jonathan gradually distanced himself from the South African regime.

Swaziland was the last of the protectorates to regain its independence, in 1968. The Swazi king, Sobhuza II, was a traditionalist of the old order, and played a much larger role in politics than his counterpart in Lesotho. Before independence, there were a number of political parties, but Sobhuza organised one of his own, the Mbokodvu Party, and manipulated the elections in 1964 so as to secure its victory. The Mbokodvu Party was proudly nationalist, and many of the younger and more radical Swazi joined it. In 1968, the British imposed a Westminster type of settlement whereby Sobhuza became, in theory, a constitutional head of state. Sobhuza put up with this until 1973, when he took over the government himself and withdrew the constitution. He reinstated a number of so-called traditional institutions which were supposed to provide an exchange of political views between the monarch and his subjects. The system became more difficult to maintain as economic and social changes gathered momentum. The king had to keep a wary eye both upon his own subjects and on the resident foreigners, among whom were many South African farmers, who owned nearly 40 percent of the land. He had also to watch the Marxist influences emanating from neighbouring Mozambique. At the time of his death in 1982, Sobhuza was the oldest reigning monarch in the world.

Despite its great size, South-West Africa, which from the 1970s on was generally known to the outside world as Namibia, had a population of less than 1 million people, of whom nearly 100,000 were whites, mostly Afrikaners, but also some of German descent. The largest group of African people were the Ovambo, who lived in the far north, astride the Angolan frontier. The other main Bantu-speaking group were the Herero, whose ancestors had suffered so severely at the hands of the Germans (see Chapter 12). There were also scattered Khoi-speakers, such as the Nama. At the end of the Second World War, the South African government refused to accept the authority of the UN Trusteeship Council over the territory, which it proceeded to govern as if it were a fifth province of the Union. The all-white electorate sent its representatives to the South African parliament, and most of the repressive legislation of the South African system was applied in the territory. The Odendaal Plan, published in 1964, proposed to bind South-West Africa even more closely to the

Republic and to create nine ethnic Homelands on 40 percent of the land, the remaining 60 percent being reserved for whites.

Meanwhile, a number of African political movements had developed, of which the South-West Africa People's Organisation (SWAPO) was the largest and enjoyed the best international connections, especially at the UN and the OAU. Faced with the Odendaal Plan, SWAPO turned to armed resistance, which started with small-scale guerrilla actions, mostly in the Ovambo country near the Angolan frontier. In 1966, the UN was persuaded to revoke South Africa's mandate, awarded by its predecessor, the League of Nations. In 1971, the International Court ruled that South Africa should end its occupation of Namibia. In the same year, the Ovambo and other African groups mounted a general strike, whereupon the South African administration declared a state of emergency and forcibly broke up the strike. In 1973, Homelands were set up for the Ovambo and Kavango, which were granted a limited form of self-government. The scale of violence mounted in the territory as the security forces used harsh methods in attempting to deal with the disruptive activities of SWAPO, which were mainly directed against the official Homeland leaders. The most significant event in the confrontation over Namibia was, however, the Portuguese withdrawal from Angola and the consequent civil war between the MPLA government in Luanda and the UNITA guerrillas operating in the south of Angola. With the help of the MPLA, SWAPO was now able to mount much more substantial military actions in Namibia from bases in Angola. South African forces retaliated from their big military base at Grootfontein in northern Namibia, from which they also aided the UNITA guerrillas opposing the MPLA.

In 1975, South Africa tried to seize the political initiative by holding a constitutional conference of 'representatives' of all the 'peoples' of Namibia, without reference to SWAPO or the UN. The Turnhalle Conference, as it was called, concluded with a statement to the effect that Namibia should obtain independence from South Africa in 1978, but that the separation into 'homelands' and 'the white area' should continue under some kind of South African guarantee, which implied the continuance of some kind of control. Neither SWAPO nor the UN would accept the Turnhalle proposals. The western members of the UN Security Council attempted mediation, but, in the end, the

South African government announced its decision to hold elections in the territory based on the Turnhalle scheme. Behind all the overt diplomacy, the real nub of the Namibian situation was that South Africa, covertly encouraged by the United States, was unwilling to remove its military forces from Namibia so long as Russians and Cubans were aiding a Marxist government in Angola. Namibia had, in fact, become a buffer zone in the Cold War, and would remain so through most of the 1980s.

During the years from 1945 to 1980 and beyond, South Africa's external relations were governed mainly by the reaction of other states to its internal policies and practices. This was not only on account of what had already happened there, but even more because of what might happen in the future. There were many states in the world where governments representing a minority of the population tyrannised over the majority, controlling the internal and external movements of their people, using secret police and informers to sniff out the slightest manifestations of dissidence, and practising torture in their interrogation chambers and assassination outside them. There were many governments in the world, many even in Africa, which had killed far more of their own citizens than the government of South Africa had yet done. What was unique to South Africa was that these crimes and injustices were compounded by the explosive factors of race and colour. When a Steve Biko died in the hands of white policemen, every black man in the world felt personally involved. The one last shooting flame in the fire of Pan–Africanism was the desire of every self-governing black nation to free its brothers in the south. Even Idi Amin sought to pose as a hero in this crusade, knowing that other African states would find it harder to criticise his internal regime if this item of his external policy was aligned with theirs.

The Breakthrough in South Africa

Faced with this situation, the white government of South Africa made some efforts to break out of its growing isolation at the tip of the African continent. While continuing to cultivate its economic links with the western countries and Japan, it tried hard to launch the notion that it could be both a valuable trading partner and a source of development aid to many countries within Africa. During the 1960s and 1970s, Verwoerd and Vorster established close relations with Lesotho and Malawi and held 'dialogues' with countries as far afield as Ivory Coast, Liberia, Ghana, and the Malagasy Republic. South African goods were on sale in many African countries which did not officially admit South African visitors or permit the overflight of South African planes. Botswana, Zambia, Zaire, and Zimbabwe were all to some degree dependent on South African railways for their access to the sea. And even Mozambique had to balance its budget by continuing to send labour migrants to South Africa in exchange for government-to-government payments in gold bullion. In 1969, a fourteen-nation conference of African states issued the Lusaka Manifesto, which reflected above all the thoughts of Presidents Kaunda and Nyerere. The manifesto laid down guidelines for future dialogue between South Africa and other African states, suggesting that this could be fruitful only after South Africa had shown itself ready to change substantially the policy of separate development. Given such readiness, other African states would recognise that there might be a considerable interval before majority rule was achieved. But, although Vorster and other ministers occasionally spoke favourably of this approach, the words and deeds of white South Africans until the late 1980s generally implied a firm rejection of what could have been a unique opportunity to escape from their self-imposed impasse.

There was, however, one kind of warning which the cabinet of P. W. Botha could not ignore, and it was that which came from the internal leaders of South African industry and commerce. It told them that with steadily growing clarity that the hitherto brilliant progress of the South African economy would soon grind to a halt unless fresh sources of skilled and semi-skilled labour could be recruited from the ranks of the black population, which already numbered some 29 million and was expected to rise rapidly by the end of the century. These would be the main consumers and producers of the future, and it was inevitable that most of them would live and work in and around the white cities and not in the countryside or the Bantustans. F. W. de Klerk, then a rising younger minister, says in his autobiography that his exposure to the management of the economy during the early eighties had convinced him that it would be impossible to maintain economic growth on the one hand and to succeed with the implementation of the homeland policy on the other. 'I firmly believe', he says, 'that economic growth was a far more powerful agent for change than any of the other factors – including sanctions and international pressure'. And he goes on with the surprising statement that a special and presumably secret committee within the cabinet developed 'a new policy framework, which constituted a 180-degree change in policy for ever away from apartheid, separate development and racial discrimination. The proposed framework accepted the fundamental principles of one united South Africa, one person one vote, the eradication of all forms of racial discrimination, and the effective protection of minorities against domination'.[1] The new framework was accepted by the Federal Congress of the National Party in Durban in August 1986 and by the restricted electorate of apartheid South Africa in 1987.

No doubt de Klerk's retrospective account of policy developments in the 1980s glosses over large differences of opinion regarding the timing of constitutional change that was actually envisaged. Nevertheless, as the memoirs of Nelson Mandela make clear, at least some of the ministers of P. W. Botha's cabinet were taking real and significant action to prepare some of the political prisoners on Robben Island for freedom to resume their political activities in civil society. Already in March 1982, Mandela and three of his fellow prisoners had been transferred to a prison near Cape Town, where they had access to newspapers and radio broadcasts. In 1985, he contacted the government, saying that in his view the time had come for it and the ANC to enter into negotiations. 'We had been fighting against white majority rule for three quarters of a century. We had been engaged in the armed struggle for two decades. Many people on both sides had already died... It was clear to me that a military victory was a distant if not impossible dream. It simply did not make sense for both sides to lose thousands if not millions of lives in a conflict that was unnecessary... It was time to talk'.[2] The government's response came slowly, but, by December 1988, Mandela had been moved to Victor Verster prison near Paarl, into a large house, with servants and a cook, and where he could receive visitors. It was clear that he

---

[1] F. W. de Klerk, *The Last Trek*, London, 1998, p. 72. Ibid., p. 109.
[2] Nelson Mandela, *Long Walk to Freedom*, New York, 1994, p. 457.

was being groomed for release within the foreseable future and for a star role in all that was to follow. All this shows that, while keeping its real views secret from the electorate, the government had appreciated that major changes could come about peacefully only by securing the cooperation of the leaders of the ANC, both those in prison and those in exile and that, among them all, Mandela would be the one with whom they could best hope to do business.

From 1988 at least, only two serious impediments to decisive action remained. The first was the presence of Cuban mercenaries in Angola, and it was settled by the withdrawal of the Cubans in 1989. The second was the personal reluctance of the aging President Botha to pull the trigger, and it was solved by his suffering a stroke in January 1989, followed by his resignation the following August. He was succeeded in mid-September by F. W. de Klerk, who on 2 February 1990 announced to an astonished world that the time for reconciliation and reconstruction had arrived, and that his government would shortly be rescinding the prohibition on the African National Congress and the South African Communist Party as well as releasing Nelson Mandela unconditionally from his long imprisonment. The most extraordinary feature of the whole episode was that, a year later, the government sought the approval of the white electorate in a referendum and won it by a handsome majority. There was a long way still to go before the actual sharing of power could begin, but the direction of change appeared henceforward to be immutable. South Africa had at last joined the rest of the continent – in intention, if not yet in fact.

TWENTY ONE. The Politics of Independent Africa

The African states which gained their independence during the 1950s and 1960s, mostly by peaceful agreement with the former colonial powers, were born in an atmosphere of political euphoria. They had inherited from their colonial predecessors working systems which, whatever their limitations in respect of personal freedom and whatever the long-drawn-out insult of alien rule, had provided a framework of internal and external security; efficient and disinterested administration; sound finance; a basic economic infrastructure of roads, railways, harbours, and airports; and at least the beginnings of modern social services in education, health, and community development. To these, the new African leadership appeared at first to have added the vital element of political legitimation by mobilising an impressive proportion of the ordinary citizens in support of political parties organised on the western democratic pattern. 'Seek ye first the political kingdom', said Kwame Nkrumah, 'and all these other things shall be added unto you'.

Leaders of the new states at first felt so confident of the internal cohesion of their countries that many of their earliest efforts were directed to foreign affairs. To secure their frontiers, they had to forge new ties with the neighbouring African states, while outside the continent, they had to develop relationships with those industrialised countries other than the former colonial powers which might help them as trading partners, as sources of investment, and as donors of aid for their educational and other needs. Ideology played some part in these contacts, with some states forming a westward-leaning

'Monrovia bloc', while others more radically socialist joined a pro-Soviet 'Casablanca bloc'. But these and other groupings proved ephemeral. Most African statesmen soon learned that it was best to cultivate relations with both eastern and western outsiders and to play one off against the other. In terms of aid, this was the period of the 'children's crusade', when many thousands of idealistic young men and women from western Europe and North America spent a year or two teaching, mostly English or French, in newly established primary schools in the rural areas of African countries from Algeria to Madagascar and from Sierra Leone to Zambia. In France and Belgium, they were known as *co-opérateurs* and given exemption from military service as an incentive. Members of the American Peace Corps enjoyed the same privilege, and service in Africa became an alternative to the Vietnam war. In Britain, the government subsidised a number of voluntary organisations, the largest being Voluntary Service Overseas. During the early years of African independence, these young people played a significant part in expanding African educational systems and in bringing a consciousness of the outside world to the new generation of African schoolchildren. The eastern-bloc countries, lacking the relevant languages, could do little to rival them.

Within the continent, Nkrumah's vision of a United States of Africa found little support, and even the tentative regional federations formed during the colonial period in French West and Equatorial Africa, the Central African Federation and the more limited East African Community, soon broke down into their component parts as soon as the element of outside compulsion was removed. For a brief period, with the attempted secession of Katanga from the Congo (see Chapter 18), it looked as though this tendency to fission might go much further, but the decisive intervention of the United Nations, using contingents from other African countries, turned the scales. In 1963, there emerged the Organisation of African Unity (OAU), a consultative body with its headquarters in Addis Ababa, which offered a useful mechanism for settling disputes between African states as well as providing a collective voice on those matters where there was substantial agreement, such as the common struggle against the remaining areas of colonialism in Angola and Mozambique, Rhodesia, and South Africa. It became a fundamental principle of the OAU that the frontiers inherited from the colonial period should be treated as sacrosanct both as to border disputes between states and to acts of secession within them.

Democracy, Autocracy, and Military Rule

Within the newly independent states, political leaders soon realised that to mobilise public support behind programmes of mass education and economic betterment presented problems very different from the simple issue of indigenous as against alien rule on which they had ridden to power. The very basis of nationality, to which all states laid claim, was nothing but a colonial superstructure hastily erected over very diverse populations still speaking many different languages, in which only a small minority of the best-educated people had any strong sense of an allegiance wider than the ethnic group. Faced with this situation, few African leaders saw any useful solution in the confrontational party politics of the western world. All of them were, by western standards, men of the political left, and most of them saw much more relevance in the Marxist–Leninist idea of a political party as the instrument of a vanguardist elite, tolerating no organised opposition, and designed to enlist the masses behind a single philosophy and political programme. In Africa, such a conception of the party could be justified as 'nation-building', and there were many observers in the West as well as the East who were ready to justify it on that score.

The idea of single-party politics seems to have entered the continent mainly through the Francophone states of West Africa, where Houphouët-Boigny in the Ivory Coast and Sékou Touré in Guinea installed what were virtually single-party regimes even before the formal transfer of power. By the middle of the 1960s, most of the other Francophone countries, with the notable exception of Senegal, had followed suit. In English-speaking Africa, it was the Ghana of Kwame Nkrumah which led the way, while in eastern Africa, the Tanzania of Julius Nyerere, the Malawi of Hastings Banda, and the Zambia of Kenneth Kaunda were not far behind. Nyerere, especially, attempted in his public speeches and writings to defend the change to 'African socialism' on the grounds of its consonance with the traditional political ideas of pre-colonial Africa, where the elders had talked things through 'under the shade of the big tree', aiming at unanimity rather than confrontation: only when consensus had been achieved did the presiding chief translate it into an executive command, which all then jumped to obey.

In practice, however, the vanguardist party proved to be an insidious growth leading to the domination of the many by the very few. Lacking opposition parties, parliaments withered, and ministers reigned without any check on their actions. Appointments and promotions in the civil services, the police forces, the judiciary, and the state corporations became subject to party patronage. The party network extended all through society and down to the village level, explaining and activating government policy, but also listening and reporting to higher authority. Suspected deviants were harried by legal and extra-legal means. Vanguardist parties had their bullyboys, often disguised as youth movements, ready to move in and rough up a village which was resisting collectivisation or a university where too much freedom of speech was being practised.

Changes in the socialist direction came not suddenly, but piecemeal. In Ghana, for example, which obtained independence in 1957 under a constitution on the Westminster model, a one-party state was not formally declared until seven years later, but, already in 1958, a Preventive Detention Act was passed, which was used not only against members of the opposition but also against dissidents within the ruling CPP. The Industrial Relations Act of the same year brought the trade unions under government control. In 1960, the country became a republic, with a new constitution which gave sweeping powers to Nkrumah, who now became president instead of prime minister. In 1964 came the declaration of single-party rule, by which time the CPP had degenerated into a party of avaricious time-servers. As western disapproval mounted, Nkrumah moved ever closer to the Soviet bloc. He maintained his support for independence movements in other countries and continued to speak and write about the need for Africa to unite, but his version of African socialism, aptly called Nkrumahism, amounted to little more in practice than the construction of some industrial and infrastructural projects which proved vastly expensive and resulted in little that was economically useful. The president himself became increasingly isolated from ordinary Ghanaians, secluding himself at first in the old Danish slave-trading

fort at Christiansborg and, later, in a military barracks on the outskirts of Accra, where he could be defended by a specially recruited
presidential guard armed with weapons superior to those of the regular army. Ironically, it was by the army that, in 1966, he was deposed
while absent on a visit to China. Nkrumah had inherited one of the
most prosperous of African countries, with a healthy balance of payments and a strong reserve of foreign currency. After nine years of
his rule, Ghana was bankrupt, food and consumer goods were in
short supply, and all government services had deteriorated beyond
recognition. He died, little mourned, as a pensioner of Sékou Touré
on an island off the coast of Guinea.

The military coup in Ghana was not the first such episode to affect independent Africa. In Egypt, the rule of King Farouk had been
overthrown by the officer corps as early as 1952. In Sudan, the army
had taken over in 1958 from the first civilian government, elected
only two years earlier. In Togo, the army had intervened in 1963 to
install a new civilian president and, in 1965, General Mobutu, who
had been a leading figure in the army mutiny of 1960 (see Chapter
18), established himself as the president of the Congo, henceforward
renamed Zaire. During 1966 and 1967, however, military coups succeeded each other right across the middle part of the continent. Military rulers took over power in Bénin, Togo, Upper Volta, and the
Central African Republic. And, in Uganda, a civilian prime minister,
Milton Obote, used the army to overthrow the constitutional government of the country. By far the most sinister of these episodes,
however, was the succession of coups in Nigeria, which brought the
richest and most prosperous of the new states of middle Africa to
the very brink of disintegration and ruin.

From Military Rule to Civil War

Nigeria's constitution, which had been negotiated with great care
by the British government with the Nigerian politicians, provided
for a federal structure with a central authority and three partially
autonomous regions. At the federal level, politics revolved around
the inescapable fact of northern predominance, by virtue of the size
and population of this mainly Muslim region. Since independence
in 1960, the federal prime minister had been the conservative and

highly respected nominee of the Northern People's Congress, Sir
Abubakar Tafawa Balewa. Two censuses and elections, held in 1963
and 1964, although alleged to have been fraudulently conducted,
merely confirmed this political reality. At the regional level, politics
was dominated by the three most numerous ethnic groups – Hausa
in the north, Yoruba in the south-west, and Ibo in the south-east.
In interregional matters, the Yoruba, having many Muslims among
them, tended to side with the Hausa. The odd men out were the Ibo,
who were solidly Christian and had the best-educated elite, whose
members became widely spread in trade and literate jobs across the
other two regions. They tended to feel both indispensable and ill-
appreciated and, in January 1966, a group of young, mostly Ibo,
army officers turned upon the politicians, assassinating Balewa and
the prime ministers of the northern and south-western regions, and
installing a military regime with an Ibo, General Ironsi, as head of
state. Resentment mounted in the other two regions. Ibo living in
the northern towns were massacred and, in July, a group of northern
officers murdered Ironsi and installed Lieutenant-Colonel Gowan, a
northern Christian, in his place. The military governor of the eastern
region, Lieutenant-Colonel Ojukwu, thereupon took steps to withdraw his region from the federation. Secession was formally declared
in May 1967, when Ojukwu proclaimed the independence of the new
state of Biafra.

There were many reasons why the federal government could not
endorse the secession, but the most urgent was the fact that the oil
fields on which Nigeria depended for its revenues and its balance of
payments were nearly all situated in Biafra. It was, in fact, a parallel
case to that of the Katanga in 1960, when Tshombe had attempted by
secession to monopolise the main mineral wealth of the Congo for
the benefit of one of its provinces. And so in Nigeria there began the
civil war, which was to last three years and to cost the lives of more
than a million Nigerians. At first, the Biafran forces, being better
prepared, were able to overrun much of the area between Benin and
Lagos. But federal troops soon pushed them back and carried the
war into Biafra. By the middle of 1968, Biafra was reduced to an
enclave in the Ibo heartland crowded with starving refugees, who
congregated around the only functioning airstrip at Uli. That the
war still lasted for a further eighteen months was due to Ojukwu's

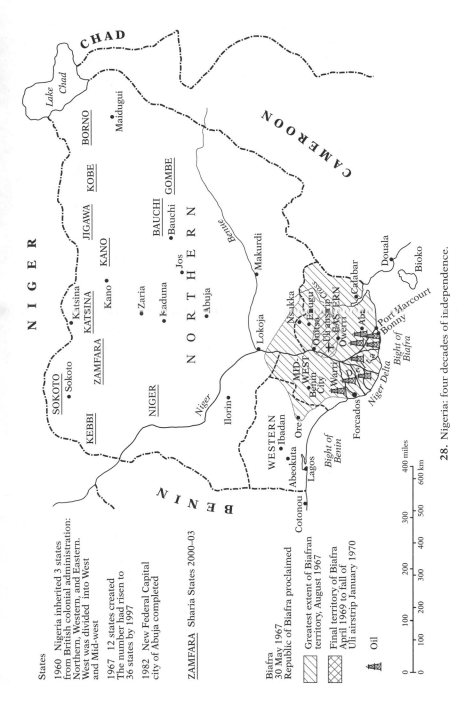

States

1960 Nigeria inherited 3 states from British colonial administration: Northern, Western, and Eastern. West was divided into West and Mid-west

1967 12 states created The number had risen to 36 states by 1997

1982 New Federal Capital city of Abuja completed

ZAMFARA Sharia States 2000–03

Biafra
30 May 1967
Republic of Biafra proclaimed

Greatest extent of Biafran territory, August 1967

Final territory of Biafra April 1969 to fall of Uli airstrip January 1970

Oil

28. Nigeria: four decades of independence.

309

skilful presentation to the outside world of Biafra as a brave little
Christian nation, hemmed in by overbearing Muslim persecutors
who were only interested in grabbing its wealth. He secured the support of four African governments, including Tanzania, and Zambia.
He obtained military supplies from France, South Africa, and Portugal, all of which were for different reasons interested in diminishing
the stature of Black Africa's most powerful independent state. He
successfully manipulated the non-governmental relief agencies into
providing cover for the airlift of arms to the enclave. But the federal
government was sustained politically by Britain and militarily by
the Soviet Union, which at that time was busily expanding its influence in the Muslim world of the Middle East and North Africa. And
the majority of African states were concerned, as always, with the
preservation of existing frontiers, and so favoured the federal cause.
At last, early in 1970, Biafra gave up the terrible charade. Ojukwu
fled to the Ivory Coast. Gowan was magnanimous in victory. There
were no major recriminations, and soldiers and civil servants were
successfully reabsorbed into the federal and regional structures. In
time, even Ojukwu was able to return to his homeland. And Nigerians in general felt themselves to be more a nation than they had
been before the war. The main political casualty of the war, however,
was civilian government, which became henceforward the exception
rather than the norm.

Military rule did not occur in every African country. A surprising number of civilian leaders – Hassan II in Morocco, Bourguiba
in Tunisia, Senghor in Senegal, Houphouët-Boigny in Ivory Coast,
Nyerere in Tanzania, Banda in Malawi, Kaunda in Zambia, and Tsiranana in Madagascar – managed to maintain themselves in power for
a quarter of a century or more without losing control of their military
forces. Moreover, where it did occur, military rule was not always or
everywhere a disaster. In Nigeria, once the civil war was over, military
rule meant merely that senior soldiers filled the ministerial posts and
the state governorships while a relatively efficient civil service went
about its accustomed tasks. Most African governments during the
first three decades of independence were autocratic, if not despotic,
narrowly based, and prone to corruption. In most cases, it made little difference whether or not the head of state wore a uniform. Military coups did, indeed, throw up a fair selection of very dangerous

and unpleasant characters. The most enduring and eccentric of these was certainly Colonel Muammar Gadhafi, who, with all the oil wealth of Libya behind him and with a very small home constituency on which to spend it, was able to engage in an extraordinary variety of external adventures. He attempted to destabilise one after another of the Muslim or partly Muslim states to the north and south of the Sahara by actively supporting opposition groups within them. He was involved in numerous attempts to overthrow legitimate governments by violence, including the assassination attempts against King Hassan in 1974 and President Sadat of Egypt in 1976. He engineered an unsuccessful coup against President Nimeiri in the Sudan in 1975, and was connected with the terrorists who finally murdered Sadat in 1979. Gaddafi provided money and training for terrorist groups in a number of West African states. He sent troops to Uganda in support of his fellow Muslim Idi Amin in 1978, this being one of the few occasions when he helped an established ruler. Although his numerous interventions appeared to be impulsive and erratic, his underlying motive was usually to export his own version of militant Islam, seeing himself as a latter-day prophet with a destiny to lead the faithful. To this end, he spent huge sums of Libyan revenue in Black Africa in campaigns to convert Christians and animists – campaigns which were sometimes surprisingly successful, as in Nigeria and Rwanda. Chad, as we shall see, he regarded as his gateway to the south – this is quite apart from his claims to the mineral-rich Aouzou Strip, which were based on colonial deals between France and Italy in 1935.

As dangerous as Gaddafi, although within a more confined space, was Macias Nguema, who ruled Equatorial Guinea – which had been Spain's only tropical African colony – for eleven terrible years, until he was arrested and executed by his own soldiers in 1979. He and his Fang henchmen from the mainland section of the country terrorised the once prosperous island of Fernando Poo (Bioko) until all recognisable civil life had been obliterated. Two other notoriously violent rulers were Jean Bokassa and Idi Amin, both of whom had come up through the non-commissioned ranks of the French and British colonial armies. Bokassa turned the Central African Republic into a mock-Napoleonic empire, spending a large part of the state's revenue on his own coronation. The French president Giscard d'Estaing was his guest and joined him for a hunting expedition; eventually in

1979, the French tired of his excesses and engineered a coup to depose him. Idi Amin's rule in Uganda during the 1970s was only one of three decades of civil strife in that country, but for the misuse of military power it was almost unsurpassed.

When Uganda became independent in 1963, it was a prosperous and well-run country, although there were deep-lying tensions, especially between the Nilotic peoples of the less developed northern half of the country and the Bantu peoples of the fertile and more densely populated south. These tensions rose rapidly to the surface in the context of national politics. Soon after independence, Milton Obote, a northerner, won power by allying himself with the parliamentary representatives of Buganda, thus dividing the south. When this alliance threatened to break up, he used the army against the Kabaka of Buganda, who was also the constitutional president of the whole country, driving him into exile and then eliminating the special status of Buganda within the state. In 1971, Obote was ousted by his army commander, Idi Amin, a Muslim from the remote Kakwa tribe living along Uganda's border with the Sudan, who represented just the kind of tough, uneducated valour that colonial armies had liked to recruit.

Amin soon brought his northern soldiery with him to the capital, and rewarded them by encouraging them to plunder the Asian shopkeepers and other entrepreneurs on whom so much of the economy depended. In 1972, in an effort to court popularity, he deported the entire Asian population, some 30,000 in all, who had to seek asylum in Britain with little more than the clothes they were wearing. Like many another guilty tyrant, Amin spent the rest of his eight-year reign trying to eliminate, one by one, the possible opponents of his rule. His first mass victims were the soldiers from Obote's north-eastern Lango tribe, who were slaughtered in the thousands. He replaced them with his own Kakwa and others from the distant north-west, whose presence in the south was even rougher. Having antagonised the southerners, especially the Baganda, he turned to repressing them. Prominent people from all walks of life were picked up in droves, incarcerated in horrible conditions, beaten, and tortured. The chief justice and the Anglican archbishop were among many others who were simply murdered. In an overwhelmingly Christian country, Amin relentlessly promoted the cause of

Islam, building a huge mosque in the very centre of Kampala, taking his financial support from Saudi Arabia and Libya, and encouraging the Palestine Liberation Organisation (PLO) to set up training camps in Uganda. Finally, in 1974, as a diversion for his feuding army, he invaded an obscure corner of north-western Tanzania on the pretext of rectifying a misdrawn frontier line. President Nyerere, who had been sheltering Obote since 1971, mounted a retaliatory invasion of southern Uganda, where the local population gave every support to the Tanzanian troops. Gaddafi rushed in Libyan reinforcements, but nothing could stop the Tanzanians, and Amin fled the country to an asylum in Saudi Arabia.

Unfortunately for Uganda, Nyerere used the prestige of his victory to push for the restoration of his protégé, Obote, who – after a dubious election – returned to the presidency. After some fifteen years of misrule by northerners, six of them by Obote himself, the southern part of the country was in no mood to extend the experiment or to wait for another election. Cells of armed opposition emerged in the countryside and were more brutally repressed by Obote than anything attempted by Amin. Gradually, the best of the opposition coalesced around the National Resistance Army built up by Yoweri Museveni, who had gained his military experience fighting with FRELIMO against the Portuguese in Mozambique. Although the incident which actually gave rise to Obote's second flight into exile arose from faction-fighting within the national army in the north, Museveni soon emerged as the leading figure and became president in 1986. The centre of power was thus restored to the south, where a large majority of the population lived. There was still no lasting settlement between north and south, but at least the huge task of moral and material reconstruction could be begun where the possibilities of a return to stability were greatest.

The southern Sudan, even more than northern Uganda, was a vast, inaccessible and deprived region, culturally and ethnically very different from the Arabic-speaking north. The inhabitants found it very difficult to identify with a government composed mainly of northerners who tended to treat them as untutored savages, to be compelled rather than persuaded (see Chapter 17). By 1967, relations between Khartoum and its southern provinces had so deteriorated that the Anyanya were demanding complete separation for the south.

A critical juncture was reached when northern soldiers massacred townspeople in Juba and the congregation of a Christian church in Wau. Fighting flared, and hundreds of thousands of refugees fled to neighbouring states. In due course, General Nimeiri, who came to power in a military coup in 1969, opened negotiations with the Anyanya, which led to an agreement mediated by Emperor Haile Selassie in Addis Ababa in 1972. This brought the first phase of the civil war to an end. A federal constitution was introduced, giving regional autonomy to the south. Southern ministers entered the central government. The Christian religion was recognised in the south and the English language given equal status with Arabic. Anyanya units were incorporated into the federal army. But this settlement lasted for only a decade before Nimeiri's regime was faced with a series of attempted coups, a declining economy, and the spread of Islamic fundamentalism. In an attempt to contain the last of these, Nimeiri proclaimed that Islamic law would, henceforth, be applied throughout the country, whereupon the Sudanese People's Liberation Army, founded by a southern colonel, John Garang, renewed hostilities against the centre. The miseries of the ensuing civil war were compounded by the great drought and famine of 1984–5, which sent fresh waves of refugees fleeing into Darfur and Kordofan, as well as into the surrounding countries. The government resorted to savage means in their attempts to pacify the southerners. In the early 1980s, the Khartoum authorities had begun to supply arms to the Baqqara Arab nomads who pastured their cattle and horses along the Bahr el-Arab and Bahr el-Ghazal. When Sadiq al-Madhi came to power in 1986, he stepped up arms deliveries to the Baqqara, who had been the mainstay of his great-grandfather's rebellion in 1881 (see Chapter 3). As they had done in the nineteenth century, Baqqara militias raided deep into the lands of the settled and mainly Christian Dinka and Nuer, burning villages, killing the men, capturing the women and children, and stealing the cattle. The impasse continued throughout the 1980s and beyond. Of all the countries of Africa, the Sudan was perhaps the one where the existence side-by-side of peoples at very different stages of development created the most intractable political problems.

One element common to both the Sudanese and the Nigerian conflicts was the political opposition between Muslim and non-Muslim communities living within the same frontiers. This element stretched out like a geological fault line right across the sub-Saharan belt, from the Senegal to the Indian Ocean. It had ancient roots in the mutual distrust between the raiders and the raided of pre-colonial times; during the colonial period, it was strengthened as the descendants of the raided were quicker than the Muslims to acquire western education and prestigious employment in the modern sector. The former slave race might thus become the ruling class, and relationships then grew worse than before. In the former French colony of Chad, for example, the southern agriculturalists, of whom the Sara were the largest group, were the chief gainers from French colonial rule. They grew the cotton which was the country's main export crop, and many of them became Christians and found education for their children. Meanwhile, the northern Muslims were doing their best to resist French rule. The three provinces in the far north – Borkou, Ennedi, and Tibesti – were not even subdued until 1930. Here, the largest group were the Toubou cattle nomads, who remained under military control until 1965. It was the southerners who took over power from the French in 1960. The first president, François Toumbalaye, soon instituted single-party government and dealt harshly with the Muslims. He embarked on a cultural Africanisation programme even more drastic than that attempted by Mobutu in Zaire, trying to enforce Sara customary law throughout the country. This led to widespread resistance and, in 1975, Toumbalaye was assassinated in a military coup which placed the northern Muslims in control. In 1979, however, a civil war broke out between rival factions of the new regime, which was to engulf the country until the 1990s, with Libya involved on one side and France and the United States on the other.

Civil War and Cold War

We have seen (in Chapter 17) that already in the 1960s, there existed the seeds of conflict in the countries of the Horn of Africa, particularly in the desire of Eritrean and Somali Muslims to be free from domination by Ethiopian Christians. Since the abolition by Haile Selassie of the federal constitution in 1962, Eritrean separatists had been preparing, with the help of Arab and East European countries,

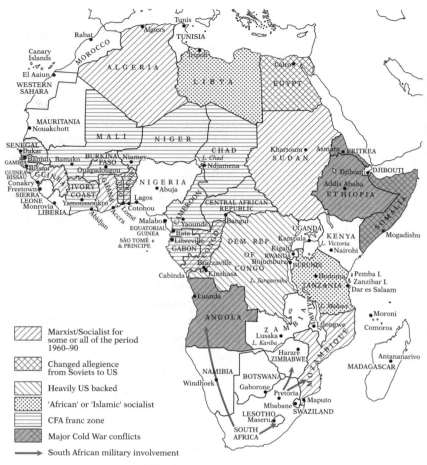

29. Africa and the Cold War.

to fight for the independence of the province. Meanwhile, the Somali population of the Ogaden province of Ethiopia was encouraged by the government of Somalia to seek a transfer of territory to its ethnic homeland. Faced with guerrilla activities on two fronts, Ethiopia leant heavily on American support, while Somalia turned to the Soviet Union. Early in 1974, however, this system of alliances was reversed when Haile Selassie's government was overthrown by a military coup, engineered by young officers of Marxist views with the help of East European embassies in the capital. There is no evidence that the Ethiopian revolution enjoyed strong popular support.

It was the work of a small military clique, encouraged and aided by eastern-bloc countries concerned to extend the Cold War in a region of strategic importance, which commanded the entrance to the Red Sea and the oil routes to the west. The revolution did nothing to solve the separatist problem in Eritrea or the Ogaden. It simply meant that American help was withdrawn from Ethiopia and accorded instead to Somalia, while the military government, known as the Dergue, was left still fighting a war on two fronts as well as facing internal opposition by the Oromo and other ethnic groups. Addis Ababa was subjected to a reign of terror, whereas members of the Dergue engaged in mutual assassination and the wholesale slaughter of opponents. By 1976, the original 120 members had been reduced to fewer than 60, and the strongman of the revolution, Brigadier Mengistu Haile Mariam, was feeling his way to power. Early the following year, he staged his own coup. This was the signal for the Soviet Union openly to switch its support from Somalia and the Eritrean separatists to the new Ethiopian government.

Between 1977 and 1990, the Soviets sent Mengistu some $12 billion in arms and military aid and also paid for most of the expenses of 17,000 Cuban 'volunteers' to support the huge Ethiopian army of some 250,000 men. These forces cleared the Ogaden of Somali invaders and reestablished a measure of control over the central part of the country. But in the north, the Eritreans fought on and were soon joined by new separatist movements in Tigre and among the Oromo. As time went on, the Mengistu regime became increasingly unpopular on account of its clumsy attempts to impose collectivised farming and by the brutal deportation of starving peasants from the famine-stricken regions to the north of the capital to untried land in the south. Moreover, by about 1986, the Soviet Union was beginning to be disenchanted with its far-flung operations from Afghanistan to Angola; from then on, the northern Tigrean separatists increasingly seized the initiative. In 1991, they were at last able to move into the Amhara heartland and occupy the capital, while Mengistu fled into exile in Zimbabwe.

Meanwhile, in Somalia, the government gradually lost control of the nation. Defeat by Soviet-backed Ethiopia in 1977 turned Siad Barre's regime toward self-destruction. Although ethnically and linguistically homogeneous, Somali society was deeply divided by territorially based clans, of which Barre had to seek the support of some, thereby alienating others. Power thus became dispersed to local warlords, and civil strife spread even to the capital. Despite large injections of American aid, Somalia by the mid-1980s was in the process of violent disintegration in a landscape increasingly crowded with starving refugees. When Siad Barre fled the country in 1991, there ceased to be a recognisable government.

Several other African countries had to endure periods of internecine violence during the early years of their political independence, including Rwanda, Burundi, Zaire, Angola, and Mozambique (see Chapter 19). No reliable estimate is available of the numbers killed in actual fighting, but, by the mid-1980s, the number of persons displaced from their homes was thought to be about 16 million, of whom 4 million had crossed international frontiers into neighbouring countries. Refugees – whether from inside or outside their countries of final settlement – were by definition destitute people, who had left behind them their houses, their standing crops, their seed-corn, and even their agricultural tools. They tended to resettle in the least accessible frontier regions, where it was hardest for governments to bring them famine relief, medical help, and education for their children. They formed the poverty-stricken underclass of nearly every African country.

The Pressures of Population Increase

The results of violence apart, every state in Africa had to face the pressures of a staggering increase in population. Between 1960 and 1990, the population of the continent more than doubled, from about 200 million to about 450 million. This resulted from a general failure to adapt established habits of childbearing to the greatly reduced death rates prevailing in pre-colonial and early colonial times. The economic consequences of this increase is discussed in the next chapter, but the political consequences were hardly less momentous. Right up to the end of the colonial period, Africa had been essentially a rural continent. Only in North Africa and limited parts of West Africa were there any large indigenous towns. Elsewhere, even the colonial capitals inherited by the new nations were mostly small places with populations of 50,000 or less. Colonial government had been about ruling rural people. Townships had been for foreigners, their support staffs, and their servants. By 1990, however, a quarter of the entire population of Africa lived in towns and, in the capital cities, their numbers were doubling every ten years. The townspeople were now those of whom governments were most aware. They were closer at hand, more politically conscious, and more dependent on public services than most countryfolk. Increasingly, governments concentrated their efforts on the cities and the adjoining countryside which supplied them with their food. In the peripheral areas, services and communications crumbled, sometimes to the point at which local food shortages turned into famines because of the inaccessibility of relief supplies. During the first thirty years of independence, the conditions of life in the villages of Africa changed very little, and even then, mostly for the worse. It was in the exploding populations of the cities that the seeds of political change were to be found.

It was in the cities that there grew up, between about 1960 and 1990, a middle class of relatively well-educated and well-to-do Africans, who were accustomed to mixing and dealing as equals with foreigners and to measuring their own material and moral condition by international standards. At the time of independence, such people had been virtually confined to the leading members of the legal, teaching, and clerical professions. Thirty years later, they included also senior civil servants, businesspeople, academics, journalists, military officers, diplomats, and many others who travelled abroad, read foreign newspapers, listened to foreign broadcasting, watched the political trends in other countries, and discussed their own national affairs within a much wider framework than that countenanced by the heavy-handed party machines designed to keep ruling coteries perpetually in power. Public dissent might still be too dangerous to be widely practised, but, by the later 1980s at least, the possibilities of it looked less hopeless than they had done before. On the one hand, there was the example of the anti-communist revolutions in eastern Europe, which showed how apparently impregnable regimes like those of Poland, Romania, and East Germany could be unseated by an alternative leadership capable of mobilising crowds onto the streets. On the other hand, there was the pressure for human rights which could be exerted by international organisations and donor governments once the Cold War had come to an end.

Increasingly, from about 1985 onwards, offers of material aid could be linked with demands for the modification of autocratic systems, with their in-built tendencies to corruption and economic stagnation. By 1992, a majority of African countries had promised in principle to abolish the political monopolies enjoyed by their governing parties. True, many of them meant to delay the implementation of reforms for as long as possible, but at least there was some light visible at the end of the tunnel. In 1992, an autocrat as decent and respectable as Kenneth Kaunda, who had held power for nearly thirty years, lost an election and passed into retirement. Here, if anywhere, there seemed to be a portent of things to come.

In South Africa, Nelson Mandela was released from jail on 11 February 1990 after twenty-seven years of imprisonment. From the steps of Cape Town City Hall, Mandela addressed the mass of people who had turned out to greet him and, by means of television, millions throughout the world. In concluding his speech, he repeated his own words during the trial in 1964:

I have fought against white domination, and I have fought against black domination. I have cherished the idea of a democratic and free society in which all persons live together in harmony and with equal opportunities. It is an ideal which I hope to live for and to achieve. But if needs be, it is an ideal for which I am prepared to die.[1]

Oliver Tambo stood down as president of the ANC on grounds of ill health, and Mandela assumed the role. All the major pieces in the apartheid jigsaw were rapidly dismantled and all political parties became legal, but a convention set up in 1991 to negotiate the future of the country proved unwieldy and divisive. It was replaced by a more manageable structure, paving the way for South Africa's first democratic elections on 27 April 1994, which resulted in a huge victory for the ANC, with 62.2 percent of the vote and gaining 252 of the 400 seats in the National Assembly. The old National Party attained just over 20 percent of the vote, getting the largest share in the Western Cape, and with support which cut across racial lines. Eighty-six percent of the electorate participated in the elections, an exceptionally high turnout. Mandela was inaugurated President on 10 May,

---

[1] Heather Deegan, *The Politics of New South Africa*, Harlow, 2001, p. 230.

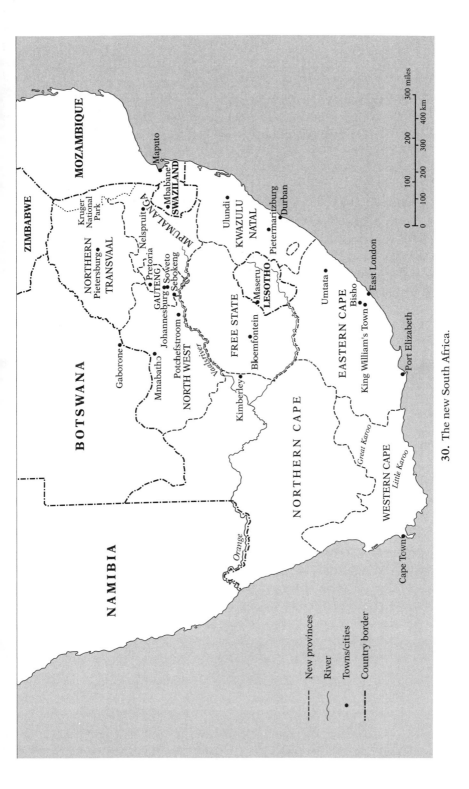

30. The new South Africa.

with de Klerk as a deputy president. Nine provinces took the place
of the Republic's four and, in time, the mainly white South African
Defence Force merged with the ANC and other resistance fighters
to form the South African army. One of the most significant acts of
the new government, and certainly the one that was held in universal esteem, was the establishment of the Truth and Reconciliation
Commission, to provide public acknowledgement of and reparation
to the victims of abuse under the apartheid regime, with powers to
grant conditional amnesty to the perpetrators of gross human-rights
violations. An exceptionally liberal and comprehensive Bill of Rights
was passed in 1996, which enshrined rights over wide aspects of social life – such as housing, education, and health care – as well as
political and legal affairs.

TWENTY TWO. Economics and Society in Independent Africa

The Years of Optimism

The wider world within which the majority of the African countries gained their independence during the late 1950s and 1960s demonstrated two apparently contradictory features. On the one hand, the Cold War between the communist and capitalist political systems was waged with grim determination by both sides and divided the world into two opposing camps. On the other hand, there was an upsurge of economic optimism which was common to the leading states on each side of the ideological divide. Experts of whatever economic persuasion – politicians, businesspeople, managers, economists, academics, civil servants – were firmly of the opinion that economic development, properly directed, could close the gap between rich and poor countries within a comparatively short time span. Prominent economists like Walter Rostow and Arthur Lewis wrote cheerfully of poor countries needing only brief injections of outside capital and technology before achieving economic 'takeoff', when they would cease to be mere suppliers of primary produce and learn to process their own commodities. Controlled industrialisation was the aim and, from both ends of the political spectrum, it was presented as something that could be determined by government action.

It was an aim which the leaders of the new African nations were happy to embrace and, for a time, it appeared that they would not be disappointed. During the 1950s and 1960s, commodity prices were generally favourable for African producers, although there were big fluctuations in the prices of some products. The price of cocoa, for example, was low during many of the early years of Ghana's independence, and this contributed to the economic disaster of the Nkrumah regime. In general, however, the volume of exports from the countries of sub-Saharan Africa grew by 6 percent a year throughout the 1960s. After 1967, especially, commodity prices boomed, and since African governments derived most of their revenues by buying produce from farmers at one price and selling it on the world market at another, the higher commodity prices were reflected in buoyant revenues. Some of this newfound affluence was ploughed back into socially beneficial causes, such as education, health services, and small-scale agricultural improvements. During the 1960s, agricultural production increased at a rate of 2.7 percent per annum, which roughly matched the growth of population. It looked as though Africa would at all events be able to feed itself and gradually become self-supporting in other ways as well.

Education nearly everywhere developed rapidly, building on the foundations laid during the last years of colonial rule. In tropical Africa as a whole, primary-school enrolment increased from 36 to 65 percent during the first two decades of independence, and secondary school enrolment from 3 to 13 percent. Universities multiplied, and large amounts of aid money flowed in to provide them with attractive buildings and well-stocked libraries and laboratories. By the end of the 1960s, Nigeria alone possessed five universities, with a total student enrolment of more than 10,000. Because most graduates were destined for careers in secondary education, it looked as though this, the worst bottleneck in the educational system, would soon be a thing of the past. In Ghana, which had three universities serving a population only one-fifth that of Nigeria, primary- and middle-school education was, in principle, free and compulsory for all children between six and sixteen, and enrolment in all educational establishments reached 10 percent of the population as a whole as early as 1961. It was remarkable that in all the West African countries, most teaching at all levels was given in either English or French. This reflected the much deeper roots of western education in the coastal regions of this part of the continent. It meant that the West African elites were more cosmopolitan in outlook than their opposite numbers anywhere else, with the exception of South Africa. There was, indeed, a great difference in the pace of educational development between West Africa on the one hand and most of eastern and central Africa on the other. Whereas the larger West African countries mostly reached independence with some thousands of graduates, countries like Uganda and Kenya had only a few hundred. Tanzania at independence had only twelve graduates, while Zaire had none at all. In those parts of central Africa where independence was delayed by long liberation struggles, the mainspring of higher education had to develop among *émigrés* and exiles, of whom only a small proportion would ever return to work in their own countries. Here, the bottleneck in secondary education was seen at its worst.

During the early years of independence, considerable strides were made in the improvement of health services, ranging from the construction of large hospitals in the capital cities to primary health care clinics in the villages. Aid donors were particularly generous in helping to establish teaching hospitals, and much effort was put into improving health, diet, and hygiene at the local level, using the help of expatriate volunteers as well as enlisting the participation of local residents. Although the struggle against endemic disease, especially malaria, proved to be much more arduous than had been anticipated, some progress was made and infant mortality continued to be reduced, with the result that every African country experienced a massive acceleration of the already serious trend in population growth (see Chapter 21). Whereas in one sense this represented a great victory over disease, in another sense it brought the entire continent face to face with its greatest economic and social problems. It meant that, until childbearing habits adjusted themselves to the new levels of life expectancy, the young nations of Africa would have 'to run in order to stand still'.

In practice, however, the gravity of the population problem was not widely appreciated during the 1960s, or even later. During the colonial period, people had become so accustomed to thinking of Africa as an underpopulated continent that it was difficult for them to imagine that the pendulum could swing so far in the opposite direction in so short a time. It was widely assumed that the fertility rate would prove to be self-adjusting with only a comparatively brief time-lag. Meanwhile, the general answer to population growth would be found in industrialisation, which would absorb the surplus

rural population into productive employment in the towns. Industrialisation would enable primary produce to be processed locally,
and so would reduce the number of necessary imports. And the key
to successful industrialisation would be cheap power, for which the
great rivers of Africa were waiting to be harnessed. Hydroelectric
dams were thus the favoured development projects both of the last
years of colonial rule and the first decade of independence. In the
impressive multi-volume brochures prepared by the international
firms of engineering consultants, dams were presented as the very
cornerstones of modernisation, supplying electricity not only to industry but also to every African household. Above the dams, huge
man-made lakes would give rise to new fishing industries, which
would supply the protein deficiencies of African dietary systems. Industrial towns would grow up beside the new lakes, and all around
them great irrigation projects would give rise to a new and much-
needed kind of intensive agriculture. Hydroelectric schemes could
be made attractive to international donors. They were also cherished
by African politicians, who could present them as powerful symbols
of economic virility and national prestige. As demonstrated by the
'High Dam' project at Aswan in Upper Egypt, which passed without
much of a strain from American to Russian sponsorship in 1956, the
outside technology could be supplied from either eastern or western
sources, just as the resultant electric power could be turned either
to a capitalist or a socialist pattern of industrial development.

   Although embarked upon with such high hopes, most hydroelectric projects proved, in practice, both costly and disappoint-
ing. The Akasombo dam built across the Volta River in southern
Ghana, which was completed in 1965 just before the fall of Kwame
Nkrumah, was financed by the government and by loans from the
World Bank, the United States, and Britain. Its largest result was
to cripple the young country with foreign debt as the costs of construction soared far beyond the estimates. The aluminium-smelting
industry, which was supposed to be among the first fruits, failed to
develop owing to the poor quality of the local bauxite. Above the dam,
the 500-km-long (300 miles) lake was soon covered with aquatic vegetation, which prevented the emergence of the predicted inland fish-
eries. Because of the discouragement to private-sector investment
in Ghana's increasingly socialist state, the manufacturing industry

planned to grow up around the nearby port installations at Tema never really got off the ground, so that the vastly expensive hydro-electric plant was left functioning at a mere fraction of its potential.

It was much the same story with the gigantic Inga project to dam the Congo cataracts below Kinshasa, which was originally supposed to be capable of supplying half of the total power needs of the entire continent. The initial phase of the project, launched in 1972, was to light the capital city and its environs, to power an iron and steel complex in the river valley above Lake Malebo, and to supply most of the electricity needs of the Zairean copperbelt, including a vast new smelting plant in Shaba province, more than 1,800 km (1,100 miles) south of Kinshasa. The total cost – all of it borrowed – was well over $1 billion, and amounted to 20 percent of Zaire's foreign debt. This sum, according to some opponents of the scheme, could have paid the wages of the country's teachers and nurses for twenty years. In practice, however, construction was first of all limited and then frequently delayed. The steel plant seldom operated at more than 10 percent of its capacity, and employed only 1,000 workers instead of the 10,000 originally envisaged. What steel it did produce was of poor quality and cost three or four times as much as imported steel. Twenty years after its notional completion date, the copper refinery in Shaba had yet to begin production. Once again, debt mounted and more useful development was forgone. The giant hydroelectric projects at Kariba and Cabora Bassa on the Zambezi were better organised and financed, but both became prime targets for the insurrectionary movements fighting for the independence of Zimbabwe and Mozambique. The Kariba dam, which served both Zambia and Zimbabwe, was often threatened by the poor political relations between the two countries, and Cabora Bassa was constantly surrounded by guerrilla action which imperilled its distribution lines. Both projects reinforced the lesson to intending developers all over Africa, that large schemes required a degree of political stability which most African countries did not yet enjoy. The dictum that 'Small is beautiful' was to be the watchword for the 1970s and beyond.

Hydroelectric projects were not, of course, the only examples of mis-spending and mis-borrowing by the governments of the 1960s. Nearly every government wished to celebrate its independence by founding a national airline, using imported aircraft and a great many foreign employees to fly routes, many of which were quite uneconomic. Again, nearly all African countries spent far more than they could afford on arms and military equipment, much of it far beyond their means to service and control. Luxury hotels built by the public sector too often stood empty for lack of reliability in the basic services like electricity, water, and drainage. Presidential palaces, yachts, hunting lodges, aircraft, and armoured motorcars absorbed grotesque proportions of some national revenues. Nevertheless, during the 1960s, and for a year or two beyond, most African economies appeared to be improving, albeit very slowly. The small farmers of Africa, who still formed more than 90 percent of the continent's population, were maintaining and even increasing their production of food and export crops. The capital cities were growing rapidly, but the first generation of city-dwellers tended to maintain their family connections with the countryside, which gave them flexibility in the means of survival and provided the urban labour market with a plentiful supply of cheap labour.

In some African countries, such as Egypt, Morocco, and parts of Nigeria, industrial production had long preceded the colonial era. Again, in many African colonies, industrial processes had been initiated by African as well as by European and Asian entrepreneurs. Nearly all of this had been low-level industry – breweries, tanneries, cotton ginneries, cigarette and match factories, motor vehicle servicing, and maintenance. Political independence, by the removal of some colonial controls such as those on urban building standards, gave a boost to these kinds of small-scale industrial activities, especially those run by Africans. This was the case even in some countries with nominally socialist or Marxist economic policies. Much of this activity was so small-scale that it slipped unnoticed through the meshes both of legal controls and economic statistics, and so made up a vast informal sector of African economies. Most of these very small industries were concerned with the processing and distribution of food, drink, clothing, and household goods, as well as with construction and household repairs and with passenger and goods transport. At the upper end of the market, however, were businesses involving imports and exports, shipping, insurance, accountancy and banking, rural plantations, and city property, which during colonial times had been managed by expatriates working for foreign companies. During the early years of independence, most of these were reconstituted as local firms, with a majority of local directors and managers. These African businesspeople formed, together with their opposite numbers in the public sector, the nucleus of a largely new African middle class, upon which the health and progress of the new national economies largely depended.

The Years of Stagnation and Decline

The economic performance of African states varied greatly from one to another, but looking at the overall picture, it becomes clear that during the second and third decades of independence, the earlier modest growth in gross domestic product (GDP) per head of population first slowed to a halt and then began to decline. There were several reasons for this, of which the most important was certainly the steadily accelerating growth of population throughout the continent. As we have seen (in Chapter 21), this was not due to any increase in the fertility rate, but simply to the fact that every year saw an increase in the number of childbearing women, of whom the great majority expected – like their parents before them – to have five, six, or seven children in the course of their married lives. During the fifteen years between 1972 and 1987, the population of sub-Saharan Africa grew from about 275 million to about 450 million,[1] with a yet more striking increase in the proportion of those who were still too young to be producers. The World Bank's study of sub-Saharan Africa published in 1989 stated the position in the starkest terms: 'By 1987 this region of some 450 million people – more than double the number at independence – had a total gross domestic product...of nearly $135 billion, about that of Belgium, which has only 10 million inhabitants'.

An analysis by country of the 1987 figures for GDP shows that there were four countries – Libya, Algeria, Gabon, and South Africa – which stood in a class by themselves, with GDP between $2,000 and

[1] These figures, assembled by the World Bank, do not take into account the five North African countries – Morocco, Algeria, Tunisia, Libya, and Egypt – with a combined population of about 110 million in 1988. The estimated population for the whole continent in 1991 was 650 million.

$7,000. Libya and Gabon were countries with small populations and large reserves of oil. Algeria and South Africa, as former colonies of European mass settlement, had attracted significantly more investment at an earlier date than other African countries, and so enjoyed more broadly based economic infrastructures. After these four came a group of eleven relatively prosperous countries, with per capita GDP between $500 and $1,000. It comprised, first, the three North African countries of Egypt, Tunisia and Morocco, which, though fairly well industrialised, lacked oil or other mineral resources. It included, next, five of the Atlantic-facing countries – Senegal, Ivory Coast, Cameroon, the Congo Republic, and Angola – all with well-developed plantation industries combined with offshore oil. Finally, it included three southern African countries – Zimbabwe, Botswana, and Swaziland – which had gained economically from their proximity to South Africa.

A third group of countries, with GDP figures between $200 and $500, included several of the largest and politically most significant countries – Nigeria and Ghana, Sudan and Kenya, Uganda and Zambia. Nigeria, at the height of the oil boom around 1980, had briefly seen its GDP rise to more than $1,000: its subsequent fall to $370 had been due to falling oil revenues, accompanied by overspending and overborrowing during the good times. Ghana and Uganda had both come to independence as prosperous countries with well-developed commercial crops and considerable mineral resources: their subsequent economic failure was due to misgovernment and political instability. The Sudan was basically a poor and undeveloped country, which had suffered nearly thirty years of civil war: it owed its modest prosperity to the efficient development of irrigated commercial cropping of long-staple cotton in a tiny economic heartland adjacent to the capital. Kenya was not well endowed with minerals, but made the most of its well-watered highlands to produce tea and coffee, and of its more arid game parks and its sunlit beaches to promote a lucrative tourist industry. The case of Zambia illustrated the danger of dependence on a single resource – in this case, copper – which provided more than 90 percent of the country's foreign-exchange earnings. When the bottom fell out of the copper market in 1975, Zambia was overwhelmed by a series of economic crises. During the 1960s, it had grown its own food and often produced a surplus; through neglect of its farmers, it became by the 1980s an importer of food. For a time, the government continued, by external borrowing, to provide these imports and maintain the social services for its mushrooming urban areas on the copperbelt; but, foreign exchange soon ran out, manufacturing output fell, and heavy debt was incurred, amounting by 1987 to $600 for every Zambian citizen, against a GDP of $470.

Several smaller African countries belonged within the same third bracket of GDP figures, including Sierra Leone, Liberia, Mauritania, Mali, Niger, Bénin, Togo, the Central African Republic, Rwanda, Burundi, Somalia, and Lesotho. There was also a fourth group of extremely poor countries with GDP figures between $100 and $200, which was remarkable for including four of the largest and best-known African states – (1) Ethiopia, the former historic empire and more recently the seat of the Organisation of African Unity; (2) Tanzania, which had led the East African countries into independence, and which under the twenty-five-year presidency of Julius Nyerere had seemed to be the great laboratory of African socialism; (3) Zaire, which had been 'the model colony' of Belgium, richly endowed with minerals and with well-watered agricultural land; and (4) Mozambique, never a rich land, but commanding the seaports and the lines of communication to a vast and rich interior in South Africa, Zimbabwe, Malawi, and eastern Zambia, a country which had borne the main weight of the struggle against Portuguese colonialism, only to go on and destroy itself in fifteen years of civil strife. It is certain that by 1990, Somalia, too, would have fallen, and for the same reason, from the third bracket to the very bottom of the fourth.

It was in a continent already experiencing the social distress of economic crisis that the HIV/AIDS epidemic erupted during the early 1980s. At first it seemed to be confined to countries in central Africa from Zaire to Kenya south to Zambia, but rapidly spread north and south from there. By the end of the decade, it had become a pandemic stretching from the Sudanic zone all the way to South Africa. Initially, it was thought to be mainly an urban phenomenon. Figures available in the late 1980s showed that 8 percent of the population of Kinshasa had HIV/AIDS and that in Kampala the number of cases reported was doubling every six months. It soon became apparent, however, that vast rural areas were also affected, particularly those which had been overrun by undisciplined soldiery in times of civil strife, or which provided labour migrants to the mines. The HIV/AIDS pandemic had serious economic as well as social consequences. Young adults – the prime labour force – were the worst hit of all age groups. Their children became orphans and their parents were left to face old age and incapacity without their support – and this at a time when the revenues of governments were still far too slender for any kind of social security safety net to be within the bounds of possibility. By the early 1990s, it was still too early to do more than guess at the ultimate scale of the HIV/AIDS calamity for Africa or to make any useful comparison of its ravages alongside those inflicted by drought, famine, and civil war. However, it could perhaps be estimated that, even in a worst-case scenario, all these natural disasters together would be unlikely to reverse the more general trend of population growth in the continent as a whole.

It is clear that many of the most crucial economic problems of African countries during the critical years after 1972 stemmed from the sharp variations in the world price of oil. During the 1960s, and until 1972, oil had been priced at less than $2 a barrel. Even at that modest price, the discovery of oil in Libya in 1965 had been sufficient to turn one of the poorest African countries into one of the richest. Even at that price, Ojukwu had thought it worthwhile to attempt the secession of Biafra (see Chapter 21). But, in 1973, the oil-producing countries of the Middle East combined to form the Organisation of Petroleum Exporting Countries (OPEC) and, by cutting supplies, drove up the price to $12 a barrel in 1974, skyrocketing to $34 a barrel in 1981, at the height of the war between Iraq and Iran. The first consequence for African countries was obviously to divide still further the fortunes of the Haves and the Have-nots. For the Haves, it meant a sudden access of prosperity, sufficient in the case of Nigeria temporarily to triple the GDP of a large and populous country. For the Have-nots, however, the effect was to multiply by fifteen times or more the cost of their most essential import, for lack of which their transport systems and many other aspects of their economy would grind to a halt. In Tanzania, for example, oil, which had previously absorbed 10 percent of the country's export earnings, had by 1980 risen to 60 percent. In more concrete terms, where a ton of exported tea had bought 60 barrels of oil, it now bought only 4.5 barrels.

But this was not all. As fast as the OPEC countries invested the surplus from their hugely increased earnings in banks and finance houses throughout the developed world, so these institutions began to 'recycle' the funds by offering loans on relatively attractive terms to governments, including many Third World governments, which sought to alleviate their growing financial problems by borrowing. Between 1970 and 1980, the external debts of African countries rose from $6 billion to $38 billion. In 1988, the total had reached $134 billion, and it was still rising. By the end of the 1980s, Africa's debt was equal to its annual GDP and 3.5 times its earnings from exports. Debt services actually paid during the years 1985–8 amounted to 27 percent of export earnings, but this represented only three-fifths of the region's obligations. From 1980 onwards, only twelve sub-Saharan countries serviced their debts regularly. But, even so, figures have been produced which show that between 1982 and 1990, Africa paid out in debt services $217 billion against net resource inflows of $214 billion: these included all bilateral and multilateral development aid, investment, new loans, and export credits.

Clearly, not all of this mounting level of African debt was attributable to the recycling of enhanced oil profits, but for about ten years, from 1975 to 1985, the availability of such funds did much to postpone the day of reckoning when most African governments found themselves unable to borrow any more money on straightforward commercial terms. During this last decade of relatively easy borrowing, many of the structural weaknesses of African economies went uncorrected, and with results that became ever more debilitating. Most obvious among these weaknesses was the steadily rising cost of the public payroll. Nearly all governments failed to control the self-generating pressures for growth in their bureaucracies and their armed forces. Many civil service posts had become virtual sinecures, held in combination with other occupations in the private sector. Again, many military and police chiefs played upon the fears of politicians, who knew themselves to be increasingly unrepresentative, to build unnecessarily large and lavishly equipped armed forces to contain civil unrest rather than to protect their countries against external dangers. In socialist-oriented states, the directors of public corporations likewise failed to control their payrolls, leading to losses and claims for subsidies from the revenue. Less obvious, but

no less hurtful, was the manipulation by nearly all African governments of the exchange rates of their national currencies, which were
in general fixed at many times their real value in the market place.
This had the effect of making imports artificially cheap, including
the luxuries enjoyed by the elite, but also the imported foodstuffs
increasingly used by the ordinary citizens of the rapidly growing
capital cities. These imports, themselves often the result of farm
subsidies in the countries of origin, undercut the prices of locally
produced foods, which meant that African farmers, despite the pressures of increasing population, concentrated on subsistence crops
for their own consumption and grew less, rather than more, food for
the local market.

The artificial exchange rates were, of course, only sustainable with
the aid of strict exchange controls and licensing systems for both imports and exports, and these in their turn provided irresistible temp-
tations to those in power, from presidents and ministers at one end of
the scale to junior bureaucrats, such as customs officers, at the other.
The prevalence of this kind of corruption – 'the 10 percent rule', as it
was often called – was one of the major causes of indiscipline in the
public services. Finally, there was the steady progress of conspicuous
expenditure by many, if not most, African heads of state. Presidential palaces proliferated; retinues increased; presidential motorcades
grew longer, noisier, and more intimidating; fleets of buses carried
rent-a-crowd audiences to ululate at presidential speeches delivered
in huge new sports stadia. The venue to the annual summit confer-
ences of the OAU was much sought after by African leaders, and
lavish sums were spent in preparation for them. For the 1965 conference, Nkrumah had built a palace containing 60 luxury units and
a banqueting hall to seat 2,000, causing some of his disenchanted
countrymen to coin the slogan 'One man, one motor-bike'. But in
1977, President Omar Bongo of Gabon constructed a row of seafront
hotels in Libreville and a new palace for himself at a cost of $200 mil-
lion. Two years later, President Tolbert spent half of Liberia's annual
budget to host the OAU summit; whereas in 1980, President Siaka
Stevens went one better by spending two-thirds of Sierra Leone's
budget on the same cause. The most lavish spender of the 1980s,
however, was surely President Mobutu, who, at a time of severe

economic crisis in Zaire, spent more each year on the presidency than on the combined budgets for roads, hospitals, schools, and social services. In 1988, he admitted to a personal fortune of $55 million, but some claimed that the true figure was probably ten times higher. Mobutu spent vast sums on rebuilding his home village at Gbadolite on the Oubangi, where he constructed a magnificent country palace for his own use, with an airport large enough for the Concorde, which he often leased from Air France. He owned châteaux in France and Belgium and estates in Spain, Italy, Switzerland, and the Ivory Coast. In later years, he spent much of his time aboard a luxury yacht in the Congo River, which earned him the nickname of 'le voisin' ('the neighbour') among his increasingly disaffected and scornful compatriots.

The Hard Road to Recovery

Although the broad picture of economic disarray in African countries was well appreciated by the larger development agencies and, in particular, by officials of the World Bank and the International Monetary Fund (IMF), their advice, tendered with increasing urgency from about 1975 onwards, was resisted by most governments for as long as any alternative sources for renewed borrowing remained open. The government of Kenya was one of the first to accept a measure of surveillance by IMF representatives, who established an office in the country's Central Bank. A wider measure of surveillance was instituted in Zaire from 1978 with officials of the World Bank and the IMF installed in the Central Bank, the Audit Office, and the Ministry of Finance. From 1981, however, the favourite client of the IMF was Ghana, where Flight-Lieutenant Jerry Rawlings, aged thirty-four, had just seized power from the incompetent civilian government which he had himself inaugurated following his coup d'état in 1979. Ghana's economy was then at an extreme low ebb. Cocoa production had fallen from 560,000 tonnes in 1965 to 150,000 tonnes in 1981. The transport system had gravely deteriorated. The railways were almost at a standstill. Very little foreign currency was available for even the most essential imports, such as spare parts for agricultural and manufacturing machinery. The factories were operating at about a quarter of their capacity. There was even a shortage of power because the level of Lake Volta had been drastically reduced by drought. Rawlings went about a recovery programme with a determination and realism that his predecessors had lacked, accepting IMF aid, control, and conditions. The grossly overvalued currency was progressively devalued until by 1988, the cedi was worth only 2 percent of its nominal value in 1982. Inflation and budgetary deficits began to fall, the balance of trade improved, and the GDP rose. Helped by good weather, cocoa production doubled between 1983 and 1989. Gold and other mining production rose, and manufacturing also recovered. New generating equipment for the Akasombo dam restored power supplies. But these substantial economic gains were only achieved at a considerable social price, in high unemployment, reduced medical and social services, and cuts in educational expenditure. The government imposed a high sales tax in order to lower consumption of imported produce, which severely affected the living standards of city-dwellers. There were several attempted coups, student strikes, and much popular unrest. But, by the early 1990s, the economy was in a healthier condition than it had been since the early days of independence, and Rawlings, under IMF prompting, slowly edged Ghana toward a more democratic form of government.

Increasingly during the 1980s, the IMF found itself in the position of being the only available lender, and so it was able to adopt a firm policy of imposing conditions in exchange for its help. Moreover, as the Cold War drew to a close, it was able to mobilise the diplomatic support of all the main donor countries in persuading African governments to accept its prescribed remedies. Most applicants were henceforward required to follow the example of Ghana in undertaking a phased devaluation of their currencies, with the principal objective of restoring a proper balance between the prices of locally grown and imported foodstuffs. While this was very much in the interest of African farmers, it weighed heavily upon city-dwellers, who were much better able than the farmers to express their discontent. Thus, when President Kaunda, for example, turned to the IMF in 1985 to rescue Zambia from near collapse, one of the remedies prescribed by the Fund was the removal of the subsidy on maize meal.

This led to such violent riots in the copperbelt towns that the government broke off its relations with the IMF and restored the subsidy. By 1990, however, it was finally forced to return cap in hand, accept the remedies, and face further riots in consequence. Similarly, in Gabon, an austerity programme prescribed by the IMF in 1986 led stage by stage to serious riots in Libreville and Port Gentil. The most unfortunate initiator of such reforms was President Thomas Sankara of Burkina Faso, who so alienated the small but powerful class of bureaucrats and urban workers in his country that he was assassinated in a coup in 1987. Most of the IMF's clients, however, fared better than Sankara and, in the continent as a whole, GDP figures improved, if only slightly, after 1985. In its 1989 report, the World Bank heaped special praise for the improvement on the contribution of the small-scale private sector which had emerged in and around the burgeoning cities:

During the recent years of economic crisis, small firms in the informal sector have provided a growing share of jobs and output. Estimates indicate that these enterprises currently provide more than half of Africa's urban employment, and as much as one-fifth of GDP in many countries. Unregulated and unrecorded, the informal sector is home to small firms in agriculture, industry, trade, transport, finance and social services. It is not static, and not necessarily traditional in its techniques, but it undertakes innovation indicated by market forces. In the informal sector enterprises find a business environment that is competitive, free from unjustified regulatory restraints and well adapted to local resource endowments and demand.[2]

Coming at a time when so much else in the African scene was redolent only of gloom and disaster, there was much encouragement to be found in this judgement by the World Bank about the enterprise shown by African townspeople. For, if the most important fact about the African condition in 1990 was that population was doubling every twenty years, then the next most important fact was that the population of the cities was doubling every ten years. In 1990, one-quarter of all Africans lived in the towns, and it was anticipated that by the end of the century, the proportion would have risen to one-half. This might still leave a great many people living in rural areas – more,

---

[2] World Bank, *Sub-Saharan Africa: From Crisis to Sustainable Growth*, Washington, 1989, p. 10.

indeed, by the year 2010 than the entire population of the continent in 1990. Nevertheless, a new Africa was being born in the towns and in the countryside immediately adjacent to them. If in these key areas economic enterprise was beginning to be self-generating, then there was every hope that from there it would spread, along with improved local government, into the peripheral regions where the worst conditions of poverty and destitution were to be found.

TWENTY THREE. Into the Third Millennium

For Africa as a whole, the final decade of the twentieth century saw little to justify the heady hopes held by many well-wishers at the end of the 1980s. True, the collapse and dissolution of the Soviet Union and of its empire in Eastern Europe had provided the indispensable condition for a radical change of regime in South Africa, from a white minority government to a democracy based on universal suffrage. Elsewhere, however, the partial disengagement of the two world superpowers did little to stabilize the internal divisions within African countries. To the contrary, it often set the scene for a sharp increase in civil violence, both in countries or regions that had already experienced Cold War conflicts and in those that up till then had remained relatively peaceful.

The Ashes of the Cold War in Angola and the Horn of Africa

In Angola, Jonas Savimbi continued – and even intensified – his twenty years of conflict with the MPLA government in Luanda by buying sophisticated weaponry and equipment from a circle of willing suppliers, who delivered them by air direct to his military headquarters in the bush in exchange for the diamonds mined in his political enclave in the southern part of the country. The MPLA government, deprived now of its Cuban mercenaries and Russian weapons, had to rearm itself by spending most of the royalties which it was receiving from its offshore oilfields – revenues which might otherwise have helped to reconstruct a war-torn economy. The

Benguela railway, which had formerly provided the main outlet of the copper mines of southern Zaire and northern Zambia, and which was important for the revenues of all three countries, remained closed throughout the Angolan civil war. Only after Savimbi himself fell to an assassin's bullet early in 2002 was a ceasefire signed by his followers which gave hope of a lasting settlement. By this time, the death toll in the war had risen to some 3 million, with an approximately equal number of refugees forced to flee from their homes.

The Horn of Africa was another region in which violence, far from abating after the end of the Cold War, markedly increased. Here, the removal of the Cuban contingent from Ethiopia, coupled with the cessation of the massive Soviet arms shipments, released pent-up tensions both within that country and around its borders. The insurgency long conducted by the Eritrean and Tigrean liberation movements in Ethiopia soon triumphed over the military dictatorship of President Mengistu, who in 1991 fled into exile in Zimbabwe. His place was taken by the Tigrean leader, Meles Zenawi, who was able to establish his authority over the disparate peoples of the centre and south of the country, on the promise of a radical devolution of powers to ten regional authorities, but who was compelled, in 1993, to grant full independence to Eritrea. Sadly, relations between the two countries worsened to such an extent that, in 1998, Eritrea invaded a small slice of Ethiopian territory known as the Yirga triangle. The Ethiopians met force with force, and the resulting war is reckoned to have cost the lives of some 30,000 combatants before Eritrea finally accepted defeat in 1998. At the height of the fighting, Eritrea was spending a third of its gross domestic product on defence, a figure unparalleled elsewhere in the world.

Meanwhile, straddling Ethiopia's eastern frontier, the Somali nation – though still united in language and by the common practice of Islam – was splintering politically into a score or more of warlordships based on the clan systems of pastoral people, who were constantly shifting the grazing grounds of their animals. During the Cold War, the Mengistu regime had managed, with Soviet support, to control the Somali inhabitants of the Ogaden province in its eastern lowlands, while the majority of Somali living in their own country paid some kind of respect to the feeble bureaucracies inherited from the former colonial rulers at Mogadishu and a few other coastal

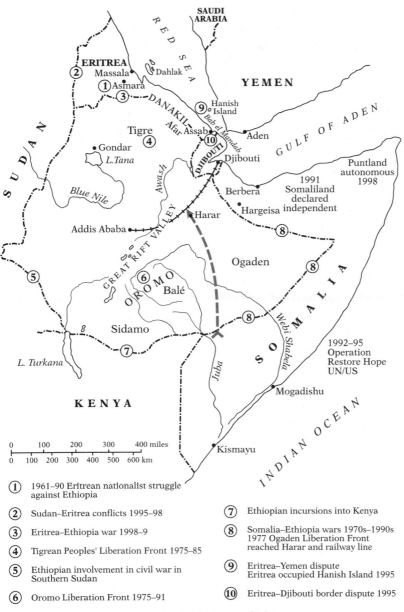

31. Conflicts in the Horn of Africa.

1. 1961–90 Eritrean nationalist struggle against Ethiopia

2. Sudan–Eritrea conflicts 1995–98

3. Eritrea–Ethiopia war 1998–9

4. Tigrean Peoples' Liberation Front 1975–85

5. Ethiopian involvement in civil war in Southern Sudan

6. Oromo Liberation Front 1975–91

7. Ethiopian incursions into Kenya

8. Somalia–Ethiopia wars 1970s–1990s 1977 Ogaden Liberation Front reached Harar and railway line

9. Eritrea–Yemen dispute Eritrea occupied Hanish Island 1995

10. Eritrea–Djibouti border dispute 1995

towns. These had been dominated through most of the first twenty years of Somali independence by President Siad Barre, who progressively became more dictatorial, especially after receiving recognition and economic and military aid from the United States, following the Soviet assumption of influence in Ethiopia. With the departure of Mengistu, American interest in the region reverted to Ethiopia, and Barre lost much of his prestige. He fled from Mogadishu in 1991 and, the following year, went into exile in Kenya. Barre's departure left the pastoral warlords to vie with each other for control of the coastal towns and of the powerless, sedentary cultivators living between the Webi Shebele and Juba valleys in the far south of the country. The northern part of Somalia – the land of the old British Protectorate – broke away and was declared independent as Somaliland and, in 1992, Muhamed Egal, one of the founders of united Somalia in 1960, was elected president of the breakaway state.

Later in 1992, a calamitous drought struck not only Somalia, but also neighbouring parts of Ethiopia, Kenya, and the southern Sudan. The UN and other western relief agencies struggled to bring food and basic medical aid to a starving and demoralised people. A multinational task force, led by the United States in the wake of its victory in the first Gulf War, landed at Mogadishu in December 1992 in an attempt to stop the fighting between rival warlords and ensure that the donated food reached those for whom it was intended. This massive foreign intervention, which at its peak numbered 31,000 troops – more than two-thirds of them Americans – merely added fuel to the fire of Somali inter-clan politics. The Mogadishu warlords battled to control the distribution of food themselves and to direct it to their own supporters. The multinational troops were caught up in major urban battles, in one of which eighteen Americans were killed. Television viewers back in America saw the dead bodies being dragged through the streets of Mogadishu. President Clinton, who had just been elected to office, promptly ordered the withdrawal of most of the U.S. contingent and, by the end of 1994, the greater part of the UN forces had followed their example. The cost of the UN mission to Somalia finally reached $1.6 billion, and its failure had far-reaching consequences in the reluctance of the United States to participate in any further African conflicts. It was no less a setback for the United Nations, which, with its meagre resources and constantly escalating responsibilities, could no longer risk military involvement in the more dangerous cases requiring its intervention. After the U.S./UN retreat, Somalia, including towns such as Mogadishu and Kismayu, was split up among some twenty-six warlords, conflicts among whom continued well into the new century. More peaceful economic activity picked up, most notably in the livestock trade. In 1998, Saudi authorities lifted the ban on Somali livestock imposed because of an outbreak of rinderpest, which had an immediate impact on the economy of the north-western regions, with the first shipment of 9,000 animals leaving the port of Berbera in Somaliland in May 1999. The south of Somalia slowly recovered from the 1997 floods of the Juba and Shebelle Rivers, which had devastated the surrounding farmlands. The new millennium seemed to bring some hope to the Somali people. Public order reemerged from the grassroots with what has been termed 'bottom-up' local administrations and, thus, even in a largely stateless society, it was possible for economic and social regeneration to take place despite the anarchy of militia politics.

The Tragedy of Rwanda and Congo

The most widespread and frightful of all the violent episodes which afflicted Africa during the last decade of the twentieth century were those which occurred in Rwanda, Burundi, and eastern Zaire. In Rwanda, this took the form of carefully prepared genocide by a hardcore of militant Hutu on their Tutsi neighbours and fellow countrymen. This was not, as in Somalia and Liberia/Sierra Leone, the internecine fighting of warlords. Rather, it was a sudden explosion of the centuries-old rivalry between Tutsi cattle owners and Hutu agricultural peasants for the control and use of land in one of the healthiest and, therefore, most densely populated corners of the continent. Hutu and Tutsi – who made up some 15 percent of the population in both countries – spoke the same language and shared the same religious and cultural traditions: distinctions between the two groups were those of class or caste rather than of ethnicity. In colonial times, it was advantageous for the Belgian administrators to reinforce the superior social and political position of the Tutsi, but even before independence, the Hutu had driven large numbers of

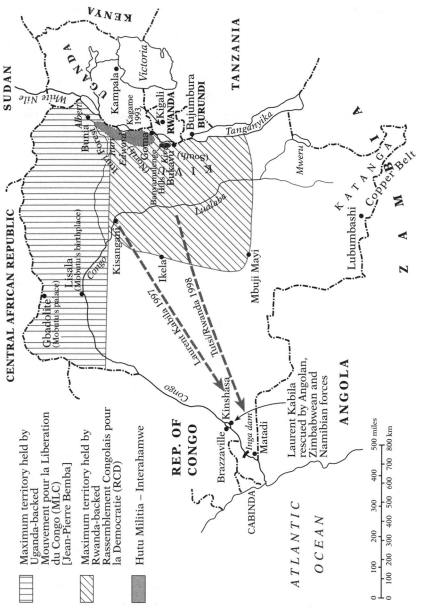

Legend:

Maximum territory held by Uganda-backed Mouvement pour la Liberation du Congo (MLC) [Jean-Pierre Bemba]

Maximum territory held by Rwanda-backed Rassemblement Congolais pour la Democratie (RCD)

Hutu Militia – Interahamwe

32. Crises in Rwanda and Congo (Zaire).

344

Tutsi from disputed territory, most of whom had taken refuge in the neighbouring districts of southern Uganda. By the early 1970s, the violence had spread to Burundi where, in 1988, a Tutsi-led government turned upon the Hutu in an attempt to eliminate all the better educated among them who might be capable of forming an alternative administration. By the end of 1993, hundreds of thousands of Hutu survivors had fled to Rwanda, Zaire, and Tanzania, while many others were living in refugee camps around the borders of their own country. Meanwhile, in Rwanda, a Hutu government had since 1990 been facing an insurgency movement launched by Tutsi refugees in Uganda led by Major-General Paul Kagame – himself a child of Tutsi refugees of the 1960s – who had served in Museveni's National Resistance Army, becoming deputy head of military intelligence. Kagame's Rwanda Patriotic Front (RPF) was already achieving considerable success in the eastern part of the country.

In April 1994, the presidents and members of the governments of both countries attended a regional conference in Dar es Salaam in an attempt to implement earlier peace accords for Rwanda. The Burundi president was persuaded to return home with his Rwandan counterpart in the latter's aircraft. The plane was shot down by a ground-to-air missile as it was approaching Kigali airport, and all on board were killed. Although it was never determined who the perpetrators were, it was rumoured that they could have been members of the Rwandan army, acting deliberately to inflame inter-communal conflicts. Following this disaster, units of the presidential militias responded by launching a pogrom against the Tutsi population of the country. Hutu citizens were incited by the virulent anti-Tutsi broadcasts emanating from a station calling itself Free Radio–Television of the Thousand Hills. Commonly known as the Hate Radio, its noisy pop-style transmissions directed poor Hutu peasants and the young urban unemployed to take up their reaping knives and incendiary torches and slaughter their Tutsi neighbours. So many did so that between April and July 1994, around 800,000 Tutsi may have been killed, while hundreds of thousands more fled their homes in the hope of saving their lives. Kagame's insurgents from Uganda took advantage of the prevailing chaos to accelerate their campaign by seizing the capital, Kigali, before moving into the southern and western parts of the country.

As a consequence, between 1 million and 2 million Hutu, shep-
herded by their own militia and the soldiers of their defeated army,
moved en masse into the neighbouring Kivu province of Zaire,
where they established themselves in makeshift encampments –
unlit, undrained, and entirely dependent on outside help for food
and even drinking water. Local resources were completely inadequate to deal with a human influx of this magnitude, and tens of
thousands died of disease or starvation before international relief
could be brought to them. It has been estimated that by the end of
that July 1994, no more than a third of the 7.5 million people who
had inhabited Rwanda three months earlier were still alive and re-
siding within its borders. The response of the outside world – and in
particular America and Europe, as well as the UN – both to the genocide and to the plight of the refugees, was largely one of helplessness.
Most neighbouring African states did little to help, and what intervention there was merely made matters worse. By the time the UN
finally launched relief operations, it was a case of too little, too late.
The newly established government of Kagame, although it claimed
to be impartial between the two communities, in practice did little to encourage the refugees to return. Those who attempted to do
so found their land and property redesignated for Tutsi occupation,
and often faced arrest or ill-treatment by the military or the police.
Most refugees, therefore, remained in eastern Zaire under the political influence of the hard-line Hutu militias, who had organized the
massacres and were now engaged in preparing a forceful return, an-
tagonising their Zairean hosts and the international aid workers sent
to help them. Naturally, the Kagame government regarded their presence so close to the frontier as a constant threat, and this feeling was
shared by the Tutsi and another Tutsi-like people called Banyamulenge living in the grassland strip of eastern Zaire between the forest
and Lake Kivu. Both groups believed that the Hutu refugees should
be driven farther away from the frontier, into the barely habitable
Ituri forest to the west. In the absence of cooperation by the government of Zaire, they felt entitled to take preemptive action themselves
to achieve this objective.

The main consequence of this situation was to demonstrate the
utter inability of President Mobutu's government in Kinshasa to defend any of its frontier regions from incursions by neighbouring

countries. Soon Rwandan troops, strengthened by army units from Uganda, were occupying all of the open country east of the forest and chasing Hutu refugees retreating up the two forest roads leading to Kisangani, some 800 km (500 miles) into Zairean territory. Simultaneously, minor warlords from the Sudan were infiltrating the country to the north of the forest, while the Banyamulenge in the south of Kivu province had found a gifted war leader in the person of Laurent Kabila, a former aide to Patrice Lumumba and a lieutenant in the Maoist insurrection of Christopher Gbenye, who had been operating as a warlord in the mountains to the west of Lake Tanganyika since 1964. Kabila's present ambition was to overthrow the increasingly unpopular regime of President Mobutu. To that end, early in 1997 he launched a brilliantly successful insurgency by moving his numerically insignificant army rapidly from one little airport town to the next, recruiting supporters as it went, until in May it reached the neighbourhood of Kinshasa. By this time, Kabila's forces had been joined by contingents from the armies of Rwanda, Uganda, Burundi, and Angola. Already a sick man, Mobutu fled with his family, first to Togo and then to Morocco, where he died a few weeks later as the guest of King Hassan. Kabila joined his victorious forces in Kinshasa and, with the approval of his Rwandan and Ugandan supporters, declared himself president of what was to be known henceforward as the Democratic Republic of Congo (Congo DR).

As president, Kabila lacked the natural charisma and political flair of Mobutu Sese Seko, and soon proved himself even less adept than his predecessor at providing beneficial rule to the huge country. Before long, Kabila turned on his Banyamulenge and Rwandan sponsors by blocking the expansion of their influence in the eastern part of the country and by declaring himself in sympathy with the Hutu rebels there. In response, the Rwandans and Ugandans in 1999 launched a new insurgency movement against him, quickly conquering most of the eastern provinces and sending troops by air to capture Congo's Atlantic ports and the power station at the Inga dam. Kabila, for his part, turned to the Angolan, Namibian, and Zimbabwean governments for troops to rescue his tottering regime. Sudan also supported him and, so too, briefly, did Chad. Thus, the Congo DR became the scene of a full-scale African war, involving the armies of six foreign states. Kabila's new allies set about reconquering the

west and the south, while the Rwandans and Ugandans extended
their control over the east and south-east. But all alike participated
in plundering the riches of the Congolese lands. Angola was interested in the offshore oil of the Congo estuary; Rwanda and Uganda
in the diamonds and coltan, ivory, and timber of the north-eastern
mountains; Zimbabwe in the copper and agricultural produce of the
south.

Early in 2001, Laurent Kabila was shot dead by a bodyguard, and
his twenty-nine-year-old-son Joseph was proclaimed president, thus
becoming the world's youngest head of the world's most chaotic state.
Father and son, however, could hardly have been less alike – Laurent
the warmonger, lazy, corrupt, drunken, polygynous; Joseph thought-
ful, industrious, sober, monogamous, surprising many by his moderation and good sense. He gradually replaced his father's sycophants
and cronies with career administrators, while western diplomats reported a willingness to take advice from outsiders. The son's economic reforms were rewarded by a promise from the World Bank
of a loan of $400 million. Slowly, the chaotic military situation in-
side the Congo clarified in favour of Joseph Kabila, so much so that
he was able to dispense with all the foreign armies that had come
to his assistance, except for his bodyguard of Zimbabweans. On the
political side, the South African government of Thabo Mbeki took
the initiative as mediator and, between July 2002 and the end of
the year, Rwanda and Uganda undertook to evacuate their forces
from the eastern Congo, whereas Kabila agreed to form an interim
government which would include the leaders of the various rebel
groups. Progress toward bringing the conflict to a conclusion was to
be monitored by an independent panel of UN and Southern African
personnel. Unfortunately, these accords soon began to unravel. Both
Uganda and Rwanda continued to arm rival militias, and both countries were ready to re-invade the north-eastern lands of the war-torn
Congo. By April 2003, when yet another peace deal was signed between the Congo government and the main rebel groups, six or seven
warlords' fiefdoms stretched from Ugandan-occupied Bunia in the
north to Rwandan-controlled Bukavu in the centre. When Ugandan
forces withdrew from Bunia in May 2003, rivalries between Hema
and Lendu groups over land in the heavily forested Ituri province
soon led to a complete breakdown of law and order. A French-led

force was assembled in an attempt to keep the warring factions apart. Peace seemed as far off as ever. Meanwhile, a leading aid agency calculated that 4.7 million people had died as a direct result of the civil war. If this figure is close to accurate, the war in the Congo claimed more lives than any other conflict since the Second World War.

Warlords in Liberia and Sierra Leone

Yet another region of the continent which suffered greatly from internal conflict during the 1990s was the area straddling the borderlands between Liberia and Sierra Leone. The violence started in 1989 in Liberia, when the country was invaded by Charles Taylor, a former high official in the Liberian government who had fled abroad following a charge of serious fraud. During his time as an outlaw, Taylor had become the political spokesman for a group of fellow exiles scattered through several neighbouring countries, known as the National Patriotic Front for Liberia (NPFL). The military leader of the NPFL was a former officer in the Liberian army, Prince Johnson, who recruited a rabble of unemployed youngsters – boys and girls, many of them orphans – whom he turned into a brutally effective force. Some 10,000 strong, these 'children' were regularly drugged with crack cocaine and trained in terrorist techniques of killing, mutilation, rape, and incendiarism. Starting from bases in the northwest of the country, the rebels moved onto Monrovia in July 1990, but Johnson's forces reached the capital before Taylor and gained control of most of the city. At this point, the Economic Community of West African States (ECOWAS) dispatched a peacekeeping force made up of troops from anglophone countries, with Nigerians well in the lead. Within weeks of their arrival, Johnson abducted President Doe from under their noses, took him to his camp, and there videotaped his torture and execution. Thus disgraced by his military colleague, Taylor's bid for the presidency inevitably failed, but he remained in control of key areas of the interior. Here, he set up a warlord economy based on the extraction of diamonds, timber, rubber, and iron ore, yielding him an income of some $200–250 million a year. During the next five dreadful years, Liberia was torn apart by warring factions. Some 60,000 armed youngsters ravaged the

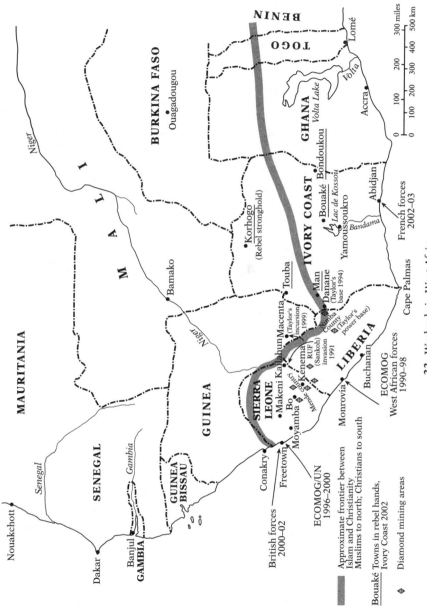

33. Warlords in West Africa.

countryside, scattering hundreds of thousands of terrified refugees into Sierra Leone, Guinea, and Burkino Faso. In Liberia, all factions were involved in shady commercial transactions, including members of the peacekeeping force. Ceasefires and disarmaments brokered by ECOWAS were, however, gradually made to stick, so that by 1997 it was possible to hold national elections. Charles Taylor received three-quarters of the vote, thus finally achieving the presidency by peaceful means after his earlier attempts to seize it by violence had failed. Unfortunately for the ruined country, however, resistance to the Taylor government soon led to a renewal of civil strife. By 2003, large parts of Liberia were once again in rebel hands, and violence spread over into the neighbouring Ivory Coast, itself the scene of similar conflicts.

During the early stages of the Liberian civil war, the Sierra Leonean president Joseph Momoh and his successor Valentine Strasser, both military men, had strongly supported the efforts of the ECOWAS peacekeepers to maintain a lawful government in Monrovia. It was thus very much in Taylor's interests to foster a similar insurgency in Sierra Leone, as it was also to get a hold over the diamond-bearing areas in that country which were much more productive than those in Liberia. A Sierra Leonean movement, known as the Revolutionary United Front (RUF), was therefore recruited, trained, and armed under Taylor's patronage in the Liberian hinterland. It was led by Foday Sankoh, a former corporal in the Sierra Leone army. The nucleus of the RUF invaded Sierra Leone in March 1991, and built up its numbers by conscripting youngsters, many of whom were committed to the movement by being made to take part in acts of terrorism against locals who opposed the Front. The practice of mutilation, in particular, sent uncompromising messages to supporters of the lawful government in Freetown. By 1994, the RUF was in control of most of the diamond mines, the product of which was exported in its raw state through Taylor's hinterland camps in Liberia, and from there by air to buyers, many of them in Israel. The profits of the trade enabled Sankoh to extend his campaigns up to the outskirts of Freetown. As happened previously in Liberia, a mainly Nigerian peace-keeping force was sent by ECOWAS, which sustained heavy casualties. The UN, too, sent in an international contingent, which was no more successful. At this point, when Sierra Leone appeared to be on the edge of total breakdown, Britain independently dispatched 1,000 crack troops to defend the capital, while a naval force stood offshore. Thus reinforced, the peace-keepers gradually gained ground, and the British-trained government forces began to disarm the rebels. In due course, Sankoh was captured and held for trial on war crimes. By the beginning of 2002, the civil war appeared to be over. Many of the rebel soldiers had been successfully reintegrated into the government forces and, in May 2002, the lawful president, Ahmad Kabbah, was re-elected by a large majority of the voters. The cost of the rebellion in human lives may never be counted, but it is thought that at its height, more than a third of the population of Sierra Leone had fled into Guinea and other neighbouring countries.

Muslim North Africa

During the 1990s, the Maghrib countries of North-West Africa – together with Libya, Egypt, and the Sudan – were able to be much firmer than many sub-Saharan states in resisting internal and external demands for political and social change and economic reform. The international and social relations of these Arabic-speaking Muslim countries formed part of a nexus embracing the Middle East as well as the Islamic areas south of the Sahara. The strength of these social and religious bonds is well illustrated by the huge growth in the numbers of people making the pilgrimage to Mecca and Medina from the entire compass of Islamic lands stretching from Morocco to Indonesia. In the early twentieth century, about 70,000 pilgrims made the hazardous journey to the holy cities each year. Thanks to cheap air travel, by the 1990s religious tourism was bringing an estimated 1.3 million foreign pilgrims a year to Saudi Arabia's holy cities, in addition to the 1.4 million coming from within the country itself. In Mecca, on the Mountain of Umar, developers were planning to clear thousands of old buildings to make way for high-rise towers of hotels and apartments of twenty to forty floors, to house the more prosperous pilgrims, and the traditional monthlong Hajj in Ramadan was being increasingly extended to include the months on each side of it. No doubt, only a handful of these pious pilgrims would return home from the Hajj fired by Islamic militancy, but nearly all would find their sense of the universal brotherhood of Islam strengthened by the experience. Nevertheless, from whatever source, all the North African lands were powerfully affected by the growth of radical Islam as both a political and religious movement. In various forms, it posed a threat to King Hassan of Morocco, to the autocratic government of Tunisia, and to President Mubarak of Egypt. In Algeria, it caused a festering civil war. Moreover, young Muslim volunteers from the North African countries had contributed powerfully to the forces of the Taliban resistance to the Soviet occupation of Afghanistan in the 1980s and when, following the Soviet retreat, their services were no longer required there, many returned home during the 1990s and greatly enhanced the military skills available to revolutionary movements in all of these lands.

The most tragic conflict between an established regime and the new surge of Islamic radicalism occurred in Algeria, where the government had been attempting since the 1980s to liberalise the socialist edifice established by Ben Bella and his successors during the previous three decades (see Chapter 17). In 1988, a 'war on bureaucracy' was declared to reform one of the largest and most all-pervasive governmental machines in Africa. But much to the alarm of the old-time leadership, the militant Islamic Salvation Front (ISF) narrowly won the first round of a general election held in 1991. The army and government apparatchiks moved swiftly to take control by cancelling the second round of the election and by formally dissolving the ISF. Thousands of militants were interned in camps in the Algerian Sahara, and mosques were placed under surveillance. The regime acted more from motives of self-preservation by an elite of generals, party bosses, and influential businessmen than from any real concern for democracy. Their coup ushered in a period of mounting unrest, culminating in an outright civil war, which by the end of the 1990s had claimed the lives of more than 80,000 Algerian civilians. In 1999, Abdelaziz Bouteflika became president and remained so after winning the 2002 election, which marked the return of a parliamentary majority for the FLN heroes of the struggle against France in the 1950s. But, by the turn of the new millennium, most Algerians had been so alienated by the manipulative nature of politics in their country as to boycott the elections. The most alienated group of all were the Berbers of Kabylia, who made up nearly a third of the population. Soon, what had started as a movement demanding

minority rights for the Berbers had developed into an outright insurrection. Meanwhile, sporadic radical Islamist violence continued,
some of it exported to France and elsewhere in Europe. In the aftermath of 11 September 2001, President Bouteflika was able to provide
the Americans with a list of several hundred extremists believed by
his intelligence service to have links with al-Qaeda.

Although seemingly less violent, a basically similar situation prevailed in the other two countries of the Maghrib. In Morocco, King
Hassan maintained his tight control of the political scene throughout
the 1990s, ruling the country through a narrow clique of courtiers
and administrative officials, still known by their pre-colonial designation as the Makhzen (al-makhzan), and concentrating his own
energies on building up a huge personal fortune, including a fifth of
the arable land, control of phosphate mining, and the expropriated
holdings of the former French settlers. Hassan's foreign policy cen-
tered on the incorporation of the Western Sahara, with its known
deposits of phosphates and its promise of offshore oil (see Chapter
17). After elections held in 1998, Hassan appointed the leader of the
opposition socialist party as prime minister. His son Muhammed VI,
who succeeded him in 1999, belonged to a more westernised generation brought up in a computer-literate age. He projected the image
of a modern, popular, jet-setting Muslim ruler, and promised greater
democratic participation in his country's politics and greater freedom of the press. Like Tunisia, Morocco's economy benefited from
a thriving tourist industry. But the Makhzen remained firmly entrenched and, in practice, dominated the scene. The revelation in
2002 by the Moroccan intelligence service of alleged plans by al-
Qaeda activists to blow up American and British warships passing
through the Straits of Gibraltar was widely seen as an acknowledgement for American support for Morocco's position over the Western
Sahara during the previous decade.

Meanwhile, Tunisia's president since independence in 1956, Habib
Bourguiba, was examined in 1987 by a panel of doctors called in by
his cabinet, who declared him too ill and senile to continue in office. His place was taken by the prime minister, Zine al-Abidine Ben
Ali, who embarked on a series of seemingly liberal and democratic
reforms. Tunisia developed its tourist industry and, by doing so, became one of the wealthiest countries in Africa. But, before long, Ben

Ali became much more dictatorial, banning all but a handful of tame opposition parties, relentlessly harassing human-rights activists, and violently cracking down on Islamic militants. In 2002, he contrived a referendum amending the constitution to allow him up to twelve more years in office and judicial impunity for life.

Egypt, to a much greater extent than the other North African countries, had more than an African role to play upon the world stage. Its population of 60 million was the largest of any Arabic-speaking country and, in cultural matters, it was still the leader. Whereas the rest of the Arab world might respect Saudi Arabia for its wealth, military power, and religious clout, it read Egyptian newspapers and books and listened to Egyptian broadcasting. Egypt, in fact, had a larger educated middle class than any other Arab country and, as a result, leaned toward liberalism in religious and political affairs. Indeed, President Husni Mubarak ushered in his long rule, when he succeeded Anwar Sadat upon the latter's assassination by militant Islamist soldiers in 1981, with promises of both political and economic liberalism. But, in the face of the growing opposition from militant groups such as the Gamaat Islamiya (Islamic Associations) and Al-Jihad, Mubarak reverted to the heavy-handed authoritarian rule of his predecessors. The militants turned increasingly to violence, not only against the state and opponents, but also against tourists, this reaching its climax with the massacre of sixty people at Luxor in 1997. Only by the end of the 1990s had Mubarak largely won the war waged on the Egyptian state by the Islamists. On the other hand, the government's policy of privatising and modernizing the economy led to the emergence of a new class of professionals and entrepreneurs, whose presence changed the Egyptian middle class more radically in the space of ten years than anything else had done in the thirty years since Nasser. The social and economic interests of this devout middle class tended to prevail over its ideological inclinations. This great shift in Egyptian society, which involved a depoliticisation of Islam, can be gauged by the springing up of new kinds of religious leaders, employing the media techniques of American televangelists. One such, Amr Khaled, was a Cairo accountant turned star televangelist. His message was inclusive and comforting rather than patronising and rough, his style coaxing rather than hectoring. The veil was to be worn, he maintained, not from fear of hellfire, but because God would love you better if you did. Khaled drew thousands of fans, most of them women, to weekly sessions at a mosque in a remote Cairo suburb, while his television show, broadcast throughout the Arab world on an Islamic satellite channel and subtitled in English, brought studio audiences to tears. But, with the mounting international tensions that ushered in the dawn of the new millennium, such urbane manifestations of religion would be sorely tried by the perception of Islam under threat from Western nations bent on avenging the terrorist attacks of 11 September 2001.

Straddling uncomfortably the landscapes of Muslim North Africa and Christian or animist sub-Saharan Africa, the tone and actions of the government of Sudan became more strident as the century wore to a close. In 1989, a military coup led by General Omar al-Bashir overthrew the government of Sadiq al-Mahdi. It soon became apparent that the real power behind the new regime was the charismatic Hasan al-Turabi and his National Islamic Front, which represented a long process of infiltration by the Islamist intelligentsia of the entire state apparatus, army, and financial system. Sudan became the first state in Africa to embrace Islamic militancy, and its relations with western countries – and with African countries that were not predominantly Muslim – suffered accordingly. Fleeing from harassment by the Saudi government, Osama bin Laden took refuge in Sudan in 1991 and became so prominent in jihadist activities that he was expelled in 1995, whereupon he moved to Afghanistan. Sudan openly supported Iraq in the Gulf War of 1991–2 and, when in 1998 the U.S. embassies in Nairobi and Dar es Salaam were attacked by terrorists, America retaliated against alleged Sudanese involvement by obliterating a pharmaceutical factory near Khartoum with cruise missiles. The influence of al-Turabi's National Islamic Front persuaded the government to reintroduce Shari'a law in 1991; although the punishment articles were not applicable to the three Southern regions, the intention was clear enough.

The interminable civil war became even more bitter and divisive following the discovery and exploitation of oil in the contested border region between north and south in Bahr al-Ghazal province. The presence of oil in commercial quantities had been confirmed in 1981, but the troubles in the south delayed full-scale production until the late1990s. The Sudan People's Liberation Army (SPLA) and the other

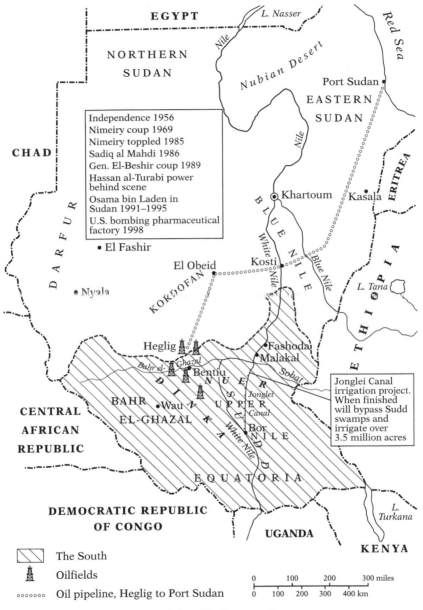

EGYPT

L. Nasser

Red Sea

NORTHERN
SUDAN

Nubian Desert

Port Sudan

EASTERN
SUDAN

CHAD

Nile

ERITREA

Independence 1956
Nimeiry coup 1969
Nimeiry toppled 1985
Sadiq al Mahdi 1986
Gen. El-Beshir coup 1989
Hassan al-Turabi power
behind scene
Osama bin Laden in
Sudan 1991–1995
U.S. bombing pharmaceutical
factory 1998

Khartoum   Kasala

BLUE NILE

DARFUR

• El Fashir

El Obeid   Kosti

White Nile

Blue Nile

ETHIOPIA

L. Tana

• Nyala

KORDOFAN

Heglig

Fashoda
Malakal

Bahr-el-Ghazal   Bentiu

NUER

Sobat

Jonglei
Canal

Jonglei Canal
irrigation project.
When finished
will bypass Sudd
swamps and
irrigate over
3.5 million acres

DINKA

UPPER

CENTRAL
AFRICAN
REPUBLIC

BAHR   • Wau
EL-GHAZAL

White Nile

NILE

Bor

EQUATORIA

DEMOCRATIC REPUBLIC
OF CONGO

L.
Turkana

UGANDA

KENYA

   The South

Oilfields

0   100   200   300 miles

○○○○○○○ Oil pipeline, Heglig to Port Sudan   0   100   200   300   400 km

34. Sudan: North vs. South.

factions in the south naturally wanted to include the oilfields in any future separate region; the regime was equally determined to preserve Sudanese unity. The construction of a pipeline to the Red Sea coast occasioned more conflicts. The government resorted to their usual savage means in their attempts to pacify the oil-bearing region, again arming the Baqqara and other nomadic groups, and encouraging them to attack the lands of the sedentary farmers. The SPLA split into two mutually hostile groups – the parent, mainly Dinka, faction under John Garang still fighting for independence, while the Nuer under Riek Machar entered into deals with the Khartoum regime. Once the oil began flowing in 1999, the government was able to more than double its military budget. Although the Khartoum regime exercised an economic stranglehold over the South, the foreign oil companies required a contented southern workforce, preferably English- rather than Arabic-speaking. Thus, the logic of the situation at the start of the new millennium was that, while the Sudan would remain one country, the Khartoum government would need to desist from its efforts to Islamise and Arabise the South and to allow it a large measure of autonomy in its internal affairs. Attempts to broker peace agreements between the two sides came and went, but one drawn up in 2002 in Nairobi appeared more likely to succeed. By then, the civil war had lasted on and off for four decades and had cost the southerners inestimable numbers of dead and maimed, as well as immeasurable disruption to the economic and social fabric of their land.

The wild card among the Muslim states of northern Africa during the 1990s continued to be the Libya of Muammar Gadhafi. Whereas during the 1980s, Gadhafi had devoted his attention to the Arab-Israeli conflict, accepting Palestinian migrants to Libya and providing moral and material support for anti-American terrorism throughout the world, he now turned to developing closer economic relations with Italy and extending his political and religious outreach to Africa south of the Sahara. UN sanctions on foreign companies investing in Libya following the Lockerbie affair did not prevent the Italian energy conglomerate AGIP from signing a contract for the annual supply of 8 billion cubic metres of natural gas, involving the construction of an undersea pipeline between the two countries. And, in 1999, Libyan financial institutions acquired an 8-percent share of the refinanced *Banco di Roma*. Gadhafi's interventions in sub-Saharan affairs had begun as early as his support for Idi Amin in Uganda (see Chapter 21), and he had long been active in supporting the Muslim north of Chad against the government of the Christian and animist south. In the early 1990s, Gadhafi was deeply involved in the supply of arms to the insurgent warlords in Liberia and Sierra Leone. He was forging links much farther south by the late 1990s. In 1998, the state-owned oil company Tamoil, acting in defiance of UN sanctions, began to supply an increasingly cash-strapped Zimbabwe with oil in exchange for the transfer of equity shares in the pipeline linking Zimbabwe with the seaport of Beira in Mozambique. Other assets transferred to Tamoil included controlling interests in Zimbabwean banks and tourist organisations.

Soon, Gadhafi's interests in Zimbabwe extended into South Africa. In 1999, Nelson Mandela was helpful in mediating a settlement of the UN sanctions on trade with Libya, and was rewarded by an invitation to South African companies to start exploring for new reserves of oil in Libya, with a view to establishing an independent source of supply. Gadhafi brought to the summit meeting of the OAU in July 1999 demands to hasten African unity, and two months later called a meeting in Tripoli to push his cherished plan for a United States of Africa. His guests showed some initial reluctance, but finally adopted a declaration advocating the replacement of the OAU by a new organisation to be called the African Union, to be governed by a Pan–African parliament. Although Gadhafi had hoped that its capital would be established in Tripoli, the majority preferred that the secretariat of the new organisation be sited in Johannesburg.

The Bumpy Path of Parliamentary Democracy: (1) West Africa

The troubles of Liberia and Sierra Leone excepted, the states of western tropical Africa emerged from the 1990s stronger and more democratic than they had been at the beginning of the decade. The narrow political and military elites which had held power since independence were now giving way to both internal and external pressures for reform. Most of the independence leaders and their supporters were either dead or retired. A new generation of voters had emerged, better educated and much more widely informed than their predecessors. Half of them now lived in cities comprising populations of many ethnic origins. The new generation had learnt to think in regional, if not yet in fully national terms, and to cast its votes accordingly. Political appointments were shifting to limited terms, so that they could be changed without military intervention. The most decisive of these changes occurred only toward the end of the decade – around forty years – therefore, after the coming of political independence.

Hitherto, the only country in West Africa which had enjoyed not one, but two, peaceful transfers of the presidency was Senegal, where Leopold Senghor had set the tone by voluntarily resigning the presidency for a chateau in Normandy in 1980. His successor, Abdou Diouf, was defeated in a parliamentary election in 2000, when the long ascendancy of the Democratic Socialist Party was broken by Abdoulaye Wade. The change of party was likewise carried out peacefully and confirmed by another election in 2001. In Ghana, which ran truer to type, there had been an alternation of civil and military governments, followed by the long presidency of Jerry Rawlings, which began with a military coup in 1980, but ended, after several electoral victories, with the defeat at the polls of his National Democratic Party in 2000 by John Kufuor's New Patriotic Party.

In Ivory Coast, the founding president, Felix Houphouët-Boigny, continued unchallenged until his death in 1993. Multi-party elections had been introduced in response to international pressures in 1990, and Houphouët was succeeded, according to the constitution, by the president of the National Assembly, Henri Bédié, who was confirmed in office at the next presidential election in 1995, after introducing a law banning any candidate who was not an Ivorian by birth. The significance of this condition was that the cocoa farmers in the southern parts of Ivory Coast had been recruiting employees from neighbouring states – especially Burkino Faso, Ghana, and Mali – who were mainly Muslims and, therefore, likely to join forces with the Muslims who lived in the north of the country. Bédié was overthrown by a military coup led by General Guei in 1999, but, in the face of international pressure, the latter called an election in 2000, which was won by the Ivorian Popular Front led by Laurent Gbagbo, who became president in the country's first democratic transfer of power. But the political manoeuvrings of Bédié and his successors had stirred bitter resentments in the poorer north, sparking widespread revolts by Muslim northerners and their immigrant allies in 2002. In an attempt to prevent the situation in Ivory Coast from degenerating into another Liberia or Sierra Leone, French troops intervened. The French government subsequently attempted to broker a peace agreement, but, at the time of this writing, it was unclear what the outcome would be. Clearly, however, the outbreak of violence posed the danger that it would inflame religious rivalry not only in Ivory Coast, but also in adjacent countries, nearly all of which had a similar fault line between northern Muslims and southern Christians. In Bénin, the government of Matthieu Kérékou, which had seized power by a military coup in 1972, was ousted at a presidential election held in 1991 by Nicéphore Soglu. As a former executive director of the World Bank, Soglu was in a prime position to dismantle the paraphernalia of the previously Marxist state. Thus cleansed, Bénin emerged as a fully democratic country – so much so that in 1996, Kérékou was reelected as president, with his rival Soglu serving as prime minister.

Nigeria, by reason of its geographical size, its variety of natural resources, and its vast population of 120 million, was clearly the most important state in tropical West Africa, but perhaps for these very reasons it had been more frequently subject to military rule than any other. President Ibrahim Babangida, who in 1985 had taken control of Nigeria from the previous unpopular military government, formed a National Electoral Commission in 1991 to oversee the transition to civilian government, but a whole series of elections was declared null and void by the regime before Chief Moshood Abiola of the Social Democratic Party won the presidental election in June 1993 with a clear majority of states. The military government, however, refused to accept Abiola's victory. Faced with a wave of demonstrations and strikes, Babangida himself stood down and a civilian non-elected head of state was appointed. After Abiola returned from a visit to Britain to a hero's welcome, Babangida's defence minister, General Sani Abacha, staged a bloodless coup and reinstated military rule. He immediately abolished all democratic institutions and political parties. Subsequently, the president issued well-worn statements about facilitating a transition to civilian rule, but, faced with threats of further coups and widespread economic disruption caused by strikes of oil-industry workers, the new government found every excuse to tighten its grip on power. In 1994, would-be president Abiola was arrested and detained in solitary confinement till his death four years later. The same year saw the intensification of the bitter campaign waged by the Ogoni people for compensation from the Shell Oil Company for environmental damage to their home-land. The violence in Ogoniland reached a climax in May 1994, when Ken Saro-Wiro and other activists were arrested by the government Internal Security Task Force. Saro-Wiro and five colleagues were tried by a military tribunal, sentenced, and executed in Novem-ber 1995, whereupon Nigeria was suspended from the Common-wealth. After brutally suppressing opposition to his rule, Abacha devoted himself to the plunder of the public revenues and especially of those which came in foreign currency from the exploitation of oil. Abacha died mysteriously in June 1998, and a subsequent investiga-tion found that he and his family had stashed away more than $3 billion in foreign bank accounts.

Following a brief period of provisional administration by the army, a return to civil government was declared and an election in 1999 was won by Olesegun Obasanjo, a retired general. Obasanjo had been the somewhat reluctant military ruler of the country from 1976 till 1979, before returning the country to a civil rule which did not last. As both a Yoruba and a Christian, Obasanjo faced the thorny problem of establishing his authority with the Muslim majority in the poverty-stricken north. In late 1999, first Zamfara, then Niger and Borno, followed by the great cosmopolitan state of Kano, indicated their in-tentions to impose the full weight of the Shari'a legal code, including its penalties of amputations and floggings (see Map 28). Local politi-cians, bereft of serious economic and social programmes, latched on to Shari'a as an easy tool to win support from a population desper-ate for an end to years of frustration, corruption, and – more than anything – hopelessness. By the first year of the new millennium, eleven of the thirty-six Nigerian states had imposed Shari'a law. The claims by Muslim leaders that Shari'a would not affect non-Muslims were misleading in that its ban on alcohol, cinemas, and integration of the sexes in most spheres of life would clearly affect everyone.

Riots inspired by religious hatreds broke out in the north and the south, while the violence surrounding the exploitation of oil in the south-east was a running sore to the Obasanjo regime. Nevertheless, the OECD in its report on the economic outlook for 2001–2 was able to conclude that the rule of law had been restored; that the courts were enforcing fundamental human rights, including freedom of speech and association; and that the independent news media had regained their freedom and vibrancy. This optimistic assessment, however, was belied by a per capita drop in income from $1,600 in 1980 (the year of President Shagari's 'boom budget') to $270 in 2000, ranking Nigeria among the twenty poorest countries in the world. Legislative and presidential elections took place in April 2003, which, if brought to a successful constitutional conclusion, would be unique: since independence in 1960, Nigeria has not transferred power from one civilian administration to another without the intervention of the military, which has ruled the country for thirty of its forty-three years as a sovereign state. In the event, Obasanjo was re-elected president, albeit in a flawed electoral contest.

(2) East and South-Eastern Africa

With one or two exceptions, the countries of east and south-east Africa survived the 1990s without serious civil violence. In Uganda, the long horror of government by plundering tyrants from the less developed northern half of the country – first initiated by Milton Obote in 1966, continued by Idi Amin from 1971 till 1979, and resumed by Obote between 1980 and 1985 – had been replaced by the gentler political ascendancy of Yoweri Museveni and his National Resistance Movement (NRM). As the NRM gradually shed its initial military flavour, showing concern for human rights and the rule of law, it continued to forbid the formation of rival parties. In 1995, however, elections by universal suffrage were held for a Constituent Assembly, with candidates standing as individuals not as party members, but with the party leaders free to engage in electioneering. This led in 2001 to a presidential election, when Museveni was confirmed in office, but with a limit of two more five-year terms. The national army remained necessarily active in repelling incursions inspired by the Sudan government across the northern frontier and, less necessarily, with its own incursions into eastern Congo. The Khartoum regime supported the Lord's Resistance Army (LRA) child fighters, many of whom were trained in camps on the Sudan side of the border. The leader of the LRA, Joseph Kony, a former Catholic altar boy, claimed to have been called by God to topple the 'satanic' government of Yoweri Museveni and to institute the Ten Commandments as the Ugandan constitution. Beginning in 1994, Kony instituted a reign of terror in parts of northern Uganda, which continues at the time of this writing. But, for most of Uganda, civil life gradually recovered from the destruction and devastation of the Amin and Obote years, and even made itself unique in Africa by achieving a reduction of 2 percent in the incidence of HIV/AIDS infection.

Kenya and Tanzania during this period were each still ruled by the same parties which had been in power since the early 1960s, but with strikingly different results. During the long leadership of President Daniel arap Moi, as earlier under Jomo Kenyatta, the Kenya African National Union (KANU) had been the party of a mainly urban elite of lawyers, civil servants, army and police officers, and businesspeople who had grown wealthy as the patrons and landlords of a middle class of artisans, traders, and transporters who inhabited the backstreets of Nairobi, Mombasa, and Kisumu. It was in many ways a vibrant and productive elite, although marred by corruption and intolerant of criticism, especially at election time. When Moi retired from the presidency in 2003 after twenty-four years, in parliamentary elections KANU was defeated by a new party – the National Rainbow Coalition – organised by the seventy-five-year-old vice-president, Mwai Kibaki. Kibaki thus succeeded to the presidency in lieu of Moi's candidate for the post. Tanzania during the 1990s was mainly engaged in conducting a staged retreat from the nobly egalitarian – but economically disastrous – policies pursued by Julius Nyerere prior to his retirement from the presidency. His successor, Ali Hassan Mwinyi, lost no time in accepting the advice of the IMF and the World Bank to float the currency, decentralize economic controls, and privatize many of the public corporations. Multi-party government was legalized in 1991, but not tested until 1995, when the candidate of the former single party – Ben Mkapa – was elected president, albeit by a narrow majority. At the turn of the millennium, Tanzania remained a desperately poor but proud country, with a strong sense of national identity, much strengthened by the continuing efficacy of Kiswahili as an African lingua franca, taught in the schools and spoken with fluency by most of the population.

In southern-central Africa, the 1990s saw the end of two lengthy presidencies which had endured since the grant of independence in 1964. In 1991, Kenneth Kaunda's United National Independence Party was defeated at the polls by the Movement for Multiparty Democracy, an alliance of some thirty fledging parties assembled by Frederick Chiluba, a trades-union leader from the Copperbelt. Chiluba substituted cabinet government for Kaunda's increasingly autocratic rule and soon addressed the main economic problem of the country – the disastrous fall in the world price of copper, almost halving the value of Zambia's exports. Embarking on a policy of retrenchment and privatization, Chiluba managed to balance the budget, but only at the cost of widespread unpopularity, which led to the breakup of his coalition. When his protégé, Levy Mwanawasa, won the December 2001 presidential election, he set about the process of prosecuting Chiluba for corruption, as earlier Chiluba had attempted against Kaunda. In Malawi, a country that had become during Hastings Banda's later years a nasty police state, the senile tyrant was at last forced into retirement in 1994. The principle of a multiparty state had been reluctantly accepted in the previous year, and elections in 1994 returned the United Democratic Front, with Bakili Muluzi, one of Banda's former cabinet ministers, as president. Like Chiluba's in neighbouring Zambia, Muluzi's government became increasingly unpopular and, in 2002, parliament rejected a proposed constitutional amendment which would have allowed Muluzi to run for a third five-year term. And, in the Indian Ocean island of Madagascar, the Malagasy Republic – the world's third poorest country – managed to survive prolonged civil unrest after a disputed presidential election in 2002.

The success story of this region was, without a doubt, Mozambique, which entered the 1990s as a war-torn disaster area. A Marxist FRELIMO government, led by Joseph Chissano, fought with a miscellaneous ethnic opposition (known by its acronym as RENAMO) armed and encouraged by the secret police of apartheid South Africa until the ANC government took full power there in 1994. The devastation of the country was such that, of its population of some

16 million, 1.5 million had fled as refugees into Malawi, Zambia, and Zimbabwe. An additional 3 million had been driven from their homes to the shelter of the exploding suburbs of Maputo, Beira, and Nova Sofala. After several previous failures, the Italian government in 1992 finally brokered the Rome Peace Accord between the warring parties. UN-supervised elections were held in 1994 and, although RENAMO contested the resulting FRELIMO victory, the fragile peace held. Chissano, who had close ties with Nelson Mandela and Thabo Mbeki in neighbouring South Africa, at their suggestion applied for membership in the Commonwealth, which was granted in 1995. During the next few years, Mozambique evinced remarkable powers of economic recovery from the devastation of the civil war. Even the migration of people fleeing violence and drought to the coastal towns proved advantageous: good agricultural land was freed for farming by modern methods, while the new townsfolk provided a willing labour force for the development of new industries, some of which had been set up by overseas companies investing in a stable country. This burgeoning industrial sector would be even more flourishing if Mozambique could benefit from the power produced by the huge Cabora Bassa dam on the Zambezi (see Chapter 19). However, under an agreement signed in 1984 by Portugal and South Africa, as well as Mozambique, the operating company was forced to continue selling most of its output to South Africa at a very low price until 2030. Meanwhile, Mozambique had to buy back its own power from South Africa, at ten times the cost.

(3) Southern Africa

In Africa south of the Zambezi, civil violence flared most obviously in Zimbabwe, where Robert Mugabe had held sway since 1980. By the 1990s, Mugabe was wielding power with steadily increasing autocracy, using the characteristic methods of a police state – misuse of the police forces, interference with the judiciary, muzzling of the press, expulsion of foreign journalists, to name only a few. The crucial issue, though, was the ownership of land, whereby a handful of white farmers owned half of the country's land – and the most fertile half at that – and used it for the production of cash crops, especially maize and tobacco. The large rural labour force was made up primarily of migrants from neighbouring Mozambique, as African Zimbabweans had long ago drifted from their poorly situated agricultural land to the towns – to work in mining, manufacturing, transport, and tourist services, in a highly diversified urban economy. Mugabe wanted to use the landed estates of the white farmers to reward his political supporters so, beginning in 1997, he authorized their seizure by gangs of thugs. The farms were turned over to mostly young and unemployed members of the ZANU/PF party, who had no experience with commercial farming and no capital to sustain it. The result – food shortages and inflation, which proliferated as land seizures multiplied from the designated estates to white-owned farms generally. The chief sufferers were the townsfolk, among whom political opposition gathered momentum, coalescing around the Movement for Democratic Change led by Morgan Tsvangirai. The general elections of June 2000 were disgraced by government-inspired violence and intimidation, which was repeated in the presidential elections of 2002. The latter returned Robert Mugabe for a fifth term of office.

The most serious aspect of the deteriorating situation in Zimbabwe was its potential repercussions on neighbouring South Africa, where a much larger and more developed economy was threatened by extreme differences in the sharing of that wealth, and where no less than 87 percent of agricultural land was still in white ownership. The ANC government of South Africa had shown admirable restraint in its Reconstruction and Development Programme drawn up in 1994, which had set a target of 30 percent of the land to be returned to African ownership within five years. With urbanization set to reach 70 percent of the population by that date, it was probably an achievable objective on the basis of reasonable compensation for the previous owners. But there was always the risk that the landless would one day take the law into their own hands and, with the Zimbabwean precedent at close hand, that risk would become larger, or so it would appear to potential investors in the outside world, where most of South Africa's external trade was with the most developed countries. This outside world was critical of President Mbeki – who took over the office from Nelson Mandela in June 1999 – for his failure to join it in denouncing Mugabe, but this was because it saw only half of the picture. The other half concerned Mbeki's strongly held view that Africa must be left to solve its own problems. South Africa, with its

population of 43 million; its mean per capita income of $2,650; and
its highly trained army, navy, and air force of some 80,000 – backed
by a thriving arms industry – enjoyed a position of leadership with
Nigeria and Libya. It was busy brokering peace between the Democratic Republic of Congo and its assailants from Zimbabwe, Rwanda,
and Uganda. South Africa was the leading member of the Southern
African Development Community and the prime mover of the New
Partnership for Africa's Development. And, as the headquarters of
the new African Union, it could not easily engage in public denunci-
ation of its own constituents.

Epilogue

Following our region-by-region survey of events in the 1990s, it seems appropriate to conclude with an overview of general factors concerning the African continent as a whole, as they appeared to stand at the end of that decade. First, despite the toll taken by the HIV/AIDS epidemic and other killer diseases, Africa's population continued to rise by 2.4 percent a year. Whereas in 1900 Africa comprised 4.5 percent of the world's total population, by 2000 this figure had risen to 10 percent of a world total of 6 billion. Largely for this reason, the people of Africa had become, statistically, the poorest in the world. Whereas the gross national per capita income of the United States stood at $34,100 and that of the UK at $24,430, Africa's *richest* country, Libya, thanks to its oil and its barely habitable deserts, hovered around $7,640. South Africa had $2,620 and Egypt $1,490. But, at the lowest end of the scale, almost nine people out of every ten in Africa's poorest countries were living on less than $2 a day; of these, two-thirds struggled to survive on less than $1 a day.

The urbanization of Africa during the 1990s had altered the whole pattern of government and society in most African countries. Although the poorer quarters of African towns might seem squalid to the passing traveller, life in them was regarded by their inhabitants as a considerable improvement over rural areas still lacking electricity, piped water, and drainage, and with most effective activity confined to the daylight hours. The urban peripheries of African towns might start out as tin shanties erected by the occupants with their own hands, but municipal authorities would soon come to realize that, if only in the interests of their more prosperous residents, streets should be laid out, paved, drained, and lit, with access to clean water if only at stand-pipes, and that schools and basic medical facilities should follow. The problem was that no sooner had one such shanty-town been made more habitable than two or three new ones would have sprung up around it. The growth in urban populations had in truth been phenomenal. By 2000, Africa boasted twenty cities with more than a million inhabitants. Lagos, with more than 10 million, was the largest, having overtaken Cairo with 9.6 million. Kinshasa, with 4.6 million, stood third. Whereas the general population of most African countries was doubling every twenty years, that of most capital cities was doubling every ten. The reason was, undoubtedly, that the capital cities received priority for all government services, for otherwise there would be epidemics, riots, and violent crime. Contrary to a widespread misconception, most of the newcomers to the cities came not from the poorest areas of the countryside, but from the rural areas immediately adjacent. These areas already enjoyed a modest prosperity by growing food for the neighbouring towns. They also benefitted from their easy access to the cities' services in education and medicine and, above all, as a source of labour at busy periods in the agricultural cycle. Thus, the family farm could be kept going by the elders as a place of retirement, receiving some seasonal help from its younger members living in the city.

In contrast, it was in the remoter rural areas that the poorest of Africa's poor were to be found. Here, central government, based in the towns and concentrating mainly on the urban population, tended to make their economies – leaving roads unrepaired; hospitals and clinics without medical supplies; schools without books, pens, or paper; the people unprotected by police or soldiers from the attentions of gangs of poachers, marauding private armies, or pastoral nomads seeking to enlarge their grazing areas. Many of the very poorest people in Africa were semi-permanent refugees, who had fled from scenes of warfare in their countries of origin and had resettled in the frontier districts of a neighbouring country, where unoccupied land was most likely to be found. The southern frontier districts of Malawi bordering on Mozambique, and the north-western frontier districts of Tanzania bordering on Burundi and Rwanda, were good examples. So too were the southern frontier districts of Burkina Faso, Guinea, and Mali bordering on Liberia and Sierra Leone. These were places where the writ of the host countries scarcely ran, and where most of the motor vehicles painfully negotiating the unpaved roads and broken culverts were those of the aid agencies of the developed world. It was likewise from scenes like these that the aid agencies took the piteous photographs of sick babies and undernourished mothers which they used to raise their supporting funds, and so helped to create an image of Africa as a continent dominated by violence, starvation, disease, and misery.

Most fearful of all the threats to Africa's well-being, and the hardest to ameliorate from the outside, was the soaring incidence of HIV/AIDS, highest in the countries of southern and eastern Africa and lowest in the ancient Islamic countries to the north of the Sahara. By 2001, more than 28 million people in Africa were infected with HIV/AIDS, and 2.3 million had already died. It was estimated that as many as 40 percent of the population in some African countries were infected, of whom most would eventually die in their late thirties or forties, having already transmitted the infection to their children. These would be left as orphans while still in their teens, or even younger, and dependent for continuing support on their grandparents or other elderly relations. Botswana, with a population of 1.6 million, had some 600,000 people infected by 2002. Average life expectancy had fallen as a result to thirty-seven years from a high of sixty-two years in the 1980s. And this in one of the richest and politically most stable states in the continent, with a gross national per capita income higher than that of South Africa, and where there was universal free education and health care. The incidence of HIV/AIDS infection among Tswana girls ages 15 to 19 was 28 percent in some areas, twice that of boys of the same age, with worrying implications for the country's future economic and reproductive capacity. One reason for it was thought to be the widespread practice of intergenerational sex, whereby older men slept with much younger girls because they thought them less likely to have been infected. Sadly, one of the commonest types of such encounters was that between male schoolteachers and their female pupils.

In neighbouring South Africa, with its population of 43 million, the situation was almost as dire, with 20 percent of adults between the ages of 15 and 49 infected and life expectancy likely to have diminished from 65.8 years to 47.9 by 2005. Here, seasonal work in mining and agriculture was often blamed as the main reason for casual sex, but next-door in Zimbabwe – where adult infection had reached 25 percent and where life expectancy was projected to be falling from a high of 66.5 years to 42.9 by 2005 – it was among teachers and health workers that the incidence was highest. Farther north, in Tanzania and Kenya, HIV/AIDS hit hardest among the more prosperous urban males and the prostitutes they frequented, and those whose occupations involved frequent travel – transport workers above all others. The reactions of those in authority in African countries and of bodies such as the World Health Organisation to this devastating epidemic were for too long in denial or overcautious, but, gradually, more positive steps were taken to grasp the deadly nettle. Uganda was the only country that actually managed to bring down the rate of infection. President Festus Mogae of Botswana was totally committed to putting all the resources of the state and of voluntary agencies, including some of the big pharmaceutical companies and of Bill Gates of Microsoft, toward eliminating the disease. His was the first African country to offer retroviral drugs to everyone who needed them, a policy which Botswana's huge neighbour South Africa was, for ideological reasons, reluctant to undertake.

By 2000, the dilemma facing most African countries was that vital cohorts of their rising human resources – men and women in their late teens, twenties, and thirties, who should have been the driving force of economic development – were those most enfeebled by HIV/AIDS and by other killer diseases such as malaria and TB. The epidemic had inflicted a crippling blow on educational systems that were already in crisis. In Zambia, for example, HIV/AIDS was killing almost as many teachers as its colleges could train. This meant that the continent was in danger of being bypassed in the race to participate in the new information technology. Whereas Europe in 2000 had 204 telephone mainlines for every thousand people, Africa south of the Sahara had only 16. The entire continent had some 10 million telephones, but half of them were located in South Africa, and the remainder were so scattered that most Africans lived two hours away from the nearest instrument. Again, there were only 2.3

Internet hosts to serve every 10,000 people in sub-Saharan Africa, whereas Latin America and the Caribbean had twice the number. One well-known expert in development economics concluded that Africa's lack of infrastructure required for integration into a global network suggested that it would be impossible to develop a globalised framework for the continent. But such top-down pessimism, though common currency among many foreign commentators, was overstated and probably mistaken. Looked at from the ground level of urban and suburban communities all over Africa, the conclusion might not be so bleak, and the gloomy statistics could have missed the mark. Turned on their head, they showed that Africans *did* have access to global communications, albeit in improvised and communal and, as yet, numerically small, ways. Indeed, the first years of the new millennium seemed likely to witness a boom in the use of mobile phones, even in countries as strife-torn as Congo DR, where the government was doing deals with international telecommunications companies to provide both the infrastructure and the availability of phones at affordable prices. Slowly, more and more people were coming to possess – or at least have access to – computers, and an increasing number of schools and colleges were teaching information technology. The Moroccan telecommunications industry, for example, had so rapidly transformed the country's outlets that the number of mobile subscribers rose from 150,000 to more than 4 million during the three years from 1999 to 2002, simply by enhancing the accessibility of their communications services, especially Internet and Broadband.

In his moving account of the civil war in Sierra Leone, Paul Richards shows how the country's youth, many of whom played a prominent and sometimes vicious part in the conflict, far from being trapped in isolating poverty, belonged within the vibrant trans-Atlantic culture. They regularly watched films and videos – war movies, Rambo, 'Agent' (James Bond), and Kung Fu being their favourites. More than 80 percent of the people in Richards' survey listened regularly to the radio. Most tuned in to the new popular FM stations, but many stayed loyal to the older AM transmissions, which carried more in the way of news, commentary, and social announcements. The Africa Service of the BBC's World Service was, by far, the leading international station to which people listened. Although the rural sample was small, the figures suggest that the alleged isolation of village dwellers and the uneducated was only relative. In Senegal in 2002, as in most other African countries, everyone seemed to be tuning in to the World Cup on radios and televisions. As a Tunisian exile remarked with some bitterness, 'We are more politically mature than our leaders'.

Now that almost half of the population of Africa lived in towns, it was only necessary to stand and observe the traffic on a main road at the morning or evening rush hour to see the extent and variety of the people and goods being carried and to realize that, even in countries with a statistical gross average income of $2 a day, many, many people must be enjoying much greater prosperity than the bare statistics would suggest. In fact, it was in and around these towns that a new African economy was being born. More than half of all employment was being provided by small firms in the informal sector, operating in such fields as construction, transport, trading, market gardening, manufacturing, and processing. One of the most striking features of the warlord empires set up from Somalia to Sierra Leone was the entrepreneurial skill of the warlords and their henchmen.

Straddling the indistinct boundary between the formal economy and that of the informal and often quasi-criminal economies were Africa's exciting cultural, sporting, and entertainment industries. Musicians from states as far apart as Morocco and South Africa, Congo and Mali, were performing in the international music arena, as well as being pop idols in their own countries. The filmmakers of Burkino Faso and other West African countries enjoyed an international reputation. And if nothing else united Africa from the Muslim north to the old colonial landscape and shantytowns around Cape Town, it was football. Quite understandably, with the wild success of their team in the competition, there was no greater instance of 'World Cup Fever' in 2002 than in Senegal. 'This victory', wrote Mamadou Kasse, the editor of *Le Soleil*,

is not just about football. It is about showing the world that when we work hard in Senegal, we can succeed in the same way as the people of Europe. A successful football team is the expression of a confident nation, one in which there is democracy, stability and human rights. You do not see Zimbabwe or Cameroun producing a winning team. Senegal is a little country, but it has very good political and democratic leadership. We are an example of an African democracy that works. Our president [Abdoulaye Wade] has led the way in the New Partnership for Africa's Development. The president is 76, but he dances like a young man.

A vast capital was waiting to be tapped in African football, and no one knew better how to make use of this populist resource than President Gadhafi. He realised that football was the quickest way for Libya to be accepted back into the international community. As one of his officials candidly put it, 'Libya wants to play her part in the international arena and show that she is not like people think, about terrorism and all that'. Football was indeed huge in Libya, with games between the biggest teams attracting crowds of 100,000. Gadhafi even used his son, al-Saddi, to front a financial investment company to buy a stake in the Italian giant Juventus and to try to take over the Greek club PAOK Salonika, so that Libyan sides could participate in the Greek league and thus qualify his country to host the World Cup in 2010.

The economic inputs of musicians, such as South Africa's Ladysmith Black Mambazo, and of world-beating football teams such as Senegal's were unlikely to find a place in the statistics published by the World Bank and other international agencies. The same could be said of most of the wealth and benefits created by each country's informal sectors and black economies. A large, but immeasurable, amount of wealth generated throughout Africa must have gone unrecorded, much of it shared by the poor as well as the rich. The reach of the World Bank, it has been said, extended only as far as a taxi ride out of Accra, and it also surely failed to comprehend the side streets and alleyways of the capital. So, when the World Bank showed Africa to be at the bottom of every conceivable index, this was true – but it was not the whole truth. Other, less measurable, standards reveal enterprising, resourceful, ambitious, humorous, canny, and conniving people getting on with their lives, and finding opportunities to do so in all the nooks and crannies of their countries' social and political structures.

It was encouraging that both the UN Economic Commission for Africa and the African Economic Outlook for 2001–2 published by the OECD reported that the continent's economies were doing better in spite of the global slowdown during these years, so that in 2001 there was an average GDP growth of 4.3 percent, compared with 3.5 percent in 2000. Average income per head across Africa rose by nearly 2 percent in 2001, boosted by lower oil prices, lower inflation, better farming methods, and increased exports to the United States arising from the African Growth and Development Act and to the European Union under similar trade agreements. Both Ethiopia and Eritrea saw their economies boom after the ending of their mutual war in 1999. Even Sierra Leone achieved a 5-percent growth after its civil war ended in 2002. A senior official of the World Bank enthused over the better management of the economies of both Rwanda and Congo DR when he visited these countries in 2002, and recommended that Congo be rewarded with a hefty helping of debt relief. Such optimistic conclusions, however, taken alone, present a distorted picture. It is important to remember that the five largest economies – those of South Africa, Morocco, Algeria, Tunisia, and Egypt – accounted for well over half of the continent's total GDP. And, although these five states all attracted satisfactory amounts of foreign investment, Africa as a whole was forecast to attract a wretched 2.3 percent of all investment worldwide. The deterrents to outside investment have been well rehearsed as comprising civil violence, political instability, *folie de grandeur* of aging autocrats, corruption at every level, and – not least – the persisting immaturity of the legal and judicial systems, which made it difficult for otherwise willing investors to enforce contracts.

With so many state structures failing to provide anything like the amenities of civil society for their people, the long-term remedies for the ills of the continent might reasonably be thought to lie with regional, continental, or even intercontinental organizations. One of the more successful examples was the Economic Community of West African States (ECOWAS), the existence of which had brought Nigerian military forces to the aid of the much weaker governments of Liberia and Sierra Leone in their struggles with political rebellions. Another had been the Southern African Development Community (SADC), which had played a useful role in strengthening the defences of neighbouring states during the final years of the apartheid government in South Africa, but which had then failed to tackle the problems posed by Mugabe's lapses into tyranny in Zimbabwe. At the intercontinental level, the Commonwealth had, surprisingly enough, proved to be a popular and potent moral club for its African members. Although it had few sanctions that could be applied to errant governments other than the suspension of their membership, this measure had, in fact, been used against Nigeria during the presidency of Abacha and against Zimbabwe following the scandalous conduct of the election of 2002. Mozambique had a foot in two such camps, having joined the Commonwealth in 1995 and having been the prime mover in the Community of Portuguese-speaking Countries (CPLP), consisting of Angola, Brazil, Cape Verde, Guinea-Bissau, Mozambique, and Portugal, which had its headquarters in Maputo.

By far, the most significant move toward more effective alignment of African states was the establishment of the African Union – the inaugural meeting of which was held in Durban in July 2002 – and the resultant expiry of the OAU after a life span of thirty-nine years. The OAU had been founded at the height of nationalistic enthusiasm in the decade of political sovereignty and the inviolability of the ex-colonial frontiers, but was much too feeble to challenge the dictators or bear down upon the warlords. Thabo Mbeki was chosen as the African Union's first chairman. The intention was to create a Pan-African parliament, a court of justice, a central bank, and a shared currency; to set out common electoral standards; and to demand that independent observers be welcomed before and during any national election. A small African Peace and Security Council was to be established, with authority to send troops to stop war crimes and genocide. Leaders who gained power by military coups would not be allowed to take part in meetings.

Almost simultaneously with the Durban conference, at the G8 meeting of donor nations in Canada, a New Partnership for Africa's Development (NEPAD) was launched. Once again, Thabo Mbeki was a prime mover in getting the new programme off the ground. NEPAD was designed to have two basic approaches: First, it was to tackle a series of specific economic projects, such as the promotion of new farming techniques and the financing and construction of a large new hydroelectric dam at Inga on the lower Congo. Second, it was to try to bring about longer-term political changes, with a serious attempt to entrench the rule of law and the observance of business codes. Projects and targets were to be set, but it was stressed that

NEPAD was a programme, not an organization. It would have no cumbersome bureaucracy. It would operate by a system of 'peer review', by which it was envisaged that governments would submit to criticism by fellow Africans according to commonly agreed standards. Mbeki wanted a small panel of eminent Africans to make such reviews, while other leaders were understandably less keen on this kind of external surveillance.

While the Durban conference was in session, the most immediate concern for its participants was the severe drought that was ravaging much of southern Africa and threatening millions of people with famine. Unlike the drought in the region of two decades earlier, this time confrontations between donors and the two countries in greatest need – Zimbabwe and Malawi – were holding up the distribution of aid to the entire region; some countries refused to receive GM maize. As one observer at Durban commented, it was as if the heads of state were occupying another universe. For Africa to survive and prosper, organizations such as the AU and NEPAD needed to demonstrate that the universe of rhetorical posturing could be subsumed by the real, live world.

Taking the continent as a whole, the economies of Africa, although still not keeping pace with the relentless growth of populations, had in absolute terms turned upwards from the stagnation of the 1970s and the decline of the 1980s. Industrialists from the outside world were slowly beginning to see a continent in which they might be able to invest more and, thereby, to help at least some African governments to stand once again on their own feet. Meanwhile, it was inevitable that Africa would continue to lose, in a diaspora to Europe and North America, the very people most capable of operating and energising the kind of regional groupings that could bring good government and sensible economies to their homelands. And, unfortunately, all experience shows that successful migrants from one continent to another seldom return to their ancestral base.

The events of 11 September 2001 restored, if not the ideology of the Cold War era, at least high moral rhetoric onto the world stage. The early reactions of the Bush administration to the terrorist attacks on New York and Washington seemed to confirm the marginalisation of much of Africa, those countries of the world which were not in the forefront of the War on Terror being of little immediate concern

35. Oil in Africa.

Major oil producing countries
Algeria
Libya
Nigeria
Angola
Middling oil producing countries
Sudan
Congo-Brazzaville
Gabon
Small oil producing countries
Egypt
Chad
Cameroon
Equatorial Guinea
Benin
Togo
Democratic Republic of Congo
Western Sahara (Morocco)

Natural gas

to America. African regimes which had a proven track record of anti-terrorist activities, however authoritarian they might be – such as those of King Muhammed of Morocco and President Bouteflika of Algeria – became the friends and allies of the United States, whereas countries that were on America's list of evil states found it prudent to slough off their old radical ways. President Gadhafi was encouraged to renounce his abetting of terrorism, while the Sudan regime cast off some of its Islamic extremism and was prepared to make peace with the South. If comments in the press were to be believed, African public opinion, while accepting with ill grace the U.S.-led campaign in Afghanistan against the Taliban and al-Qaeda, was outspokenly hostile to the preemptive war against Saddam Hussein in Iraq. 'Were preemption to become the rationale for just war', wrote one South African columnist, 'then one can imagine the endless can of worms this would open up for much of Africa. No peace process would be safe'. Nevertheless, once the dust has settled, African leaders will have to put their compunctions about the policies of the Bush administration aside and come to terms with the cosmic shift in international relations that has taken place since the end of the Cold War, with the United States becoming fully conscious of its status as the world's only superpower and determined to pursue policies which reflect this preeminence.

One exception to Africa's low-profile participation on the world stage was the exploitation of oil. The U.S. determination to find an alternative energy source to the Middle East generated a new oil rush in sub-Saharan Africa. After September 11, American companies became much more aggressively involved in the opening up of new fields throughout the Gulf of Guinea, especially in Angola, Equitorial Guinea, and Nigeria. Nevertheless, the economic, social and environmental consequences of oil exploitation, substantial and grave as these might be, affected only fairly limited areas (many of the new fields were offshore) in a small number of countries. By mid-2003, the United States showed signs of renewed interest in the continent. President Bush pledged to spend $15 billion to fight HIV/AIDS in poor countries and even contemplated sending U.S. troops to troubled Liberia. In July 2003, he paid his first visit to the continent, taking in Senegal, South Africa, Botswana, Uganda, and Nigeria. In August 2003, after the arrival of Nigerian peacekeeping forces in Monrovia, Charles Taylor left Liberia for exile in Nigeria. For a time, U.S. troops were deployed in the country, before the arrival of a large number of UN peacekeepers. Gyude Bryant was chosen to head an interim administration, pending elections. After nearly two decades of conflict, Liberia seemed poised for a more peaceful future. Likewise, the United States took steps to bring the even longer-running conflict in the southern Sudan to a conclusion. In October 2003, Secretary of State Colin Powell persuaded government and rebel leaders meeting in the Kenyan town of Naivasha to sign a comprehensive peace treaty by the end of the year.

In the aftermath of the Iraq War, the American government took steps to become more actively engaged with African issues. Even if many people were sceptical of American intentions toward their continent, Africans could turn being less in the forefront of world politics and conflicts to their own advantage, manipulating the deep divisions in the ranks of the world's privileged countries. Indeed, there was much to be gained from being left alone. It may be that what was, above all, necessary, was for Africa to revive its belief in itself and in its own power to identify and address its problems, and to be master of its own development, instead of being dependent on and subservient to outsiders to effect this development. Many serious Africans were pinning their aspirations on an African Renaissance, which, if it were to be anything more than humbug, would require people in all walks of life, up and down the continent, to emulate the example of the old master: 'We have not taken the final step of our journey', wrote Nelson Mandela at the end of his story, 'but the first step on a longer and even more difficult road. For to be free is not merely to cast off one's chains, but to live in a way that respects and enhances the freedom of others. The true test of our devotion to freedom is just beginning'.[1]

Recent Events in Sudan and Darfur

In the huge Darfur region of western Sudan, low-level conflicts between agricultural and pastoral communities had become endemic since the 1950s, if not earlier, and intensified as a result of the widespread drought in much of Sahelian Africa in the early 1980s. The basic element in these conflicts was the gradual desiccation of the region, with the Sahara encroaching ever further onto usable land. Farmers shared the more fertile mountainous regions around Jebel Marra with pastoralists, who also roamed to the north (camel nomads) and to the south (cattle nomads). In many cases these people occupied the same territory, intermarrying with one another as well as competing for land and water. The two communities were Muslims, and physically they were indistinguishable. The pastoralists

---

[1] Nelson Mandela, *Long Walk to Freedom*, New York, 1994, p. 544.

spoke Arabic as their first language, the farmers as their second. Only after the Fur and other groups launched a series of revolts against the Khartoum government, and after the nomads were called upon to suppress these, did ethnic distinctions become politically significant, with the former being spoken of as 'Africans' and the latter as 'Arabs'. The settled people of Darfur had felt excluded from the peace process which ultimately led to the signing of the Naivasha agreement in May 2004 between the government and the southern insurgents, and early in 2003 two rebel groups mounted a series of attacks on government posts.

The government's response was to arm 'Arab' militias – known in Darfur Arabic as *Janjawiid* – and these acted with such ferocity, by destroying villages and crops, killing men and boys, and raping women, that by the middle of 2004 many hundreds of thousands of people had been displaced from their homelands and tens of thousands killed or maimed. Large numbers of refugees fled to neighbouring Chad, where they were put up in makeshift camps, and to where they were often pursued by the Janjawiid. Preoccupied with Iraq and with the wider war on terror, the outside world was slow to wake up to the magnitude of the crisis in Darfur. Not until well into 2004 did aid agencies begin to organise significant amounts of relief to the refugee camps in Darfur and Chad or did the African Union attempt to mediate. And not till the middle of the year did the international community bring serious pressure on the Sudanese government to take steps to end the violence, by disarming the Janjawiid and by negotiating with the rebels.

Suggestions for Further Reading

GENERAL

J. F. Ade Ajayi (ed.), *General History of Africa IV: Africa in the Nineteenth Century until the 1880s*, Paris, UNESCO, 1989.

John E. Flint (ed.), *Cambridge History of Africa V, c1790–c1870*, Cambridge, 1976.

Roland Oliver and G. N. Sanderson (eds.), *Cambridge History of Africa VI, c1870–c1905*, Cambridge, 1985.

A. A. Boahen (ed.), *General History of Africa VII: Africa under Colonial Domination 1880–1935*, Paris, UNESCO, 1985.

A. D. Roberts (ed.), *Cambridge History of Africa VII: 1905–1940*, Cambridge, 1986.

Michael Crowder (ed.), *Cambridge History of Africa VIII: 1940–1975*, Cambridge, 1984.

A. A. Mazrui (ed.), *General History of Africa VIII: Africa since 1935*, Paris, UNESCO, 1993.

Thomas Pakenham, *The Scramble for Africa*, London, 1991.

Suzanne Miers and Richard Roberts (eds.), *The End of Slavery in Africa*, Wisconsin, 1985.

L. H. Gann and Peter Duignan (eds.), *Colonialism in Africa 1870–1960*, 5 vols., Cambridge, 1969–75.

Bill Freund, *The Making of Contemporary Africa: The Development of African Society since 1800*, Boulder, CO, 1998.

Frederick Cooper, *Africa since 1940*, Cambridge, 2002.

John Iliffe, *The African Poor: A History*, Cambridge, 1987.

Patrick Manning, *Francophone Sub-Saharan Africa, 1880–1995*, Cambridge, 1999.

David Killingray and Richard Rathbone (eds.), *Africa and the Second World War*, New York, 1986.

Prosser Gifford and Wm Roger Louis (eds.), *The Transfer of Power in Africa: Decolonisation 1940–1960*, New Haven, CT, 1982.

David Birmingham, *Decolonisation in Colonial Africa*, London, 1995.

John D. Hargreaves, *Decolonisation in Africa*, 2nd ed., Harlow, 1996.

Adrian Hastings, *A History of African Christianity 1950–1975*, Cambridge, 1979.

Paul Darby, *Africa, Football and FIFA: Politics, Colonialism and Resistance*, London, 2002.

J. F. Ade Ajayi and Michael Crowder (eds.), *Historical Atlas of Africa*, London, 1983.

World Bank, *Can Africa Claim the 21st Century?*, Washington, 2000.

NORTH AND NORTH-EAST AFRICA

J. M. Abun-Nasr, *A History of the Maghrib*, 2nd ed., Cambridge, 1975.

C. R. Pennell, *Morocco since 1830: A History*, London, 1999.

Benjamin Stora, *Algeria, 1830–2000: A Short History*, Cornell UP, 2001.

John Ruedy, *Modern Algeria: The Origins and Development of a Nation*, Bloomington, 1992.

Charles-Robert Ageron, *Modern Algeria: A History from 1830 to the Present*, London, 1991.

Derek Hopwood, *Habib Bourguiba of Tunisia: The Tragedy of Longevity*, London, 1992.

Ali A. Ahmidam, *The Making of Modern Libya*, New York, 1994.

M. W. Daly (ed.), *The Cambridge History of Egypt II: Modern Egypt, from 1517 to the End of the Twentieth Century*, Cambridge, 1998.

Afaf Latfi al-Sayyid Marsot, *A Short History of Modern Egypt*, Cambridge, 1985.

Robert Collins and Robert Tignor, *Egypt and the Sudan*, Englewood Cliffs, 1967.

Douglas H. Johnson, *The Root Causes of Sudan's Civil Wars*, Oxford, 2003.

Deborah Scroggins, *Emma's War*, Atlanta/London, 2003.

Bahru Zewde, *History of Modern Ethiopia, 1855–1991*, Athens/Oxford, 2002.

Donald Crummey, *Land and Society in the Christian Kingdom of Ethiopia from the 13th to the 20th Century*, Oxford, 2002.

Ruth Iyob, *The Eritrean Struggle for Independence: Domination, Resistance, Nationalism, 1941–1993*, Cambridge, 1995.

I. M. Lewis, *A Modern History of the Somali*, Oxford, 2002.

WEST AFRICA

J. F. Ade Ajayi and Michael Crowder (eds.), *History of West Africa*, vol. 2, London, 1974.

A. G. Hopkins, *An Economic History of West Africa*, London, 1973.

Richard L. Roberts, *Two Worlds of Cotton: Colonialism and the Regional Economy in the French Soudan, 1800–1946*, Stanford, 1996.

Janet Vaillant, *Black, French, and African: A Life of Léopold Sédar Senghor*, Cambridge, MA, 1990.

John Peterson, *Province of Freedom: A History of Sierra Leone, 1787–1870*, Evanston, IL, 1969.

Paul Richards, *Fighting for the Rain Forest: War, Youth and Resources in Sierra Leone*, London, 1996.

Astride R. Zolberg, *One-Party Government in the Ivory Coast*, 2nd ed., Princeton, 1969.

Ivor Wilks, *Asante in the Nineteenth Century*, Cambridge, 1975.

David Kimble, *A Political History of Ghana: The Rise of Gold Coast Nationalism 1850–1928*, Oxford, 1963.

Dennis Austin, *Politics in Ghana 1946–1960*, London, 1964.

John Carmichael, *Gold Coast to Ghana*, London, 1993.

Richard Rathbone, *Murder and Politics in Colonial Ghana*, New Haven, 1993.

Richard Rathbone, *Nkrumah and the Chiefs: The Politics of Chieftaincy in Ghana, 1951–60*, Athens, 1999.

David Birmingham, *Kwame Nkrumah: The Father of African Nationalism*, Athens, 1998.

James S. Coleman, *Nigeria: A Background to Nationalism*, Berkeley, 1968.

J. D. Y. Peel, *Religious Encounters and the Making of the Yoruba*, Bloomington, 2000.

Julius O. Ihonvbere and Timothy Shaw, *Illusions of Power: Nigeria in Transition*, Rochester, 1998.

Toyin Falola, *Nigeria in the Twentieth Century*, Carolina Academic Press, 2002.

EASTERN AND WESTERN CENTRAL AFRICA

Vincent Harlow, E. M. Chilver, and Alison Smith (eds.), *History of East Africa*, vol. 2, Oxford, 1965.

D. A. Low and Alison Smith (eds.), *History of East Africa*, vol. III, Oxford, 1976.

Robert L. Tignor, *The Colonial Transformation of Kenya*, Princeton, NJ, 1978.

Bruce Berman and John Lonsdale, *Unhappy Valley: Conflict in Kenya and Africa*, London, 1992.

Wunyabiri O. Maloba, *Mau Mau and Kenya: An Analysis of a Peasant Revolt*, Bloomington, 1998.

Valerie Cuthbert, *Jomo Kenyatta: The Burning Spear*, Harlow, 1982.

John Iliffe, *A Modern History of Tanganyika*, Cambridge, 1979.

Annie Smyth and Adam Seftel (eds.), *Tanzania: The Story of Julius Nyerere*, Kampala, 2000.

Michael Twaddle, *Kakungulu and the Creation of Uganda, 1868–1928*, Oxford, 1993.

René Lamarchand, *Rwanda and Burundi*, London, 1970.

Ruth Slade, *King Leopold's Congo*, London, 1962.

Osumaka Likaka, *Society and Cotton in Colonial Zaire*, Wisconsin, 1997.

Crawford Young, *Politics in the Congo: Decolonisation and Independence*, Princeton, NJ, 1965.

George Nzongola-Ntalaja, *The Congo, from Leopold to Kabila: A People's History*, New York, 2002.

Michela Wrong, *In the Steps of Mr Kurtz*, London, 2000.

SOUTHERN CENTRAL AFRICA

David Birmingham and Phyllis Martin (eds.), *History of Central Africa: The Contemporary Years since 1960*, Harlow, 1998.

R. J. Hammond, *Portugal and Africa 1815–1910*, Stanford, 1966.

Douglas L. Wheeler and René Pelissier, *Angola*, New York, 1971.

Tony Hodges, *Angola from Afro-Socialism to Petro-Diamond Capitalism*, Oxford, 2001.

Malyn Newitt, *A History of Mozambique*, London, 1995.

Allen F. Isaacman, *Cotton Is the Mother of Poverty: Peasants, Work and Rural Struggle in Colonial Mozambique, 1938–1961*, Portsmouth, NH, 1996.

Merle Bowen, *The State against the Peasantry: Rural Struggles in Colonial and Postcolonial Mozambique*, Charlottesville, VA, 2000.

Martin Chanock, *Law, Custom, and Social Order: The Colonial Experience in Malawi and Zambia*, New York, 1998.

Andrew Roberts, *A History of Zambia*, London, 1976.

B. S. Krishnamurthy, *The Making of Modern Malawi*, London, 1992.

John Flint, *Cecil Rhodes*, London, 1976.

Robert Blake, *A History of Rhodesia*, London, 1977.

T. O. Ranger, *Revolt in Southern Rhodesia 1896–7*, London, 1967.

Charles van Onselen, *Chibaro: African Mine Labour in Southern Rhodesia 1900–1933*, London, 1976.

Richard Gray, *The Two Nations: Aspects of the Development of Race Relations in the Rhodesias and Nyasaland*, London, 1960.

James P. Barber, *Rhodesia: The Road to Rebellion*, London, 1967.

Patrick Bond, *Uneven Zimbabwe: A Study of Finance, Development and Underdevelopment*, Trenton, NJ, 1998.

Hevina S. Dashwood, *Zimbabwe: The Political Economy of Transformation*, Toronto, 2000.

W. Minter, *King Solomon's Mines Revisited*, New York, 1986.

Helmut Bley, *South-West Africa under German Rule*, London, 1971.

Raymond Kent, *From Madagascar to the Malagasy Republic*, Westport, CT, 1976.

SOUTH AFRICA

Monica Wilson and L. M. Thompson, *The Oxford History of South Africa*, 2 vols., Oxford, 1969–71.

William Beinart, *Twentieth Century South Africa*, Oxford, 1994.

James Barber, *South Africa in the Twentieth Century*, Oxford, 1999.

Rodney Davenport and Christopher Saunders, *South Africa, A Modern History*, New York, 2000.

Noel Mostert, *Frontiers: The Epic of South Africa's Creation and the Tragedy of the Xhosa People*, London, 1992.

Colin Bundy, *The Rise and Fall of the South African Peasantry*, London, 1979.

Charles van Onselen, *Studies in the Social and Economic History of the Witwatersrand 1886–1914*, 2 vols., London, 1982.

W. K. Hancock, *Smuts*, 2 vols., Cambridge, 1962–8.

Peter Walshe, *The Rise of Nationalism in South Africa: The African National Congress 1912–1952*, London, 1970.

Francis Wilson, *Labour in the South African Gold Mines 1911–1969*, Cambridge, 1972.

H. J. and R. E. Simons, *Class and Colour in South Africa 1850–1950*, Harmondsworth, 1969.

Deborah Posel, *The Making of Apartheid, 1948–1961: Conflict and Compromise*, Oxford, 1991.

A. Adedeji (ed.), *South Africa and Africa: Within or Apart?*, London, 1997.

A. Guelke, *South Africa in Transition: The Misunderstood Miracle*, London, 1999.

Jack Spence (ed.), *After Mandela*, London, 1999.

Nelson Mandela, *Long Walk to Freedom*, London, 1994.

F. W. de Klerk, *The Last Trek*, Johannesburg, 1999.

Index